The Decline of the English Musician
1788–1888

The Decline of the English Musician 1788–1888

A Family of English Musicians in Ireland, England, Mauritius, and Australia

A. V. BEEDELL

CLARENDON PRESS · OXFORD
1992

Oxford University Press, Walton Street, Oxford OX2 6DP
Oxford New York Toronto
Delhi Bombay Calcutta Madras Karachi
Petaling Jaya Singapore Hong Kong Tokyo
Nairobi Dar es Salaam Cape Town
Melbourne Auckland
and associated companies in
Berlin Ibadan

Oxford is a trade mark of Oxford University Press

Published in the United States
by Oxford University Press, New York

British Library Cataloguing in Publication Data
Data available
ISBN 0–19–816294–4

Library of Congress Cataloging in Publication Data
Data available
ISBN 0–19–816294–4

Typeset by Joshua Associates Ltd., Oxford
Printed in Great Britain by
Biddles Ltd., Guildford and King's Lynn

ACKNOWLEDGEMENTS

I WOULD like to thank the librarians and other officers in the following institutions. In Ireland, the National Library of Ireland (Dublin); the Limerick City Library who forwarded my request for information from the Vere Hunt Diaries to the appropriate agency; Mid-West Archives, Limerick, who supplied extracts from the Vere Hunt Diaries; The Church of Ireland Dean of St Canice's Cathedral, Kilkenny, for permission to view the First Entry Book of St Mary's Church, Kilkenny, and other records; also my friends Gael Fogarty and Brian Docherty in whose home I was able to stay in Dublin.

In England, The British Library, Bloomsbury; the British Library Newspaper Collection, Colindale; The British Library Manuscripts Department; The British Library India Library and Records, Blackfriars Road; The Public Records Offices in both Chancery Lane and Kew; Greater London Records Office; Lambeth Archives Department, Minet Library, Brixton; The Local History Library of Central Westminster Library, Buckingham Palace Road; The Principal Probate Registry, Somerset House; The General Records Office, St Catherine's House; University of London Library; The Institute of Historical Research; Corporation of London Guildhall Library; English Heritage; Victoria & Albert Theatre Museum, Covent Garden, and Picture Library; The Library of the Society for Theatre Research at the V&A Theatre Museum, also Mr Derek Forbes, Hon. Sec. of STR for some very useful information and offers of help; the Royal Society of Musicians, particularly the Hon. Archivist, Mrs Betty Matthews, and the Secretary, Mrs Marjorie Gleed MBE; Sue Highley, Research Assistant for The Huguenot Society; the Hertfordshire Records Office, particularly Mrs Gillian Sheldrick; Mr M. G. Fookes of the firm Rumball Sedgwick; Mrs Christine Shepperson for her information on John Horner Rumball and his firm; Mrs Brenda Harrison for genealogical information on the Rumball family.

In Mauritius, Dr P. H. Sooprayen, Chief Archivist of the Government of Mauritius Archives Department for typescript extracts from shipping records, newspapers, and books.

In Sydney, The State Library of New South Wales, especially Mr John

Graham; the Dixon Library; the Mitchell Library; the New South Wales State Archives; the New South Wales Supreme Court, Probate Division, Sydney, for permission to use the Cavendish Papers, and the Public Trustees, Sydney, especially Mr John Dick, whose friendly efficiency in finding me a spot to work in his crowded office, and supervising access to the material, made the job that much easier.

My thanks also to Dr David Walker of the School of History, University of New South Wales, now Professor of Australian Studies at Deakin University, Geelong, Victoria, for his support for the thesis which is the basis of this book.

CONTENTS

LIST OF ILLUSTRATIONS

LIST OF ABBREVIATIONS

Bibliographic References

ADB	*Australian Dictionary of Biography*
Aust.	*Australian* [Sydney]
BL	British Library
BM	British Museum
CWL	Central Westminster Library
DEP	*Dublin Evening Post*
DNB	*Dictionary of National Biography*
EC	*Ennis Chronicle*
FDJ	*Faulkner's Dublin Journal*
FJ	*Freeman's Journal* [Dublin]
FLJ	Finn's Leinster Journal [Kilkenny]
GDA	Gazetteer and New Daily Advertiser [London]
GL	Guildhall Library, City of London
GLRO	Greater London Records Office
GRO	General Records Office [London]
HRO	Hertfordshire Record Office, Hertford
HC(C)	*Hibernian Chronicle* [Cork]
HC(D)	*Hibernian Chronicle* [Dublin]
LAD	Lambeth Archives Dept., Minet Lib., Brixton, London
MA	Mauritius Archives
ML	Mitchell Library [Sydney]
Mon.	*Monitor* [Sydney]
NLI	National Library of Ireland [Dublin]
NSWSA	New South Wales State Archives [Sydney]
PRO	Public Record Office [London]
PPR	Principal Probate Registry [London]
QMMR	*Quarterly Musical Magazine and Review*
RAM	Royal Academy of Music
RSM	Royal Society of Musicians
SCNSW/PD	Supreme Court of New South Wales, Probate Division
SG	*Sydney Gazette*
SH	*Sydney Herald*

ST	*Sydney Times*
V&A	Victoria & Albert Museum
WH	*Wexford Herald*
WHM	*Walker's Hibernian Magazine*

Names of Chief Correspondents Referred to in the Text

AHC	Alfred H. Jones Castell
SEC	Susannah Elizabeth Castell
WJC	William Joseph Castell
W Jones C	William Jones Castell
EJ	Ellen Jones
THJ	Thomas H. Jones

INTRODUCTION

THIS book is, of course, a social history of music. Its focus is the obscure but interesting Castell family—professional English musicians with careers over five generations and five countries, spanning a period of English musical history (1789 to 1889) as famous for its breadth of activity as it was notorious for its failure of creativity. Central to the story is William Joseph Castell (1789–1839), otherwise known as Cavendish, a musician whose talents were modest, whose ambitions were limitless, and whose ultimate failure may well have been his own fault. Thanks to the burgeoning power of England's ever-expanding empire he had a world over which to range, protected under the umbrella of English culture and English arms. Thanks to the failure of English musical culture, though, he had, arguably, no place at home. This failure of culture at a time of unprecedented national prestige and influence, even more than the failure of Castell, is the pervading theme of the book. The core of it, though, is the Castell narrative, pieced together from a variety of sources, but most particularly from the letters of Castell's wife Susannah.

Telling the story of any unknown individual, using what can only be described as intimate resources, runs the risk of becoming not history but historical voyeurism. Hopefully, though, the detail that emerges from this approach may help to draw a fuller picture of the lives and worlds of a group of individuals otherwise almost invisible in history: the rank-and-file professional musician—the cultural worker if you like—whose capital resided not just in the labour of his hands and/or voice, but in something more intangible and ultimately more fragile—what Susannah, in the parlance of the day, called 'genius'.

Thus I hope that this study will provide a little more of the kind of data which will permit generalizations about the social history of music to be made with more certainty. Lawrence Stone, commenting on collective biography in his book *The Past and the Present* (Boston, 1981, p. 57), comments that,

In any historical group, it is likely that almost everything will be known about some members of it, and almost nothing at all about others; certain items will be lacking for some, and different items will be lacking for others. If the unknowns bulk very large, and if, with the serious incompletes, they form a substantial majority of the whole, generalizations based on statistical averages become very shaky indeed, if not altogether impossible.

Cyril Ehrlich, in his *The Music Profession in Britain since the Eighteenth Century: A Social History* (1985), follows up Stone's remarks, suggesting some elementary safeguards for the social historian of music in using this approach. Veneration for genius and appetite for gossip should not be allowed to dominate any representative survey. Institutional education records should not be presumed more important than those of other, less accessible, forms of education. Care should be taken to allow for distortion of surviving facts about a musician's social origin, which could well have been suppressed, and for natural documentary bias towards high birth and education.

In her study, 'A Profession of Artisans: The Careers and Social Status of British Musicians, 1750–1850' (Ph.D. thesis, Pennsylvania, 1983), itself based upon the concept of collective biography, Deborah Rohr points up other problems, acknowledging that the 'unknowns' bulk so large as to make generalizations from the 'knowns' a precarious exercise. Her primary source was her own catalogue of 6,587 musical biographies, gleaned from biographical dictionaries, memoirs, biographies, and from the records of the Royal Society of Musicians.

Thus, with these problems in mind, the opening up of the Castell/ Cavendish records, with all their spontaneous diversity, and ingenuousness, cannot help but avoid some of the pitfalls listed by Ehrlich while at the same time redressing Rohr's imbalance between knowns and unknowns.

The letters and other documents from which the Castell story has been constructed comprise a bundle of private papers and documents created by the Curator of Intestate Estates in Sydney between 1839 and 1841. They were unearthed through the identification of Roger Therry's 'Devenish', in his *Reminiscences of Thirty Years Residence in New South Wales and Victoria* (2nd edn., 1863, pp. 114–16), as the Sydney musician, known as William Joseph Cavendish. Therry, in recalling Devenish's story in the chapter on notable 'criminals' (a classification loose enough to include crimes against morality as well as those against law), had made a specific reference to his private papers having been confiscated by the Curator of Intestate Estates at the time of his death. By a rather remarkable fluke (so I am told), the file, now held by the NSW State Archives, is still extant. All of the personal correspondence is reproduced as Appendices to my Hons. MA thesis, 'William Joseph

Castell, o. k. a. Cavendish (1789–1839), Musician. His Origins, Life and Career in Ireland, England, France, Mauritius and Australia', vol. 2 (University of New South Wales, Sydney, 1990).

Note: For Therry's 'revelations' in full, see the Appendix, and for brief details of his life and career see Chapter 6, n. 195.

1
Ireland, 1788–1792

Whatever expression (in a moment of irritation) escaped my
lips in reference to your <u>own birth</u>, I can solemnly protest you
<u>extorted</u> . . . I retorted in self defence only.

SEC to WJC, Dec. 1827.

WEXFORD: A PREAMBLE

ON 2 April 1789, the *Wexford Herald* reported that the ships *Sirius* and
Supply, together with the transports, had made good their voyage to
Botany Bay.

As Terra Incognita, New Holland, or The Great South Land, Australia
had for centuries been the repository of imagined horrors—of demonic
abnormality—a Hieronymus Bosch landscape of infernal retribution.
Now it had become something else—more credible but only marginally
more appealing—the dumping ground for one of the first major waste
products of industrial civilization—the English so-called 'criminal
classes'.[1]

It was an event that was exciting enough for its sheer physical achievement in the face of the unknown, but an event nevertheless heavily tinged
with macabre unreality. Mrs Castelli, who at that time was appearing in
Wexford with Smithson's troupe of players, could scarcely have believed
it possible that her unborn child was destined to end his life at that almost
unbelievably distant point on the globe where now 700 convicts and
their guards were founding the penal colony of New South Wales.

In her condition, Mrs Castelli may have surrendered to perhaps a flush
of prescient melancholy upon hearing the news; but the age was one of
sense and energy, and even in the green rooms of provincial theatres,
conversation would probably have dwelt more on matters of science and
'oeconomy' than upon superstition and horror, which were the stuff of
popular novels and the contemporary English theatre and nothing to do
with life.

---

[1] See Robert Hughes, *The Fatal Shore. A History of the Transportation of Convicts to
Australia, 1787–1868* (1987), 43–4.

Smithson and his troupe had opened in Wexford the previous December to a rather cool reception, which had warmed, however, with the help of a little controversy in the press between 'Theatricus' complaining of 'languor', and 'Mores' of 'Snakes in the grass'.[2] Mrs Castelli was an undoubted star. The *Wexford Herald* had quickly singled her out for praise. She added much, it said, to the amusement of the audience, and her vocal abilities 'justly merited applause'.[3] It later went on to affirm that 'this lady, when Time has made her more acquainted with the Stage, will probably excell in the Vocal Line'.[4] But Mrs Castelli was not all that new to the stage. She had made her début in Dublin at Daly's Smock Alley on 26 November 1787 and had travelled with that company when the Dublin season ended, to Cork in August/September 1788, when owing to some unrecorded circumstance she parted company with Daly's relatively prestigious troupe to end up by Christmas with the much less prestigious Smithson.

William Joseph Smithson (the father of the actress Harriet Smithson who became the wife of Hector Berlioz) was a country actor-manager usually based in Ennis and Galway, but who frequently enough resorted to the road. And it was to his itinerant company that Mrs Castelli affixed herself after her break with Daly, obviously with mutual benefit. But life as an itinerant player was tough and precarious. It depended not only on health and talent, but on the 'protection' of an often fickle public and the vagaries of often unprincipled managers. Separated from society by their rootlessness and by their ancient threat to authority and moral convention, there was little protection for players, and their undoubted freedom was often bought dearly in social neglect and frequent deprivation.

Life on the road may have had its romance; but its pleasures of freedom and conviviality could best be enjoyed by men. The tales of hilarity and high adventure that feature in reminiscences by John Bernard or Charles Lewes can be set against the commentaries of Eliza Winstanley or Ann Holbrook, or those of Charlotte Charke, who likened touring, in the previous generation, to 'engaging in a little dirty Kind of War'. It was 'more reputable', she thought, 'to earn a Groat a Day in Cinder-sifting at Tottenham Court'.[5]

[2] *WH* 12, 19, 22 Jan. 1789.
[3] *WH* 29 Dec. 1788, p. 4d.   [4] *WH* 19 Jan. 1789, p. 4c–d.
[5] John Bernard, *Retrospections of the Stage* (1830); Charles Lewes, *Memoirs* (1805); Eliza Winstanley, *Shifting Scenes in Theatrical Life* [1859]; Ann Holbrook, *The Dramatist; or Memoirs of the Stage* (1809); Charlotte Charke, *Narrative of the Life of Charlotte Charke* (2nd edn., 1755), 187, in Robert Hume (ed.), *The London Theatre World 1660–1800* (1980), 157.

Smithson's company was probably a cut above the average. The *Wexford Herald* certainly claimed that, for itinerant performers, the 'present company are much superior to the general run of this part of mankind'.[6] But even so, for Mrs Castelli it was definitely a decline in status, which would suggest that her departure from Daly had not been voluntary, or, if so, then brought about as a result of some kind of pressure. Richard Daly was Ireland's foremost theatrical entrepreneur, possessing a virtual theatre monopoly in Dublin, then still a significant city on the English theatrical circuit. He was also notorious for his sexual exploitation of his female employees. But we shall be dealing with Richard Daly later. It is enough to say here that he may have rid himself of Mrs Castelli in Cork due to her pregnant condition, a condition which he himself may have engendered.

In Wexford, she played a variety of musical roles: Rosetta in *Love in a Village*, Leonora in *The Padlock*, Wilhelmina in *The Waterman*, Laura in *The Agreeable Surprise*, Louise in *The Deserter*, and Yarico in *Inkle and Yarico*, and sang 'The Trump of Fame' and 'Tis Beauty Commands Me' between the acts on other nights. She looked 'charmingly and sung admirably',[7] and was probably the subject of convivial toasts at Corrick's tavern over many a pint of porter, one too many of which, 'diverted by the conversation of some Players', occasioned a wifely rebuke for at least one Wexford citizen.[8]

Mr Castelli was also in Wexford at this time, employed by Smithson as the 'keeper of the Pit door', in which capacity he suffered on one occasion the abuse of a drunken butcher's boy—that scourge of the theatre—who threw stones and dirt at him, 'with an intent to wound him'.[9] He was later the box-keeper.

The season ended with the usual round of benefits.[10] On 13 February 1789, Mrs Castelli assisted at Mr Power's night by singing 'Tally Ho', but also, and this is rather singular, by performing a Concerto on the Piano-Forte;[11] an indication that here was no illiterate itinerant, but a person with pretensions to musical education. Mrs Castelli gave her own benefit on 6 March, supported by the full cast in *Inkle and Yarico* and *The Brave Irishman*, and after Smithson's benefit on 30 March, the

---

[6] *WH* 12 Jan. 1789, p. 2d.   [7] Ibid. 2 Feb. 1789, p. 4d.
[8] Ibid.   [9] Ibid.
[10] These were not charitable performances as 'benefit' concerts are termed today, but performances got up by and on behalf of members of the company by special arrangement with the manager (i.e. payment). Benefits were an opportunity for the public to bestow largess, or not, upon individual performers, upon the results of which often depended their livelihood between seasons. See St Vincent Troubridge, *The Benefit System in British Theatre* (1967).   [11] *WH* 12 Feb. 1789, p. 4d.

company set out for Kilkenny, fifty miles to the north-west, the town where Mrs Castelli was to give birth to William Joseph Castell.[12]

KILKENNY

Politics and culture

Kilkenny, the ancient city of Ossory, was the largest inland town in eighteenth-century Ireland.[13] The Hightown, or English section, extended from the castle on the River Nore (begun in Norman times under Strongbow in 1176) down to the low-lying Watergate, where the smaller Bregagh River had once marked the outer limit of Norman fortifications against the native Irish. Significantly, beyond Watergate, the town was, and still is, called Irish Town. Except for a dramatic natural escarpment upon which crouches the sombre medieval pile of St Canice's cathedral, it was low-lying and undistinguished; 'mostly composed of sorry houses and poor cabins'.[14] It was the Hightown from which Kilkenny took its character and which was to express its post-Norman history as well as its eighteenth-century prosperity—a prosperity which was very much an Anglo-Protestant affair.

From the time Cromwell bedded his horses down in St Canice's cathedral in 1650, or perhaps more specifically from the time of the Penal Laws which followed in the wake of the Battle of the Boyne in 1690, native Irish and English Catholics had found it almost impossible to share a common culture with the new Anglo-Protestant ascendancy, and in Kilkenny, the town that Lady Morgan referred to as the 'Versailles of Ireland',[15] as elsewhere, the distinctions of race and creed were materially felt.[16]

[12] The Royal Society of Musicians, London. MS Members' Files [W. J. Castell]. Baptismal certificate; son of Peter and Sophia Castelli on 27 May 1789 at St Mary's church [Church of Ireland], Kilkenny, Ireland. Surviving records in Kilkenny consist of a 'First entry book', apparently a rough draft, which refers to Peter and Sophia Castella, a mistake which was evidently rectified when transferred to the main register from which the RSM certificate was extracted in 1813. The register itself was lost during the 1920s. The 'First entry book' is held at St Canice's cathedral, Kilkenny.

[13] Katherine M. Lanigan and Gerald Taylor (eds.), *Kilkenny, its Architecture & History* (1987); R. W. Lightbown, 'Some Eighteenth and early Nineteenth Century Visitors to Kilkenny, Part One', *Old Kilkenny Review*, 3 (1984), No. 1 (2nd ser.), 3–16; John Hogan, *Kilkenny, the Ancient City of Ossory* (Kilkenny, 1884).

[14] [Thomas Campbell], *A Philosophical Survey of the South of Ireland* (1777), 99.

[15] *Lady Morgan's Memoirs: Autobiography, Diaries and Correspondence*, i. 114.

[16] See William Lecky, *History of Ireland in the Eighteenth Century*, 141 ff. for an account of their provisions and of the social, economic, and cultural effects of the Penal

A predictable extension of Anglo-Protestant hegemony was the wholesale importation of cultural artefacts from England, among which was the theatre. Dublin was not only a significant extension of the English theatrical circuit, but a lively source of players, playwrights, and musicians. The London stage would indeed have been much poorer without the formidable roll-call of such names as Woffington, Macklin, Sheridan, O'Keefe, Moore, Jordan, Kelly, Cooke, and many more. But such triumphs, however gratifying to the individuals concerned, merely reinforced the English cultural domination of Ireland, since Irish success was strictly contained within the limitations of English taste. Dublin remained, for all its dynamic contribution to English drama, a mere appendage of London, and where London, and indeed English, provincial players could often gain lucrative employment between English engagements. So too the Irish circuit of Cork, Limerick, Wexford, Kilkenny, Belfast, and even Galway and Ennis in the west, which also served as a testing ground for theatrical neophytes both English and Irish. With this caravan came the latest London stage hits as well as the stock repertoire of the English stage.

The pieces played by Mrs Castelli and the troupe in Wexford were fairly typical. *Inkle and Yarico*, for example, a comic opera by Samuel Arnold in the favoured English form of spoken dialogue and jokes, interspersed with ballads and songs of a loosely generic disposition, had only had its London première at the Theatre Royal, Haymarket, in August of 1787. *The Farmer*, with music by Shield and text by the Irishman John O'Keefe, and produced in Wexford for Smithson's final benefit, was also a recent London hit (Covent Garden, 31 October 1787); while other pieces like *Love in a Village*, *The Waterman*, *The Padlock*, and *The Deserter* were popular pieces of English theatre from the 1760s and 1770s. Interspersed with this essential fare would have been an occasional bowdlerized Shakespeare, or a serious melodrama in quasi-Shakespearian mode like Nicholas Rowe's *Jane Shore*, or a classic comedy like Fletcher's *Rule a Wife and Have a Wife*, or Congreve's *The Way of the World*, decently sanitized.

As in England, the popular repertoire was heavily loaded with musical pieces and even straight drama was often embellished with songs and

Laws on the majority of Catholics in Ireland; also more recent works like Maurice O'Connell, *Irish Politics and Social Conflict in the Age of the American Revolution* (1965), ch. 5; Michael McConville, *Ascendancy to Oblivion. The Story of the Anglo-Irish* (1986); J. C. Beckett, *The Anglo-Irish Tradition* (1976). See also period works like Arthur Young, *Tour of Ireland* (1776–1779), ed. A. W. Hutton (1892), especially vol. 2; or period fictional works like Maria Edgeworth, *Castle Rackrent* (1800) and *The Absentee* (1812).

music, so much so that it has become difficult to be able to draw a line with great confidence between what was loosely termed 'opera' and what was not. In 1791, Mrs Castelli, with Mr Palmer and Miss Brett, was billed singing 'the celebrated and much admired DUET and TRIO from THE CRITIC of "Little Nancy said unto me one Day" '.[17] Sheridan's play is nowhere categorized as an opera, and yet as performed then it was probably not so different from his *The Duenna*, which was. White, in the introduction to his *Register of First Performances of English Operas*, refers to 'the insuperable problems of definition'.[18] The ramifications of this, as we shall see in Chapter 2, were to be ultimately beneficial neither to English music nor to English drama.

Irish music itself, with its ancient traditions, survived the onslaught almost solely as a folk idiom, sentimentalized by fashionable taste or shamelessly plundered to provide 'tunes' for English 'operas' and plays; the English, as we shall see in Chapter 2, having come to believe the legend that English tunes no longer existed. Perhaps the most notable exploitation of the Irish musical idiom was Tom Moore's *Irish Melodies*, published in Dublin and London between 1808 and 1834, which became a touchstone for civilized 'sensibility' throughout musical Europe. A collection of not very ancient Irish poems set by various mediocre composers in pseudo-Irish style, they captured, somehow, the poignant melancholy of Irish innocence and grief without giving offence to mainstream cultural prejudices, or confronting the political and economic issues that lay behind Irish suffering. Not even the musical iconoclast Hector Berlioz was proof against their anaesthetizing sentimentality. 'Hymns of resigned love', he called them, 'to which one listens inexplicably moved, dreaming of solitude, of grand nature, of beloved beings who are no more, of the heroes of ancient times, of one's suffering country, even of death itself . . .'.[19] Ultimately such usage served only to trivialize a musical culture which possessed no formal means of development—no educational tools other than those imposed by the declining English cathedral tradition or *ad hoc* secular instruction on either English or Continental lines. It is therefore hardly surprising to find that Paul Lang, in *Music in Western Civilization*, singles out two Irishmen, Michael Balfe (1808–1870) and William Vincent Wallace (1812–1865), as epitomizing the best in English opera of the mid-

[17] *FDJ* 17 Dec. 1791, p. 120.
[18] Eric Walter White, *A Register of First Performances of English Operas and Semi-Operas from the 16th Century to 1980* (1983), p. v.
[19] Hector Berlioz, *Memoirs*, ed. Ernest Newman (1935), 335.

nineteenth century, a musical form which was otherwise declared to be 'virtually dead'.[20]

On 4 April 1789, Smithson announced in the columns of *Finn's Leinster Journal* that, 'actuated by every Duty that can guide a grateful Heart', he was about to throw himself and his Company of Comedians upon the protection of the ladies and gentlemen of Kilkenny and its vicinity, promising 'proper Attention to his Business—strict Assiduity to please—and a careful Watch in arranging the Characters so as to correspond to the Strength of the Company'. On the same day, the paper carried a four-column report on the new settlement at Botany Bay, dealing at length with the strange ways of the Aborigines: a people destined to win even less cultural respect than the natives of Ireland. Still on the subject of Botany Bay four days later, the *Journal* noted drily: 'The Settlers in New Holland are likely very soon to be rid of all the bad habits of their former profession. There is very little to pilfer at present, and soon the richest among them will have nothing to lose.'[21]

In Kilkenny the season opened at the Court House on 24 April with *Love in a Village*, the leading role of Rosetta being played by Mrs Castelli, who was billed 'from the Theatres Royal London and Dublin', London obviously being thought more likely to impress Kilkenny audiences than the Norwich claim of her Dublin début in 1787. Mr Castelli acted as Box-Keeper, allocating places in the boxes (at 3*s*. 3*d*. each) from 11 till 9 o'clock at his lodgings at Kehoe's. The pit places were 2*s*. 2*d*. and the gallery 1*s*. 1*d*.[22]

The mood in Kilkenny, in the recent past troubled by the Whiteboys and other marauding bands of quasi-tribal guerrillas still at war with occupying landowners and their agents, seemed easy enough. Outrage appeared to be confined to Lieutenant Holmes of the 12th Light Dragoons who was claiming that Nathaniel Watts, 'Dog teacher', born at County Cork, 'a short, thick fellow about 36' and wearing 'an old light-coloured coat, a white Marseilles Waistcoat, and white Cashmere Breeches; the latter much too big for him', had stolen his white pointer bitch called Belle.[23] Other news of interest to Kilkenny readers concerned the sitting of the Irish Parliament in Dublin, where Major Doyle, a well-known figure in Kilkenny as the member for Mullingar, was presenting

[20] Paul Lang, *Music in Western Civilization* (1942), 930–1.
[21] *FLJ* 8 Apr. 1789.
[22] *FLJ* 18 Apr. 1789, p. 3c.
[23] Ibid.

several motions; also Salomon was in Dublin, where he was giving a series of concerts at the Rotunda, and the fact was duly noted, also in Dublin, that 'every gentleman is to wear embroidery at the Ball of Brooke'.[24]

Farther away, in London, the first of the great colonial magnates, Warren Hastings, was on trial in Westminster Hall, and it was noted that 'Mr Pitt's favourite liquor is red port. Like Sir John Macpherson he is a six-bottle man. He can knock down both the chancellor and Lord Mulgrave. The minister will yield the baccanalian palm to none but Dundass.'[25] It was also thought to be of interest to the newspaper readers of Kilkenny that Count Alman was lying wounded at the Horns Tavern after a duel on the Common at Kennington. An extensive report was provided.[26]

Birth and origins

After Mrs Castelli's first appearance in Kilkenny on 24 April, there is no further mention of her until 27 May, when it was announced that, having 'recovered from her late indisposition', she would appear on 3 June in *Inkle and Yarico* in her usual role of Yarico.[27]

In the meantime, William Joseph Castell, son of Peter and Sophia Castelli, had probably been born and certainly had been baptised on 27 May at St Mary's church, Kilkenny. He shared his Christian names with his parents' employer, Smithson, who more than likely acted as his godfather, although William, as we shall see, was also the name of Sophia's father. But William's origins are perhaps not as clear as the parish records of St Mary's would indicate. As already suggested, his natural father may have been the Anglo-Irishman, Richard Daly. Laxity in such matters was not uncommon at the time, and members of the theatrical profession were considered to be less scrupulous than most. It is even remotely possible that his father may have been the member for Mullingar, the then Major John Doyle. These two gentlemen were prominent if not equally distinguished members of the Anglo-Irish élite, but before looking more closely at their credentials, let us turn first to Peter and Sophia Castelli, who must share the official and therefore the historical responsibility for the parentage.

Sophia, as we have already noted, made her Dublin début with Daly at Smock Alley on 26 November 1787. She was billed at the time from the

24 *FLJ* 25 Apr. 1789, p. 2b, c.   25 *FLJ* 2 May 1789, p. 2a.
26 *FLJ* 9 May 1789, p. 2.   27 *FLJ* 27 May 1789.

Theatre Royal, Norwich,[28] indicating that she had begun her theatrical career if not in Norwich then at least in England. Norwich was one of the major provincial English theatres with a large and remunerative circuit, but an advertising puff was no guarantee of veracity. Nevertheless, as we have already seen from her performance of the concerto on the piano-forte in Wexford, she did have an educational background which gave her claims to superiority some basis.

Her father was in fact William Jones,[29] probably the trumpeter of that name who was performing in London in the second half of the eighteenth century. The *Biographical Dictionary of Actors, Actresses, etc.* cites him as the teacher of Master [?Robert] Green, the young trumpeter who performed at Finch's Grotto Gardens, Southwark, in about 1765 and at Marylebone Gardens in 1770 and as a regular player in the Covent Garden and Drury Lane orchestras up to about 1796. He was also cited as a trumpeter in the Handel Memorial Concerts at Westminster Abbey and the Pantheon in May and June 1784.[30] A member of the Royal Society of Musicians from 1770, he was, according to that Society's records, a performer in the Grand Musical Festivals (or Handel Memorial Concerts) up till 1790, and was also on the 1799 Royal Society of Musicians' 'List of the Benefactors and Subscribers Honorary and Professional to a Fund for the Support of Decayed Musicians and their Families'.[31]

The supposition that Sophia's father was a musician is certainly strengthened firstly by the fact that after his death in 1811, two prominent musicians, Charles Jane Ashley and his brother Richard, were called upon as witnesses to his handwriting to enable his unsigned will to be proven, and secondly that his 'tried friend' and executor, Samuel Munro,[32] was probably the theatre musician of the 1790s of that name, and fellow member of the Royal Society of Musicians.[33] It would not

[28] *FDJ* 29 Nov. 1787 indicates that her début occurred on 26 Nov., in *Love in a Village*. Other sources supply the 'Norwich' information, i.e. William Smith Clark, *The Irish Stage in the Country Towns* (1965), Appendix B; and *A Biographical Dictionary of Actors, Actresses, Musicians, Dancers, Managers and other Stage Personnel in London 1660–1800*, comp. Philip H. Highfill and others (1973–).

[29] William Jones, his will, proved 16 July 1811, indicates that WJ was the grandfather of WJC and his brother Peter. PRO PROB. 11/1524.

[30] *Biog. Dict. Actors, Actresses etc.* vii. 244.

[31] RSM, *List of Members 1738–1984* (1985), 83.

[32] William Jones, above, n. 29.

[33] RSM, *List of Members*, 104. Jones refers to Samuel Munro as 'M.P. at Dover', but there is no evidence that he was ever an MP. See *Biog. Dict. Actors, Actresses, etc.* for information on Samuel Munro, violinist and violist.

only explain Sophia's musical education but the future preparation of her own son for music. But Sophia's education had also included French and Italian,[34] and while the latter was especially useful for musicians, particularly singers, music and languages were becoming fashionable in polite society in the late eighteenth and early nineteenth centuries as normal components of female education. So whether or not the trumpeter, who seems to have been in comfortable enough circumstances (his future granddaughter-in-law would later refer to him as 'sainted'), intended his daughter to follow a musical, let alone a theatrical, career with such accomplishments is rather problematical. Whether or not he approved of her marriage to Peter Castelli is also uncertain. On the face of it, Castelli does not seem to have been much of a catch, although his son's later claim to 'great family' might suggest some hidden glory.

Castelli was not a common name in England and of course had a distinctly foreign flavour—hardly unusual in musical circles. There had been a Signora Anna Castelli, a singer who had come to England with an Italian burletta company in 1754–5 and may have stayed on;[35] and in the 1820s and 1830s another female singer of the same name appeared at Covent Garden and King's theatres.[36] But in the 1780s the name Castelli was more closely associated with a less exalted form of entertainment, namely with a troupe of performing animals, known generically as the 'Dancing Dogs' but also including performing monkeys and the celebrated 'learned pig' on whose condition Dr Johnson himself stooped, in justifying the cruelty of its training, to make the profound observation that Life, on any terms, even the Pig's, was preferable to death. However, it was the 'Dancing Dogs' themselves (on whose account Dr Johnson, as far as we know, was never asked to adjudicate) that caught the public imagination. Although publicly advertised as Sieur Scaglioni's,[37] at least two contemporary commentators referred to them only as Castelli's (or Costello's) dogs.[38] And it was as Castelli's 'CELEBRATED DOGS FROM PARIS'

---

[34] Her ad offering to teach these languages, *FLJ* 15 July 1789, p. 3b.

[35] *Biog. Dict. Actors, Actresses etc.* iii.

[36] King's Theatre, 'Concerts Spirituels', 5 Mar 1824, *QMMR* vi (1824), 75; Harold Rosenthal, *Two Centuries of Opera at Covent Garden* (1958), 45, cites a performance of Signora Castelli on 12 July 1833 at Covent Garden as Adalgisa in *Norma*.

[37] BL, Collections relating to Sadler's Wells. The Percival Collection, II. 193–224, newspaper cuttings, *c.* 1784–5.

[38] W. T. Parke, *Musical Memoirs* (1830), ii. 292–3, refers to Castelli's Dogs; F. Reynolds, The *Life and Times of Frederick Reynolds* (1826), i. 261, refers to 'a subordinate, but enterprising actor by the name of Costello' having 'collected at the great fairs of Frankfort and Leipsic a complete company of Canine performers . . .'.

that they appeared in Dublin in November 1784 at Daly's Smock Alley, sometimes on the same bill as the celebrated Signora Sestini from Covent Garden, London, and Maria Theresa Romanzini (later Mrs Bland) in her début season in Ireland.[39] Indeed a notice of Miss Romanzini in Francis Higgins's *Freeman's Journal* of 13 November was rather overshadowed by being immediately followed by a eulogy upon the 'Learned Dogs'.

From the amazing curiosity and attention thro' all the town which one exhibition only of the *Learned Dogs* has excited, a correspondent is of opinion, that Mr Daly should permit them to be shown at least three times a week during their engagement, as there can be no doubt but every person, man woman and child in Dublin and within ten miles of it, will embrace some opportunity or other of going to see their performances. So singular and surprising an exhibition was never before seen in this kingdom and may never again, perhaps, after these wonderful animals have quitted it.

As we shall see, Higgins and Daly were closely associated. Perhaps they had a vested interest in the 'Dancing Dogs'.

Graphically represented in a broadsheet of the period,[40] the dogs' special forte appears to have been the impersonation of humans in various social situations; dancing an allemande, spinning wool, drawing, driving and being driven in a carriage, paying social visits, all dressed in the height of fashion. But what most struck audiences, it would seem, when the dogs first appeared at Sadler's Wells at Easter in 1784, was their re-enactment of the popular theatre piece *The Deserter*, originally a French ballet but adapted by Charles Dibdin in 1773 into a successful 'musical drama' for Garrick's Drury Lane.[41] And two scenes in particular seem to have created a sensation. One was the storming of the fort led by the intrepid canine 'Moustache' in the role of Skirmish, with the dogs scaling ladders and then at the sound of the retreat tumbling back down again in mad disarray. The playwright Frederick Reynolds (1764–1841) was particularly struck with this.

I see him now [Moustache], in his little uniform, military boots, with smart musket and helmet, cheering and inspiring his fellow soldiers, to follow him up scaling ladders, and storm the fort. The roars, barking, and confusion which resulted from this attack, may be better imagined than described.

---

[39] *FJ* 2–13 Nov. 1784.
[40] See Fig. 1.
[41] *A New Musical Drama* by C. Dibdin [music and text], after Sedaine. Two Acts. An adaptation of Monsigny's *Le Deserteur*, Drury Lane, 2 Nov. 1773; White, *Register of First Performances*.

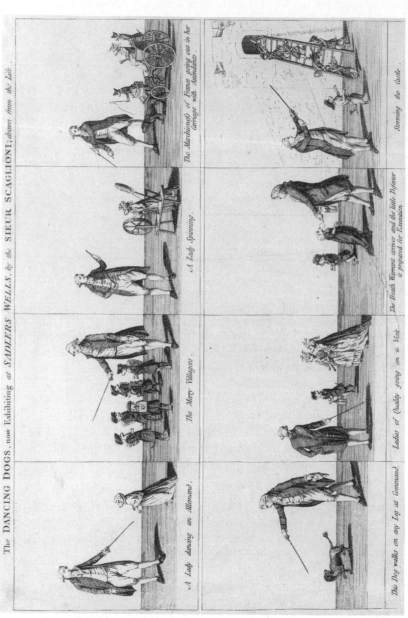

The DANCING DOGS, now Exhibiting at SADLERS WELLS, by the SIEUR SCAGLIONI; drawn from the Life.

A Lady dancing an Allemand. | The Merry Villagers. | A Lady Spinning. | The Marchioness of France going out in her carriage with Attendants.

This Dog walks on any Leg at Command. | Ladies of Quality going on a Visit. | The Death Warrant arrives and the little Defaster is prepared for Execution. | Storming the Castle.

1. A series of pictures illustrating some of the routines performed by the Dancing Dogs. Engraving, 1784. Ref. Beard

At the moment when the gallant assailants seemed secure of the victory, a retreat was sounded, and Moustache and his adherents were seen receding from the repulse, rushing down the ladders, and staggering towards the lamps in a state of panic and dismay . . .[42]

A variation of this performance, not noticed by Reynolds, was announced on 2 September 1785. One of the dogs had been trained to play the part of a 'spy' and was to 'mount the ladder backwards, which has never been seen in the Kingdom before'.[43]

The other scene which excited interest was the execution of Moustache, as the deserter, where he is marched out to be shot by his fellow musket-bearing canines. The Covent Garden oboist William Parke was suitably impressed:

after he had fallen, [he] writhed about in convulsive agonies till apparently relieved by death, when he lay as still as a defunct mouse; and so perfect was his performance to the end that though he was held up by the tail for the audience to view him, he never moved a limb till his master had gently thrown him off the stage (at one of the side scenes) when he got up, and wagging his tail, ran into the green room for his reward—a good supper.[44]

Sadler's Wells, said Reynolds, in point of fashion, resembled the Opera House on a Saturday night during the height of the season, with 'princes, peers, puppies, and pickpockets all crowding to see what Jack Churchill, with his accustomed propensity to punning, used to term the illustrious dog-*stars*'.[45] Not since Mrs Midnight's Oratory in the 1750s, when her Animal Comedians caused 'Every boarding-house romp and wanton school-boy [to] be employed in preventing the end of the canine creation',[46] had performing animals enjoyed such a vogue. They eclipsed even Breslaw's singular display in Cockspur Street in 1775 of the Deserter Bird, who, like Moustache, 'The moment the explosion took place' (this time from a miniature cannon lit by another military canary), 'fell down and lay apparently motionless, like a dead bird, but at the command of his tutor . . . rose up again'.[47]

But in spite of their celebrity, such spectacles were held in contempt by the theatrical profession as well as by the discerning theatre-going public,

[42] Reynolds, *Life and Times*, i. 263–4.
[43] BL, Collections relating to Sadler's Wells, i. 209.
[44] Parke, *Musical Memoirs*, ii. 292–3.
[45] Reynolds, *Life and Times*, i. 261.
[46] Quoted in Thomas Frost, *The Old Showmen and the Old London Fairs* (1874), 170.
[47] Vide Strutt, *The Sport and Pastimes of the People of England from the Earliest Period* (new edn. 1801), 200.

who considered them worthy of the fair booth, 'where sense and reason
are set at defiance, and where an admirer of the drama would be ashamed
to appear'. They were considered to be on a level with tumblers and all
those other 'minor amusements' that 'vitiated taste and debased
society'.[48] And the Dancing Dogs themselves did not escape opprobrium.
Their appearance in Ireland was labelled as an 'affront' and as proof that
Daly had 'vilely disgraced—and abused' the Irish stage.[49]

The dogs, however, had a long career. In May 1784 they were
advertised at Astley's at the Royal Grove, Westminster.[50] And a 1786
handbill looking very similar to Scaglioni's advertised the 'Dancing
Dogs', again at Astleys, under the auspices, though, of 'Signor and
Signora Maisa'.[51] Then John Bernard in 1793, when managing the
theatre in Plymouth, recalled hiring for a night 'from an Italian' a company of dogs who performed *The Deserter*. The canine actor who played
Skirmish was, said Bernard, 'so full of characteristic fun, that I don't
think my old friend Vandermere, the richest colourist of the part in the
opera I ever witnessed, could have looked at the "Comical Dog" and sat
with complacency'.[52]

There is a story associated with Moustache, told almost a hundred
years later by that self-styled chronicler of canine wonders, the Revd
Charles Williams,[53] which suggests that the dog once belonged to a
French soldier. So famous had his personality and tricks become—
especially his impersonation of the deserter, 'with dropped tail and ears,
going through his trial . . . standing upright to be shot at; and at the
sound imitating the discharge of guns, suddenly falling down, and lying
stretched on the floor as if he was actually dead'[54]—that the soldier was
offered a large sum for him by a high-ranking officer. According to
Williams, the offer was refused and the dog was later poisoned by 'some

---

[48] Robert Hitchcock, *An Historical View of the Irish Stage from the Earliest Period down
to the Close of the Season 1788* (1788–94), ii. 145; James Boaden, *Memoirs of the Life of
John Philip Kemble* (1825), i. 361.

[49] *Candid Remarks upon the Stage-bill, Now Depending* (1785).

[50] May 25, 1784, 'Several extraordinary manoeuvres of the Dancing Dogs', in J.
Decastro, *The Memoirs of J. Decastro* (1824), 'Scarce advertisements', 25.

[51] V&A Picture Library, Negative S.1783. Engraving, 'The Original and Amazing Troop
of Dancing Dogs, from Italy and France, added to the Entertainments at Astley's,
Westminster-Bridge, which will be continued every Evening, during the Season, by the
much celebrated Signor and Signora Maisa'. Date given by V&A. There may, of course,
have been two distinct troops of dancing dogs performing at the time.

[52] Bernard, *Retrospections*, ii. 288.

[53] See Charles Williams, *Dogs and Their Ways* (London, 1863); *Anecdotes of Dogs*
(London, [1869]).

[54] Williams, *Anecdotes of Dogs*, 66–7.

miscreant'. The story goes that years later, whenever Moustache was mentioned, the owner, who was known, Williams said, to a friend of his, 'could scarcely refrain from tears'.[55]

Although Moustache is even today a popular dog's name in France, it is unlikely that there were two of such distinction. We could therefore twist Williams's hearsay story a little and suppose that the famous dog had indeed been sold—perhaps to Castelli—who might after all have been what his son later claimed: a colonel and of 'great family'.

Castelli was certainly never a colonel in the English army. The only colonel who was, and who may also conceivably have been Castell's father, was Colonel John Doyle, the member for Mullingar, who as a Lieutenant-Colonel was to sign a commission in the 1790s appointing Peter Castell, gentleman, a cavalry quartermaster to the 87th Regiment—of which more later.

How a colonel, then, in the pre-Revolutionary French army should have come to be connected with a troop of performing animals in England and Ireland is a perplexing question. It certainly would have represented a distinct loss of social caste—remembering, though, that it was Sieur Scaglioni not Castelli himself who was the public showman. Castelli was in all likelihood the entrepreneur and as such would have preserved at least a modicum of social dignity among his erstwhile peers. It may indeed have been his 'breeding' and connections, legitimate or otherwise, which contributed to the success of the enterprise and brought even members of the Royal family out along the robber-infested roads from the West End to Spa Fields.

And it seems to have paid in financial terms as well. Reynolds reckoned that the proprietor of Sadler's Wells, Wroughton, made £7,000 out of the show.[56] Perhaps Castelli made enough to set himself up in London as a gentleman of 'great family' and win Sophia Jones, perhaps with a view to promoting her talents as he had done those of his dogs.

As box-keeper to Smithson and later probably to Vere Hunt's company, Castelli was once again involved in an essentially entrepreneurial occupation. In the days before numbered seats and matching tickets, the theatre-goer could only reserve his or her seat in the box through negotiation and payment of gratuities to the box-keeper. It was an arrangement which also suited the theatre management since the box-keeper was himself a source of revenue rather than a paid servant. In the larger London theatres, according to the theatre historian W. J. Lawrence, the rent the box-keeper paid the theatre could be as high as

[55] Ibid.   [56] Reynolds, *Life and Times,* 264.

£500 a year, which meant that he had to extort quite appreciable sums from patrons in order to make a decent return on his investment. To do this, he often created the very obstacles he was paid to relieve.[57] A delicate trade obviously, and one usually plied by men of maturity and judgement, although Luttrell's diary entry for 25 January 1705 records at least one woman. 'Last night Captain Walsh quarelling with Mrs Hudson, who keeps the boxes in the playhouse, she pulled out his sword and killed him.'[58]

That the trade could be a lucrative one is suggested by a story that when the celebrated manager Colly Cibber (1671–1757) was imprisoned, his box-keeper, Mr King, actually offered to raise bail for him of £10,000 and reckoned he should have been sorry if he could not have raised twice that sum.[59] Perhaps theatre managers had curbed such capacities since those times, but it would also seem to have been a position of some authority in the hierarchy of the theatre itself. It was the box-keeper along with the guardsmen, during the riots at Covent Garden of 1801, who entered the gallery and quelled the rioters.[60] It was a profession, then, which evidently called for demonstrable talents: cunning, courage, and not a little belligerence among them; talents which would not have been out of place in a military environment.

Indeed, notwithstanding the occasional violent persecution of provincial theatres to the point of extinction, and the sometimes very real threat to female favourites posed by over-enthusiastic military admirers for whom harassment and even abduction of female members of theatrical companies were modes of behaviour not wholly inconsistent with gentlemanly codes of conduct, there existed between the military and theatrical life in the eighteenth and early nineteenth centuries a distinct cultural connection. It was observable not only in the fact that the military was itself possessed of a distinctly theatrical air, or in the fact that theatre companies were often run by martinets, but also in the prominent role the military played as patrons of the theatre.[61] Perhaps in

---

[57] W. J. Lawrence, 'The Old Box-Keeper . . .', *Birmingham Mail*, 1 Feb. 1824, in W. J. Lawrence, MS, 22 vols. of Miscellaneous Papers concerning the History of the Theatre in Ireland, comp. by W. J. Lawrence. INL MSS 4292–4314, xiv. 1; The Old Stager, 'Box Office Bilking', *The Stage*, 7 Feb. 1935, in Lawrence, Miscellaneous Papers, xx. 2.

[58] Narcissus Luttrell, *A Brief Historical Relation of State Affairs from September 1678 to April 1714* (1857), v. 513.

[59] Extract from Thomas Davies, *Dramatic Miscellanies . . .* (3 vols. 1784) in *Gentleman's Magazine* liv (1784) pt. 1, p. 364.

[60] Henry Saxe Wyndham, *The Annals of Covent Garden Theatre from 1732 to 1897* (1906), i. 287.

[61] See Arnold Hare, *The Georgian Theatre in Wessex* (1958), 15–16.

acknowledgement of this, the language of the theatre was often couched in military terms, with frequent references to campaigns and battles, generals and troops. Officers often enough donned the sock and buskin in charity performances. In 1783, on 8 August, Wolfe Tone performed at Kirwan's Lane, Galway, in a performance in which the cast, except for the ladies, was wholly comprised of officers;[62] and actors certainly liked dressing up as soldiers even off the stage. John Kemble took a special pleasure in parading in his Volunteer's uniform in Ireland in the 1780s,[63] and the favourite but wayward actor George Frederick Cooke, suffering from the results of his 'irregularities' (drink), was returned to England, given a 'private' situation, and put to bed in Chatham barracks.[64]

This association may certainly help to explain the relationship between Castelli, the theatre box-keeper, and Doyle, the career soldier and politician—and even more so the possible relationship between Doyle and the box-keeper's wife.

Final days

When the Kilkenny season ended in July 1789, perhaps constrained by the obligations of motherhood, or perhaps simply because there were no other options open to her, Mrs Castelli announced that she intended to reside in the town and undertook to 'instruct a few young ladies in the FRENCH and ITALIAN Languages, in a correct and Superior Stile; also MUSIC, VOCAL and INSTRUMENTAL'.[65] In December she was still there and performed in leading roles in special performances on behalf of the Charitable Society.[66] But whether by desire or necessity, she was soon to be on the move again.

In January 1790, Smithson had set up a refurbished theatre in Ennis,[67] and in April Mrs Castelli advertised her benefit there for the 26th. The *Ennis Chronicle* had already reminded its readers of the duties owed to performers in the matter of their benefits. The benefit was to the actor, it said, his harvest: 'if that fails him it renders him liable to innumerable inconveniences and distresses, as the failure of an entire crop does the farmer.'[68] Perhaps this agricultural analogy appealed to the people of Ennis, for on 17 May, Smithson offered his sincere thanks to his public

---

[62] Playbill published in Frank Macdermot, *Theobald Wolfe Tone and his Times* (1939; reprint, 1980), facing p. 82.
[63] Bernard, *Retrospections*, i. 250–1.   [64] *Monthly Mirror*, Apr. 1795, p. 373.
[65] *FLJ* 15 July 1789.   [66] *FLJ* 5 Dec. 1789, in Clark, *Irish Stage*, 181.
[67] *EC* 15 Jan. 1790.   [68] *EC* 1 Apr. 1790.

for a successful season, and returned for another season later in the year, when the *Ennis Chronicle* was again supportive, with a friendly puff for Mrs Castelli's August benefit.

It seldom occurs that an Actress of Mrs Castelli's merit deigns to visit small towns like this, and to ensure us a return of that excellent actress, we have now an opportunity of rewarding those talents and abilities which we so much admire and applaud: her Benefit has been announced for Wednesday next, and we hope to see it attended in such a manner as to evince our desire to encourage and protect merit.[69]

The company was due to visit Galway, planning to return to Ennis for the races, but circumstances intervened and as far as is known, in spite of the *Chronicle*'s supplication, Mrs Castelli never did come back to Ennis.

While Smithson and his company were away in Galway, Sir Vere Hunt and his Company of the United Theatres of the South stole a march and installed themselves in the town. Adding insult to injury, it also looks as if Sir Vere may have attempted to poach Smithson's talent as well, since Mrs Castelli was forced to deny publicly that she was leaving Smithson, presumably to join Hunt. The report, she said, was 'totally groundless, and only fabricated for sinister views'.[70] The usurpers opened on 13 September with Mrs Achmet playing Mrs Castelli's role of Yarico in *Inkle and Yarico*.

Sir Vere Hunt's intrusion into Smithson's territory cannot have been welcome. Smithson had invested capital in his Ennis theatre which he may not have recouped, and he had certainly intended returning.[71] More galling, perhaps, was the fact that although Hunt's company was professionally run, he himself was a dilettante—a wealthy baronet who did not live from his company's earnings. Like Daly in Dublin, though, he was probably an inveterate gambler. Daly used to turn his theatre after the play into a high-class gambling resort frequented by the most notorious 'bucks' of the town, among whom was Sir Vere Hunt.[72] Very possibly he used his own theatres in the same way. Whether, also like Daly, he had trouble as a result in paying his actors' salaries, is a hypothetical possibility.

---

[69] *EC* 16 Aug. 1790.

[70] *EC* 13 Sept. 1790.

[71] *EC* 19 Aug. 1790.

[72] *An Answer to the Memoirs of Mrs Billington with the Life and Adventures of Richard Daly Esq, and an Account of the Present State of the Irish Theatre* (1792), 36. 'Mr Daly . . . has nightly suppers in the theatre when the performances are over, at which Sir V——H——, G—— M——, and the most notorious gamesters are invited.'

On paper he paid Mrs Achmet his top salary of £1. 11s. 6d. per week, which was 6d. more than he paid his top male actor, and £1. 1s. more than he paid the other female members of the company.[73] Mrs Achmet, born Catherine Egan, daughter of an Irish surgeon, was the wife of the exotic Dr Barumdad Achmet. A clever self-publicist and impostor, whose real name was William Cairns, Achmet had won some notoriety before quitting wife and country, but is chiefly remembered for having introduced Turkish baths into Dublin. Apart from her marriage, Mrs Achmet's celebrity seems to have consisted in her handsome physiognomy, recorded in Walker's *Hibernian Magazine* in 1788, and in her performances of the minuet. She had subsequently tried her attractions on London at Covent Garden, but her powers seem to have failed her on that occasion and she returned to Ireland, evidently to be snapped up by Sir Vere.[74]

How much Mrs Castelli was earning with Smithson we do not know— nor do we know whether Hunt actually approached her with an offer. As a performer, Mrs Castelli may well have been superior to Mrs Achmet, but the latter enjoyed those advantages of nature and notoriety already alluded to, which Hunt obviously felt warranted his generosity, and if he had indeed offered Mrs Castelli an engagement it may well have been as an also-ran at 10s. 6d. a week. In any case, Smithson determined to put as much space between himself and Hunt as he could, and by 8 November 1790 the Company of Comedians, with Mrs Castelli, were back in Kilkenny. On 22 November the company gave *He Would be a Soldier*, by desire of a person (perhaps Major Doyle, the member for Mullingar) 'of the First Distinction'. Probably playing Charlotte, Mrs Castelli was prominently advertised.

Mr Castelli was still the box-keeper, but when, in early January 1791, one of a series of 'Gentlemen's Plays' was given for the benefit of the company, Mr Smithson himself took charge of the boxes. The cast comprised lady and gentlemen amateurs 'of consequence', the only two professionals being Mr Brennan and Mrs Scott.[75] It was events such as these that perhaps led Lady Morgan to describe Kilkenny as the 'Versailles of Ireland'. The 'richness and magnificence of the dresses' were particularly noted. The orchestra was composed of 'gentlemen of the first musical talents' who performed in the execution of some of the

[73] Vere Hunt, MS 'Account Books', in Clark, *Irish Stage*, 61. Quoted for the 1789/90 Limerick season.
[74] Lawrence, Miscellaneous Papers, viii. 98a; ix. 77.
[75] *FLJ* 5 Jan.; 12 Jan. 1791.

pieces with 'great taste', which, combined with the abilities of the dramatis personae, 'produced a striking influence of the "force of harmony, the feast of reason, and the flow of soul" '.[76]

This appears to say very little for the professionals upon whom such encomiums were never lavished. The 'gentlemen's' repertoire consisted of Hannah More's tragedy, *Percy*, Fletcher's comedy, *Rule a Wife and Have a Wife*, and the farce *Bon Ton*. But, apparently unabashed, Smithson reopened the theatre on 31 January for his own benefit, *As You Like It*, in which Mrs Castelli played Celia. The season of benefits went on till 4 March, ending with another for Mr Smithson which included 'some very expensive pantomimical entertainments, founded on the subjects of the *French Revolution*, called the "Triumph of Liberty or the Destruction of the Bastile", exhibiting one of the most grand and interesting spectacles that ever engaged the feelings of mankind'.[77]

Mrs Castelli made her last appeal to the gentility of Kilkenny in late January 1791. Her benefit was to take place on 3 February, in which, however, she herself would be unable to perform, being again 'indisposed'.[78] It was also to be her last season with Smithson. By 23 February, with another of Smithson's players, Mr Brennan, she was in Limerick in the enemy camp, with Sir Vere Hunt's company under the management of William Moss.[79]

The pregnancy implied in Mrs Castelli's 'indisposition' and non-appearance at her own benefit in February seems not to have interfered significantly with her itinerary. In this she was not remarkable. If anything she was perhaps less robust than many other women in similar circumstances, who sometimes went directly from the stage to the delivery couch with some pomp, and back again without too much delay. This was doubtless also a tribute to the audiences of the time, who quite happily coped even with the sometimes obvious dramatic contradictions that a heavily pregnant heroine could inflict upon their credulity. Tate Wilkinson records, for example, the case of Mrs Osborne, who right up to the moment she was carried off to the couch had been playing the role of a heroine whose nuptials had been tragically prevented.[80]

We can only speculate on the reasons why Mrs Castelli left Smithson. It may have been because he was planning to return to the west,[81] which

---

[76] *FLJ* 12 Jan. 1791.   [77] *FLJ* 19 Feb. 1791.
[78] *FLJ* 29 Jan. 1791.   [79] Clark, *Irish Stage*, 63.
[80] Tate Wilkinson, *Memoirs*, ii. 96–7, quoted in Hare, *Georgian Theatre in Wessex*, 51, with other examples and comments on the same subject, 110–11.
[81] Clark, *Irish Stage*, 182.

may no longer have suited her, or it may simply have been that Vere Hunt offered her more money. In March, there is a record of his paying her only 16s. 8d., but by 30 April her salary seems to have risen to £1. 5s. 0d. Not quite in Mrs Achmet's league but far better than the 10s. 6d. he usually paid female members of the company. It would appear also that Hunt employed Mr Castelli in some capacity. He paid him £4. 11s. 0d. on 8 March 1791 and lent him £1. 2s. 9d. on 5 May.[82]

The season in Limerick was short, ending on 18 March, and after a month the company moved on to Cork, opening at the 'New Theatre Royal', Princes Street, on 26 April.[83] It was a far cry from 1788, when Mrs Castelli had first appeared in Cork with Daly and a first-rate company at the Theatre Royal, George Street. This 1791 return with Hunt hardly seemed to make an impact. Cork was a significant mercantile city and there were other diversions. Astley's 'Living Rarities' was at the Royal Tent, where for a British shilling, half price for 'trades-people and the Younger Members of Families', admittance, only with the utmost difficulty, could be gained.[84] The Theatre Royal itself, in George Street, had initially been engaged by the amateurs who put on *Lionel and Clarissa* on 25 April, and Breslaw's was offering 'New Various Entertainments' (perhaps his famous military canaries) and Roasted Leg of Mutton.[85]

On 12 May, however, it was noted that Vere Hunt's company was to put on the old standard, Mrs Centlivre's *The Wonder a Woman Keeps a Secret*, for Mrs Wells's benefit, for which Mrs Castelli was to sing 'Tally Ho'.[86] But trouble had been brewing, and a final disagreement between Hunt and his manager, Moss, left the 'troops' disbanded and without leadership. Sir Vere Hunt had 'retired', presumably to the comforts of Dublin.[87]

As fate would have it, it was Daly who then had control of the Theatre Royal in George Street.[88] With Hunt's company out of the way (Ezra Wells had taken what was left of it to Youghal),[89] Daly opened at the Theatre Royal in August, engaging Mrs Billington 'to perform a few

---

[82] Vere Hunt, MS 'Account with John Booker, 28 Aug. 1790–22 June 1791', extract, courtesy Mid-West Archives, Limerick, Ireland.
[83] Clark, *Irish Stage*, 128.
[84] HC(C), 9 May 1791.
[85] HC(C), 25 Apr. 1791, for 'the Amateurs'; 16 May 1791, for Breslaw's.
[86] HC(C), 12 May 1791. Actually advertised for 11th; obviously a misprint.
[87] Clark, *Irish Stage*, 63.
[88] HC(C), 30 June 1791 advertised Mr Hurst's benefit at Mr Daly's theatre, Theatre Royal, George Street.
[89] Clark, *Irish Stage*, 129.

nights in the ensuing Season for Fifty Pounds per Night'. Engaged as well were Incledon and other musical celebrities.[90] There is no evidence either that Mrs Castelli was engaged in some minor capacity with the Daly company in Cork or that she went to Youghal with Ezra Wells. But by November 1791 she was certainly back with Daly for the winter season in Dublin.

RICHARD DALY AND THE IRISH THEATRE

Richard Daly came from a 'good', which is to say Protestant landed family near Galway—the second son of an affluent farmer—and was educated at Trinity College, Dublin,[91] where according to most sources he was something of a disturbing influence, rendering himself obnoxious 'by the extreme looseness of his manners and principles'.[92]

In Daly's time, Trinity 'bucks' were a formidable element in Dublin society, frequently terrorizing the inhabitants and often descending upon the theatre, creating riot, confusion, and even death. The lawyer and eventual judge of the High Court of the Admiralty in Ireland, Sir Jonah Barrington, himself once a student of Trinity, considered such activities to be no more than youthful high spirits which arose merely 'from the fire and natural vivacity of uncontrolled youth: No calm deliberate vices,— no low meannesses,—were ever committed.'[93] But the plebeian view was different. In 1759, the singing actor Joseph Vernon witnessed a cold-blooded murder in the Brown Bear Coffee House next to the theatre. Trinity students burst in and without provocation stabbed a young man to death, after which they calmly adjourned to the theatre. One of their number was subsequently arrested, tried, and acquitted. Vernon himself, though, did not give evidence, considering it prudent to leave the country.[94] Such was the tradition of élitist Trinity which Daly inherited and which he seemed to have taken to his heart. In his own day, he was regarded as 'so given to commotion that he was the terror of all public places'.[95] In 1772, he led a raid on the green room of the theatre,[96] and it was noted that several watchmen (traditional objects of student animosity) were murdered in the streets of Dublin, during the period of Daly's 'youthful pranks'.[97]

---

[90] *HC*(C), 8 Aug. 1791. [91] *DNB* (1888) [Richard Daly].
[92] *Answer to the Memoirs of Mrs Billington*, 24.
[93] Barrington, *Personal Sketches*, ii. 200. [94] Lewes, *Memoirs*, ii. 151–5.
[95] John O'Keefe, *Recollections of the Life of John O'Keefe* (1826), ii. 44.
[96] Ibid. [97] *Answer to the Memoirs of Mrs Billington*, 24.

Temperamentally, Daly was what the actor and playwright John O'Keefe rather generously liked to call 'naturally ardent and impatient', and on a personal level 'a man of great humanity and a zealous friend'.[98] O'Keefe, however, was virtually alone in this assessment. In line with the social mores of the day, he was certainly accorded something close to respect for his courage and panache as a duellist, fighting, so it was said, sixteen in two years with swords and pistols. He dressed up always in a pea-green suit and presented his full front, 'conspicuously finished with an elegant brooch'.[99] But he also possessed a capacity for spontaneous generosity and *bonhomie* which even his enemies acknowledged. John Bernard, usually no admirer of Daly, recounts how after having left Daly's company in disgust, he met him by chance along the road. Bernard's actress wife was ill, and his finances were in a poor state. Daly expressed regret at their having become estranged, and to Bernard's great surprise made him a gift of £20.[100] He was more usually, though, reviled as a murderer, swindler, rapist, and debauchee.

There was the unfortunate billiard-marker at Mara's table in Cope Street. After giving a decision against Daly a billiard ball was thrown at the man with such violence that hitting him in the eye, it killed him.[101] The law, it seems, was impotent. Then there was the famous case of the 'pigeoning' of the results of the lottery; which is to say, conspiring to get early news of the draw in London, before insuring the numbers in Dublin to the tune of £6,000.[102]

But the crimes for which he was probably most reviled were those reputedly committed against women, using either physical or economic force to gain sexual advantage. The comedian William Oxberry, for whom Daly was 'a weak-minded villain, an unjust manager and an unprincipled libertine', in a memoir of Mrs Jordan, wished, 'even now when that weak villain's bones have returned to the corruption that best befitted them . . . to call them from the grave, to be burnt as a sacrifice to offended decency'. Mrs Jordan, he recognized, turned out in her subsequent career to be less than 'a straight-laced moralist', but it was not simply sensualism that Oxberry condemned—for he was not averse, he

---

[98] O'Keefe, *Recollections*, 43–4.

[99] J. T. Gilbert, *History of the City of Dublin* (1861), ii. 105, quoting from an unspecified title of Boaden.

[100] Bernard, *Retrospections*, i. 302.

[101] *Answer to the Memoirs of Mrs Billington*, 25; This is also one of the crimes ascribed to Daly by John Magee from 1789, according to Gilbert, *History of the City of Dublin*, iii. 31. The date of this event is not specified.

[102] *Answer to the Memoirs of Mrs Billington*, 55; also *DNB* [Richard Daly].

The Irish Manager.

2. Richard Daly. Originally
published in *Town and Country
Magazine*, xviii (1787), 625,
beside a portrait of 'The Tomboy'
[Mrs Jordan]. Ref. BM DG 7190.

said, to conquest 'gained by favour'—but rather Daly's meanness and
violence.[103] It was in his capacity as theatrical manager that Daly was
apparently most callously exploitative in his relations with female
members of his companies, and where he earned most disapproval.

Georgian theatre managers were notoriously tyrannical and unpopular (Oxberry reckoned the only 'good fellow' of all the managers he
ever heard of was Tate Wilkinson), and certainly it is necessary to
consider this in relation to the accusations made against Daly. The
manager in relatively recent years had usurped many of the roles
previously performed collectively by the company. He had also usurped
the right to take all the profits of the company, previously shared among
all the members. This had been achieved by the manager turning
capitalist—a trend that was becoming apparent in England in many

---

[103] William Oxberry, 'A Memoir of Mrs Jordan', *Oxberry's Dramatic Biography and
Histrionic Anecdote*, i (1825), 198.

other fields of endeavour as well.[104] It turned him from being just another member of the company into an employer. The risk involved in his initial outlay undoubtedly made him a hard taskmaster in this respect and necessitated legally binding contracts and sanctions to control employees unused to the discipline of such rational methods of profit-making. It was these contracts and sanctions which Daly was accused of abusing in relation to women, and the near-universality of the accusations would suggest more than a grain of truth.

After Trinity, Daly had been sent to London to study law, but quickly exhausting his patrimony he turned to the stage, studying for some time with Macklin and making an inauspicious London début as Othello. Returning to Dublin, he began his serious career under Ryder in 1780–1. He had married, however, the celebrated Miss Barsanti, then Mrs Lyster, who had had the good fortune to be widowed and left in possession of some capital with which Daly launched himself as manager, ousting the unfortunate Ryder in a somewhat controversial coup in October 1781.[105]

That Daly's style of management was despotic there can be little doubt. There was the story of his ordering the horns in the orchestra to be forfeited because in a particular section of the score they had a 'rest'.[106] It may have been apocryphal. The same story was told against Astley as far away as New South Wales as late as 1835.[107] But considering Daly's recorded problems with his band, and his inclination to dispense with them where possible, it does have plausibility.[108] And Daly's forfeits were considered at the best of times to be overly punitive. They included the following:

Refusing a part, first time	£5. 0. 0
On a second refusal it is the manager's option to discharge you	
Looking through the green curtain	10. 6
Being absent in any scene of the play at rehearsal	2. 6

[104] Oxberry, 'A Memoir of Mrs Jordan', 199; see Hare, *Georgian Theatre in Wessex*, 85–9; and for a general view, James J. Lynch, *Box, Pit and Gallery. Stage and Society in Johnson's London* (1953), ch. 7, 'The Manager'.

[105] *Thespian Dictionary or Dramatic Biography of the Present Age* (2nd edn., 1805); Henry Boylan, *A Dictionary of Irish Biography* (1978).

[106] *Answer to the Memoirs of Mrs Billington*, 4.

[107] *Aust.* 11 Dec. 1835.

[108] See treatment of the theatre orchestra later on in this chapter. Daly was also castigated by Magee in 1789 for his failure to provide an orchestra for his theatre in Limerick. *DEP* 29 Aug. 1789. The author of *Candid Remarks upon the Stage-bill* reckoned that Daly was musically ignorant.

Not being ready at the time of beginning	10. 6
Coming to business intoxicated	£5. 0. 0
Looking at the Viceroy when he comes to the play	10. 6
Going on the stage improperly dressed	10. 6
Playing imperfect	£1. 1. 0
Striking, or returning a blow in the theatre	£5. 5. 0

Cum multis aliis &c[109]

But it was not simply the forfeits themselves which were objectionable. Other theatres had similar disciplinary provisions and it should be noted that in the 1799/1800 season at Covent Garden, James Harris increased the fine for refusing a part from £5 to £30.[110] It was rather the manner in which Daly operated them. Like the £200 bond or 'articles' required by most theatre managers, it was his abuse of the legal sanction, not the sanction itself, which gained him his reputation for ruthlessness and corruption.[111]

Daly's strategy, according to report, was first to attempt to seduce by his charms and by his power to offer prestigious roles. Failing this, he would instruct the prompter to deliver to the recalcitrant a set of roles which she could not out of pride accept. He would then forfeit her. Deprived of her income (a forfeit of £5 being more than the usual weekly wage for all but the most illustrious), and dunned by creditors, she would flee, only to be pursued by the law and thrown into prison for default of her 'articles', where she might repent at leisure her rejection of the manager's simple demands.[112]

Even by the standards of the day, Daly's promiscuity was apparently rather excessive. By his own celebrated and apparently amiable wife he had nine children, but could not resist, it would seem, any sexual opportunity that presented itself in the form of attractive members of his company over whom he had such awesome economic power. The names of Jordan, Esten, and Billington figure prominently in the chronicles of Daly's predilections,[113] but according to Boaden he was nothing less than

---

[109] *Answer to the Memoirs of Mrs Billington.*

[110] *The London Stage 1660–1800. A Calendar of Plays, Entertainments & Afterpieces* ... (1958), part 5, p. 2202.

[111] *Answer to the Memoirs of Mrs Billington*, 45–7.

[112] Ibid. 49–50; Oxberry reckoned his method was to advance small sums of money and then sue for debt as a form of leverage. 'Memoir of Mrs Jordan', 198.

[113] For Mrs Jordan, see Oxberry, 'Memoir of Mrs Jordan'; James Boaden, *The Life of Mrs Jordan* (1801); for Mrs Billington, *Answer to the Memoirs of Mrs Billington*, and [James Ridgway], *Memoirs of Mrs Billington, from her Birth, containing a Variety of Matter, ludicrous, theatrical, musical and —— with Copies of several Letters now in the*

'the general lover of his theatrical company'.[114] A spectacularly attractive man, except for a rather unpleasant squint[115] (although one contemporary described him as resembling more a hairdresser or *valet de chambre* than a gentleman),[116] it is possible of course that many of his conquests were achieved without recourse to managerial prerogatives.

Daly, like so many other eighteenth-century managers, was not essentially a business man, but an actor who shared the same stage as his subordinates and suffered likewise the judgement of the same audiences. He had, of course, certain material advantages; his talent was not his only recommendation, as John Bernard, who was in Daly's company in 1782, recalled: 'Daly, our manager, had a good memory, a good person, and a good wardrobe, with good parts to play—which were the entire constituents of his good acting; but he was a manager and could give away orders to get himself applauded.'[117]

Daly, however, was no shirker when it came to capital investment. In 1788, with his friend Francis Higgins (1746–1802), solicitor and proprietor of the *Freeman's Journal*, he spent £12,000 on refurbishing the Crow Street theatre in Dublin,[118] which, in the currency values of the times, was a speculative investment of serious magnitude. But by then he had secured a legal theatrical monopoly. By an Act of the Irish Parliament in 1786, 'for the establishment of a well regulated theatre in the City of Dublin', he had been declared Master of the Revels with control of theatrical proprietorship. Anyone who wished to build or rent a theatre had first to gain his consent.

This rather powerful piece of leverage, both cultural and commercial, bestowed so generously by government ought to suggest that Daly had friends in high places, or that Francis Higgins did. Certainly the bestowing of such a monopoly presupposes if not a total compliance then at least a demonstrable loyalty to the ruling clique at Dublin Castle, a notion not inconsistent with the fact that Francis Higgins, popularly known by the sobriquet of 'The Sham Squire', was to become, if he was

possession of the Publisher, written by Mrs Billington to her Mother, the late Mrs Weichsel (1792); for Mrs Esten and the accusations against Daly by John Magee, the editor of DEP, see Scaramuccio, 'The Adorable Mrs Esten', *Irish Life*, 1 Aug. 1913, in Lawrence, Miscellaneous Papers, ix. 12a.

[114] Boaden, *Mrs Jordan*, i. 12.
[115] Gilbert, *History of the City of Dublin*, ii. 105.
[116] *Answer to the Memoirs of Mrs Billington*, 44.
[117] Bernard, *Retrospections*, i. 235.
[118] Gilbert, *History of the City of Dublin*, ii. 208.

not already, one of the government's most reliable and useful informers in the years of political agitation and turmoil that were to follow.[119]

The monopoly turned out, however, not to be as powerful as it might have been. Probably because of a loophole in the 1786 law which permitted the Lord Mayor to exercise some remnant of his old prerogatives (which had not been given up without a struggle), Astley's circus managed to circumvent it. As a result, Daly was forced in 1787 to take out leases on 'every other vacant place in the city suitable for a circus', in an attempt to forestall what was to become quite serious competition.[120] But he was unsuccessful. Astley managed to get a spot in Peter Street, where he met with extraordinary success well into 1788. Scandalous paragraphs subsequently appeared in 'some of the papers against Mr Astley ... skulking under the mask of public criticism'.[121] One of Astley's performers, the comedian John Decastro, recalled the affair with some bitterness in his 1824 *Memoirs*, describing 'the great Mr Daly's' management of the Dublin theatre in very unflattering terms. Daly, he said, 'then kept that place of entertainment in a most wretched, filthy and degraded state. The men performers he nearly starved on playhouse pay, performing once or twice a week instead of every night; and the women he kept by the same means, in a state of compliance to his desires.'[122] Monopoly, it would seem, had brought with it its own problems, not only of artistic complacency but of public disquiet and private jealousy.

The reference to Daly's 'desires' was a slight variation on the usual theme. Mrs Castelli was at that time in Daly's company, but seemed in robust enough health. In May she appeared at the Philharmonic Society's benefit for distressed debtors, conducted by Giordani, along with other

---

[119] Gilbert, *History of the City of Dublin*, ii. 207; *Thespian Dictionary*; for Higgins's role as a government informer, see W. J. Fitzpatrick, *A Note to the Cornwallis Papers Embracing with other Revelations, a Narrative of the extraordinary Career of Francis Higgins, who received the Government reward for the Betrayal of Lord Edward Fitzgerald* (1859); and T. J. Walsh, *Opera in Dublin 1705–1797* (1973). See also the entry for Francis Higgins in *DNB*, but in the matter of the betrayal of Lord Edward Fitzgerald, see Michael MacDonagh, *The Viceroy's Post-Bag. Correspondence hitherto unpublished of the Earl of Hardwicke First Lord Lieutenant of Ireland after the Union* (1904), 366–9: the letter of 23 Aug. 1803 from Hardwicke to his brother Charles Yorke, then Home Secretary, which makes it clear that Higgins was only the conduit. The £1,000 reward did actually go to Higgins, but was meant for the real informer Francis Magan. At Higgins's death though, the money had still not been paid over.

[120] See petition of the Commons, 'put under the city seal' against the bill, presented to the Irish House of Commons, Dublin, Assembly Roll, 27 June 1785, in *Calendar of Ancient Records of Dublin*, ed. by Lady Gilbert (1907), xiii. 424, 435–6; *Candid Remarks upon the Stage-bill*, esp. p. 30; for Astley's, see Gilbert, *History of the City of Dublin*, i. 45.

[121] *FDJ* 4 Apr. 1788.

[122] Decastro, *Memoirs*, 51.

leading ladies from Daly's company. She played June in the burletta *Midas*.[123] On 2 June, she was presumably the Signora Castelli making her first appearance at the Rotunda with Messrs Weichsel and Ashe.[124]

Her career with Daly till then, however, had been rather patchy and may well have reflected those managerial manipulations to which the females of his company were said to have been subject. Initially, in November 1787, her appearance had been greeted with enthusiasm, perhaps at Daly's behest, by *Faulkner's Dublin Journal*. She had played Lucinda in *Love in a Village*—an important, but not a leading role. 'We understand', said *Faulkner's*, 'she has been but a short time on the Stage, nevertheless her youth, figure and voice will we doubt not in a short space of time place her in a most respectable rank in the theatre.'[125] But this prominence was short-lived. Almost immediately she was relegated to the role of Colombine in the pantomime *The Triumph of Mirth; or Harlequin's Vagaries*, in which she was effectively upstaged by Chalmers and O'Reilly as Harlequin and Clown.[126] This was probably the 1783 Drury Lane production with the elder Grimaldi and music by T. Linley, doctored to suit Irish audiences by Chalmers.[127] It was probably also the production described by Dawson (one of Daly's lieutenants, one-time proprietor of Capel Street theatre) in Bernard's *Retrospections* in which a 'dog-cart' was introduced, drawn by four mastiffs and attended by an ape postillion dressed in livery. It had featured in an elopement scene to Gretna Green, carrying off Harlequin and Colombine. 'It accordingly circuited the stage once or twice, the Clown and Pantaloon pursuing . . . contributing by its run . . . to the run of the pantomime.'[128] Shades of the 'Dancing Dogs' and Mr Castelli?

When the new theatre in Crow Street was opened in 1788, the *Triumph of Mirth* did not transfer there. Its last advertised appearance was on 28 January, just as the benefit season was about to begin—a season in which Mrs Castelli's name does not appear, except on 5 April in support of Mrs Molloy when she appeared as Sophia in *The Lord of the Manor*.[129] But she bounced back in June with several leading roles at

[123] *HC(D)*, 21 May 1788.

[124] Ibid. 2 June 1788.   [125] *FDJ* 29 Nov. 1787.

[126] *DEP* 8 Dec. 1787, comments only on Chalmers and O'Reilly, ignoring the role of Colombine altogether.

[127] According to Allardyce Nicoll, *A History of Late Eighteenth-Century Drama, 1750–1800* (1927), *Triumph of Mirth; or Harlequin's Wedding*, was first performed, Drury Lane, 26 Dec. 1782; the *Public Advertiser*, 13 Oct. 1783, refers to it as a 'new Panto' at DL with Grimaldi; Clark, *Irish Stage*, 124, claims it was written by Chalmers and notes special stage effects, snow storm, etc.

[128] Bernard, *Retrospections*, ii. 284–6.   [129] *HC(D)*, 26 Mar. 1788.

Crow Street: as Isalinda in *Busy Body*, the name part in *Rosina*, her old role of Lucinda in *Love in a Village*, Clare in *The Duenna*, and Clorinda in *Robin Hood*. When the Dublin season ended, she opened the Cork season as Clorinda with a formidable cast,[130] but once again faded from the scene. This burst of activity may have been due to sexual politics, there being some circumstantial evidence that Mr Castelli was engaged elsewhere. The Cork *Hibernian Chronicle* noted on 25 August that 'The Dancing Dogs have done more for Bernard in Plymouth than a different species of beings could accomplish—this may be owing to the *refinement* of the times . . .'.[131] The supposition that Daly, in the absence of her husband, bought Mrs Castelli's favours with grateful roles then dumped her when she became pregnant, and perhaps difficult, remains only that—supposition—but it is far from implausible, considering that her child was born in April or May of the following year.

However, by the time Mrs Castelli returned to Dublin and to Daly's company in 1791, Daly's star was decidedly on the wane. Not only was his monopoly about to crumble, but, inflamed by a campaign waged against him by John Magee (d. 1809), editor of the *Dublin Evening Post*, audiences were becoming increasingly hostile towards him.

The Dublin theatre of this period was in almost every respect identical to the Georgian theatre in England, with its aggressively entrepreneurial yet monopolistic economic structure, and its social and cultural ambivalence—at once adored and abhorred, and patronized by almost the full spectrum of the community: from royalty (in Ireland the Viceroy and his entourage) to the perennially obstreperous butchers' boys. The physical design of most Georgian theatres, and certainly of The Smock Alley and Crow Street theatres, reflected, however, the rigid demarcation lines of class and money: boxes for the élite (including those often on the stage itself), the pit for the merely respectable, and the gallery (sometimes more than one and usually invisible to the rest of the house) for the rest. For all the physical separation, however, the general ethos transcended it in a universal liveliness verging on volatility. Rowdy to the point of riot and sometimes beyond, critical and self-consciously aware of its right to be pleased, Georgian audiences were far from the largely passive audiences of today. Frequently they intruded upon the action on the stage, provok-

---

[130] *HC*(C), 4 Aug. 1788. The cast included Messrs Bowden, Duffy, O'Reilly, E. King, Johnston, and Cornellys; Mrs Dawson and Mrs Hitchcock. Also engaged for that season were Mrs Pope, Mr Holman, Mr Clinch, Mr G. Mahon, Miss Hughes, and Mrs Esten.

[131] *HC*(C), 25 Aug. 1788.

ing or encouraging the players. Uproariously censorious or rapturously enthusiastic, the audience was very much a part of every performance.[132]

Reynolds tells how during the first night's performance of *Mysteries of the Castle* at Covent Garden in 1795—a year in which the war with France was going badly and there had been serious domestic unrest at home—the audience, towards the close of the third act, had expressed 'considerable disapprobation at a passage which they conceived to be political—it alluded to "the government's secret enemies"'. Recalling that there was a passage in the next scene using the same words, Reynolds rushed round from his box around to the green room and 'earnestly requested the actors omit the objectionable sentence': which they did and there was no further interruption.[133]

If anything, Dublin audiences were even more attentive. Bernard's *Retrospections* of his days in Ireland give ample testimony to the authority of the audience. He tells how, because the band had walked out, Crawford, the manager of Crow Street during the 1782–3 season, although he was already dressed for his role as Hamlet, was made to play jigs on his fiddle before the play itself was permitted to begin: for which, however, he was good humouredly encored.[134] Nor were actors' physical characteristics spared. The singing actor Bowden apparently had a very protuberant nose which the 'light of the house seemed to converge upon', distracting all eyes by its luminous redness. When he was in Dublin performing in *Robin Hood*, according to Bernard, he suffered considerably from this defect. 'The Smock-Alley House was long and narrow, and whenever he came on, the audience were in the habit of holding conversations from the opposite stage boxes as to the authenticity of his great feature . . .'.[135] 'Such interruptions in the middle of a sentimental song must have been', mused Bernard, who was not a fan of Bowden's, 'vastly pleasant to the singer'.[136]

The two soldiers with fixed bayonets, standing, as Barrington described, 'like statues' on each side of the stage, close to the boxes to keep order, were helpless enough in that kind of situation, as they were apparently in most others.[137] In 1787, during Mrs Castelli's first season in Dublin, *Faulkner's Dublin Journal* fumed at the 'outrages' committed in the upper gallery—the 'hissing, hooting, calling to the Band for

[132] See H. B. Baker, *History of the London Stage* (1904); J. Doran, *'Their Majesties' Servants'. Annals of the English Stage from Thomas Betterton to Edmund Kean* (1888); Hare, *Georgian Theatre in Wessex*; Hume, *London Theatre World 1660–1800*.

[133] Reynolds, *Life and Times*, ii. 198.

[134] Bernard, *Retrospections*, i. 297. [135] Ibid. i. 224–5.

[136] Ibid. [137] Barrington, *Personal Sketches*, i. 197–8.

improper tunes, using the most obscene language, abusing every person within reach of their observation; throwing apples, oranges, nay sometimes glass bottles'.[138]

Actors, who were not always the dolts 'who have scarce human reason' of Pasquin's dispensation,[139] certainly had a lot to contend with and must have possessed at least a modicum of wit to have survived at all. It was of course the age of great actors, if not great plays—the age of the illustrious Kemble family of John, Stephen, and Sarah Siddons, of the Sheridans, the elder Macready, of Lee Digges, Macklin and Munden; of Mrs Crouch, whose father had been an attorney-at-law and friend of Dr Johnson;[140] of Joseph Holman, who had been educated at the Soho School and was a graduate of Queen's College, Oxford;[141] of the self-taught Mrs Inchbald—all of whom at some stage appeared upon the Dublin stage and faced the same vociferous and critical Dublin audiences.

The orchestra was always a very important element in any season. In Dublin it was probably directed at this time by Tommaso Giordani (?1733–1806), one of Dublin's foremost musical residents—violinist, composer, teacher, and co-founder in 1779–81 of a somewhat premature 'national' opera in Capel Street.[142] It would have comprised, on and off, the cream of Dublin's professional musicians, native and imported: Charles Weichsel, James Billington, Andrew Ashe, John Fisher, Henry Mountain, Mahon, and Reinagle were probably all engaged from time to time. Its quality may perhaps be judged from the fact that in the next generation it was to produce a cluster of prodigies to enliven the London musical scene, among whom were Tom Cooke, its leader at the age of 15, and William Vincent Wallace.

Its turbulence was also worthy of note. In December 1787, Daly sacked the whole of it 'for some misbehaviour' and brought in a band from London. Its members and supporters, however, created mayhem from the gallery and only the 'energy' of Daly restored order, so that 'a very crowded and brilliant audience' could enjoy their evening's entertainment, 'without further molestation, or having their ears wounded by indelicacies, more savage than the war-hoop of Indians whom the piece presented [*Inkle and Yarico*]'.[143]

[138] *FDJ* 29 Dec. 1787.
[139] Anthony Williams (pseud. Pasquin), *The Children of Thespis. A Poem* (1792), 243.
[140] i.e., Mr Peregrine Phillips. See *Oxberry's Dramatic Biography and Histrionic Anecdote*, v (1825, 1826), 235.   [141] Boaden, *Kemble*, i. 218.
[142] Flood, *History of Irish Music*, 307–8.   [143] *DEP* 13 Dec. 1787.

From about 1789, however, Daly was faced with a different sort of turbulence. Resentment seems to have been building up towards him, perhaps because of his monopoly, perhaps because of his tactics against Astley, perhaps because of poor standards, or perhaps because of his association with the unpopular and nefarious Francis Higgins. John Magee sustained the growing animosity, accusing him, as 'The Dasher', of the billiard-marker's death, of 'pigeoning' the lottery, and, with his friend and partner, Francis 'The Sham' Higgins, of numerous other malefactions.[144] In August 1789, Magee had played the role of protector to Mrs Esten, who was having the usual difficulties with Daly. She had apparently been forced to flee and had been arrested. Magee used his paper to warn and advise her.[145] At about the same time, Magee was openly calling Daly by such names as 'blackleg' under the guise of musical criticism of his company in Limerick.[146] Frequently 'rendered imbecile by these defaming publications',[147] Daly's response, along with Higgins and two others, was to sue, and perhaps it was the fact of Magee's subsequent imprisonment without bail on the basis of hefty fiats—totalling £7,800—handed down by the Chief Justice, John Scott (1739–98), Lord Earlsfort, later Earl Clonmel and personal friend of Higgins, that aroused the sporting passions of the Dublin rowdies, who proceeded to make sure that the duo's heavy investment in Crow Street, in spite of this blatant testament of establishment support, should bear few fruits: 'numbers of ruffians armed with bludgeons, pistols, and old swords, usually came into the gallery immediately on the opening of the doors and interrupted the performance by shouting—"a clap for Magee, the man of Ireland; a groan for the Sham"'.[148] There were groans for 'the Dasher' as well. Never a man to temporize, Daly, in the trial that eventuated in June 1790, claimed damages of £8,000 against Magee but was finally awarded only £200, plus 6d. costs. Magee, however, remained in prison for some time for contempt of court.[149]

The culmination of all this antagonism was a full-blooded riot in late

---

[144] Gilbert, *History of the City of Dublin*, iii. 31; *DNB* [Richard Daly].

[145] Scaramuccio, 'The Adorable Mrs Esten'.

[146] *DEP* 29 Aug. 1789, quoted in W. J. Lawrence, 'Stories of the Old Limerick Stage', *Evening Telegraph*, 25 Nov. 1922, in Lawrence, Miscellaneous Papers, xiii. 29.

[147] Gilbert, *History of the City of Dublin*, ii. 212.

[148] Ibid. ii. 211–12.

[149] Ibid. iii. 32–3. The issue of the tyrannical fiats imposed upon Magee turned out to be a critical point in Scott's career. Due to agitation, legislation was enacted controlling their application—a direct censure on Scott. His influence subsequently declined. See *DNB*. See also Brian Inglis, *The Freedom of the Press in Ireland 1784–1841* (London, 1954) for a discussion of the case.

December of 1791. Incledon had been advertised to appear at Dawson's benefit but owing to illness could not perform. A violent tumult broke out and apologies were made; but some 'young bucks' in the boxes 'grew outrageous, and most provokingly insolent; they insisted on the manager asking pardon of the house on *his knees*'. Daly of course 'very properly and spiritedly refused', with which:

the lamps and benches began to experience a general demolition. Mr C. D——, the councellor [Daly's brother] was in the front of the house and naturally incensed . . . [he] took a decided part in the business; and seizing hold of the first aggressor . . . very properly punished him for his wantonness and presumption. Mr R. D—— feeling his brother in imminent danger from the superiority of numbers, came to his assistance, and drove the *principal rioter* from the house . . .[150]

The upshot, rather surprisingly, was that Charles Daly was sentenced to one year's imprisonment and Daly to six months.[151]

This event should have meant the forfeiture of his theatre, or at the very least his official monopoly, which was conditional upon good behaviour.[152] But, perhaps unsurprisingly, given his possible connections with the government through Higgins, this was not to be the case. Daly's hold on both his theatre and his monopoly continued till his voluntary 'retirement' in 1797 when Frederick Jones bought him out on very advantageous terms to Daly.[153] Those last years, however, had been made increasingly difficult.

In 1792 James Ridgway, after he had been refused 'hush money', published a scurrilous attack on Mrs Billington which brought up some ancient and undoubtedly unwelcome scandals involving Daly's connections with the singer. They were meant to defame Mrs Billington rather than Daly; indeed he was depicted by Ridgway as a totally honourable husband and father, corrupted by the licentiously wicked Mrs B. 'It is now generally agreed that public performers, whose morals are flagitious, are the proper objects of general censure. Then should not the Public join in the most indignant reprobation of a wretch, who has been the sole cause of alienating the affections of an indulgent husband, from an amiable, virtuous wife, and a numerous beautiful offspring?'[154] But—indicative, even then, of the cynicism inherent in this strand of journalism (of which, regardless of the publisher's other virtues, this work was certainly a fair example)—Ridgway titillated his readers with much

---

[150] *Answer to the Memoirs of Mrs Billington*, 57–9.   [151] Ibid. 59.
[152] Gilbert, *History of the City of Dublin*, ii. 207–8.   [153] Ibid. ii. 218.

prurient sexual innuendo concerning Mrs Billington's relations with her father, brother, and husband, and dragged up against her not only that she had been raped at the age of 12 but that she gave evidence at her attacker's trial with '*accuracy* and *feeling*'. None of which, by the immutable laws of association in the public mind, could have done Daly any good.

It resulted, in any event, in the publication of a defence of Mrs Billington 'by a Gentleman well acquainted with several curious Anecdotes of all parties' which took the opportunity to attack Daly not only for his past crimes against the female sex ('Actresses, who visit the Irish stage, are more subject to be *seduced* than *seduce*') but against the Irish theatre itself. Much more measured and believable than the Ridgway pamphlet, it cannot have bolstered Daly's tottering credibility.[155] In the same year, in response to the claim that the shambles at Crow Street had become too much for gentle sensibilities, Frederick Jones won the right to open a 'private' theatre for the gentry in Fishamble Street.[156]

Daly died in Dublin in September 1813 on £800 a year, paid assiduously by Jones[157] (£400 of which reverted to his children on his death),[158] and with a government pension of £100.[159] To this extent, compared with many others in his profession he was a successful man. Unlike his less successful predecessors, Ryder and Mossop, he seemed, however, never to have won affection or sympathy. Perhaps these verses, written in his heyday of 1785, in part explain why.

> Strange! That a Manager's o'erbearing pride
> The public judgement should presume to guide!
> And, vainly fond of his own precious self,
> Let merit lie, neglected on the shelf,
> To force his pretty person on our sight,
> As if that alone could fill us with delight.[160]

Mrs Castelli's contribution to the company when she returned to Dublin in late 1791 had been slight. She had been very much relegated to minor roles and soon disappeared from sight altogether. With Daly in prison in early 1792, it was probably an appropriate time to leave

[154] Ridgway, *Memoirs of Mrs Billington*, xv.
[155] *Answer to the Memoirs of Mrs Billington*.
[156] Gilbert, *History of the City of Dublin*, ii. 214; Stockwell, *Dublin Theatres*, 161.
[157] Gilbert, *History of the City of Dublin*, ii. 239.
[158] Ibid. ii. 218.
[159] *DNB* [Richard Daly].
[160] Quoted in Gilbert, *History of the City of Dublin*, ii. 108.

Ireland. She may have gone to Edinburgh, where Stephen Kemble and Mrs Esten were competing for John Jackson's relinquished management and where Bowden and other Irish sojourners later turned up.[161] Or she may have gone to Bernard in Plymouth or to any one of the provincial theatre companies around the country. By 1793, however, she was engaged, for £1 a week, at Covent Garden, where a Mr Castello was a door-keeper.[162]

IRISH POSTLUDE

The Irish connection was not altogether severed, however, for in 1793 when the energetic Major Doyle, Member for Mullingar, soon to be Lieutenant-Colonel and later, in 1796, Secretary at War in Ireland, raised the 87th Prince of Wales Regiment in Kilkenny and the surrounding districts ('where his name is yet remembered with affection'),[163] it seems he did not forget Mr Castelli, the box-keeper.

The 87th had a startling initial career, which it is to be hoped Castelli missed. In its first campaign in Holland in 1794 it was part of a general débâcle,[164] and according to the *Gazetteer* (London) of 17 March 1795, out of the 1,500 brave fellows of 1794, only '11 privates now remain'. In 1795, undaunted, Doyle was again recruiting; this time in Dublin,[165] where he helped celebrate St Patrick's Day by giving out relief to the wives and children of the men still held prisoner in Holland.[166] According to War Office Records, Castelli, now Peter Castell, was in a muster, 25 June–24 December 1794, and listed as Quartermaster of Cavalry—on leave.[167] He appeared in subsequent musters up till 1797—always 'on leave'. The actual commission, undated because of damage, was preserved and found with his son's personal papers in Sydney in 1839.[168]

Doyle, if not of 'great family' in the received sense, was at the very least a distinguished Anglo-Irishman who went on to greater things. A lifelong

---

[161] Lewes, *Memoirs*, iii. 85, 204.
[162] *Biog. Dict. Actors, Actresses etc.*; *The London Stage 1660–1800* does not cite Mrs Castelli (or Castelle as she is sometimes called) till 1795, when she was earning £1. 5s. od. a week.
[163] Francis Hastings Doyle, *Reminiscences and Opinions* (1886), 365.
[164] *DNB* [Sir John Doyle].
[165] *GDA* 17 Mar. 1795.
[166] *GDA* 21 Mar. 1795.
[167] PRO, WO 12/8949, Muster Roll, 87th Prince of Wales (Irish) Regiment, 25 June–24 Dec. 1794.
[168] Supreme Court of New South Wales, Probate Division (SCNSW/PD) 968/1, Cavendish Papers.

bachelor, he eventually became a general, a baronet, and a governor of Guernsey. Whether he also became the father of William Joseph Castell will, however, never be known. The likelihood is that he did not. In these stakes, Dick Daly is the more likely contender. But it is far from unlikely that a connection of some kind had been formed. The 'patronage' or 'protection' of actresses was, as we have seen, common enough. It did not automatically signify concubinage or even occasional sexual 'favours'. In the 1820s, following what was presumably a family tradition, Sir John's younger brother, Lieutenant-General Sir Charles Doyle (1770–1842), Master in Chancery in Ireland, took up the young daughter of the manager of the Galway theatre, Harriet Smithson, in a patronage relationship which was probably perfectly chaste.[169] Perhaps the same was true in the case of the then Major John Doyle, MP for Mullingar, and Sophia Castell. The odds though are against. It would be very surprising indeed if the Quartermaster's Commission (or warrant) was not the box-keeper's reward for his indulgent compliance.

The impact of these Irish beginnings upon Castell's future life—upon his perceptions, aspirations, and personality—is difficult to judge. Yet there is in Castell's later deportment a definite, if faint, echo of the Anglo-Irish, pistol-toting hothead, duellist, gambler, dandy, and lecher that was Richard Daly; and not a little of his passion for personal dominance. Unfortunately, however, there is little evidence of Daly's singularity of purpose, nor, it must be said, of his capacity to survive in a hostile environment.

But perhaps the greatest legacy of those early years of wandering in Ireland may have been to lay the seeds of that restlessness of spirit which finally led him to Australia, a country which, like Ireland, was to have a foreign culture imposed upon it in a process which brought to Australia, as it had brought to Ireland, the traditions and limitations of the cultural life of Georgian England.

[169] William Oxberry, 'Memoir of Miss H. C. Smithson', *Oxberry's Dramatic Biography and Histrionic Anecdote*, ii (1825), 206.

2

England: The Land Without Music

> We are not a musical country whatever may be said to the
> contrary.
>
> SEC to WJC, December 1830

MUSIC AND THE LONDON STAGE, 1793–1804

FROM 1793 until about 1804, apart from appearances at Birmingham
and in London at the Haymarket and Royalty theatres, Sophia Castelli
appears to have been engaged chiefly at the major houses, Covent
Garden and Drury Lane, where she performed regularly in very minor
roles.[1] Such a position, although by no means illustrious, was nevertheless desirable enough and was probably gained through some form of
patronage. But it is unlikely, whatever the nature of such patronage, that
it was ever powerful enough to push her beyond a relatively secure place
in the lower echelons. Regardless of her talents ('a very pleasing actress
[who sang] with great spirit'),[2] there is no evidence that with whatever
patronage she did have access to she ever ruffled the feathers of the
established stars as aristocratic patronage for her old Irish colleague, Mrs
Esten, had done those of Mrs Jordan.[3]

She was earning £1 a week in 1793, and in spite of the high inflation of
the war years, only £1. 10s. 0d. in 1799–1800;[4] a rate of pay that the
playwright and biographer James Boaden was too embarrassed even to
acknowledge. 'All the salaries below £3 per week I purposely omit', he

---

[1] *London Stage, passim.*
[2] Quoted in *Biog. Dict. Actors, Actresses, etc.*
[3] Mrs Esten was under the 'protection' of the Duke of Hamilton. Doran, *'Their
Majesties' Servants'*, iii. 95–6. Through his influence the Duke of Clarence (later William
IV and Mrs Jordan's *de facto* husband for many years) apparently prevailed upon Mrs
Jordan to permit the intrusion into what were her popular roles; see also *Thespian Dictionary* under the entry for Mrs Esten; and Thomas Gilliland, *The Dramatic Mirror* (1808),
ii. 756–7.
[4] *Biog. Dict. Actors, Actresses, etc.; London Stage*, iii. (1792–1800), 11 Sept.–11 June
1799–1800.

said', 'that I may not seem to discredit the names of very deserving people.'[5] Mrs Jordan, still in the early stages of her career, was averaging about £31. 10s. 0d. a week.[6] The theatre in England at this time was, however, in an anomalous condition, unable to produce plays without music, or operas without speech, and catering for an audience determined to have spectacle and sensation rather than either. Indeed by 1800 the legitimate drama had lost much of its intellectual momentum. It had, in the words of James Lynch, 'sold out to spectacle and music'. It had 'abandoned literary drama and poetic illusion for acting scenario and scenic display'.[7] Certainly it was true that music from about the mid-eighteenth century had become broadly popular as a consumer product. It was noted in 1775 that the love of music had descended even to common servants, 'who pretend as much judgement of an opera tune as my lady Duchess'.[8] In September 1798 the *European Magazine* expressed concern that music's great popularity, corrupted by 'false taste', could destroy 'our national prosperity, and introduce a secret rot into the very bone and nerve of the State'. By 1800 it was declared by another journal to be the 'age of music', and, even though not 'possessing music of our own', the taste for it was said to be 'universal' and it had become as regular a branch of female education as any other necessary qualification.[9] Even Anthony Pasquin had observed and deplored what he referred to as the 'musical mania which tortures the times':

> Oh! I'm sick to the soul, to see MUSIC alone,
> Stretch her negligent length on the Drama's gay throne.
> Where Muses more honor'd by Wisdom should sit,
> To adorn the heart's mirror, and fashion our wit.
> Let the Wench have her place, as a Wench worth respecting,
> But to wound her OLD SISTERS, is base and affecting.[10]

Even the 'mania' itself became the subject for the stage when Thomas Hurlstone in his farce *Crotchet Lodge* 'very happily ridiculed the fashionable rage for music',[11] and Bowden, on one occasion, was commended

---

[5] Boaden, *Kemble*, ii. 354.
[6] Ibid.   [7] Lynch, *Box, Pit and Gallery*, 308.
[8] *An Inquiry into the Melancholy Circumstances of Great Britain* (1775), quoted in E. D. Mackerness, *Social History of English Music* (1964), 109.
[9] 'On the Present Taste in Music', *European Magazine*, xxxiv (Sept. 1798), 158–60; *Universal Magazine*, cvii (July–Dec. 1800), 264. Quoted in Thomas B. Milligan, *The Concerto and London's Musical Culture in the late Eighteenth Century* (1983), 15.
[10] Williams (Pasquin), *Children of Thespis*, 20.
[11] *Gazetteer and New Daily Advertiser* (London), 16 Feb. 1795, p. 3d.

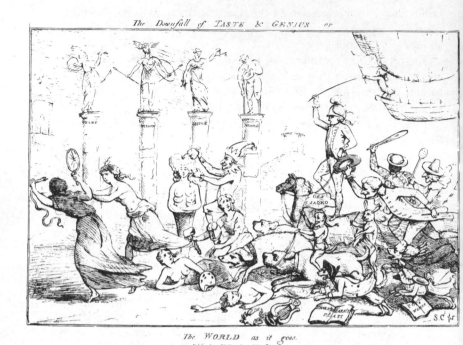

3. Cartoon *c.*1784 by S. Collings showing the flight of the dramatic as well as the other muses, overwhelmed by vulgarity. Note the learned pig and the Dancing Dogs as part of the invading throng. Ref. BM DG 6715.

for his good articulation by which he was able to rescue 'the most beautiful images in the language' from 'the usual prevalence of the music'.[12]

But if music was the late eighteenth-century rage, if it usurped the position of the legitimate drama, it gained little by it. Instead of stimulating English music to greater heights, the very opposite occurred. English music was actually about to confront its nadir. For if literary imagination had somewhere else to go—to the novel, or to poetry— musical imagination was severely circumscribed. The Church had long since ceased either to encourage or to inspire, domestic music had yet to be reinvented, folk music in England had slipped out of sight and out of mind, and the great European forms—the opera (or at least opera

---

[12] *Gazetteer and New Daily Advertiser* (London), 8 Nov. 1795, p. 3a.

without spoken dialogue), the symphony, instrumental chamber music, and the *Lied*—seemed totally alien to English propensities. Apart from the Bible, from which had sprung the oratorio tradition of Handel, and which itself lay like a dead hand upon English musical consciousness, the vitiated and debased drama was to become, for a period, music's only viable inspiration and support.

It is unlikely that Mrs Castelli would have had any notion of the depth of the problem. Indeed, given the vast popularity of music at the time, she could hardly have felt unjustified in preparing her son for a career which ought to have offered him every prospect of material success. Such, however, was not to be the case.

THE PHILISTINE INHERITANCE

The musical tradition to be offered to William Joseph Castell had always exhibited a certain fragility. Even an apologist like Ernest Walker had to admit in 1907 that 'the lack of steady continuity is one of the most striking features of English musical history'. English musical genius, he acknowledged, 'oscillated violently', from the greatness of the 1540–1620 period down into the trough to rise again with the 'brief efflorescence' of Purcell, followed by a 'dark stretch' which did not end till the later part of the nineteenth century.[13] This 'dark stretch' lasted, in effect, from the death of Purcell in 1695 to the emergence of Edward Elgar in the 1890s (and some might argue well beyond even this)—a period of almost two hundred years.

Several theories have emerged to explain this embarrassing trough, made even more noticeable by the astounding musical advances achieved in continental Europe by the great rival cultures of France, Italy, and Germany. The most popular theory is encapsulated in the view that it was the fault of the Puritans whose hatred and suppression of music froze the seeds of creativity. W. J. Turner is fairly representative of this particular prejudice, taking refuge in the belief in a previous golden age and quoting Erasmus to show that in 'Merrie England', before the rise of Puritanism, the 'English could lay claim to be the best-looking, the most musical and to the best tables of any people'.[14] The fact that Percy Scholes in his two books[15] on the subject was at great pains to defend the

---

[13] Ernest Walker, *History of Music in England*, 3rd rev. edn. (1952), 394.

[14] From *Morae Encomium*, in W. J. Turner, *English Music* (London, 1941), 9.

[15] Percy A. Scholes, *Music and Puritanism* [1934]; and *The Puritans and Music in England and New England* (1934).

Puritans from this imputation has probably not put much of a dint in an argument which, although obviously simplistic, has a thread of historical truth and is still pervasive.

Wilfred Mellers, on a similar but more subtle tack in 1946, put it down to the 'wicked distinction between religion and life, between God and art, which would have been unintelligible to the mediaeval mind'.[16] The enemy for Mellers was not so much the Puritans themselves as the development of what the socio-historian Max Weber saw as their intellectual child, 'Big Business'.

In a footnote on English music in his *Protestant Ethic and the Spirit of Capitalism*, Weber too remarked its decline from a promising and far from unimportant early period to the absolute musical vacuum 'which we find typical of the Anglo-Saxon peoples later, and even today'.[17] Without stopping to discuss the issue further, Weber by inference also calls the Puritan ethos to account.

Michael Foss, in his *Age of Patronage. The Arts in Society 1660–1750* (1971), blames the philistinism of power, whereby art was meant to serve a practical function. Music, being perceived to fail in this regard, was, his argument goes, largely ignored, and allowed to go its way, which was the way of Italy and France, the English idiom being very much despised.[18] This view has something in common with that of Mellers, since power and politics in the late seventeenth and early eighteenth centuries were very much about 'Big Business'.

Certainly, in spite of its superficial popularity, by the mid-eighteenth century music in England had lost much of its intellectual status as an art form. And it is difficult to escape from the idea that the Puritan ethos, insofar as it was powerfully materialistic and pragmatic, did seriously undermine the position of music, which in England was so bound up with the mystical elements of both the English Court and the English Church. The decline in music's intellectual credibility in England *does* parallel the rise of secular materialism and the Lockian rejection of the metaphysical and the hypothetical in favour of the observable and the measurable. From Thomas Browne's 'Musick of the spheres', in which there was 'something of divinity more than the ear discovers, [an] hiero-glyphical and shadowed lesson of the whole world',[19] it had become, in

---

[16] Wilfred Mellers, *Music and Society. England and the European Tradition* (1946), 117.
[17] Max Weber, *The Protestant Ethic and the Spirit of Capitalism* (1930), 222.
[18] Michael Foss, *The Age of Patronage. The Arts in Society 1660–1750* (1971).
[19] Thomas Browne, *Religio Medici* (1642), in *Works*, ed. by Simon Wilson (1836), ii. 106.

Locke's own analysis, a waste of time and an incitement to join 'odd' company. 'And I have among Men of Parts and Business so seldom heard any one commended or esteemed for having an Excellency in Musick, that amongst those Things that ever come into the List of Accomplishments, I think I may give it the last place.' Unlike dancing, which, apart from the useless 'Jigging part, and the Figures', contributed 'Manliness and a becoming Confidence to young Children', music in the Lockian scheme of things had no intellectual or social function.[20]

Locke profoundly influenced the eighteenth-century mind. In the words of Ernest Tuveson, he inaugurated or made necessary 'a re-thinking of every aspect of the personality: soul, conscience, reason, imagination, even immortality itself'.[21] What Newton did for the Universe, Locke, it may be argued, did for the European consciousness. Not that Locke was a lone prophet. He was no Blake. He was rather the mouthpiece for a pervasive restlessness already present within his society, concerning established ideas on the nature of hierarchy and of intuitive faith, ideas which had already to some extent been exchanged for an experimental pragmatism by which authority, rather than descending from above, ascended from below through the agency of human reason. The mystical and metaphysical were already under attack, and the reign of 'nature' and 'sense' already begun. 'All Faiths', wrote Charles Blount in 1683, 'have been shaken but those only which stand upon the Basis of Common Reason.'[22]

One may hear many later resonances of Locke's indictment against music, not just from an incipient Puritan bourgeois like Campbell, the author of London Tradesman, who in 1747 warned parents and guardians against encouraging any musical interest in a young man on the Lockian grounds that it 'certainly takes him off his Business [and] exposes him to Company and Temptation to which he would otherwise have been a stranger';[23] but from the urbane and sophisticated aristocrat Lord Chesterfield as well. Just two years after Campbell, Chesterfield was writing to his natural son, Philip Stanhope, warning him in pointedly Lockian terms of the dangers to his status as a gentleman in performing upon any musical instrument. It was all very well to enjoy music

---

[20] John Locke, *Some Thoughts concerning Education*, introd. by R. H. Quick (2nd edn., 1884, p. 174; para. 197 in orig. edn. of 1693).

[21] Ernest Lee Tuveson, *The Imagination as a Means of Grace. Locke and the Aesthetics of Romanticism* (1960), 5.

[22] In Basil Willey, *The Eighteenth Century Background. Studies in the Idea of Nature in the Thought of the Period* (1940), p. 6 of 1980 edn.

[23] R. Campbell, *The London Tradesman* (1747, facsimile edn. 1967), 92–3.

performed by a hired musician, but a gentleman should not demean himself by active participation. 'It puts a gentleman in a very frivolous contemptible light; brings him into a great deal of bad company; and takes up a great deal of time, which might be better employed.'[24]

Early in the eighteenth century, Addison, through the *Tatler*, the *Spectator*, and other journals, had tirelessly promoted the Lockian point of view among the denizens of the clubs and the coffee-houses of London and linked it inextricably with the English virtues (later to be perceived specifically as 'middle-class' virtues) of prudence and reasonability, and with a defence of English intellectual achievements. Addison was of course no musical philistine, yet he could argue energetically if not passionately that if the English had no opera, it was because opera was a lesser form of art than those arts practised by Englishmen. 'If the Italians have a Genius for Musick above the *English*', he suggested, then 'the *English* have a Genius for other Performances of a much higher Nature, and capable of giving the *Mind* a much nobler Entertainment'. Indeed Music was not only a lesser art, it was also potentially dangerous.

Music is certainly a very agreeable Entertainment but if it would take the entire Possession of our Ears, if it would make us incapable of hearing Sense, if it would exclude the Arts that have a much greater Tendency to the Refinement of Human Nature; I must confess I would allow it no better Quarter than *Plato* has done, who banished it out of his Common-wealth.[25]

Musicians themselves were not unaware of the implications. The musician John Potter in 1762 refers to the 'contempt thrown upon music' due to notions of its unprofitability, its object of mere pleasure, and the crucial factor of the time required to become proficient in it. Potter remained unrepentant and defiant, claiming his art to be 'most delightful, advantageous to many and hurtful to none',[26] but it is not surprising to find Dr John Brown in 1763 accepting without apology or apparent regret the notion that the English had no native music. The Anglo-Saxons, he argued, were a colonizing people and had somehow left behind the parts of their culture which had given music its political authority. In the new environment music had become peripheral, capitulating to more useful arts, while remaining to some extent suspect

---

[24] Philip D. Stanhope, 4th Earl of Chesterfield, *The Letters of the Earl of Chesterfield to his Son*, ed. by Charles Strachey (1901), i. 324; 19 Apr. 1749.

[25] *Spectator*, No. 18, 21 Mar. 1711.

[26] John Potter, *Observations on the Present State of Music and Musicians* (1762), 61–70.

in the eyes of the State as a residual challenge to its rational purpose.[27] Brown's theory was entirely consistent with English 'Enlightenment' thinking about the necessary relationship between art and power, a relationship largely defined in terms of the subordination of the former to the latter. The end of all art must be somehow to reflect and serve Polity, otherwise called the public good.[28]

Nor was Brown alone in this view. No less a musical authority than Dr Burney concurred. He not only failed to acknowledge the existence of English folk music but referred to those 'wild and irregular Melodies . . . such as the rustic tunes of Wales, Scotland and Ireland' as the kind of music that was best learned 'in the nursery and on the street'. *Real Music*, he declared, 'arises from a complete scale under the guidance of such rules of art as successful cultivation has rendered respectable and worthy of imitation'.[29] Music for Dr Burney was little more than a pleasing and highly refined embellishment to a civilized life-style: 'an innocent luxury unnecessary, indeed to our existence, but a great improvement and gratification to the sense of hearing.'[30] A view not inconsistent with that of Lord Chesterfield; a view, indeed, which made music all the more easily dismissed by the seriously assiduous middle classes. Upwardly mobile, clever, wealthy, but frustrated people, even when they were not Unitarians, Quakers, or Dissenters of other persuasions, tended, with exceptions of course, towards an attitude to music which associated it with frivolity and even vice.

The worldly, middle-class philologist and political reformer, John Horne Tooke, educated at Westminster, Eton, and Cambridge, took holy orders in 1760 in order to placate his ambitious parents made wealthy in the London poultering trade. Tried for High Treason in 1794 as the *éminence grise* behind the supposedly revolutionary plots of the London Corresponding Society against the British State, Horne Tooke was the epitome in many ways of the middle-class professional man of that period, whose god was Locke and reason and who could see no good reason to bend the knee to those who were clearly his intellectual

---

[27] John Brown, *A Dissertation on the Rise, Union, and Power, the Progressions, Separations and Corruptions of Poetry and Music* (1763), 183–4.

[28] See Foss, *Age of Patronage*, 106–9; Rapin, in Willey, *Eighteenth Century Background*, 22, 'Poetry being an Art, ought to be as profitable by the quality of its own Nature and by the Subordination that all Arts should have to Polity, whose end in general is the public good.' (*Reflections on Aristotle's Treatise of Poesie* (1674), Rymes' translation, 1706 edn., ii. 163.)

[29] Charles Burney, *A General History of Music* (1789), ii. 220.

[30] In Mackerness, *Social History of English Music*, 2.

inferiors. But he was no Puritan. The father of at least three illegitimate children, in his youth an inveterate card player and in his maturity the focus of a highly sophisticated circle of men and women, he nevertheless considered that the education of an 'English gentleman' should consist of Greek, Latin, Italian, French, Anglo-Saxon, and Mesogothic, travel to France, Italy, Germany, Holland, and Flanders, which would take him up to the age of 30, but absolutely

> No Music, very little dancing.
> No drawing, No Painting. No Manège [horsemanship]
> No cardplaying, No Virtú [collecting *objets d'art*]. No fencing.[31]

Note the first place given to the interdiction against music.

Eighteenth-century England was in fact a field where a rather subtle war was being waged between two antipathetic cultures: between the aristocracy, still perceived for such purposes as 'Norman', and the 'Anglo-Saxon' middle class.[32] (Note Horne Tooke's inclusion of the Anglo-Saxon and Mesogothic languages.) It was a conflict which was still in its more subtle and cultural stages. The middle class, apart from some notorious individual exceptions, was not yet clamouring for power in a technical sense—rather it was establishing its claim to the moral and intellectual high ground. By 1804, in the voice of Don Estriella, Southey (whose subject, perhaps, was not altogether unrelated to his potential market) could in any case claim for the middle class an unequivocally superior position in the scheme of things.

The English people, by which I mean, as distinguishing them from the populace, that middle class from whom an estimate of the national character is to be formed, have that wonderful activity and courage, that unless the superiority of numbers against them were more than tenfold, they would put out an insurrection as they put out a fire . . . The people then, are the security of England against the populace.[33]

While Southey explicitly excludes the 'populace', he implicitly excludes the aristocracy as well. But the aristocracy, unlike the 'populace', was in

---

[31] BL, Horne Tooke Collection of Pamphlets, vol. 2, MS 'Mr Horne Tooke's Plan to rear an *English* gentleman'. It is possible of course, given his famous wit, that he had his tongue a little in his cheek, if he ever knew that his sentiments on the subject were reverentially being recorded, perhaps by one of his daughters, to be preserved for posterity. Nevertheless, given his severely materialistic individualism, such prohibitions do not seem out of character.

[32] See Christopher Hill, 'The Norman Yoke', in which Hill traces the development of the Anglo-Saxon 'golden age' mythology from the 17th to the 19th century. In *Puritanism and Revolution* (1958), pp. 58–125 of 1986 edn.

[33] Robert Southey, *Letters from England* (1807, this edn 1984), 375–6.

a position to resist, and did so with a hardening of those class lines which are still visible in contemporary Britain. Breeding was the one thing that the middle class, for all its other virtues, could not claim, and as Lord Chesterfield remarked, 'Nobody was ever loved that was not well-bred.'[34]

The position of English music in this conflict was an unhappy one: for between Lord Chesterfield's 'Whenever I go to the opera I leave my sense and reason at the door with my half-guinea and deliver myself up to my eyes and ears', and Dr Johnson's 'the Italian opera, an exotic and irrational entertainment which has always been combatted and always has prevailed', there seems almost a conspiracy.[35] Here were the two arch-priests of two opposing worlds in virtual agreement.

Both men throughout their lives, in their very different ways but in the best Lockian tradition, attempted to make sense and order their priorities. Chesterfield, by a rigid attachment to rules of external social forms, tried to establish the identity of the gentleman in society in a not dissimilar way to the gentlemen of the Royal Society who were striving to identify other classes in the natural world. Sir Joseph Banks, it was rumoured, boiled fleas in the hope that if they turned red he would be able prove they were of the lobster class. They didn't. ('Fleas are not lobsters, damn their souls!'[36]) Lord Chesterfield might have commiserated with him in his disappointment, for his own experiment on the hapless Philip Stanhope, his son by a French governess, turned out badly too. He never lived up to his father's expectations and died in early middle age without having achieved an understanding of those principles so dear to Lord Chesterfield.

Chesterfield's rules of gentlemanly conduct consisted of a fastidious attention to the minute banalities of life, to all those little 'riens' as he called them—those social particulars which, perhaps rather like Newton's atoms, created the universe. Never laugh, he admonished, for laughter was the province of the senseless masses, 'and that is what people of sense and breeding should show themselves above'. Never miss

---

[34] In F. L. Lucas, *The Search for Good Sense. Four Eighteenth-Century Characters, Johnson, Chesterfield, Boswell, Goldsmith* (1958), 151.

[35] Stanhope, *Letters*, i. 200; Samuel Johnson, *Lives of the Most Eminent English Poets*, ed. Peter Cunningham (1854), chapter on John Hughes, ii. 184.

[36] William Gardiner tells the story in good faith in *Music and Friends* (1838), i. 122–3. It was almost certainly a fantasy. Earl Stanhope in his *Life of the Right Honourable William Pitt* (1861), i. 286, ascribed it to John Wolcott (Peter Pindar) whose 'grotesque' humour specified that there were fifteen hundred fleas boiled in a saucepan—a joke probably directed at the gentlemen amateurs of the Royal Society as a whole.

the dancing master, he advised his son, for although dancing itself was a 'very trifling silly thing', it was one of those 'petit riens, which in arithmetical account, added to one another, *ad infinitum*, they would amount to nothing, in account of the world, amount to a great important sum'.[37] Thus for Chesterfield art and pleasure, laughter, music, and dancing must serve his sense of social propriety and sustain class distinction.

The more plebeian Dr Johnson, a figure who became, in spite of himself, a touchstone of Anglo-Saxon, middle-class intellectual virtue, attempted to create in his Dictionary— also from minute particulars, this time of language—a great rational tool with which to fashion that natural and even classless 'truth' to which all art was subject. Poetry, said Dr Johnson, is 'an art of writing pleasure with truth by calling imagination to the help of reason'.[38] For both men, any art that could not bear witness to his ultimate objective was at best irrelevant and at worst pernicious.

Yet in spite of their fundamental agreement in the matter of the arts— their fundamental philistinism, if you like—it was their class-related antagonisms which became more famous and which represented in many ways the broader conflict of class and culture which dominated the age and which ultimately ended in economic and cultural victory for the heirs to Johnson rather than for those of Chesterfield.

The Victorians owed more, after all, to Addison, Steele, and Dr Johnson than they ever owed to Lord Chesterfield. Indeed Chesterfield was much vilified by the newly emerging middle-class moral propagandists as the 'Grey-beard corrupter of our list'ning youth',[39] although one suspects it was less because of the ridiculousness of his snobbery, which was to some extent absorbed, than because of his lax and cynical approach to sexual morality. But the transition was not sudden—nor was it all that simple. Aspiration, not only to wealth but to property ownership and social status, led often to affected imitation of aristocratic life-styles. Indeed Harold Perkin has suggested that it was this very impetus towards emulation in all social strata which was the driving force behind what we call the Industrial Revolution.[40] And certainly while the intrinsic puritanism of the middle class may have remained in

[37] Stanhope, *Letters*, i. 212, 9 Mar. 1748; ibid. ii. 127, 11 Mar. 1751.

[38] Johnson, *Lives of the English Poets*, quoted in Tuveson, *Imagination as a Means of Grace*, 1.

[39] William Cowper, *Progress of Error*, i. 342.

[40] Harold Perkin, *The Origins of Modern English Society 1780–1880* (1969), p. 97 of 1985 edn.

evidence in its moral sensibilities, in its material aspirations it undoubtedly softened. Its more affluent members took on with a vengeance the aristocratic mantle of conspicuous consumption, albeit with a greater seriousness of purpose.

It would be wrong of course to imagine that while this cultural transition and exchange was taking place that music as an entertainment was (with the exception of some fundamentalist religious groups) in any sense discouraged. As we have seen, it became, in the last half of the eighteenth century, virtually a boom industry. Nor did private music-making among most classes—from the royal family to the cottager—disappear. Indeed the portraits of the élite painted by Johan Zoffany (1733–1810) illustrate continued enthusiasm in upper-class circles, while the recollections of eighteenth-century musical amateurs like William Gardiner and Thomas Bewick describe lively interest among provincial gentry, townsmen, and cottagers.[41] Yet it has to be said that the trend was away from the old forms of convivial music-making. Fashionable aristocratic males did not as a rule engage in music-making. Indeed Garret Wesley, the 1st Earl of Mornington (1735–81), the father of the Duke of Wellington, is the well-known exception which proves the rule, being, it was said, the only peer of the realm to be seen carrying a fiddle-case under his arm in the streets of London. Perhaps less well known is the story that his son, a talented musician in his youth, upon taking up his military career threw his fiddle into the fire: a dramatic illustration of the alienation that had taken place between music-making and the life patterns of the élite. Fashionable middle-class males took their cue from their betters, while those so disposed among the working population, once able to organize their own working lives to accommodate music-making within the framework of their local community, found themselves subjected to the discipline of the factory; at least according to William Gardiner.[42]

Certainly the old catch and glee clubs remained and many English composers contributed to these vocal ensemble pieces. They were designed, however, for amateur performance either in the home or the club rather than for public display and did not survive far into the nineteenth century, wilting beneath the all-consuming sun of the Italian virtuoso *buffa* ensemble. In their place, socially if not musically, evolved the mass choirs of the oratorio tradition—a substitute which reflected the

---

[41] Gardiner, *Music and Friends*, i, *passim*; Thomas Bewick, *A Memoir of Thomas Bewick*, ed. by Ian Bain (1979).
[42] Gardiner, *Music and Friends*, i. 47.

changed condition of English society, represented not by the agricultural village but by the industrial city.[43]

English professional musicians, for reasons which are not altogether clear, had never enjoyed the direct patronage of the aristocracy as they had done in Europe. Even in Tudor times, as Woodfill points out, the number of households which kept resident musicians as part of their establishment was relatively small;[44] explained perhaps by the deliberate centralism of the Tudor court which established London as the cultural as well as the political and economic capital of England.

We might have imagined, then, that professional musicians would quickly have turned to the increasingly influential commercial, moneyed classes of the late seventeenth and eighteenth centuries, and for a moment it seemed almost as if this might happen. London's early concert life began in the taverns during the Commonwealth with a clearly middle class following, and with John Bannister's entrepreneurial efforts from 1672 on, it quickly became a source of private profit. But increasing virtuosity on the one hand and consumer passivism on the other led to greater use of exotic and more 'exciting' foreign models and, not unnaturally, of foreign musicians. Concerts became increasingly élitist, with private subscriptions replacing public access.[45] Aristocratic exclusionism tended to reinforce this. The English musician and English music became the province of the English theatre where it wallowed in the social and aesthetic shadow of the Italian Opera. It was to be a long time before the middle class became once again the natural support of English music and musicians.

Underlying all this, as has already been suggested, was the larger social and cultural conflict between a still powerful aristocracy and an emerging, self-conscious, middle-class culture, seen in both the emulation and the rejection of each other's values and expressed by both parties with reference to a Lockian epistemology which offered little comfort to a profession already struggling against so many odds.

---

[43] See E. D. Mackerness, *Somewhere Further North. A History of Music in Sheffield* (1974); Reginald Nettel, *Music in the Five Towns 1840–1914* (1944).

[44] Walter L. Woodfill, *Musicians in English Society from Elizabeth to Charles I* (1953), 59.

[45] See Robert Elkin, *The Old Concert Rooms of London* (1955); Reginald Nettel, *The Orchestra in England* (1946), 20–6; Stanley Sadie, 'Concert Life in Eighteenth Century England', *Proceedings of the Royal Musical Association*, lxxxv (1958–9), 17–30; William Weber, *Music and the Middle Class. The Social Structure of Concert Life in London, Paris and Vienna* (1975), 2–4; Percy M. Young, *The Concert Tradition from the Middle Ages to the Twentieth Century* (1965), 73–87.

Musicians were not of course a group set apart from the social and economic flux. In the nineteenth century, they too, as educated and often sophisticated people, sought the middle-class goals of respectability and financial independence. Yet their task was impeded not only by social attitudes towards music of ingrained philistinism but by their own incapacity, also ingrained, to come to terms, either professionally or aesthetically, with changing social and economic conditions. For impinging upon the ideological prejudices of both patrician and plebeian antagonists were other historical forces: the power and influence of foreign musical models; the defection of the Church from its musical responsibilities; the social and cultural limitations of the English theatre; the perception of music as being outside of the mainstream of intellectual and political life; and finally there was the historical failure of the institutions of the profession itself to win for musicians, firstly, freedom from dependence upon an aristocratic patronage which was itself reluctant and even hostile, and secondly, more significantly, control over their own profession. Before continuing with the Castell narrative it is appropriate to pause to take a brief look at these problems.

THE ENGLISH MUSICIAN

The foreign threat

Native English musicians, from the advent of Handel and the Italian Opera in 1711, had occupied an ambivalent position in their own country. In the midst of one of the most musically active capitals of Europe, London, they constantly struggled for recognition in the face of an overwhelming preference among musical patrons for foreigners.[46] Italians, Frenchmen, and Germans were all in demand, attracted by English affluence and an expanding cultural market. As wealth brought status and leisure to greater numbers, music as a purchasable commodity became an affordable luxury to an enlarged élite. The leaders of fashion, however, remained the aristocracy, and aristocratic preference was not only for foreign musicians but foreign music. Continental commentators

---

[46] See Deborah Rohr, 'A Profession of Artisans: The Careers and Social Status of British Musicians 1750–1850', Ph.D thesis (Pennsylvania, 1983), 97; Simon McVeigh, 'Felice Giardini: A Violinist in late Eighteenth-Century London', *Music & Letters*, lxiv (July–Oct. 1983), 162–72; Cyril Ehrlich, *The Music Profession in Britain since the Eighteenth Century* (1985), 16–19.

like Von Uffenbach, d'Archenholtz, and Wendeborn all remark upon the preponderance of foreign musicians in London.[47] Quite apart from the singers, names like Pepusch, Handel, Abel, Bach, Cramer, Clementi, Salomon, Giardini, Dussek, Viotti, and Haydn dominated the instrumental sphere throughout the century. In 1728, Daniel Defoe, a man whose Presbyterianism never interfered with his love of music (so long as music did not interfere with the serious side of life), ever practical, was moved by the presence of the 'heaps' of foreign musicians in London to put forward a proposal to found a conservatorio on Italian lines to train English foundlings into the profession. Only this, he believed, would avoid 'the expensive importation of foreign musicians'.[48] But his plan came to nothing.

The most expensive, exclusive, and arguably the most musically important institution in eighteenth-century London was the Italian Opera at the King's Theatre in the Haymarket. It was considered to be the musical sun from which all else took energy and life. From this institution English men and women were all but excluded, and inevitably it was resented and attacked. In 1728 Swift can be heard with classic cantankerousness referring to 'Italian Effeminacy' and 'Italian Nonsense'. We want, he said, 'nothing but Stabbing or Poisoning to make us perfect Italians'.[49] And in 1774 the same tone can still be detected in Joel Collier's *Musical Travels*. Taking the opportunity of a satire on Dr Burney, 'Joel Collier' attacked 'The Directors of our Opera, for having at last condescended to permit an *Englishwoman* to be called Signora, and by virtue of that title to share some of the princely incomes which have been hitherto lavished on Italians'.[50]

The most successful counter-attack had come with the production of Gay's *The Beggar's Opera* of 1728, the success of which did not, however, enhance the development of any alternative English lyric drama. Its success was due not to any strength of its own as a viable art form but largely to its mocking inversion of the Italian form and to the verbal satire on contemporary politics. It was a literary rather than a musical coup, and its influence was, as Wilfred Mellers suggests, ultimately philistine.[51] English music was left with little of intrinsic value.

[47] Von Uffenbach, *Die Musikalische Reisen des Hern Von Uffenbach* (1710); M. d'Archenholtz, *A Picture of England* (1791); and G. F. A. Wendeborn, *View of England* (1785, 1791 in London).

[48] Daniel Defoe, *Augusta Triumphans* (1728), title-page, and p. 17.

[49] *Intelligencer*, No. III, 1728.

[50] *Musical Travels through England by Joel Collier, Organist* (1774), p. iv.

[51] Mellers, *Harmonious Meeting*, 266–72.

Indeed the tradition of ballad opera which *The Beggar's Opera* spawned was to become, as we shall see, yet another stick with which to beat it.

The decline in morale had been arrested but not stemmed. It continued throughout the century, exacerbated by other social factors, noticeably by the decline of the Church of England.

Musicians and the Church

The Church had been the cradle of English music. Less important than the Crown as an active patron,[52] its cathedral schools were nevertheless the intellectual and creative nurseries of the English musical idiom.[53] Nearly all the great names of the past, Dunstable, Tallis, Byrd, Purcell, and many more, had been educated in the Cathedral schools or the Chapel Royal. Both before and after the Reformation, music had been an important part of the Church's ritual, and it was the function of the Cathedral schools to ensure musical continuity and excellence in worship. It was from these schools that the Court skimmed off the cream for the Chapel Royal.

Traditionally, choristers were given a sound musical education which included composition and instrumental skills, as well as an academic education sometimes leading to one of the universities and frequently enough to successful careers outside either the Church or music.[54] The usual pattern, though, was for boys to remain as choristers till their voices broke, during which time they might have attended the local grammar school for their Latin and mathematics. Then they would either have been apprenticed to a music master or to some other trade, or, if favoured, perhaps sent to one of the universities, usually with a view to taking orders and becoming either cathedral precentors or vicars choral.[55] Thus a talented boy from almost any social class might once have found himself on the road to gentility as a chorister at one of the

[52] Woodfill, *Musicians in English Society*, 158.

[53] See, for example: John Skelton Bumpus, *A History of English Cathedral Music* (New York, 1908); Henry Davey, *History of English Music* [1921]; Edmund Horace Fellowes, *English Cathedral Music from Edward VI to Edward VII* (London, 1941); Peter Le Huray, *Music and the Reformation in England 1549–1660* (1967); Mackerness, *Social History of English Music*; Mellers, *Music and Society*; Sydney H. Nicholson, *Quires and Places Where They Sing* (London, 1932); Henry Raynor, *Music in England* (1980); Nicholas Temperley, *Jonathan Gray and Church Music in York, 1770–1840* (1977); Walker, *History of Music in England*; Samuel Sebastian Wesley, *A Few Words on Cathedral Music and the Musical System of the Church* (1849).

[54] Woodfill, *Musicians in English Society*, 173, gives several examples of secular success of ex-choristers, including Richard Hooker and John Milton the elder.

[55] Ibid. 144–50; 172–3.

forty cathedrals or collegiate chapels throughout the country. Even without a university education, those lucky enough to return as singing men found a niche in the world that while not grandly remunerative offered satisfaction, respectability, and security. Not unnaturally, parents had been keen to offer their sons in this capacity, and not unnaturally competition had kept standards high.

This was the system many in the early nineteenth century wished to see preserved and strengthened, largely because England possessed no other institutionalized form of music education. The only alternatives to a cathedral education for a musician were either the apprenticeship system or private tuition, neither of which possessed any intrinsic social prestige or advantage.

It was indeed becoming much bewailed that the Church was failing to provide musicians with either the status of a proper education or a proper living and that the system was in danger of imminent collapse. Parents of likely children who had once 'esteemed themselves fortunate in placing them under the superintending care of the Dean and Chapter' no longer did so to the same degree, and according to a member of the Chapter in Chichester in the 1820s the cathedral was forced to accept boys from 'humble circumstances'.[56]

In the climate of eighteenth-century materialist scepticism, the Church had partially withdrawn into a scepticism of its own, often indulging in what Trollope in the middle of the nineteenth century could still identify as 'the comfortable arcana of ecclesiastical snuggeries'.[57] There was little place in such arcana for church musicians, who were by then almost entirely secular. Very few precentors were musicians, and their role for many years seems to have been as antagonist to the secularly trained organist, whose job it had become to train the boys and organize the music for the services.[58]

In 1813 one such organist, Dr Joseph Pring, took the Dean and Chapter of Bangor Cathedral to Chancery because he claimed that the increased value in the cathedral tithes was not being spent, according to the provision of the endowment, on the choir, but on a building project. At that time the organist was receiving £60 per annum; the four singing

---

[56] Quoted in Rohr, 'Profession of Artisans', 146.

[57] Anthony Trollope, *The Warden* (1855; Minster Classics, 1968), 47.

[58] See Wesley, *A Few Words on Cathedral Music*; Chapter Book, Bangor Cathedral, 26 Dec. 1811, in Joseph Pring, *Papers, Documents, Law Proceedings of the Choir of the Cathedral Church of Bangor* (1819), 14f. 'The organist is required to instruct the Singing Boys in the Arts of Singing two hours on every Saturday; And . . . take all Directions relative to the Choir, from the Precentor and to submit to the same.'

men, £10 each; the four choristers, £10 between them; and eight other boys who appeared in surplices, £2 each per annum.[59] In reply to Dr Pring's action, the Dean and Chapter argued in court that the organist had no rights in terms of the tithes or the endowment since he was their 'superior servant' in the same category as the Church Yardman, the Bell-ringer or the Organ-blower.[60] It was argued that £60 was quite enough for the organist, since it was understood that such salaries as organists received were never intended to be large enough for themselves and their families to subsist upon. It was always understood that they would teach 'the younger branches of families Music, which an Organist can teach, and it is in *that* way they make up a sufficient maintenance'.[61]

In other words, the Cathedral accepted that it was no longer common practice for cathedral organists to dedicate their energies entirely to the services of the Church, any more than it was common practice for cathedrals to provide a living wage for their musical servants. The case won a modest increase in income for the organist and his choir but left the Dean and Chapter with ultimate discretionary power in the matter of its own tithes, which had increased incidentally, by over 400 per cent, from £400 to £1,787. 14s. 9d.[62]

It was certainly true that cathedral organists often had several paying posts and could earn good money teaching music in their neighbour-hoods. There was the case of Robert Jones, the organist at Ely, who was reputed to have earned £2,000 a year in his peripatetic wanderings on horseback among the local gentry, teaching singing and keyboard.[63] But this, it was argued, was part of the problem. What could possibly be left over for the cathedral and its music when its organist and choristers were so frantically occupied seeking the means of worldly survival? The result could only be yet a further decline in standards of performance, and even less commitment from the Church to either its music or its musicians.[64] As it was, the system, said J. E. Cox, recalling his own days as a chorister, had managed to produce one of the most neglected classes in society. No longer a candidate for higher things, the chorister had become no more than a singing machine, who, when his voice had broken, was 'cast out only half educated upon the world'. Cox himself was particularly bitter at the failure of the Church to provide him with a 'liberal' education.[65]

[59] Pring, *Papers, Documents*, p. viii.

[60] Ibid. 73.   [61] Ibid. 81.

[62] Ibid. 9.   [63] Rohr, 'Profession of Artisans', 294.

[64] 'The Present State of Music in England', *QMMR* vi (1824), 283–4; Rohr, 'Profession of Artisans', 184–96.

[65] John Edmund Cox, *Musical Recollections of the last Half Century* (1872), 50–2.

At about the time that Dr Pring was challenging the authorities at Bangor, Maria Hackett had taken up the plight of the boys at St Paul's Cathedral, who, she claimed, were exploited and neglected and, excluded from the Cathedral school, were left in ignorance and idleness until their voices broke and they were apprenticed out. She was not arguing for a 'liberal' education, merely for the rudiments.[66]

The effects of this situation were noticeable and many were the complaints about the standards of musical performance in the English cathedrals—once the glory of English musical tradition. 'Oh! my country,' cried one distressed contributor to the *Quarterly*. 'What wonder that our cathedrals are desolate . . . what wonder that the singers are often of the lowest order of society? . . . that our secular musicians consider it a disgrace to be attached to the service of the church?' Music, he or she declared, was now only to be heard in the theatre.[67] And this was not an inaccurate assessment.

Nor had the Evangelical movement within the Anglican Church enhanced the position of the church musician; nor helped to confirm church authorities in a proper commitment to music. Indeed, in an age of contention, it was a subject that produced some heat.[68] There was resistance to popish ritual, to organ voluntaries, and to specialist choirs. The Methodists, close relatives of the Evangelicals, had actually dispensed with the latter altogether,[69] in favour of congregational participation and the introduction of rollicking secular tunes of purportedly 'execrable taste'.

We should do well to consider, whether this divine art [music] might not be rendered more available than it is now, in heightening the interest in our own form of worship . . . even the Dissenters read us a very useful lesson; notwithstanding the execrable taste which they frequently display, in selecting tunes from the playhouse and the street, and in appropriating them to the praise of Him.[70]

---

[66] Maria Hackett, *A Brief Account of the Cathedral and Collegiate Schools* (1827); and *Correspondence and Evidences respecting the Ancient Collegiate School attached to Saint Paul's Cathedral* (1832).

[67] ΘΥΤΙΣ [Thetis, i.e. Richard Mackenzie Bacon], 'On the Present State of Church Music in England', *QMMR* i (1824), 458–9.

[68] See Minimus [Edward Hodges], 'On Church Music', *Bristol Mirror* reprinted as a series in *QMMR*, beginning iv (1822), 33; also Jonathan Gray, *An Inquiry into Historical Facts Relative to Parochial Psalmody. In Reference to the Remarks of the Right Reverend Herbert, Lord Bishop of Peterborough* (York, 1821).

[69] Temperley, *Jonathan Gray*, 8.

[70] 'Present State of Music in England', *QMMR* vi (1824), 285.

It was noted that while the Methodist chapels were full to overflowing and the Catholic chapels of foreign embassies filled with Protestant musical dilettanti,[71] in the Anglican Cathedrals the officiators often outnumbered the congregation.[72] Not unexpectedly, conditions in the parochial churches were even worse. Isaac Nathan questioned, 'whether any thing can so powerfully put harmony to flight as the psalms in a country church. The nasal twang of the clerk, unaided by any instrument, the discordant voices of the whole group of singers, and the monotonous airs to which the words are adapted, instead of promoting devotional inspiration, torture the ears of those who . . . possess an iota of taste.'[73]

Although the status of the cathedral organist was never completely eroded (it was to make something of a comeback in the mid to late nineteenth century), in the short term, the economic and social status of the cathedral musician in the first decades of the nineteenth century had arguably not been worse since the days of Cromwell's Commonwealth, when church, college, and cathedral organs had been smashed, sold, or removed to public houses (Cromwell himself appropriated the organ of Magdalen College, Oxford), and church musicians turned out of their livings.

The implications in all this for musicians were very serious. The cathedral musician had long been the high-status branch of the profession. It was he who had justified the position of music as a 'liberal art'. It was on him that the universities had, since 1463 at Oxford, conferred their degrees. It was from his ranks that had come the greatest products of English musical creativity. Now it would seem that all the most prestigious could do was to ride about the country, seeking pupils among the daughters of the gentry to whom they could teach the rudiments of pianoforte and the singing of fashionable ballads, and, in all probability, for a pittance, employing a deputy to perform the drudgery of the church service in their place—a practice that was to become quite common and attract much criticism.[74] Nor did it appear that the Church intended any remedial action, either in the education or in the payment of its musicians. Unequivocally, the profession had been deserted by the very

---

[71] 'Sketch of the State of Music in London', *QMMR* ii (1820), 391; and vi (1824), 254.

[72] 'Twelve single and double Chants . . . by Z. Buck', *QMMR* vi (1824), 276–7.

[73] Isaac Nathan, *An Essay on the History and Theory of Music* (1823), 29. Isaac Nathan (1790–1864), who attained some celebrity for his settings of Byron's *Hebrew Melodies*, went to Australia in 1841, where he came to be considered the 'father' of Australian music, composing settings of Aboriginal songs, the opera, *Don John of Austria*, and other miscellanies. One of his descendants is the conductor Charles Mackerras.

[74] See Rohr, 'Profession of Artisans', 195–8.

institution which many believed was music's legitimate inspiration. And it certainly seemed that the theatre was the most likely substitute.

Musicians and the theatre

But this situation proved to hold its own hazards for the musician. In an age of industrial discipline and renewed puritanism, the theatre, rather like bull-baiting, bear-baiting, cock-fighting, fairs, and football, was on the reform list of the Evangelicals.[75] It was closely associated with the unruly mob, with easy virtue and moral contamination. Its appeal to baser instincts and its nocturnal habitude made it highly unsuitable as an organ of social amelioration. In self-defence, the theatre might attempt to cut its coat to fit by presenting what Charles Lamb in 1807 called 'insipid levelling morality' on the stage—plays presenting a 'puritanical obtuse-ness of sentiment, a stupid infantile goodness', which audiences might lap up as reflection of their own virtues[76]—but the theatre itself remained an institution of dubious moral quality. It was still the 'vortex' into which 'the million have lost their moral sense in the delirious whirl of public applause and fallen victims to private solicitation, to seduction, and to dissolute pleasures'.[77] Not unnaturally, since music formed such an important part of the English theatre of those times, musicians were clearly implicated in the theatre's vicious influence. The association, maintained the *Quarterly Musical Magazine and Review*, was 'irremedi-able'.

Musicians were unfortunate in their relationship with the theatre in another sense as well, in that they failed to create an English opera—a much hoped-for product in an age when opera came to be perceived as a flagship of nationalist culture. By the 1820s, it had become a much-ventilated theme in the *Quarterly*. Out of the 'prodigious mass' of music written for the English stage, nothing save Arne's *Artaxerxes*,[78] it was believed, could qualify for the title of a genuine opera. 'England is yet possessed of anomalous intermezzi only of song and scenery, plot, incident and equivoque, which though agreeable . . . gives us no title to anything even remotely bordering upon the regular structure of a genuine opera.'[79] Yet only a national opera would do. Only an opera would serve

[75] Robert W. Malcolmson, *Popular Recreations in English Society 1700–1850* (1973), 100–7.

[76] Roy Park (ed.), *Lamb as Critic* (1980), 122.

[77] Vetus [Richard Mackenzie Bacon], 'On the Character of Musicians', *QMMR* i (1819), 285.

[78] Thomas Arne (1710–1778), *Artaxerxes*, produced Covent Garden, 2 Feb. 1762.

[79] Timotheus [Richard Mackenzie Bacon], 'To the Editor', *QMMR* ii (1820), 1.

to prove English musical superiority over its foreign adversaries and disprove the slander that the English were an unmusical nation. National honour demanded as much.[80] 'I want to see', cried one frustrated contributor,

fine poetry combined with fine music; then indeed we might judge of the genius of the English composer and of the national disposition for music . . . Let us then, Mr Editor, seek to diffuse this grand and comprehensive idea as alone affording the true notion of opera. Let us seek to convince poets and musicians, artists and lovers of the arts, the conductors of our public amusements, and the NATION itself, that they owe it to the NATIONAL CHARACTER to demonstrate this proposition, and that we—the English—understand and admit its truth.[81]

But for all the argument, and the brave words of the *Quarterly*, England's first journal dedicated to the art and profession of music, no national opera was forthcoming, and in the clash of interests that marked early nineteenth-century England, the sound of English musicians being ground into dull uniform particles between the stones of public indifference and foreign competition could scarcely be heard. The English composer, it was acknowledged, sank calmly 'into the humble character of a teacher, which the public calls upon him to assume . . . consenting to be respectable and happy, rather than great'.[82] And the composer who did step on to the precarious ladder of fame became, said the embittered Thomas Worgan, no more than 'a drudge, an underling, a caterer for the music shops, a ladder for the vocal and instrumental performer, an obscure scribbler, or a panderer to a corrupt taste'.[83]

Certainly after the flurry of successful composers for the theatre of the mid to late eighteenth century—successful, that is, within the limited terms imposed by the English stage—composers like Arne, Shield, Arnold, Storace, and even Dibdin, with their lively and melodious pastiches, the early nineteenth century produced only Henry Bishop and a handful of professional hacks, among whom Isaac Nathan was probably not the least.

But Bishop's ultimate fate, as official 'composer' to Covent Garden and later at Drury Lane, was to become the purveyor to London audiences of dozens of anglicized versions of Continental operas, of which he later said in defence, 'I have been a slavish servant to the public . . . had the public remained loyally *English*, I would have remained so

[80] 'Sketch of the State of Music in England', *QMMR* iv (1822), 249.
[81] R, 'Opera', *QMMR* v (1823), 290.
[82] An Observer, 'On the Present State of the English Musician', *QMMR* v (1823), 439.
[83] Thomas Danvers Worgan, *The Musical Reformer* (1829), 21.

too.'[84] He might also have said, had the proprietors of theatres shown more interest in musical originality or excellence and less in the cheapness of the product. Isaac Nathan's court case of 1828 demonstrated the meanness of theatre proprietors when it came to music.

Nathan sued Price, the proprietor of Drury Lane, for commissioning him to write *The Illustrious Stranger* in 1827 and then refusing to pay him for it. In defence, Price claimed that it was not usual for the patentees of the large theatres to pay anything to composers for their music if they themselves kept the copyright, for it was considered that the performance of their music at the theatre was of 'infinite advantage to them, inasmuch that it gave a popularity to their pieces which could not otherwise be obtained'. The court decided, reluctantly it must be said, for the defendant.[85]

It would seem that Worgan had been right. The composer was no more in the eyes of theatre managers than a pedlar with an eye to marketing his songs to the music shops. Hardly a helpful climate in which to create a national opera. Neither were composers helped by the existence of a workable body of librettos. Most were no more than artificial concoctions. One of the best of the 'poets', James Planché, excused himself on the same grounds as Bishop, that the public demanded as much. He maintained audiences could not bear more than a few minutes of music at a stretch. Anything longer would be greeted by calls of 'Cut it short' from the gallery and 'obstinate coughing or other significant signs of impatience from the pit'.[86] But the *Quarterly* castigated Planché's very first effort, his *Maid Marion* of December 1822, as 'trash' and sympathized with Bishop for having to give expression to 'nonsense and inanity'.[87]

The musician and the intellectual climate

All these factors combined to make the English musician less than influential in English society and culture of the early nineteenth century. In the great debates of the age music had little or no voice. Where, after all, did musicians stand in the great ideological disputes of the day—reason versus faith; liberty versus authority; capital versus land; labour

---

[84] BL MS Eg. 2159, fo. 96, in Rohr, 'Profession of Artisans', 309.
[85] 'Court of Common Pleas, Westminster, May 29 . . .', *The Times*, 30 May 1828, p. 3d.
[86] J. R. Planché, *Recollections and Reflections* (rev. edn. 1901, reprint 1978), 55.
[87] 'The Music of the legendary Opera called Maid Marion or the Huntress of Arlingfield . . .', *QMMR* v (1823), 93.

versus capital; man versus machines? What did English music and musicians have to say about the Poor Laws or the Corn Laws, about Malthus or Ricardo, Hume, Burke, John Wesley, or Tom Paine? The ballad singers of the streets clearly had decided opinions about basic political questions, especially during the long French wars. Thomas Bewick recalled how on this account they had been suppressed in Newcastle and in London, with those not pushing the official patriotic line often summarily silenced;[88] but the musical establishment could offer little more than the patriotic lip-service to 'king and country' of Charles Dibdin's square-rigged tunes for which he was rewarded with a government pension.[89]

Individual musicians like the Samuel Webbes (father and son), who belonged to the eventually suppressed London Corresponding Society,[90] may have been active enough, with opinions of their own, and the fact that the Philharmonic Society when it was formed in 1813 incorporated

[88] See Thomas Bewick, *Memoir*, 41, where he describes how the ballad singers of Newcastle were suppressed during the French Revolutionary Wars; also the *Gazetteer and New Daily Advertiser*, 9 July 1795, p. 3c, reports a riot in London caused by a crowd attacking troops come to cart off one of the local London ballad singers. Not content with rescuing him, the crowd proceeded to smash the windows and demolish the furniture of the arresting constable, one Slade. On the other hand, Thomas Holcroft, the dramatist and friend of Godwin, complained, not of the suppression of the ballad singers but the use of them made by the government. They were, he said, 'drilled, paid, and stationed at the ends of streets, to chaunt the downfall of the Jacobins, the glorious administration of Mr Pitt, and the victories of the Duke of York'. *A Narrative of Facts, relating to a Prosecution for High Treason* (1795), 11.

[89] See Mackerness, *Social History of English Music*, 135, for Dibdin, 'instructed' by Pitt; *DNB* notes that Dibdin was awarded a pension of £200 for his trouble which was withdrawn by the Grenville government of 1806–7.

[90] See Rohr, 'Profession of Artisans', 356, for this supposition. She bases it on the evidence of Francis Place who recalls borrowing a French book from Webbe junior, whom he identifies as a musician, like his father. The London Corresponding Society, founded in 1792 by the shoemaker Thomas Hardy and wound up by 1798, did have two Webbes who were members. But in a membership register confiscated by the Treasury Solicitor's office in 1794, both are shown to have belonged to other trades (PRO TS11 951/3495). They may have registered in this way, of course, to preserve some kind of anonymity and thus protect themselves from loss of patronage. Or they were perhaps working for the government and did not wish their professions known to the general LCS membership. The government spy John Taylor was indeed introduced to the LCS by Samuel Webbe. 'The Trial of Thomas Hardy' in T. B. Howell and T. J. Howell, *Complete Collection of State Trials and Proceedings for High Treason . . .* (1817), xxiv. 24.

Another member of the LCS, however, was one Alexander Wills, a dancing master. He was also a member of the socially more prestigious but similarly prosecuted Society for Constitutional Information ('Trial of Thomas Hardy', Howell, *State Trials*, xxiv. 984). On the whole, though, musicians, unlike some actors and even artists, perhaps for obvious economic reasons, seem to have kept themselves aloof from politics.

certain egalitarian principles into its original structure[91] does suggest an awareness by individual musicians of the political issues of the day. But music itself did not enter the debate. Music was perceived in intellectual circles as irrelevant. Jane Austen, although she played the piano, was derisive,[92] and figures like Wordsworth, Keats, Hazlitt, Hunt, Southey, Byron, and Shelley attached no real intellectual significance to music. Even Coleridge's early interest was chiefly recreational. The American, Ralph Waldo Emerson, perhaps summed up the Anglo-Saxon attitude when he complained, 'How partial, like mutilated eunuchs, the musical artists appear to me in society! Politics, bankruptcy, frost, famine, war— nothing concerns them but a scraping on a catgut, or tooting on a bass french horn.'[93] But the problem lay not simply with the musicians. It lay equally with the English mind. That energetic social chronicler Thomas Creevey records that the sophisticated Princess Lieven, normally quite at home among the English ruling élite, was on one evening occasion so peeved at the indifference that greeted her musical accomplishments that on being shown the next morning the glories of her host's stables she remarked to Creevey, 'I have as much pleasure in looking at these horses as you Englishmen have in hearing music.'[94] There was even a kind of pride amongst some aristocrats in their philistine credentials. The influential Whig peer, Henry Richard Vassal Fox, 3rd Baron, Lord Holland (1773–1840), while being equivocal about pictures, was reported by the banker and poet Samuel Rogers as actually hating music.[95] So whereas in France, and certainly later in Italy, music was recruited as a powerful agent in the dissemination of political ideas, and whereas composers themselves sometimes flirted with ideology,[96] in England music remained irrelevant.

Musicians were considered to be practitioners of a refined but inessential art. Their skills were seen to cater not to the mind but to sensual

[91] Rules, quoted in Nettel, *The Orchestra in England*, 106–7; Myles Birket Foster, *History of the Philharmonic Society of London, 1813–1912* (1912), 5.

[92] See *Jane Austen's Letters to her Sister Cassandra and Others*, ed. by R. W. Chapman (2nd edn., 1952).

[93] Quoted in Julius Pornoy, *The Philosopher and Music. A Historical Outline* (1954), 208.

[94] Thomas Creevey, *Papers*, selected and ed. by John Gore (1903, this edn. 1985), 277.

[95] *Reminiscences and Table-Talk of Samuel Rogers*, collected by G. H. Powell (1903), 219.

[96] See Peter Anthony Blom's review in *Journal of Interdisciplinary History*, xix (No. 1), 128–30, of Ralph P. Locke's *Music, Musicians and the Saint-Simonians* (1986) for composers like Halèvy, Nourrit, Hiller, Mendelssohn, and Berlioz who were influenced by the Saint-Simonian call.

pleasure, which those with money and leisure could purchase and dispense with at will. Among the aristocracy, there was also the need to establish the claims of breeding over innate talent, or the need to confront the possibility that a skill mastered somehow took precedence over the genius of blood, even when repressed by lack of application and therefore skill.[97] In the years after the French Wars, there was certainly a heightened consciousness of caste among the aristocracy and their emulators which, as we shall see in Chapter 4, appears to have aggravated the already strained relationship between the aristocracy and English musicians.

For the successful man of business, superficially emulating his betters, music was a luxury and a commodity with which to indulge his wife and his daughters. At best, for those whose social credentials did not equal their social ambitions, music was a way of demonstrating cultural authority. Indeed, as we shall see, in Sydney in the 1830s, music used in this way briefly formed part of the political discourse. Certainly, for women, for whom it had become something with which they were permitted to fill the hours rendered empty of meaningful work by the necessities of newly acquired status, music was considered morally a more elevated pursuit than the reading of novels or attending the theatre, even if it sometimes took on an obsessional quality in the lives of women who were otherwise starved of intellectual stimulus. But music remained nevertheless peripheral, as women themselves mostly did, to the dynamics of English economic and cultural life.

The *Quarterly* might strenuously, if self-consciously, assert that music was a fundamental building-block of a decent society without which the sanctity of family life might have one less support, but the argument was a strained one; 'there is a stabilizing, refining power inherent in music which cannot fail to be ultimately connected with the affections concerned in the support of domestic happiness.'[98] Had not music along with the other arts been responsible for exchanging the selfish, sensual, and exclusively masculine delights of the former age—the dinners, the suppers, the clubs, and the reverence for the 'six-bottle man'—for the delights of a mixed society in the home, where female virtue was at its most powerful and affecting? According to the *Quarterly* it had.[99] The journal might assert with equal conviction that it was wrong to consider music 'merely as an amusement (as it too commonly is by the volatile and

---

[97] My thanks to Dr A. D. Harvey for this suggestion.
[98] Vetus [Richard Mackenzie Bacon], 'To the Editor', *QMMR* i (1819), 421.
[99] Vetus, 'Music as a Pursuit for Men', *QMMR* ii (1820), 7–10.

the ignorant)', when it was in reality 'an intellectual pleasure', a 'rational delight', and an 'elegant science'.[100]

The *Quarterly* might claim that music 'moderates the excesses of a high natural temperament, elevates our devotion, chastens our affections', and might declare with more than a sniff of moral superiority that compared to such boorish upper-class pursuits as hunting, shooting, and fishing, music was wholly safe as well as cheap,[101] but its voice was small and if not wholly undistinguished (its founder and chief writer was the provincial newspaper proprietor and editor Richard Mackenzie Bacon (1776–1844) of the *Norwich Mercury*, author of a private biography of his friend, Edward Harbord, 3rd Baron Suffield), then far too circumscribed by narrow speciality. The voice of the *Quarterly* was as insignificant as that of a sparrow above the boom of the ocean. And it is curious, at least to us now, that Bacon, in an attempt to amplify his message, felt it necessary in one of his first 'Vetus' articles to state that he himself was not a musician.[102]

Professional organizations, 1604–1822

The history of the musical profession's attempts, from the Middle Ages right through to the nineteenth century, to normalize its relations with the rest of society, and to regulate, through its institutions, professional and social standards, education, remuneration and competition, makes a sorry tale. Its first significant effort was the creation of the old medieval guild company, incorporated in 1604 by Letters Patent by James I as the Company of Musicians. It governed apprenticeships and was empowered to summon periodically all its members, including masters, to be tested for standards.[103] But it was never a wealthy, influential, or powerful guild.[104] Its chief professional function outside the apprentice-

---

[100] C.T., 'To the Editor', *QMMR* i (1819), 280.

[101] Vetus, 'Music as a Pursuit for Men'.

[102] Vetus, 'On the Character of Musicians', 293, 'I am Sir, not a musician'. Richard Mackenzie Bacon also published a series of his 'Timotheus' letters to the Editor of the *QMMR* as a book entitled *Elements of Vocal Science, being a Philosophical Enquiry into some of the Principles of Singing* [1824]. William Ayrton's *Harmonicon*, founded in 1823 with a more popular format, also added its voice to the defence of music and musicians against the philistine assumption of its uselessness. See e.g. 'Miscellaneous Thoughts on Music' (i, 1843, p. 141), which makes much of music's key role as fund-raiser for charity, asserting also that music 'tends to keep us out of mischief and to blunt the edge of care'.

[103] O. Jocelyn Dunlop and R. D. Denman, *English Apprenticeships and Child Labour* (1912), 217.

[104] Woodfill, *Musicians in English Society*, 25–6; H. A. F. Crewdson, *The Worshipfull Company of Musicians* (1956).

ship system seems to have been to attempt to protect the livelihoods of city musicians from the encroachments of outsiders. As far as Charles Burney was concerned, this just meant 'empowering the company to keep out of processions and city-feasts, every street and country-dance player of superior abilities to those who have the honour of being styled the *Waits of the Corporation*'. Burney's other charge was that it afforded 'aliens an easy and cheap expedient of acquiring the freedom of the city, and enabling them to pursue some more profitable and respectable trade than that of fiddling'.[105]

Records of the Company certainly bear out this latter claim.[106] From the last half of the eighteenth century, few of its members were actually musicians. Burney himself was, and so were the Ashleys—a significant musical family and significant also in the records of the Company. John Ashley was elected Master in 1803[107] and three of his sons were members. But the majority of apprentices listed to be articled to 'citizens and musicians' were destined to become ballast officers, periwig-makers, brewers, coach-makers, pastry-cooks, and cordwainers.[108]

The entire apprenticeship system was of course in a state of decline in the late eighteenth century, with the apprenticeship clauses of the Statute of Artificers being repealed in 1814,[109] but, in any case, the Company of Musicians had always been held in opprobrium by those, like Sir John Hawkins, who considered its trade associations an affront to music's 'liberal' tradition. 'The only one of the liberal Sciences that conferred the degree of Doctor was itself degraded [by association with the Company of Musicians] and put on a footing with the lowest of the mechanic arts.'[110] By and large, the musical élite—members of the Chapel Royal, for example—had always eschewed it.

Founded in 1738 by three London musicians in response to witnessing the hardships suffered by two children of a deceased colleague, the Royal Society of Musicians might at first sight appear to have been a step in the right professional direction. It was, as Pippa Drummond has pointed out,

[105] Burney, *General History of Music*, iii. 359.

[106] Guildhall Library, MS 3094/1–2, Corporation of London, Company of Musicians, Apprentice Books (1765–1832); Guildhall Library, MS 3098, List of Freemen (1743–1831).

[107] Guildhall Library, MS 3087/1–3, 5, Court of Assistants, Minute Book (1772–1839), 12 Oct.

[108] See also Ehrlich, *Music Profession in Britain*, 26–7.

[109] K. D. M. Snell, *Annals of the Labouring Poor* (1985), for his chapter on the decline of the apprenticeship system.

[110] John Hawkins, *General History of Music* (1776, this edn. 1853), i. 481 f.

'the first sustained attempt by musicians (outside the Guild system) to protect themselves, their families and their fellows from the misfortunes of infirmity, accident and old age'.[111]

But it had very limited professional usefulness. In the first instance it was a charity, supported not only by members' subscriptions and public performances but by the munificence of wealthy non-musicians. Its job was to invest and protect assets on behalf of its members and to ascertain degrees of need, and, as it turned out, to resist claims wherever possible.[112] That it survives today (in very changed form, certainly) is probably a testament to its efficiency rather than to its generosity of spirit. The fact that musicians as a group were notoriously indigent made the Society's task certainly very difficult. The reasons behind such indigence it was not part of its charter to inquire into. Its response was rather to minimize liability by careful screening of applicants for membership. This, as we shall see in another chapter, turned the Society into something of an élite, but made no contribution to the development of the profession itself. It insisted that its members should have studied music for seven years, and that they should be healthy and in employment, but beyond this it was unable to go. Many professional musicians remained outside its umbrella, either because they could not meet the seven-year requirement, or because they were too poor to afford the subscription, or perhaps because they could not twist the arm of any member of the Society to recommend them, an important consideration, since it was certainly not in the interest of existing members to recommend musicians who were likely to need the Society's assistance.

Formed by the cream of London instrumentalists in 1813, to promote new instrumental music, the Philharmonic Society was, in professional terms, altogether more significant. For the first time, here were professional musicians declaring themselves to be leaders of musical taste and the intellectual superiors of their social betters. Programmes initially eschewed solo concertos and vocal music, which virtually guaranteed the abstention of all but the musical intelligentsia from their concerts. The aristocracy were mostly notable for their absence. The Society was, in

---

[111] Pippa Drummond, 'The Royal Society of Musicians in the Eighteenth Century', *Music & Letters*, lix (1978). As reprinted in RSM, *List of Members*, 191.

[112] RSM, MS Members' Files; Rohr, 'Profession of Artisans', came to this conclusion using these files; Ann Beedell, 'William Joseph Castell, o. k. a. Cavendish (1789–1839), Musician. His Origins, Life and Career in Ireland, England, France, Mauritius and Australia', MA thesis (2 vols., Univ. of New South Wales, Sydney, 1990), Appendix 1, Letters, Susannah Castell to William Castell, on the Society's meanness, 10 June 1828, pp. 3–4; Dec. 1830, pp. 3–4; 3 Feb. 1831, p. 6.

effect, supported by the profession itself, a fact which the *Quarterly* considered 'not honourable to the patronage [i.e. the aristocracy] of the country'.[113] But its power actually lay in the fact that it was organized by musicians and for musicians and their friends. Its rules and structure were determined by musicians themselves, and as already noted, incorporated certain elements of egalitarianism. Originally, leadership of the group was not based on any hierarchy of talent or reputation, but was on a purely rotational basis. All members, no matter what instrument they played, or how prominent in the public eye, were technically equal. 'There shall not be any distinction of rank in the orchestra and therefore the station of every performer shall be absolutely determined by the leader of the night.'[114] Furthermore, despite the scarcity of aristocratic patronage, the Society flourished both artistically and financially.

But the Philharmonic Society did not extend its egalitarianism to the public at large. As the *Morning Chronicle* of 19 March 1819 pointed out, their concerts were not 'public' in any strict sense. They were for subscribers only, and subscribers were only admitted by the directors upon the nomination of a member, 'who becomes responsible for the rank and character of those names he gives in'. The aim of this exercise was to make it impossible for any 'objectionable person' to gain admittance. 'Hence the audience is of the most select kind, and being distinguished by a pure love of excellent music, silence and attention are preserved during the whole of the performance.'[115] Thus, although the programmes were selected and performed on their terms, 'tremblingly alive' as members were 'to every circumstance that may diminish their own general reputation, judgement, care, and discipline',[116] musicians were still insensitive to the potential of mass audiences and were unable to rescue themselves from the need to flatter and cajole the class sensibilities of their social superiors.

That the Philharmonic Society saw itself as the potential leader of the profession may be judged by its plan (devised by the composer and teacher Thomas Forbes Walmisley (1783–1866)) to establish an Academy of Music. But even as these plans were being matured, they

[113] 'Sketch of the State of Music in London, May 1823', *QMMR* v (1823), 242.

[114] Quoted in Nettel, *Orchestra in England*, 107. Whether because of personal acrimony within, or pressure from without, this situation soon gave way to a stricter hierarchy and differentiated pay scales. See BL MS Loan 48.9/1. Philharmonic Society, Account Book, 1813–1866.

[115] In Robert Elkin, *Royal Philharmonic. The Annals of the Royal Philharmonic Society* [1946], 20.

[116] 'State of Music in London', *QMMR* vii (1825), 201.

were 'jostled off the course by the superior strength and activity of the noblemen and gentlemen originating the Royal Academy of Music'.[117]

There could be little that expressed more powerfully the lack of control exercised by musicians over their own profession than the setting up in 1822 of the Royal Academy of Music. Led by the amateur composer of Italian operas, Lord Burghersh (1784–1859), later the 11th Earl of Westmorland, a group of interested dilettanti conceived and executed their plan for the Royal Academy of Music without any consultation or co-operation with leaders of the musical profession. And although the *Quarterly* echoed the general dismay of musicians in its columns, arguing that any plan which 'estimates even the highest professional ability and character [of musicians] as articles to be bought and commanded' rather than to be deferred to, consulted, and respected, was unwelcome, the exclusion of the profession from the effective management of the Academy was publicly approved as preserving it from 'mere professional hands'.[118] The Duke of Wellington featured prominently in the list of aristocratic names that made up the directing Committee. But keeping a tight rein on the actual running of the show was Lord Burghersh, who made himself Chairman of the all-powerful Sub-Committee.

Adding insult to injury, one of Lord Burghersh's protégés, the French harpist Nicolas Bochsa (1789–1856), was appointed Secretary to the Board in spite of the fact that he could neither speak nor write English.[119] This was unacceptable not only because Bochsa was a foreigner, but because it was fairly widely known that he had been convicted in a French court of law for fraud and theft on a large scale, and sentenced in his absence to be branded and sent into forced labour for twelve years. Bochsa was undoubtedly a man of great musical talent—a big man, with great personal charisma, though the oboist William Parke took exception to such a 'gigantic sort of personage like Mr Bochsa playing on so feminine an instrument as the harp'.[120] But his elevation to such a position was met with much public opposition, culminating in *The Times* publishing in 1826 an extract from the *French Moniteur* detailing the charges, verdict, and sentence of the French courts.[121] He was also

---

[117] 'The Royal Academy of Music', *QMMR* iv (1822), 393.
[118] Quoted in Rohr, 'Profession of Artisans', 168.
[119] 'The Royal Academy of Music', *QMMR* iv (1822), 524: '... absurd ... can neither write nor speak the English Language'.
[120] Parke, *Musical Memoirs*, ii. 183.
[121] 'Court of Assize Paris', *French Moniteur*, 19 Feb. 1818. Reprinted in *The Times*, 6 Dec. 1826, p. 3c.

accused, although not publicly, of abduction and bigamy.[122] In 1827, public opinion eventually forced Bochsa out of the Royal Academy, where he had also been professor of harp, but the incident demonstrated the degree to which the aristocracy was capable of maintaining its indifference to the claims not only of English musicians but of middle-class morality. Bochsa continued in aristocratic patronage and went on to hold positions of authority in that bastion of aristocratic privilege, the King's Theatre.

One of the Philharmonic Society's first directors, founder of the *Harmonicon*, and music journalist, William Ayrton (1777–1858), in 1827 privately accused Bochsa's patrons of 'utter contempt for virtuous feeling', and went on to warn that when persons of high rank were inclined to 'throw their broad shield' over crimes which not even the king himself could pardon, 'that moment, a feeling will be excited the consequences of which I dare not venture to foretell'.[123] Yet it was really only when the 50-year-old Bochsa eloped in 1839 with the singer Anna Bishop, the wife of his friend Henry Bishop, and went into voluntary exile, that outraged morality was vindicated. Bochsa died in Sydney in 1856 while touring with Anna Bishop.

The foundation of Britain's first national school of music was thus greeted with a certain ambivalence. The *London Magazine*, a journal very friendly towards music, in May 1823 called it a 'farce got up by "particular desire of several persons of distinction"'. Indeed it was viewed with suspicion not least by rank-and-file musicians, who were also unhappy at the prospect of a new élite emerging which was likely to increase rather than diminish competition for jobs. Susannah Castell's response was probably fairly typical. The 'Academy Boys', as she called them, by 1830 were, she said, patronized by royalty and superseded 'good and experienced players'. They would all be 'sure of a birth in one of the Orchestras not infrequently being instrumental to the removal of One that had remain'd there for years and in all respects a very superior performer'. Their emergence, about twenty a year, she was sure would be incalculably detrimental to the interests of musicians presumably like her own sons, who had no such natural advantages. Neither was Susannah anything less than cynical about the purpose of the Academy. 'He [Lord Burghersh] was the first to patronize the Academy at its rise, and he has

[122] BL Add. MS 60370. William Ayrton, Draft letter to J. S. Mack, 28 Nov. 1827. Ayrton, it should be remembered, had been ousted from the management of the King's Theatre in 1822 by the Italian, Petracchi, so had his own reasons for resentment.
[123] Ibid.

never lost sight', she said, 'of the object—the boys <u>can</u> well afford the time to practise his music . . . hence the patronage afforded to these half taught and worse educated youths.'[124]

It is not possible to assess the degree to which Susannah's fears of unfair competition were realized. The Academy suffered in its first decades what Cyril Ehrlich describes as a 'meagre and precarious existence',[125] its product was on the whole undistinguished, and by 1866 of about 419 English players performing at the Royal Italian Opera, Her Majesty's Theatre, the Philharmonic Society, the Musical Society, and the New Philharmonic Society, only 72 were ex-RAM students.[126] As Ehrlich points out, however, these figures (published in the *Athenaeum*, whose music critic was Henry Chorley (1808–72), an avowed enemy of the RAM) were potentially biased and used a rather selective sample. But certainly the RAM had its problems, not least of which was funding. The Government offered only minimal assistance and the bulk had to come from private subscription.

Walmisley's plan, much more modest in scale, was meant to have been largely self-supporting, and had acknowledged, by its smaller intake provision, the fear of oversupply that had so troubled Susannah Castell, and, we may infer, many other rank-and-file professional musicians in similar positions to her sons. Certainly, for Susannah, the problem of oversupply and the consequent low wages earned by musicians were, as we shall see, a continuing and regretful theme throughout her correspondence of the 1820s and 1830s. She was to look on bitterly as tailors and other 'cheating' tradesmen prospered while her 'boys' were insulted and impoverished. But, above all, Walmisley had vested authority in the hands of the profession itself, rather than in a group of aristocratic dilettantes, who, totally ignoring not only Walmisley's plan but, by default, the professional integrity of leading musicians, proceeded to take 'all power out of the hands of the profession' and to insist on 'the introduction of a large number of musicians to the profession at once as it were . . . [which] entails an enormous expense'.[127]

It is difficult to assess whether Walmisley's modest plan would

---

[124] Beedell, 'William Joseph Castell', Appendix I, Susannah Castell to William Castell, Dec. 1830, pp. 4–5; 3 Feb. 1831, pp. 2–3. All correspondence from these papers (reproduced in Beedell, 'William Joseph Castell', Appendix I) will henceforward be denoted only by initials of correspondents and the dates of letters. See List of Abbreviations for full names.

[125] Ehrlich, *Music Profession in Britain*, 79.

[126] Ibid. 80.

[127] *QMMR* iv (1822), 396.

ultimately have been more successful than that of the aristocrats. Probably not. But it is arguable that the near failure of the RAM was due not simply to lack of funding by the State (although this, as Ehrlich has shown, together with the low levels of private money secured, was to be damaging), but to those very social attitudes towards music personified by the arrogance of Burghersh[128] towards the professional aspirations of musicians, which led musicians themselves to fear and even to despise their own Academy.

But for better or worse, secular institutionalized musical education had begun in Britain and, in spite of its ambivalent start, would prevail. And for professional musicians, the age of respectability loomed. Felix Mendelssohn and Queen Victoria would finally set the seal, the latter bestowing England's first musical knighthood upon Henry Bishop in 1842. It is hard to see that respectability did any more for English music, or for the professional integrity of musicians, than disrepute had. And even with the subsequent consolidation of the Royal Academy of Music, music remained a less than serious profession compared to those other burgeoning professions of the nineteenth century—medicine, law, engineering, pharmacy, architecture, or even art.[129] Yet, although Susannah would not live to see it, at least one of her 'poor boys' would end his days with his name in the Court section of the London Post Office Directory.[130] But his father, who belonged essentially to another age, would have an altogether different end.

---

[128] Dr A. D. Harvey has suggested to me that Lord Burghersh (John Fane (1784–1859), later the 11th Earl of Westmorland) was particularly class-conscious and that he had probably been the most unpopular officer in the whole Peninsular army between 1810 and 1813. Perhaps musicians were simply unlucky, then, that a man with such qualifications should have pursued composition as his hobby and should have interested himself, for whatever reason, in the foundation of a national school of music.

It is interesting to note that whenever the *QMMR* reviewed any of Burghersh's Italianate works, it always made a rather ambivalent point of mentioning his noble and/or his amateur status. See *QMMR* iv (1822), 258, 263; and especially a long review of his '15 Pieces' which took the opportunity to comment on the low status music was accorded among the great, generally, and ended by remarking, rather disingenuously, that Lord Burghersh's works were worthy enough to place him 'upon the list of amateurs who have dignified music by adopting it as a pursuit'. *QMMR* v (1823), 209–13.

[129] Cf. H. Byerley Thomson, *The Choice of a Profession. A Concise Account and Comparative Review of the English Professions* (1857); A. M. Carr Saunders and P. A. Wilson, *The Professions* (Oxford, 1933).

[130] *Post Office London Directory for 1879*, 'Court Directory', Wm Jones Castell, 90 St Petersburgh Place, W.

3
William and Susannah

You was the dearest object, tho others had pretensions; the
first and so shall be the last.

SEC to WJC, 24 Aug. 1827.

PRELUDE TO THE MARRIAGE

IN 1804 Pitt, with the oblique and surprising assistance of Fox, had
ousted the fretful Addington and resumed control of the nation and of
the war with France.[1] The previous year, almost certainly due to fears of
a French invasion and general mobilization, Peter Castell had rejoined
the ranks of Doyle's 87th Regiment as quartermaster on half-pay.[2]

Far away in Australia, in between these two events, in March 1804,
Irish convicts had staged what was the first and only uprising against
military authority in mainland New South Wales. It had taken place at
Vinegar Hill, not far from Parramatta—a spot named to commemorate
one of the bloody battles of the unsuccessful Irish uprising of 1798. The
bodies of the chief insurgents, hanged for their crime, dangled for months
rotting in their chains—a sight and smell meant to edify the remainder of
the convict population even at the expense of the comfort and sensibility
of the innocent and free; at least, that is, until Mrs Kent, a new arrival
with her husband from India on board the *Buffalo*, finally prevailed upon
Governor King to have 'the Martyrs' cut down and decently buried.[3] For
even at that early stage, the colony was assuming some of the pretensions
of civilization. Mrs John Macarthur's tinkling piano was heard at
Parramatta even before the sound of the crude drums of the Irish
insurgents forced her to take flight with Mrs Samuel Marsden down the

---

[1] See A. D. Harvey, *Britain in the Early Nineteenth Century* (1978); Clive Emsley,
British Society and the French Wars, 1793–1815 (1979); Creevey, *Papers*, 16–17.
[2] War Office, *A List of Officers of the Army and Marines . . . and a List of the Officers . . .
on half-pay . . .* (1803) [henceforth *Army List*].
[3] National Library of Australia, Canberra, Grant Papers, MS 737, John Grant, Journal,
pp. 47–8, quoted in Hughes, *Fatal Shore*, 193.

river to Sydney. Yet as the two ladies, the veritable mothers of the nation, drifted downstream, they must have wondered what new barbarism lay veiled just beyond the next dawn. As it turned out, however, they need not have been concerned; the New South Wales 'the Rum' Corps did a professional if bloody job, thus saving the colony for future generations in the name of law and order, the Protestant religion, and the sheep industry.

News did not reach London till July,[4] where it seemed to cause only the merest ripple of interest. In the English consciousness, as Swift had observed, the Irish were always rebelling,[5] and it was probably viewed with some satisfaction that the rebels, such as they were, were safely 16,000 miles away and not just across the Irish Sea, where Ireland still represented a weak point in England's defence against the 'Corsican Monster'.

Peter Castell did not long enjoy his return to half-pay. In May 1805, the quartermaster died, leaving an estate of £20.[6] At that time the family were living in Tottenham Court Road in the Parish of St Pancras, an area described by Planché a little later as 'dingy' and as an 'out of the way [and] humble neighbourhood'.[7] But the northern or St Pancras end of Tottenham Court Road ran into the relatively more genteel realms of Fitzrovia and it may have been here that the Castells resided, probably, however, in a state of some financial decay. When Sophia died in March of the following year, joining Peter in the graveyard of St James's, Piccadilly,[8] there was no record of any surviving estate.

William, at almost 17, and his brother Peter, some years his junior, seem to have been the only surviving children, their grandfather's will making no mention of any other siblings. The sister he later claimed to

---

[4] Report in London, *The Times*, 27 July 1804, p. 2c.

[5] According to the English, said Swift, a tradition among the Irish was 'that every Forty Years there must be a Rebellion'. *Drapier's Letters to the People of Ireland* (1724), in Maxwell, *Dublin under the Georges*, 14.

[6] PRO PROB. 6/181/454. Administration of the Estate of Peter Castell . . . late of Tottenham Court Road in the Parish of St Pancras . . . a Quarter Master in His Mty's 87th Reg[t] of Horse . . . July 1805.

[7] Planché, *Recollections and Reflections*, 64; referring to the environs of the Prince of Wales Theatre, Tottenham Court Road, in the 1820s.

[8] St James's Church, Piccadilly. Parish Records. Burials, 6 Mar. 1806. It is possible that they were buried here and not in the graveyard at St Pancras either because of overcrowding (burial was becoming a problem in London at that time) or because of the activities of body-snatchers. Old St Pancras, situated in a relatively unpopulated area due to the constant flooding of the nearby Fleet River, was a popular venue for the 'resurrectionists'. See Ruth Richardson, *Death, Dissection and the Destitute* (1988), p. xiii.

possess, the woman he lived with in Mauritius and Sydney, Mary, who was somewhere between fifteen and twenty years his junior, would have had to have been born at the very earliest in 1804, and could not have been born after Sophia's death in March 1805—in either scenario, a mere child when her grandfather died in 1811, and unlikely to have been entirely unmentioned in his will of the same year.[9] But this belongs to a later part of the narrative.

William was liable at that age to be registered as an able-bodied male and to be drafted by ballot, in the event of an invasion, into the home militia or regular fencible regiments. If one had money or connections, a way of avoiding the possible drudgery and hardships of a foot-soldier was to join one of the fashionable regiments of volunteers which by law exempted one from arbitrary conscription.[10] That William was able to do this using what remained of his father's connections is probably unlikely. Throughout his life, though, there remained always a military thread. In the 1820s and early 1830s, he sent letters from France to Susannah via Horseguards in London,[11] and later in Mauritius he had intimate connections, as we shall see, with his father's old regiment, the 87th Foot. Whether voluntarily or not, by 1811 his younger brother Peter had ended up in the Royal Navy, on board, it was thought, HMS *Diomede*, in the East Indies.[12]

But whatever may have been William's youthful military pretensions in an age obsessed with such matters, there can be little doubt that it was intended that he should become a musician. When he joined the Royal Society of Musicians in 1814 he declared that he had studied and practised music for at least seven years,[13] and by the time of his mother's death we can presume that he was already at work, as his eldest son was

[9] William Jones, his will. PRO PROB. 11/1524.

[10] The Levy-in Mass Bill; 'all those persons of the first and second classes, who are not enrolled in any Corps of Volunteers will be called out and *compelled to join any regiment of Regulars in any part of the Kingdom*; separated from their friends and neighbours and subject to all the hardships and discipline of a common soldier'. *The Times*, 26 July 1804, p. 2c.

[11] SEC–WJC, 10 June 1828, p. 5; 27 Mar. 1839, pp. 1–2; 10 Apr. 1829, p. 4. WJC also sent letters probably through Sir William Codrington, who in 1826 was a Captain in the Coldstream Guards. SEC–WJC, 12 Nov. 1829, p. 6.

[12] PRO PROB. 11/1524/337. William Jones's will. The doubt expressed here about the whereabouts of Peter, 'now supposed to be serving on board His Majesty's Ship Diomede in the East Indies', might suggest that he was pressed into service, a real risk for young men, especially in the riverside areas of London like Lambeth. Or perhaps he 'ran away to sea' after the deaths of his parents.

[13] RSM, MS Members' Files. Castell's application to join.

to be at the same age, in some theatre orchestra; for in spite of the war, life in London was not dramatically altered.

Although concerts had been somewhat curtailed because of the war, and although the aristocracy had not always had access to their usual supplies of French dancers,[14] the English theatres, both major and minor, had been largely unaffected. So had the Italian Opera at the King's Theatre. In 1804 the capital witnessed the début of the Italian contralto Giuseppina Grassini, who in May appeared at the King's Theatre with Mrs Billington in a celebrated performance of Winter's *Il Ratto di Proserpine*.[15] In 1806 the 20-year-old Henry Bishop had his ballet *Tamerlan et Bajazet* produced at the King's Theatre, and in the same year the arrival of the young Angelica Catalani created a sensation with the sheer volume of her instrument, and put many noses out of joint by her blatant exploitation of the foreign opera singer's much-criticized prerogative of charging high fees. The popular balladists of the day took up the cause of poor old John Bull with verve.

> A Concert she gives, but don't think her a ninny,
> She makes John Bull pay for each ticket a guinea,
> Don't talk of hard times, and high taxes, 'tis wrong,
> When five hundred pounds can be got for a song.[16]

In somewhat less controversial and also less illustrious circumstances, in 1805, at one of the Lenten Oratorio concerts at Covent Garden, the 'young Orpheus', Nicholas Mori, the eight-year-old made his public début as a violinist.[17] Much later, the talented, if choleric, Mori would prove himself less than friendly towards Castell, about whose life at that time we can only conjecture. Unlike Mori, who was to remain, until his untimely death in 1839, a high-profile musician, Castell was invisible. Like so many other competent, even talented, working musicians of the period, he lived and worked in a world that has left no record of his activities. Indeed, of his life from about 1793 to this time, virtually nothing is known, except that he was, presumably, living with his parents in London.

---

[14] Parke, *Musical Memoirs*, ii. 190, mentions the decline in musical performances throughout the war years; *re* ballet dancers, the failure of the 1794–5 season was attributed in part to the 'impossibility of getting dancers from the Continent'. *Gazetteer and New Daily Advertiser*, 30 Mar. 1795, p. 2b.

[15] See Michael Kelly, *Reminiscences*, ed. by Roger Fiske (1975), 279.

[16] *Later English Broadsides* (1979), 247, 'More Miseries! Or the Disappointment at Bath'.

[17] Parke, *Musical Memoirs*, i. 341.

London was even then a giant European city with much still about it of Hogarthian third-world confusion and contradiction; still possessing much of the tumultuousness and anarchy described by Smollett in *Humphry Clinker* a generation earlier: 'the hod-carrier, the low mechanic, the tapster, the publican, the shop-keeper, the pettifogger, the citizen, the courtier, *all tread on the kibes of one another*; actuated by the demons of profligacy and licentiousness, they are seen everywhere, rambling, riding, rolling, rushing, jostling, mixing, bouncing, cracking, and crashing in one vile ferment of stupidity and corruption—all is tumult and hurry.'[18] It was a city, though, fast sorting itself out into two broad sections—East and West. In the East—the old commercial heart of the city—all was narrow, crowded, and frequently derelict. In the West all was space, grace, and order and becoming increasingly the exclusive province of wealth, both new and old.[19] The spacious Georgian squares of the West, an affront to old habits of close, multi-layered, organic urban settlement, were to many older heads a sign of the profligacy and licentiousness of the new affluence, but to a foreigner like Archenholz they were a revelation. If all London were as well built, he said, 'there would be nothing in the world to compare with it'. But as it was he could not help but remark the appalling contrast with the East.[20]

The new desire for space was also a desire for distance to be placed between the élite and the 'mass'. The old hierarchical interdependence, bound up in the medieval concept of paternalism and *noblesse oblige*, had, under the stress of industrialism and population growth, finally given way to the new liberal economics of Adam Smith and to the fears of Malthus. Traditional notions of the moral economy, of a 'fair wage' based on the cost of living, collapsed beneath the weight of newly discovered 'natural' laws of supply and demand, by which dictum was created for the first time the somewhat bizarre notion of a surplus or redundant population, destined, if it was not to threaten the entire fabric of society, to be (through the 'natural' agencies of poverty, starvation, and *laisser-faire*) the victim of its own powers of reproduction.[21]

The implications for music and musicians in these changed social and economic relationships and values—which we shall call for want of a

[18] Tobias Smollett, *Humphry Clinker* (1771, this edn. 1895), 95.
[19] See George Rudé, *Hanoverian London, 1714–1808* (1971); M. Dorothy George, *London Life in the Eighteenth Century* (1925, this edn. 1966).
[20] T. W. Archenholtz, *A View of the British Constitution and of the Manners and Customs of the People of England* (1794), 119, in Rudé, *Hanoverian London*, 10.
[21] For the concept of 'fair wage', see E. P. Thompson, *The Making of the English Working Class* (1963, this edn. 1966), 72, 244.

better name the Industrial Revolution—were profound. Music, the most socially based, was arguably also the most commercially exploitable of all the arts. Well before the Renaissance and the emergence of the other arts into the commodity market, the minstrels had been rebuked for profiting by and thus debasing music. But by the end of the eighteenth century, the secular English musician in a secular age found himself in a market which, as we saw in Chapter 2 and as we shall see again in Chapter 4, spurned and even denied the existence of English indigenous music. For the newly emerging social and economic order, the English 'folk' itself had all but ceased to exist. In its place was an alien body of people—the landless proletariat—whom Malthus had taught it to fear. For the English musician this peculiar situation was to build a formidable wedge between his creative imagination and his cultural roots, and to create at the same time a market with an inbuilt preference for the imported over the home-grown product; a combination which devastated English musical output for at least the next hundred years.

The new shape of London—in essence the East–West divide—reflected something of this problem in its rejection of responsibility by the rich for the provision of the poor. Private charity there certainly was, and an awakening sense of the horror of poverty and of the cruelty of much of life for the very poor—an awakening humanitarianism in fact—yet at the same time, there were new Draconian laws for the protection of private property against a growing tide of dispossessed[22] and this desire for detachment and isolation. It was a process that William Castell was probably not deeply conscious of, but which moulded him nevertheless, and directed his aspirations. Musicians were, after all, precariously balanced on the divide between the two worlds—often working in one and living in the other. And the great aim was to make the total transition, out of the abyss and into the light, no matter what the cost.

On the death of Sophia in 1806, assuming that William was not after all lured into any military commitments, it is very likely that he went to live with his maternal grandfather, William Jones, in Lambeth. He may at that time also have been placed under George Veale, perhaps a friend of Jones's. It was Veale who recommended him to the Royal Society of Musicians in 1814. A violinist and viola player, Veale was, we must assume, a reasonably sound professional musician. He had been

---

[22] Thompson, *The Making*, notes the increase in the late 18th century of crimes which carried the death penalty. In 1785 the death penalty was inflicted almost exclusively for economic offences.

employed at various times at both Covent Garden and Drury Lane, and had performed at the Grand Musical Festivals between 1788 and 1790. Like Jones, he was on the 1799 Royal Society of Musicians' 'List of Benefactors and Subscribers', having joined the Royal Society in 1788. And if he was the same George Veal who is thought to have collaborated with 'Jeremy Collier Redivivus' in a 'new edition' of *Musical Travels* in 1818, satirizing J. B. Logier, then he may have moved in literary circles as well as in musical ones.[23]

Like many other professional musicians of his day though, Veale's career did not sustain him to the end of his life. In 1823 in an application for assistance to the RSM he described himself as a 67-year-old string player, who for no reason that he could see, except his age, was 'deprived of every engagement'. Consequently,

he is reluctantly compel'd to solicit your assistance and kind consideration, to aid him to obtain the necessaries of life, in the latter part of those days, the indulgence of Heav'n may grant him, assuring you most solumnly, that no pains care or attention has been spared on his part to save and obtain from the wreck of a humble fortune (which he possess'd in right of his late wife) a small annuity which he gladly brings forward, and joyfully acknowledges, to lessen his claim to that aid that nothing but the most poignant necessity & accumulated misfortune could have induced him to Solicit. Y^r Petitioner has fifty pounds a y^r encumbered with many debts.

The Annuity I have is encumbered with debts that without the kind assistance of the Society I must unavoidably sell it to pay them. Severe indeed will be my fate if I am obliged to part with all I have in this world, of any value to entitle me to the aid and assistance of that Society that I have ever served, esteem'd and venerated.[24]

In 1829, according to Susannah (she considered herself an especial favourite with him), his motto had been 'Tho wounded am not conquered', a motto which at that time she thought fit to appropriate to herself as well.[25] In 1831 she described him as 'very infirm' and noted that the Royal Society had curtailed his allowance to 'a mere stipend as they discovered that his father left him a trifle'.[26] He died in 1833.[27]

It was probably at his grandfather's house in Stangate Street that William first met Susannah Humble, the widow of another musician,

---

[23] For RSM membership, see RSM, *List of Members*, 147; for his collaboration with Collier, see *British Library General Catalogue of Books to 1975* (1980), entry for Joel Collier. It is thought George Veal provided 'notes applying the satire'.
[24] RSM, MS Members' Files [Veale].   [25] SEC–WJC, 14 Feb. 1829, p. 4.
[26] Ibid. 3 Feb. 1831, p. 6.   [27] RSM, *List of Members*.

Maximilian Humble, who, with her son Augustine, lived there perhaps in the capacity of housekeeper. When Susannah came is uncertain, but it was evidently some time before August 1810, when, on the 19th, at St George's, Hanover Square, by banns, she was married to William.[28] He was 21: she, about 36.

SUSANNAH CASTELL

Susannah Elizabeth Castell, as she now became, was in many discernible ways William's antithesis. For a start, he was the child of the feckless muses, while she was of solid Huguenot stock. He embraced opportunism, she industry—he notoriety, she respectability. He was the hedonist, she the moralist. His guiding principle was pleasure, hers virtue. Their marriage almost from the start became a battleground of opposing values and represented in its own way the cultural conflicts of the wider world in which they lived, a world in which the old libertine ways of the eighteenth-century 'Enlightenment' were under siege from the big guns of nineteenth-century middle-class 'decency' and aggressive Evangelicalism.

On another more subtle level, however, the conflict between them was also the conflict between the butt-end of classicism and nascent Romanticism. From what we know of him—at least in his relationship to Susannah—he was the cold and remote autocrat—self-conscious and artificial, while she was, in her own words, a 'child of nature'— uncompromising, passionate, and free. Indeed, he might even be seen as a faint and confused echo of Lord Chesterfield—she, as we shall be considering below, of Rousseau.

Susannah was born probably in 1774, the last of her mother's children by a second marriage.[29] Apparently a descendant of the Huguenot Henri IV of France,[30] her mother belonged to one of three branches of this princely connection, either the LeContes, the Navarres or the LeSeaurs.[31] The fact that Susannah's son, William, included the first of these in his own children's names would suggest LeConte. Perhaps she was Marie LeConte, born 20 October 1741 and baptized at L'Église de Londres,

[28] CWL, Parish Records of St George's Church, Hanover Square, London, Marriages, 10 Aug. 1810.

[29] SEC–WJC, 8 Feb. 1831, p. 2.

[30] Ibid. Thomas H. Jones [henceforward THJ]–SEC, 27 Nov. 1827, p. 1; SEC–WJC, Dec. 1827, p. 14.

[31] SEC–WJC, 13 Oct. 1830, p. 2.

Threadneedle Street, on 11 November, daughter of Pierre Le Conte and Jeanne Robert.[32]

On her father's side, she may have been one of the Portal family. Her son by Maximilian Humble was christened Augustine Edward Portal Humble,[33] which supports this possibility. A distinguished Huguenot family which quickly became 'established', contributing a number of quite scholarly and altogether worthy individuals to the ranks of the Anglican clergy, as well as a renowned company of paper manufacturers[34], the Portals also threw up at least one 'non-conformist' in the littérateur and eventual box-keeper of Drury Lane Theatre, Abraham Portal. A failed silversmith and bookseller, he was a friend of Hogarth and Sheridan and writer of plays, poetry, and treatises of only moderate distinction.[35] Born in 1726 and dying in 1809, he could indeed have been Susannah's father. But of his numerous children there is no record of a daughter called Susannah. He did have a son Edward[36] who may have been the one remembered in Augustine's christening. But then so too did Abraham's brother William.[37] Interesting as the idea of a Portal connection may be, the only hard evidence for it is the name on Augustine's baptismal record.

From Susannah's letters,[38] despite lapses of syntax and spelling of which she was aware and for which she frequently and sometimes rather incongruously apologized, it is evident that she was highly literate. William, certainly for his own purposes and not as a compliment, had himself referred to her as a 'sensible and well educated woman'.[39] Sterne, Goldsmith, Count Gramont, Bunyan, Nathaniel Lee, Milton, Thomas Percy, Dryden, Mrs Inchbald, Aesop, and the Book of Job all make entrances in various guises throughout the correspondence.[40]

---

[32] *Registers of the French Church Threadneedle Street*, iv, ed. T. C. Colyer-Fergusson (London, 1916).

[33] CWL, Parish Records of St Anne's Church, Soho, London, Baptisms, 1 Jan. 1797 (born 30 Nov. 1796).

[34] See Sir William Portal, *Abraham Portal, born 1726, died 1809 and his descendants* (1925); Francis Spencer, *Portals. The Church, the State and the People, leading to 250 years of Paper-Making* (1962).

[35] *Biographia Dramatica, or, The Companion to the Playhouse* (1812), i. 577; Portal, *Abraham Portal*.

[36] Baptized 20 Jan. 1765.

[37] Baptized 3 Mar. 1768.

[38] Reproduced in Beedell, 'William Joseph Castell', Appendix I.

[39] Quoted in SEC–WJC, 25 June 1829, p. 3.

[40] Sterne, SEC–WJC, 24 Aug. 1827, p. 1; Goldsmith—ref. to *Vicar of Wakefield*, 10 June 1828, p. 2; Count Gramont—ref. to Count Grammond, 10 July 1828, p. 1; Bunyan—ref. to 'Vanity Fair' (*Pilgrim's Progress*), 9 June 1829, p. 2; Nathaniel Lee—ref. to his *The*

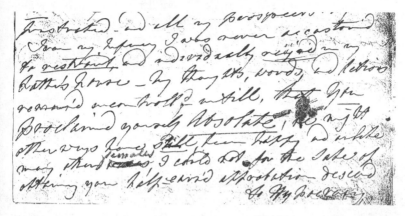

4. Extract from letter, SEC–WJC, Dec. 1827. Note WJC's pencilled emendation of the word 'wives' to read 'females'.

She had had, by her own account, an intellectually untrammelled childhood. It was only William, she claimed, who had ever tried to control her mind and feelings. 'From my infancy I was never accustom'd to <u>restraint</u> and individuality reign'd in my father's house—My thoughts, words, and Actions remained uncontroll'd untill, that <u>you</u> proclaimed yourself <u>Absolute</u>.'[41] Here indeed is the voice of early Romanticism—of Rousseau's natural child perhaps, essentially good and endowed with divine 'conscience', brought up protected from the harmful influences of civilization; buffered by nature and allowed the freedom to develop his or her individuality and to reach balanced conclusions about the world. Was this the philosophy of her 'father's house'? Over and over again in her letters we hear its echoes. Twice she declared herself 'Born a child of nature',[42] by which, we presume, she did not mean that she was illegitimate. (Although perhaps she was.) She was, she said, incapable of

Rival Queens (1677), 10 Apr. 1829, p. 5; Milton—probable ref. to *Paradise Lost*, 24 Aug. 1827, p. 2; Thomas Percy—ref. to 'Babes in the Wood'—probably from Percy's *Reliques*, 25 June 1829, p. 5; Dryden—SEC's 'Spanish Proverb', 11 Feb. 1828, p. 4, very close to 2.1. ii of Dryden's *Conquest of Granada* (1690):

> Forgiveness to the injur'd does belong;
> For they ne'er pardon who have done the wrong.

Mrs Inchbald—ref. in Dec. 1830, p. 1; Aesop—ref. in 27 Mar. 1829, p. 7; Book of Job—SEC's quote; 'Where the wicked cease from trouble and the Weary are at rest', 15 Feb. 1828, p. 3.

[41] SEC–WJC, Dec. 1827, p. 17. [42] Ibid. 11; 14 Jan. 1828, p. 2.

concealing her 'real feelings'. She could not descend to female 'fascinations' to win the affections of men and had ever 'kept the key to the
actions arising from impulses of my own heart—the master key to which
is inclination'.[43] For her, conscience, even though sometimes lulled by
over-conceit, was ultimately decisive.[44] She could not live, she said,
without something to love,[45] but above all was the desire for freedom.
'Those who really know me', she declared, 'are convinced that I can
never yield to a despotic government.'[46]

The impact of Rousseau and the philosophy of the natural were
seminal influences upon the development of Romanticism. Both were at
their height in the 1770s, 1780s, and 1790s, the period of Susannah's
childhood and youth.[47] Other influences, however, were evidently at
work. Perhaps from Sterne's surrealist evocation of the Lockian world-
view in *Tristram Shandy*, she had learned to yearn for the 'Age of
Reason', of which, she declared, 'I have never despaired'.[48] She had
obviously not perceived that that age had already been and that another,
less full of its certainties, was about to replace it. But we may be forgiven
for thinking that one of the grand influences on her mind was Bunyan's
Pilgrim's Progress. The work had become not so much a classic but, as
Edward Thompson points out, a moral banner. For many, it was not
merely their first adventure story but their 'book of books'. It became,
remarked Thompson, 'the spiritual landscape of the poor man's
dissent'.[49] It is not so much Susannah's occasional references to the work
that suggest its influence, but rather its general tone and its ideological
starting-point seem to pervade her letters. In many respects, she is herself
the eternal pilgrim, constantly rebuffed by the world, alone and trusting
in nothing save her own conscience and her personal righteousness—
headed for another world beyond the reach of human reproach, 'and
unkind treatment of inmates of a world in which I have received nothing
but ingratitude and trouble'.[50]

Like Christian, Susannah learns to despise the vanities of the world of
men and to distrust human motives.

---

[43] SEC–WJC, 10 Apr. 1829, p. 3.   [44] Ibid. 20 Feb. 1830, p. 1.
[45] Ibid., Dec. 1827, p. 17.   [46] Ibid. 9 June 1829, p. 2.
[47] The influence of Rousseau and 'Primitivism' on early Romanticism is widely accepted.
The *Oxford Companion to English Literature* (5th edn., 1985), 843, considers that
Romanticism 'expressed an unending revolt against classical form, conservative morality,
authoritarian government, personal insincerity, and human moderation'.
[48] SEC–WJC, 31 Oct. 1827, p. 4.
[49] Thompson, *The Making*, 34.
[50] SEC–WJC, 10 Apr. 1829, p. 10.

My experience (during the last two years in particular) has almost taught me to despise my fellow creatures and the conflict between grief and indignation without bounds [?was] severe—at times my heart has swell'd with gratitude for offers of services and pretended kindnesses—but it afterwards turned out that more pretended friends were only serving themselves . . . my disgust for society is extreme and I seek no other than my children.[51]

And when moved to deliver to William her more abstract reflections on the inner life of the soul, it is almost impossible not to hear the moral resonances, if not the syntactical economy, of Bunyan, as in the following observation about the efficacy of wisdom.

But it is never too late to study wisdom. Her path is so sure that those who seek never fail to find her. Her paths 'tis true are not strewed with flowers (and 'tho beautiful to behold are fleeting as the hour and day lilly) but Wisdom furnishes our minds with the seeds of perpetual spring which propagate and bloom and unlike all other exotics will not desert its possessor in the 'fall of leaf' and like a long beaten track that after death leaves her traces behind—you will have fall'n a martyr to credulity and a mistaken notion of mankind in general—Vanity too (which I can readily pardon) has had her sway—and done much mischief . . .[52]

The contrast of influences between the almost hard-hearted self-interest of Christian on his undeviating way to the 'Celestial City', consistently overcoming the vices of human nature, and of Rousseau's Émile or Julie discovering inner goodness through natural emotions, is dramatic but not necessarily contradictory. Bunyan and Rousseau were after all branches of the same Calvinist tree. But if we were to attempt to rationalize the two influences, we might conclude that although the latter had the victory over her youth, the former was to claim her later years. In this respect her life may be said to mirror the progress of Romanticism in England which, like Susannah, never did ever quite escape from the grim reductionism of the *Pilgrim's Progress*. What began as the canonization of nature and sense ended in evangelizing utilitarianism: what began with Rousseau and Wollstonecraft ended, by way of William Godwin, Hannah More, Jeremy Bentham, and John Stuart Mill, in Samuel Smiles.

Susannah's son Augustine was born on 30 November 1796[53] when she was about 22 and presumably married to the musician Maximilian Humble, son of Maximilian Emmanuel Humble, member of the Royal

[51] Ibid. 18 Oct. 1828, pp. 3–4.   [52] Ibid.
[53] RSM, MS Members' Files [Augustine Edward Portal Humble].

Society of Musicians, who died in 1777. His mother, or some other close relative, may, just conceivably, have been one of the infamous Ambrose sisters, well-known actresses of Anglo-Portuguese Jewish origin who performed in Dublin and London from the 1760s. One subsequently became professionally known as Mrs Kelf and then as Mrs Egerton. Both were perhaps more famous for their amorous adventures than for their acting.[54] The evidence is tenuous indeed, but of four Humble children buried in 1778 in St James's church, Piccadilly, where Maximilian Humble senior had been buried the previous November, one (on 21 December) was a Sarah Ambrose Humble. Years later, Susannah recalls, in her correspondence to Castell, a household relic that had once belonged to 'Miss Ambrose'—her calash, of which more will be said.[55]

From 1767 to 1796 compositions by Maximilian Humble were published in London, the earliest of them by Peter Welcker of Gerrard Street and Longman Lukey & Co. These, presumably up to his death in 1777, were composed by the older man since the younger was only 5 at that time. In 1783, Maximilian made what appears to have been his first public appearance at the age of 11, playing a harpsichord concerto and a sonata at the Crown and Anchor Tavern in company with the Leander brothers,[56] later celebrated horn players but then little older than Humble himself. After this time compositions by him appeared in London, published privately.[57] His last known work was published in the year of his son's birth, 1796, when he was living at No. 4 Bateman's Building in Soho Square,[58] one of the smaller houses of this rather cramped development of the 1770s.[59]

Nothing else is known of Maximilian Humble, but it is possible that he may have been on the verges of the fashionable musical world. That he enjoyed patronage of some kind is suggested by the evidence of at least two dedicatees: Lady Milner in 1783 and Mrs Heywood in 1796. Lady Milner was presumably the wife of the York MP Sir William Mordaunt Milner, who took his seat in the House of Commons on the interest of Earl Fitzwilliam, a prominent Whig peer of the Portland faction. Mrs

[54] See *Biog. Dict. Actors, Actresses, etc.*

[55] CWL, Parish Records of St James's Church, Piccadilly, Burials.

[56] Information received from Simon McVeigh, Calendar of London Concerts 1750–1800, Goldsmith's College, University of London.

[57] BL, *Catalogue of Printed Music in the British Library to 1980* (1987).

[58] *Horwood's Plan of London, Westminster, Southwark & Parts adjoining, 1792–1799* (reprint, 1966).

[59] According to the *Survey of London*, xxxiii. 113, these buildings were spec-built between 1773 and 1776 on the site of Monmouth House. Some were apparently incredibly small. The Horwood map shows No. 4 as one of the smaller ones.

Heywood may have been Susannah, the wife of the Serjeant-at-Law and Foxite writer, Samuel Heywood (1753–1828), son of the Unitarian banker Benjamin Heywood.[60] That his father had also enjoyed some form of patronage is suggested by his Sett of Six Sonatas for two violins and a thorough Bass, *c.* 1770,[61] which were bound in volumes of works used by royal households, in this instance probably that of the Prince of Wales.[62] Included in the same collection were trios by Carl Friedrich Abel, Felice Alessandri, and Felice Giardini, all prominent foreign musicians in London in the 1780s, with aristocratic patronage. Between Maximilian's father's death in 1777 and his own, *c.* 1796, patronage, never comparable in England in any case with that enjoyed by musicians on the Continent, declined even more, leaving musicians even further exposed to a market economy which as yet had no mechanisms for bridging the yawning social gap that would get wider before it began to narrow.

Through, either one or both of his parents, Humble may have been Jewish or of Jewish origin, which would explain in Susannah a certain ambivalent preoccupation with the subject of Jewishness. When Lee and Absolon became the new proprietors of Drury Lane in 1830, she remarked that being Jews, 'we may expect they will not spare the "Knife"'.[63] But on the other hand we hear her only a few months before this expressing a guarded sympathy. 'We Christians!! scoff at the Jew', she had said, 'for his exactions and time has sanction'd the prejudice against him—he has at length become callous to accusation—his sole object is, retaliate and amass as much money as he can get. Are there not millions of every nation and sect doing the same thing. Aye from the king to the beggars—'tho totally distinct from the "seed of Abraham".'[64] Attitudes to Jews in England at that time were extremely negative. The

---

[60] Lady Milner, for *A Sonata and an Overture for the Piano Forte . . . (c.* 1783), BL Music Lib. g. 141(7); Mrs Heywood for *Six Ballads for the Piano Forte . . . (c.* 1796), BL Music Lib. G.369 1–11(1); for Sir William Mordaunt Milner see R. G. Thorne (ed.), *History of Parliament: The House of Commons 1790–1820* (1986). Humble was only a child in 1783, but it is curious that the dedicatee of *c.* 1796 was possibly the wife of a man, once again, active in Whig politics. Samuel Heywood, a Unitarian, had been educated at The Warrington Academy (partly financed by his father) and pursued a successful legal career. See *DNB* [Samuel Heywood].

[61] BL Music Lib. RM 17.a.2(7). *A Third Sett of Six Sonatas for two violins and a thorough Bass (c.* 1770).

[62] They form part of a 'Royal Music' Collection donated to the BL in 1957. These particular volumes—a separate one for each of the three parts—are gilt-embossed on the front with the Prince of Wales's emblem.

[63] SEC–WJC, 25 May 1830, p. 4.

[64] Ibid. 26 Jan. 1830, pp. 2–3.

attempt of 1830 by the House of Commons to ameliorate their official disabilities had failed.[65] They were the butts of cruel pranks by street urchins and generally the victims of spontaneous unthinking and insensitive prejudice.[66] Even within 'enlightened' circles, tolerance was often strained.[67] Thus it is not surprising that Susannah should express a certain impatient irritation at an obtuse comment from William in December 1830 suggesting that he was stirring up family ghosts. 'I offer no apology', she said, 'for this long digression [on woman's love], and I hope you will find it as <u>entertaining</u> as your narration of the "Jewess" was to me!'[68]

But in all Susannah's correspondence, there is only one direct reference to Maximilian Humble. In a long rambling letter of ambiguous syntax and textual dishevelment indicative of warmth of feeling, she says, 'I feel at a loss to discriminate as regards your predecessor, Humble, whom you say "could never love" you might be right in your conjecture all I know is that he always treated me with the greatest kindness and apparent affection but what of that . . .'. A line is here crossed out and is unreadable but she concludes, 'This affair is <u>your own</u> and nothing to do with him.'[69] For Susannah this was a most economical response. It was either a subject which had little power to provoke, or one she felt uneasy about pursuing.

It is possible that Humble did not long survive the birth of his son. His final composition appeared in the same year, 1796—perhaps a last-ditch attempt at commercial success. It was a work of somewhat Rousseau-esque simplicity—the one dedicated to Mrs Heywood: a set of six ballads with pianoforte accompaniment. Of the poems, which were by E. Bell, at least four also suggest a primitivist influence. The potential market was evidently female and probably even Evangelical (if not Unitarian).[70] The front cover bore a bold illustration of three plump cloud-borne cherubs

---

[65] 'Bill for the Relief of Jews', rejected by majority of 63: 165 for, 228 against. *The Times* report, 18 May 1830, p. 3b.

[66] See Henry Mayhew, *London Labour and the London Poor* (1851), ii. 115 ff., 'Of the Street Jews'.

[67] According to Tom Moore, Lord Byron's friendship with Isaac Nathan was tinged with private distaste for him as a Jew. See Catherine Mackerras, *The Hebrew Melodist. A Life of Isaac Nathan* (1963), 30.

[68] SEC–WJC, Dec. 1830, p. 3.

[69] Ibid. 25 June 1829, p. 7.

[70] *Six Ballads for the Piano Forte*. They were 'Mary Queen of Scots' (with a flute obbligato); 'Virtue', a song about simple morality; 'Yarico', about the black heroine of *Inkle and Yarico*; 'The Happy Cottager', more about simple morality; 'Jenny', a patriotic ballad about Jack Tar's girl-friend; and 'The African', a celebration of the 'Noble Savage'.

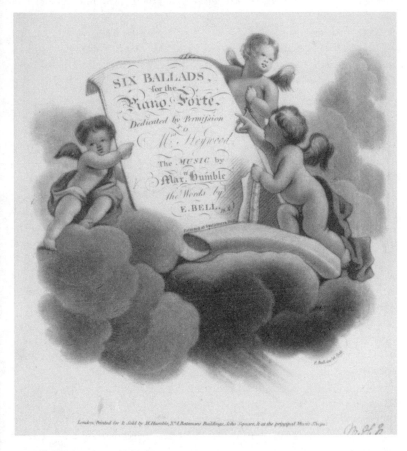

5. Note Humble's initials in the right-hand corner followed presumably by the number of the copy. Ref. BL G.369(1).

supporting and evidently admiring the title scroll: also the work of E. Bell.

Up to the time of Augustine's birth, or some time between then and her marriage to William, Susannah may have been an actress or at least may have made a brief foray into the theatrical world, although she later vehemently denied that this was so. 'I was <u>NO ACTRESS</u>, but always responsible. Tell them to <u>prove</u> that I <u>EVER WAS</u>. If they <u>can</u> I will acknowledge it.'[71] It was with 'grief and much indignation' that she heard she had been made the victim of this 'most flagrant and cruel untruth'.[72] It would seem there was no creature so lowly in Susannah's eyes as a 'public actress'. She greets the slur almost with the kind of horror and indignation that a nineteenth-century Australian might have greeted the accusation of convict origins. It was a slur that obviously represented a threat to caste.

For a respectable woman, any paying profession outside the home was hardly an option—a profession in the theatre, one of the very few viable economic options for a woman, tended to push her completely beyond the pale of respectability, unless, that is, like the inimitably chaste Miss Stephens, she became a duchess.[73] But Susannah's obvious hostility to the idea may have been less a disparagement of the profession itself and more a desire to suppress an aspect of her past. In one almost unguarded moment we are certainly led to believe that even she had once succumbed to a youthful folly of some kind—perhaps a fleeting flirtation with the stage. Speaking of the dangers of young girls being let out of the nursery prematurely, she draws a picture of a youthful female with a 'primer in one hand and fan in the other'. So equipped she 'adopts the first stage dress offer'd and presumes to a character in the public stage of life. On this point I may be permitted feelingly to urge the case in question and that in a Double sense of the meaning . . .'.[74] The 'double sense' perhaps refers to the literal as well as the figurative 'stage of life'. But in any case, her connections with the theatre were surely too close for her to have maintained a too scrupulous aversion. It is difficult to know whether Humble ever performed in one of the theatre orchestras. It is very likely that he did. Indeed it may have been in recalling such a connection rather than her own that Susannah declared herself familiar with some of the more pernicious influences of the theatre. 'You say that you have in the orchestra', she says to Castell, 'the character of a "hen pecked" [?husband] that appellation arose entirely from your disinclination to accompany them to the public houses—and is the common slang used by blagards to mortify the husbands into compliance. I have long been in the school and unfortunately am but too well acquainted with these matters.'[75]

[71] SEC–WJC, 13 May 1828, p. 2.
[72] Ibid. SEC–THJ, draft letter forwarded to WJC with SEC–WJC, 11 Apr. 1828, p. 4.
[73] Catherine Stephens (1794–1882) married the 5th Earl of Essex in 1838.
[74] SEC–WJC, 8 May 1828, p. 3.
[75] Ibid. 4 June 1829, pp. 3–4.

Among potentially many theatrical connections in a life inextricably associated with the theatre—not only through her two husbands, but perhaps through a father and certainly through her two sons—the names of Miss Ambrose and Mrs Inchbald also occur in contexts that would suggest some intimacy. Both belonged to the previous generation. The former, as already mentioned, may have been a relative of her first husband and as previously suggested may have been the actress of that name. Her calash, one of those large folding hoods built up on arches of cane, large enough to cover the rising height of fashionable coiffure in the 1770s-1790s,[76] survived, perhaps as a sentimental family heirloom, to become the subject in 1831 of a family dispute.[77] The latter, Mrs Inchbald, also became the subject of family dispute, with Susannah expressing some irritation that William should have commandeered the connection in support of one of his arguments against the female sex. 'You allude to once hearing Mrs Inchbald say "that there is no medium in a woman's love",' she wrote in 1830. 'I much doubt you did hear her so say, but if she did [?she] must, as a female [?have] known and felt the springs which actuate their feelings, neither was it necessary or incumbent upon you to enter into explanations . . .'.[78]

Elizabeth Inchbald was an altogether different proposition from Miss Ambrose. She was a self-taught intellectual; a friend of Godwin and Maria Edgeworth; a playwright, novelist, and critic, and above all a virtuous wife who after her actor husband's death gave up the stage where she herself had been a popular figure, and concentrated on writing, from which she sustained herself till her death in 1821. She was an enthusiast of the primitive school of education and wrote a novel on that theme called *Nature and Art* (1796) and a stage work entitled the *Child of Nature* (1788).[79] Unfortunately the nature and extent of the connection with the Castells is not explained. It may have been ephemeral, but it was at least one theatrical association of which Susannah could have had no reason to be ashamed. It should be remembered, however, that Susannah's family roots were in Huguenot

[76] See Willett C. Cunningham and Phyllis Cunningham, *Handbook of English Costume in the Eighteenth Century* (2nd edn., London, 1972), 350: 'The calash, from 1770–1790 was a large folding hood with a short cape; made of silk and built up on arches of cane large enough to cover the rising height of fashionable coiffure.'

[77] SEC–WJC, 8 Feb. 1831, p. 5.

[78] Ibid., Dec. 1830, p. 1.

[79] See *Oxford Companion to English Literature*; Bernard, *Retrospections*, i. 275; *Biographical Dictionary of the Living Authors of Great Britain and Ireland* (1816); portrait in *Walker's Hibernian Magazine*, Oct. 1787, p. 505.

Calvinism, which had no fondness for the theatre. On the whole, except for individuals like Abraham Portal, it produced a sober and industrious race more famous for commercial enterprise and independence than for dramatic flamboyance. Susannah's ambivalence towards the theatre, in spite of her intimate involvement, may indeed have stemmed from family pressures.

She was, as she said, the child of her mother's second marriage. She had a brother, perhaps the Edward Portal after whom Augustine was named, who apparently had some pretension to higher learning,[80] but who died propertyless sometime before 1828.[81] Other siblings, whether full or half, included at least two sisters, the ignorance of whom, she said, even William well knew.[82] One of them, Sarah, Susannah refers to as 'narrow minded and of too suspicious a nature'.[83] One of these, possibly Sarah, must have been connected, perhaps by marriage, to the firm of Meyer & Miller[84]—from 1826 listed in Pigot as boot-makers of 9 King Street, St James.[85] Susannah does not appear to have been on intimate terms with them. Pride, she said, forbade her to call upon them in the hard years after William's desertion in 1826.[86] It was a pride perhaps born of fear of censure. It is possible that her immediate family had disapproved of both her marriages, boot-making probably being seen as a more likely conduit to affluence and respectability than music-making.

THE MARRIAGE

Mrs Inchbald once wrote a farce called *Young Men and Old Women*, produced at the Haymarket in 1792. It could hardly have been inspired by William and Susannah's marriage of 1810, but it is fair to say that such a marriage, then as now, would have been considered, except by the participants, as a proper subject for farce.

Susannah was not as old nor as rich as the banker's widow Mrs Coutts would be when in 1827 she married the young Duke of St Albans, upon which lady, Creevey, perhaps recalling that she had once been an actress, had rather ungallantly pronounced that 'a more disgusting, frowsy, hairy

---

[80] SEC–WJC, Dec. 1827, p. 15.   [81] Ibid. 10 July 1828, p. 4.
[82] Ibid., Dec. 1827, p. 15.   [83] Ibid.
[84] Meyer & Miller for some reason had possession of WJC's plate on which account he paid them £1 per annum. In another context it is evident that Meyer & Miller were members of Susannah's family. WJC–SEC, 30 Jan. 1828, p. 2, and SEC–WJC, 12 Aug. 1829, pp. 1–2.   [85] Pigot & Co., *London & Provincial Directory for 1826–27*.
[86] SEC–WJC, 12 Aug. 1829, pp. 1–2.

old B. could not have been found in the Seven Dials'.[87] Nor have we any
reason to suspect that Susannah's physical appearance would have
warranted such unflattering epithets—yet the disparity in their ages does
invite speculation.

Widows with property found themselves courted often enough by
fortune-hungry males. The following advertisement was not unique.

A Young nobleman, who through his relation's avarice is kept in a condition of
beneath his rank, would be glad to render himself independent of them by
marrying a lady of Fortune.[88]

Nicholas Mori married the widow of Louis Lavenu of the firm of music
publishers. Daly, as we have already seen, married Mrs Lyster. And of
course the Duke of St Albans claimed the hand of the amazingly wealthy
Mrs Coutts. Doubtless the males brought something to such marriages—
an aristocratic title, or perhaps physical allure.

In Susannah and William's case it is difficult to see exactly what the
motivation was. On Susannah's part it would seem a straight case of
infatuation. Hence her 'You was the dearest object, tho others had
pretensions; the first and so shall be the last';[89] and 'When I gave you my
hand, you received with it my whole and entire Heart and Soul'.[90] On
William's side the picture is less clear. There is some evidence that
property of some kind may have been involved. In a letter in 1829
Susannah speaks of signing away to William, to her everlasting regret,
'The Dane Hill Estate'.[91] And there had perhaps been talk of the family
estates in France, which, presumably in the wake of the bloodletting of
the French Revolution, had become dormant and were the subject of
possible litigation by Susannah's family.[92] Perhaps there was also an
attraction in 'royal' connections, which while they held no fascination
for Susannah[93] evidently did for William. He boasted when in France of
his 'connection' to a female descendent of Henri IV, and once remarked
to Susannah, ' 'Tis not to be wonder'd at that you feel your royal blood.'[94]
But if Susannah rejected such fatuousness and believed any possible

[87] Creevey, *Papers*, 287.
[88] *Gazetteer and New Daily Advertiser*, 3 Feb. 1795. Another similar ad, 9 Apr. 1795.
[89] SEC–WJC, 24 Aug. 1827, p. 3.
[90] Ibid. 13 Jan. 1829, p. 6.
[91] Ibid. 27 Mar. 1829, p. 9.
[92] Ibid., Dec. 1827, p. 14; 13 Oct. 1830, pp. 1–2.
[93] Ibid., Dec. 1827, pp. 14–15.
[94] THJ–SEC, in SEC–WJC, 27 Nov. 1827, p. 1; WJC quoted in SEC–WJC, Dec. 1827,
p. 15; and it would appear from some of SEC's responses that he was asking her for more
information about the estates.

material benefit from such considerations to be highly unlikely—'I shall
never be one farthing richer'[95]—William may have entertained hopes on
her behalf.

On the other hand there is a case for believing that he genuinely
believed himself to have been in love with Susannah. That he had wooed
her on this basis is clear enough. She had been to him 'My Heaven'.[96]
Years of bitterness had intervened, but almost twenty years later he was
still claiming that he had indeed once loved her, a claim about which she
was by then understandably cynical.

It is a wonderful thing <u>such</u> love as you describe having formerly experienced for
me . . . that you could conceal it from me is surprising. I must indeed have been
very dull to have never discover'd it. But you describe it as a 'Religious Love' and
'Love became your Religion'. Now as I recollect right you were a sceptic . . .[97]

In a convoluted but intrinsically rather perceptive and revealing
retrospective analysis, she claimed that he had '<u>thought</u> he lov'd', and
that that passion on dying a '<u>violent</u> death' left a void which turned to
disgust which then led to alienation. To cover his error and to render his
own conscience more palatable to him, he then proceeded to try to make
her feel the same way (presumably about him). This ploy failing, he then
began, she said, a war of attrition. First he degrades her, after which he
expects and demands perfection, launching a battery of complaint. Such
was the scenario of their marriage according to Susannah. In essence, she
believed he had wooed her as a caprice and then meant to incarcerate her
love for him in the prison of his guilty hatred. Any woman, she said, who
could bear with that was 'either an Angel or an Ass'. By her own account,
she was neither.[98]

It is unfortunate that we do not have William's direct reply to this.
Indeed the only evidence we have of his attitude to the marriage comes,
except for one lone letter, through Susannah's responses. But the
dialogue was obviously lively, and even from this necessarily unbalanced
evidence a broader perspective does emerge.

The marriage itself was about conflict and dominance, but the role
each decided to adopt expressed an inherent confusion about the
fundamental nature of the battle. Susannah, the elder of the two—
vehement, unselfconscious, and passionate—seems indeed to be the
dominating figure and yet in her own eyes she was and always would be

---

[95] SEC–WJC, 13 Oct. 1830, pp. 1–2.   [96] Ibid. 10 Apr. 1829, p. 10.
[97] Ibid. 8 Aug. 1829, p. 9; also Dec. 1827, pp. 10–11; 10 July 1828, p. 2; 13 Jan. 1829,
p. 5.   [98] Ibid., Dec. 1827, pp. 10–13.

the victim. 'I do and always <u>shall</u>', she said, 'consider myself the most injur'd party.'[99] William, already in a crisis of authority due to his inferiority of years, plays at being the tyrant husband. He had, she said, 'express'd a determination to reign absolute (and you kept your word)'.[100] But in the end, it is she who stays and he who claims to have been driven out of his home and his country by her 'manners'. She, he claimed, had been instrumental in banishing him from all those delights that were his entitlement.[101] She for her part claimed only self-defence against his depredations.

Denied authority in her own household, humiliated by his attentions to her own servants, excluded from his social entertainments, injured by the physical results of his 'incontinence', insulted by his reproaches, physically coerced into obedience, subjected to his rules of silence and disquieted by other unnamed cruelties and 'ingenious mortifications', life at times was rendered unbearable enough;[102] but perhaps worst of all from her point of view was his practice of commencing domestic hostilities by 'separating beds, and <u>beginning</u> where you ought to leave off'.[103] For Susannah sexual denial was evidently a particular hardship. She loved him, she said, most fervently and his 'unnatural' treatment had at times nearly driven her to distraction, 'for my feelings as you <u>know</u> are strong'.[104] It was only under provocation such as this, she claimed, when labouring under such dilemmas and mortifying restraints, that 'self-possession fled', and that she indulged in those 'faults in manners' of which he was to complain and which led him, in a foreign country, to speak of her disparagingly and to encourage 'strangers' to view her as the 'Fiend' and 'Tiger' who had forced him into exile.[105]

Susannah's complaints, addressed as they were to the author of her dissatisfaction, and not to some third party, we need not trouble to dispute. Indeed Castell does not seem to have contradicted them, admitting on one occasion, as if in justification of his behaviour, to wanting to be 'master in moderation in his own house'.[106] Evidently it had been his need to feel himself master that had prompted his harshness.

---

[99] Ibid. 24 Aug. 1827.   [100] Ibid. 9 June 1829, p. 1.

[101] Ibid., Dec. 1827, p. 4; 14 Jan. 1828, p. 3; 12 Nov. 1829, p. 4.

[102] See SEC–WJC: lack of authority, 14 Jan. 1828, pp. 3–4; 9 June 1829, p. 3; his attentions to her servants, 4 June 1829, p. 5; exclusion from his social life, Dec. 1827, p. 11; physical result of 'Incontinence', 24 Aug. 1827, p. 2; reproaches, Dec. 1827, p. 12; silence, Dec. 1827, p. 12; coercion, Dec. 1827, pp. 10–11; ingenious mortifications, Dec. 1827, p. 15.

[103] SEC–WJC, 9 June 1829, p. 6.   [104] Ibid. 9.

[105] Ibid., Dec. 1827, pp. 11, 15–16.   [106] Ibid. 4 June 1829, p. 4.

And evidently it had been Susannah's intrinsically dominating personality that had led him to feel his mastery under threat.

Susannah, however, consistently removed herself from the dynamic of the relationship. Her love, devotion, and loyalty had all been placed at his disposal to do with as he willed. She placed in him all creative or destructive power. Even her one fault—her 'manners'—it had been in his power to remedy. 'Did you ever', she asked him, 'try to remove the obstacle you complain of?' and she answers her own question: 'No'.[107] The failure of their relationship had therefore been due, in her eyes, entirely to his actions. It was his errors which had after all 'led to what you call my faults in "manners"'.[108] It had been his incontinence, his cruelty that had been to blame for everything. She is unequivocal. 'All all, all has been your doing.'[109]

Such a passionately held view of her own impotence ought to have assuaged his manly vanity. Yet it did not—could not—because behind it lay what was probably the root cause of the conflict—Susannah's overwhelming certainty in her own moral position. It was an element so deeply embedded in her personality that it was entirely impossible for her to see it objectively as one of the fundamental causes of the argument itself. Castell himself did not seem to recognize (not at any rate comprehensively) this intrinsic impediment to reconciliation. He seems only to have attacked it piecemeal. But, like a hydra-head, after each assault upon it, it sprouted fresh provocations.

Indeed, one can see how Susannah's unconventional emotional directness—partly the result perhaps of an unconventional 'primitivist' education—may at first have attracted Castell. One can also perceive how it eventually developed into something less attractive; how it became unfettered righteousness, endorsed by 'feeling'; how her moral position became unchallengeable simply because it was 'felt' and being felt had become emphatic and tactless. All action of hers stemmed from good feeling. She could confess herself 'high spirited', but not 'vindictive'.[110] She is able in all sincerity to declare her total ingenuousness. 'You will excuse my plainess of style,' she writes to Castell; 'what I dare write to you none other would presume to and you must feel assured that the motive is a good one.'[111] While she may say, obviously in answer to Castell's challenges, 'I am no more immaculate than yourself',[112] or may

---

[107] SEC–WJC, Dec. 1827, p. 12.   [108] Ibid. 9 June 1829, p. 6.
[109] Ibid. 13 Jan. 1829, p. 4.   [110] Ibid. 5 Nov. 1827, p. 2.
[111] Ibid. 28 May 1831, p. 3.   [112] Ibid. 14 Feb. 1829, p. 3.

deny that she offers herself to the world as any model of virtue,[113] these
are but feints—mere quibbles. Her fundamental stance is quite
different—quite unassailable: 'thro' life but one principle will I
acknowledge—I have fearlessly done my duty regardless of punishment
and uninfluenced by gain—I am no hypocrite and have frequently
suffer'd for my adherence to candour and truth'.[114] She asked for no
forgiveness, for she had 'fearlessly performed my duty in any department
of life and it was your own Fault that you did not conceive me to be what
I really was, an "unchanging friend"'.[115] His behaviour, unlike her own,
had been arbitrary, unjust, and cruel. But she, unlike him, was without
any thirst for vengeance. 'Only endeavour', she once said to him, 'to
merit my love and my Heart and Arms shall be ready to receive you.'[116]
And even while she acknowledged that all faults of hers were produced
by 'strong causes'—namely his wrongdoings—she could find proper
forgiveness and could 'conclude with those emphatic words, "Go and sin
no more"'.[117]

So for the eight years of the correspondence it went on as it had
apparently throughout their marriage. He, striving, as he said, to 'make
her feel'[118] (presumably) that she was the legitimate object of his
contempt; she, constantly subverting his argument with 'feeling' and
moral self-immunization. His attempt to wound her, she said, had
ultimately failed, 'and my moral character cannot be affected by it'.[119]
His 'dictatorial Style', so 'vindictive, cruel and unfeeling',[120] still
presumably seeking to exert authority, met the solid and unyielding wall
of her moral impotence—an impotence which, rather like his authority,
was more an emotional fantasy than an observable reality.

But in the beginning it had been different. Their home had been a
'mansion of peace', before it had become a 'seat of discord'.[121] His
'knock at the door' had once exhilarated her spirits and softened the
alarms of the infant at her breast.[122] They had been born worthy of each
other, said Susannah, and she had often regretted 'that we should have
ever fall'n from that State of paradise wherein we were placed'.[123]

Who then, in 1810, was the 21-year-old William Castell with whom

---

[113] Ibid. 25 June 1829, p. 3.
[114] Ibid. 12 Nov. 1829, p. 2.   [115] Ibid., Dec. 1827, p. 16.
[116] Ibid. 5 Nov. 1827, p. 2.   [117] Ibid. 3 May 1828, p. 2.
[118] Ibid. 12 Nov. 1829, p. 3.   [119] Ibid. 20 Feb. 1830, pp. 1–2.
[120] Ibid. 10 Apr. 1829, p. 6; 12 Nov. 1829, p. 2.   [121] Ibid. 24 Aug. 1827, p. 2.
[122] Ibid. 4 June 1829, p. 4.   [123] Ibid., Dec. 1827, p. 17.

the mellowing but still yearning Susannah Humble so evidently fell in love and who by his own testimony saw in her his 'heaven'? He may have been, like Dick Daly, extravagantly handsome (hopefully without the disfiguring squint), masterfully persuasive, fashionably gallant in high blacked boots and spurs. He may in the age of the 'fop' have participated in the battle of the latest tailors' cut, or, sauntering down Bond Street flourishing the *de rigueur* cane, club, or bent twig, engaged in other bizarre games of social emulation which so characterized that period of wartime affluence.[124] On the other hand, he may have been an apogean vision of things to come—perhaps a dark brooding youth of Byronic sensibilities who eschewed the stiff crop of the fop for the soft cravat of the dreamer seeking universal truths in self-contemplation.

Perhaps there was something of both in his make-up. He was born, after all, just as the light went out on the old order in Europe, and grew up in the sporadic and sometimes garish flares of the new which blinded as often as they illuminated, and which mingled confusingly in the long afterglow of autocracy and privilege. Nearly all of his conscious life he had known nothing but a war waged on behalf of the forces of reaction, a war which, nevertheless, when it finally ended would leave little as it had been before. Perhaps it was the manifestation of a confused vulnerability which had so appealed to Susannah. She never lost, after all the betrayals and vicissitudes she had suffered on his account, the image of him as a child playing in a dangerous adult world for which he was not equipped to deal. Whether, though, this was as a man or merely as a musician she seems either unwilling or unable to resolve.

Her son Augustine was then just reaching his teens. Was he affronted on behalf of his father's memory or on behalf of his own future prospects? Or did the entry of Castell (only seven years his senior) into the little family bring with it a promise of heightened existence and glamour? Either may have been true, but in any case it is unlikely that he was consulted.

The 'State of paradise' seems to have lasted for about two years. When their first child, William Jones, was born on 18 April 1812[125] Susannah was already showing signs of insecurity. She suggested that William's devotion to the child represented a 'transfer' of his affections. Later, she explained away her reaction as no more than a 'mere declaration' having no real substance. And as she said, 'Had you appeared less indifferent

---

124 For affectations of fashion, see Southey, *Letters from England*, 290.
125 GLRO, Parish Records, St Mary's Church, Lambeth, Baptisms, 14 June 1812.

6. Portrait of an unknown man, Sydney, *c.* 1835; possibly William Joseph Castell. Reproduced from Cedric Flower, *Duck and Cabbage Tree* (Sydney, 1968).

7. Stangate Street, Lambeth, drawn in 1949 by B. Shawcroft. No. 38 corresponds to No. 19 of Susannah Castell's period. The street no longer exists. Ref. *Survey of London*, xxiii, pl. 59.

towards <u>such</u> a child, you would be unworthy of him. He was a <u>picture</u> and "cast in beauteous mould". He was the offspring of Love, who presided at his birth.'[126] Nevertheless, just as surely as Napoleon's retreat from Moscow of that year was a turning-point in the war, it would seem that a turning-point had also been reached in their marriage.

At the time of William Jones's birth in 1812, they were living at 19 Stangate Street, Lambeth, in the house of Castell's grandfather, the 'sainted' William Jones.[127] The house was on the southern side of the street not far from its intersection with Upper Marsh. A long back garden was contiguous with acres of farmland and the demesne gardens of Lambeth Palace, providing a rather pleasant rural aspect. It was a neat two-storeyed Georgian terrace house with a kitchen basement and probably a loft. A short flight of stairs linked the pedimented front door with the street, forming, as with other houses in the row, a bridge above the basement and cellar below.[128]

[126] SEC–WJC, 13 Jan. 1829, p. 7.
[127] LAD, Minet Library, Brixton, Records of St Mary's Church, Lambeth, MS Poor Rate Books. Shows William Jones to be the householder at that time. The houses are not numbered, but are entered in the appropriate sequence. Also see below, n. 135, for probate details which confirm address.
[128] Cf. *Horwood's Plan of London*, 1799 and 1819 edns.; and *Ordinance Survey of London*, Sheet XLIV, 1872; according to these, No. 19 was the No. 38 shown in *Survey of London*, xxiii, Pl. 59, Strip elevation of Nos. 2–46 Stangate Street of 1946. Its rural aspect is illustrated by a water colour View of London of Capon's of 1804, showing, in the foreground, the Lambeth area near Stangate Street (in *Survey of London*, xxiii, frontis). There is also a pencil drawing by Patrick Nasmyth in the Lambeth Archives Department, LP. 12/170 Stan. S.2, sometime before 1831, showing Arcadian rear gardens in Stangate Street.

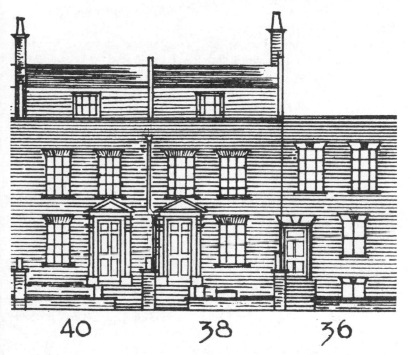

8. Detail of the drawing by B. Shawcroft (Fig. 7) showing No. 38, then No. 19.

It was a popular area for musicians and theatre people. John Macintosh the eminent bassoonist lived next door, and the clown Joe Grimaldi senior had once lived and died at the other end of the street. Philip Astley lived at the bottom of it in what was then known as

Amphitheatre Row.[129] This is to name but a few. It was not surprising, since the area had since the seventeenth century spawned a variety of public entertainments—from Cuper's Gardens in the north down to Vauxhall in the south. There was Finch's Grotto Gardens in Southwark, and the Apollo Gardens (or Temple of Apollo) just north of Westminster Bridge Road with its music, concerts, *fantoccini*, and Grand Apollonian Promenade. Just by the river at Westminster Bridge, a stone's throw from Stangate Street, was Astley's Amphitheatre, and the Royal Circus, later to become the Surrey Theatre, had opened in 1782 and was at St George's Circus by the Obelisk and toll gates. It was also relatively close to the theatres of the West End. Before the opening of Waterloo Bridge in 1817, access had been less convenient, but boatmen and their wherries had been ubiquitous and cheap and Westminster Bridge not such a long detour.

In May 1818, the Coburg Theatre (now the Old Vic) was opened just by the Cut on Westminster Bridge Road, exploiting the greater access afforded to patrons by the new bridge. This made the Lambeth area even more popular with musicians and actors. It is no idle detail in Thackeray's *Pendennis* that has Charley Podmore, the 'pleasing tenor singer from T. R. D. L. and Back Kitchen Concert Rooms', moving, upon his marriage, from his lodgings in Shepherd's Court to Lambeth.[130]

The area's attraction lay in its cheapness rather than its fashionability. Musicians, actors, artists, and obscure Swedish barons shared it with boatmen, coalheavers, hat-makers, floorcloth-weavers, clerks, and bricklayers,[131] although in the quasi-rural hinterland there were traces of lesser gentility. The houses in Stangate Street were all valued rather modestly at an annual rent of between £9 and £25. Number 19 was somewhere in the middle of the range, at £15 in 1809 and £20 in 1815.[132]

Up to 1811 the household presumably comprised grandfather Jones, Susannah and Augustine, William, and perhaps at some stage William's brother Peter. Susannah by her own account had a very amicable relationship with the old man. She had enjoyed at sylvan Stangate Street, she said, the 'uninterrupted friendship' of Castell's 'sainted grandsire'.[133]

[129] For Grimaldi, see Edward Walford, *Old and New London. A Narrative of its History, its People and its Places* [n. d.], vi. 417; for Astley, see LAD, Records of St Mary's, Lambeth, Poor Rate Book, 1809.
[130] William Thackeray, *Pendennis* (1849), ii. 34.
[131] From GLRO, Parish Records of St Mary's, Lambeth, Baptisms, 1812–25.
[132] LAD, Records of St Mary's, Lambeth, MS Poor Rate Books.
[133] SEC–WJC, 15 Dec. 1828, p. 3.

To him she was 'Dear Bell' and it was he who had advised her that she should consider herself upon the same level as the rest of the world and cease retreating from those who were her inferiors—an admonition she accepted as truth while yet admitting that she 'could never to this day emerge from diffidence—and I tremble at speaking to a stranger'.[134]

Curiously, however, when William Jones died in 1811, his will, also written in 1811 and witnessed by Augustine, referred to Susannah, to whom he left a small bequest, as Mrs Susannah Humble[135] when, as we know, in August 1810 she had become Mrs William Joseph Castell. With William Jones's death and Peter's absence in the navy, the control of the Stangate Street property passed into Castell's hands. Ten months later his first child was born and, as we have already noted, 'paradise' was beginning to crumble.

It could not have been long after this, or even before, that Castell joined the orchestra of the Surrey Theatre. Since 1809 it had been under the proprietorship of William Elliston (1774–1831), who had changed its name from the Royal Circus to the Surrey and had tried to move it into the realms of the legitimate theatre—failing which, on account of the licensing laws, it had become the home of burletta and melodrama.[136] By 1814, Castell was the chorus-master there as well as performing in the orchestra.[137]

For Susannah, however, the Surrey engagement represented an ominous landmark in their relationship. 'There is no reason for liking that theatre', she says, 'as experience taught me the contrary. We were then living happily and without an excuse for 'alienation' on account of my "manners".'[138] It was then she reckoned that a 'sudden alteration' took place which changed the complexion of their marriage.

It says something for Castell's reticence that it was not until 1829 that he told Susannah the reason; that he had been dubbed by his colleagues 'hen pecked'.[139] It was a charge which, as we have already seen, Susannah brushed aside as the machinations of 'blagards' to ruin him in the public houses.[140] It was William's own 'disinclination' in this regard, rather than her admonitions, that led to his persecution. As usual,

[134] Ibid. 25 June 1829, p. 4.
[135] PRO PROB. 11/1524/337, Will of William Jones of No. 19 Stangate Street, Parish of Lambeth. Proved, Surrey, July 1811.
[136] Edward Westlake Brayley, *Historical and Descriptive Accounts of the Theatres of London* (1826), 73; Walford, *Old and New London*, vi. 369.
[137] RSM, MS Members' Files.   [138] SEC–WJC, 10 Apr. 1829, pp. 9–10.
[139] Ibid. 4 June 1829, pp. 3–4.   [140] Ibid.

VIEW of the SURREY THEATRE, MAGDALEN, &c &c.

9. Engraving, 1812, at about the time Castell first worked there. Ref. GLRO. Southwark H 12866.

ROYAL CIRCUS.

10. Later the Surrey Theatre. Hand-coloured aquatint after Rowlandson and Pugin. 1809. Ref. GLRO. Southwark H 13175.

Susannah removes any action of hers from the equation. Yet in all probability, Susannah may have been central to any problems Castell was having in the orchestra of the Surrey. It is not difficult to imagine what else they may have said about Susannah to mortify a young man so fragile to criticism. Nor is it difficult to imagine that such criticism may have been the catalyst which stirred slumbering misgivings about the nature of his marriage, until then subdued perhaps by the novelty of bliss in that 'State of paradise' to which Susannah had referred. Did he suddenly wake out of a dream to find himself exposed to the world's ridicule? Did he suddenly see Susannah as the world saw her, as a middle-aged virago? Perhaps, but it was to be with some difficulty and not without emotional turmoil that he finally extricated himself.

Both Susannah and Richard Mackenzie Bacon of the *Quarterly Musical Magazine and Review* would have agreed that it was just another case of virtue succumbing to the pernicious influences of the undiluted company of fellow musicians.

... the early character of the musician is liable to be tinged by opposites; by an overweening opinion of his own accomplishments, and by vulgar and dissolute habits acquired during the season of obscurity. It will now hardly be disputed, that excellence in the fine arts calls into exercise a larger portion of sensibility than belongs to excellence in any other pursuit, considered of itself, and that this sensibility receives nourishment and strength every day from the practice of music. It follows that the science not only trains its professors to this superior power of perception, but also throws them into the company of others, who are the objects of similar excitement. If these premises be true, it will, and does in point of fact, account for the moral aberrations of those employed in the fine arts, which though they sometimes terminate in gross sensuality, will be almost always found to begin in sentiments, the offspring of an excitability that may fairly be termed morbid.[141]

Susannah would not have expressed it like that, but, as she said, she had been 'long in the school' and well knew the dangers.

The first major rupture apparently occurred when Susannah was pregnant with their second child, Alfred, sometime between June 1813 and February 1814.[142] It was the perennial enemy 'incontinence' and it had been doubly offensive to Susannah since she herself suffered 'direfull effects' as a result—presumably some form of venereal disease, which although not proving fatal to herself and her unborn child left the latter

---

[141] Vetus [Richard Mackenzie Bacon], 'On the Character of Musicians', *QMMR* i (1819), 289.

[142] SEC–WJC, 13 Jan. 1829, p. 7.

not wholly unscathed.[143] A 'long train of irregularities succeeded', and the chasm in their affections formed.[144]

Yet even then, she maintained, 'all would have subsided in tranquility' had William renewed his 'affectionate behaviour and wonted kindness of manners'. But this did not happen. Her further humiliation seemed to be his object. Stung by the injuries she had received and without any sign of a renewal of affection, she felt 'under such circumstances no great inclination to give quarter'.[145] The die, it would seem, had been cast.

---

[143] Ibid. 24 Aug. 1827, p. 2.
[144] Ibid.
[145] Ibid. 13 Jan. 1829, p. 7.

4

A Professional Man, 1814–1826

Neither was it necessary in separating from me that you
should part with all your property and return home a begar.

SEC to WJC, 9 June 1829.

PROFESSIONAL CRISIS, 1815–1826

Free-market music

BY 1815, when the war in Europe finally ended, English musicians found
themselves in an expanding market for their product but with most of the
in-built problems of the previous century and a half still unresolved. The
new opportunities were also fraught with peculiar difficulties. Expectations of technical excellence had risen continuously since the late
seventeenth and early eighteenth centuries. Roger North had complained
then of the alteration in taste which had rejected the 'easy, temperate air,
practicable to moderate and imperfect hands' in favour of technical
perfection, so that 'even masters, unless of the prime cannot entertain us,
the plain way becomes ridiculous and must therefore be laid aside. By
this you may judge what profit the public hath from the improvement in
music.'[1] But in the early nineteenth century it was not only the plain way
that had become ridiculous—so had the technical. Haydn and Mozart
and the German school had already made quite extraordinary demands,
but now virtuosity for its own sake had taken over the salons—'mere
animal sensation', declared one critic, and Minimus (Edward Hughes)
wrote that it delighted in nothing but 'noise and bustle':

rapidity is more recommended than precision, and force more highly valued than
feeling, the genius of harmony or some other pretending to that title, has
converted the piano-forte into a velocipede [a prototype bicycle, then a new
invention and something of a fad], and reckons her success by the number of

---

[1] Roger North in his *Autobiography*, ed. by A. Jessop (1887), 70, in Christopher
Hogwood and Richard Luckett (eds.), *Music in Eighteenth-Century England*, 2.

miles which she can traverse in an hour, not regarding the awkwardness or ungracefulness of her method of travelling.

Words like 'infection', 'depraved', and 'perversion' flowed readily from Minimus's pen.[2] The florid school of Henri Herz and Johann Pixis was indeed about to vie with the Herculean romanticism of later Beethoven, and concert singers as well as instrumentalists 'truckled' to the perverted obsession, sacrificing sentiment to the thrill of velocity. And the fact that the very best professional English musicians were capable of the new technical standards did little to assuage the fear that England's musical traditions, let alone its virtually non-existent music education system, could not support the demand for musical prodigiousness—for the phenomenal. The appearance of opportunists like J. B. Logier with his chiroplast invention, designed to mass-produce masters of the keyboard, tells its own story. Nor, as we have already seen, did the emergence of the Royal Academy of Music in 1823 provide any immediate source of native genius.

Technical excellence, moreover, was being purchased in a very competitive market. Within a culture that was avowedly materialist, but where wealth had little value unless it could be converted into social status, leisure as the badge of gentility was often the aim. Thus music, insofar as it was associated with leisure, had value. But while music as a commodity may have become more highly valued, musicians as the mere adjuncts to production were often as little regarded as producers in other sectors of the emerging industrial economy, and were as often exposed to the vagaries of the market in rather the same way. Unlike other manufacturers of crafted products, though, musicians did not suffer direct competition from machines but were rather at risk of becoming machines themselves in competition with each other—for mechanical superiority, and also with foreign musicians who came flooding into London in the post-war period.

Since the days of Henry VIII, foreign musicians had been coming to England in significant numbers and, at least since the Restoration, English musicians had registered their unhappiness about it. And, of

---

[2] 'Sketch of the State of Music in England, May 1822', *QMMR* iv (1822), 246; Minimus [Edward Hodges], 'On Church Music', *QMMR* iv (1822), 179; 'Sketch of the State of Music in London, May 1823', *QMMR* v (1823), 244. Young, *Concert Tradition*, 103–4, comments on the decline of technical ability in musical amateurs *vis-à-vis* professionals as a factor in concert development. William Weber, *Music and the Middle Class*, 11, also refers to what he calls the 'professionalization' of the musician in the early nineteenth century.

course, the inroads of Italian opera had long been the subject of native resentment. But in the post-Napoleonic period, although there are no figures, it would seem that saturation point had been reached. The 'flood-gates', according to George Rodwell, had been flung open by 1824.[3] It was this problem, even more than the aesthetic and technical ones, which most exercised minds, and, while there were no petitions to Parliament or commissions of inquiry into the issue, it was nevertheless a vexatious one for those relatively few persons outside the profession itself who were tuned in to it. The suggestion that native musicians perhaps needed to be protected provoked uncompromising opposition which echoed the fundamental economic premises that so bewitched that generation. 'Fair Play' in 1822 expressed his view in familiar ideological language. 'Quality and cheapness', he declared, 'are what a nation ought alone to regard, and these properties are only to be obtained by the most open competition. All other principles are foolish and fallacious.' Readers were urged not to encourage 'indolence by any exclusive privilege indulged to birth-place'.[4]

Poor Vetus (Richard Mackenzie Bacon) from his 'heart's core' as an Englishman wanted nothing more than to see Englishmen 'as eminent in art as in arms', and was ready to adopt eagerly every possible means of kindling to a flame the 'spark divine'. But even he (especially as a staunch liberal) could not envisage any other method by which this could be achieved than by open competition with all comers.[5] It was to be a kind of Common Market of Art—a tariff-free Europe of 1992, 170 years before its time. But what it meant for English musicians was that they were to be judged by the standards of what was still considered, in many respects, to be a foreign musical culture. The English composer, in particular, was 'told to write symphonies like Haydn, Mozart or Beethoven; to compose operas like Cimarosa or Paisiello, and *then* he shall have patronage!'[6] Indeed he was asked to write operas, period: and this, as we have already seen, he did not readily seem able to do. Advice was at hand. 'We should', said one enthusiast, 'be able at once to discover, invade and conquer the El Dorado of the Italian dramatic

---

[3] See Henry Raynor, *A Social History of Music from the Middle Ages to Beethoven* (1972), 145, and Blom, *Music in England*, 108. George Rodwell, *A Letter to the Musicians of Great Britain* (1833), 30, in Rohr, 'Profession of Artisans', 24.

[4] Fair Play, 'Competition with foreign talent', *QMMR* iv (1822), 298.

[5] Vetus [Richard Mackenzie Bacon], 'Encouragement of English Musical Talent', *QMMR* iii (1821), 282; 'Sketch on the State of Music in London, May 1823', *QMMR* v (1823), 242.

[6] An Observer, 'On the Present State of the English Musician', *QMMR* v (1823), 435.

treasure. Nothing . . . would so speedily conduce to our becoming a really musical people . . .'[7] To this end, imports would not only provide healthy competition but act as a cultural stimulus to national greatness. It is perhaps not too surprising that educated musical amateurs and dilettanti looked to the Continent for their fount of culture. The 'Grand Tour', so much a feature of élite education in the eighteenth century, had for its aim, after all, the instillation of a deep regard for aesthetic models that were not English. And as Southey's Don Estriella had noticed, England was not the country of the arts: music had no place in the amusements of the ordinary people, who, he mused, were perhaps too deprived of leisure for such pursuits.[8] As a result it had become almost automatic to turn to the Continent for ability that had been acknowledged there as of the highest order, 'and', as the *Quarterly* commented, 'to yield it the loftiest place and precedence amongst ourselves'.[9] But of course much of this was mere aristocratic exclusivism and parvenu emulation. Surely the new era was at hand—surely the romantic brotherhood of art would sweep all this aside. Poet would speak to poet—romantic spirit to romantic spirit within the exclusive temple of the initiates.[10]

Not so in England. Insofar as nineteenth-century Romanticism was a restatement of pre-Enlightenment spirituality and a rejection of the values of pragmatic materialism,[11] England barely had a Romantic Age at all, except in the superficial sense of fashion. The English remained staunchly Lockian in their intellectual stance—eschewing the hypothetical and the theoretical with what amounted almost to prejudice. John Stuart Mill recognized as much in tailoring his works so as to avoid their seeming to constitute a single hypothetical argument. It would seem that an ideology 'through-composed' (if I may borrow the term) was no more acceptable than an opera. Coleridge, with his interest in German philosophy, arguing for his 'clerisy' of artists and philosophers, made obeisance at the throne of German Romanticism[12]—but in music, the silence was deafening. There is an early overture by Samuel Sebastian

---

[7] Common Sense, 'On the Means of giving an Opera to the English', *QMMR* iii (1821), 162.

[8] Southey, *Letters from England*, 40; ibid. 413.

[9] Vetus, 'Encouragement of English Musical Talent', 277.

[10] See E. T. A. Hoffman, 'A Tale of Don Juan', in Jacques Barzun (ed.), *Pleasures of Music. An Anthology of Writing about Music and Musicians from Cellini to Bernard Shaw* (London, 1954), 36.

[11] See Warren Dwight Allen, *Philosophies of Music History* (1939, this edn. 1962), 15.

[12] S. T. Coleridge, *Church and State* (1830).

Wesley (1810–76), son of Samuel Wesley, that shows an extraordinary readiness to explore the romantic idiom of Carl Maria von Weber[13]—but its impetus was still-born. The Church claimed the considerable talents of perhaps the only English musician of that generation who had the capacity to drag English music on to a level with the best of the European mainstream. And despite the strange paranoia inherent in Nicholas Temperley's assertion in 1981 as editor of *Music in Britain. The Romantic Age 1800–1914*, that somehow this failure was mythical and the product of 'Forces hostile to British musical achievement', working both then and now to undermine the reputation of British composers,[14] no evidence produced as yet, certainly nothing in *Music in Britain*, serves to contradict this otherwise universally accepted view of English music in the so-called Romantic Age.

Moral dilemmas

English musicians suffered also from another more subtle yet arguably more serious problem. They had fallen foul of newly emerging moral sensibilities and were generally considered to be unequal to the cultural improvements of the age. The neo-Puritanism of middle-class Evangelicalism had created a climate of moral 'refinement' in which English musicians on the whole found little acceptance, but in which foreign musicians with their polished manners learned at the aristocratic courts of Europe were welcome. As the *Quarterly*, ever ready to supply advice and admonition, remarked, 'English musicians must yield the palm to foreigners, who are generally educated people—and as a friend of mine once observed, "a foreigner can make himself friends by his agreeable vivacity, and his general attainments, where an Englishman would go unnoticed"'. And the playwright and novelist Charles Maturin (1782–1824) (lionized in 1820 with the publication of his Gothic novel *Melmoth the Wanderer*), in his otherwise unexceptional novel of 1818, *Women; or Pour et Contre*, should have given the English musician much food for thought, had he or she ever read this story of the fabulously well-bred singer, Madame Dalmatiana. Her native Englishness is only discovered at the climax, so heavily has it been overlaid with the refinements of a Continental education—this, and not her English origin, being the key to her acceptance, almost as a social equal, in soirée society:

---

[13] In E. Major, *c.* 1830. It was either an early work by S. S. Wesley, or a late one by his father S. Wesley. Probably the former.

[14] Temperley, *Music in Britain. The Romantic Age 1800–1914* (1981), 1.

a Siddons, a Catalani, a Gabrielli, a La Tiranna, with all the graces embodied, in the beautiful slender form of a female about 20; but the talent that excited most wonder was her perfect knowledge of the English language and literature, and her marked preference of the characters of English tragedy, which she played alternately with those of the Italian opera.

It was important of course that her high-society 'friend', Lady Longford, believed her to be 'a woman of rank and fortune in Italy; immensely rich, quite independent', who only performed on the public stage 'from habit'. Indeed so independent was she that her guests dared not even ask her to sing to them in private because such a request 'would be committing her as a public performer'.[15] But perhaps even more important—she was not *just* a singer. She was also a Siddons—a tragedian—conversant with the highest models of literature. Music of itself was not enough to recommend her as the perfect ideal of the artist.

This was entirely consistent with the views promulgated by the *Quarterly*, forever passionate about the plight of English musicians, left to wallow in their philistinism. Indeed, it was Bacon himself who drew their attention to Maturin's novel, to the model of Madame Dalmatiana contained therein, and to the lesson, that no amount of natural talent, or assiduous application, even that of a Madame Catalani, was sufficient to counteract the lack of a broader education. It was here, in this lack, that the problem for musicians lay.[16] Whereas once in the Cathedral schools the musician had been endowed with a 'liberal' education, that is to say, with an education suitable for a gentleman—Latin, Greek, and mathematics—now no such education was offered. The *Quarterly* argued that what was needed was a return to this ideal: the musician as gentleman first, and musician after.

It accepted that contemporary musicians were far from such an ideal and exhorted them to be 'more industrious . . . more retiring in manners and more circumspect in every particular of their lives'.[17] But it was not the musician's fault, the journal argued, if he lacked sophistication and

---

[15] 'Plan for the formation of an English Conservatorio', *QMMR* iv (1822), 133; Charles Maturin, *Women; or Pour et Contre* (1818), 151, 177, 179.

[16] Bacon noted the novel in the article, 'On the intellectual cultivation necessary to a singer', *QMMR* v (1823), 141, reproduced in his 1824 *Elements of Vocal Science* at p. 273. The reference to Madame Catalani, whose lack of intellectual training, according to Bacon, prevented her becoming a Dalmatiana, may have been prompted by the knowledge that Maturin's wife was a singer who had studied with Catalani. Bacon fails to mention the moral of the tale though, that Madame Dalmatiana, for all her great capacities, like another fictional singer, Madame Alcharisi in George Eliot's *Daniel Deronda*, signally fails as a mother, and thus, by extension, as a human being.

[17] Equalization, 'Singers and Instrumentalists', *QMMR* iv (1822), 432.

polish, for he could find no better associates 'than those of his own condition'. Thus, 'the polite and informed who are induced to enter into conversation with him, discover at once that his recommendations are confined to his fiddle or his voice'. The mortification that such encounters would necessarily inflict upon the hapless musician, which he was 'doomed to experience for evermore', could only be prevented if music, that 'liberal art', were to be aided and supported by a 'liberal education'.[18]

Surprisingly, the disgruntled English composer Thomas Danvers Worgan agreed. One might have expected a rejection of such qualifications from such a total devotee of his art, but he declared: 'Give musicians a liberal education and they will not in any wise be deteriorated by the study and practice of music.'[19] A far cry from Potter's defiant reproach of 1762 to those 'who are engaged in the plunder of the world' to respect the musician for his 'love and close attachment to music', and for his choice of music above 'the love of wealth and grandeur'.[20] It would seem that musicians themselves had come to believe that music, studied by itself, could indeed lead to that deterioration of manliness and dignity that Locke, Campbell, and Chesterfield had claimed it would.

Yet this loose, vapid creature, so suspect in the Lockian scheme of things, was now, in the hour of its greatest demoralization, about to be held hostage to quite a different archetype, which tended towards the plodding but correct Sir George Smart (1776–1867), or towards that acerbic pedant Dr William Crotch (1775–1847), who once tersely accused Beethoven of breaking the rules of composition, without 'the least good obtained from it';[21] while English music, perhaps as some kind of intrinsic reproach, clung to a churchy provincialism which was meant to express not the flights of romantic imagination, but the solid virtues of the English character.

'An Englishman' writing in 1823 felt motivated to speak of how English music 'from the earliest to the latest times' had always been a moderate and temperate expression which tempered all the passions and emotions which the music itself attempted to convey. 'This sobriety', he went on, 'regulating even our warmest feelings, is as I conceive it the

[18] Vetus [Richard Mackenzie Bacon], 'On the Character of Musicians', *QMMR* i (1819), 290–1.
[19] Worgan, *Musical Reformer*, 45.
[20] Potter, *Observations*, 69–70.
[21] His 'Lectures', 1831. In Carl Engel, *Musical Myths and Facts* (1876), i. 143.

national disposition.'[22] With Addisonian certainty, another writer could see that the very lack of an operatic form was a reflection of virtue. 'For we have been and are a warlike, a philosophical, and a religious people— but never OPERATICAL.'[23] English music may have failed dramatically, but this was only because of an intrinsic moral quality. It was the 'temperance which sobers imagination, restrains passion and chastens all productions of Englishmen who never regard vehemence as sincerity or volubility as allied to truth of expression'. As the *London Magazine* put it, proudly, but with just the slightest tinge of regret, the sterling metal of the English style 'properly so called, is conversant with none of the modern arts of voluptuous insinuation'.[24] Thus, of the foremost English dramatic composer of the day, the *Quarterly* could comment without rancour that Mr Bishop rarely ever reached the heights or plumbed the depths, 'but his genius is more in accordance with the equability of English habits of thinking and English affections'.[25]

This might have been well enough if English appetites had been easily satisfied by such home-grown moral integrity, but they were not. Indeed they craved the very voluptuousness that English music and English musicians were meant, apparently in obeisance to the national character, to eschew. Why, asked the *Quarterly*, could not the English, who possessed genius of the most polished erudition, like Dr Crotch's, whose oratorio, *Palestine*, could command such admiration, or like Mr Horsley's whose glees were the product of such sensitive and delicate taste, or Mr Bishop's whose operas so abounded in merit, produce *morceaux* of real delight? Why, it was really asking, should three little pieces by Paër give so much pleasure and the combined efforts of the best of English genius give so little?[26]

But it was hardly the English musician's fault if he or she felt constrained to act the part of the sober pedant or chaste performer in order to win social approbation and therefore economic security. It was all very well for the already 'respectable' to pick any musical delicacy they fancied from the Continental platter with perfect impunity—but altogether a different one for English musicians to supply them. Even the English language itself posed a threat to decency when set to music. Not

[22] An Englishman, 'On the Character of English Music', *QMMR* v (1823), 442.

[23] An Observer, 'The State of Music in England', 286.

[24] An Englishman, 'On the Character of English Music', 445; *London Magazine*, i (June 1820), 620.

[25] Review of Bishop's music for Shakespeare's *Two Gentlemen of Verona*, at Covent Garden. *QMMR* iv (1822), 83.

[26] Review of 'Three Works' of Paër. Paris. *QMMR* ii (1820), 95.

even a Moore or a Stephenson, it was felt, could obliterate the 'primal vulgarity' of the words of some English songs, no matter how beautiful the melody.[27] In 1821, the young 'English' composer Pio Cianchettini (1799–1851), son of the Bohemian pianist Katerina Dusikova and nephew of Jan Dussek, was severely rebuked for setting Shakespeare's 'Take oh! take those lips away', because the words (though Shakespeare's) contained 'indelicacies of allusion, which in this refined age will hardly be tolerated'.[28] And the language was also seen as one of the drawbacks of English 'opera', where 'our comic songs are all vulgar . . . [and] the language and manners of the lowest classes are the objects of description'. The practical jokes of a wagoner or a representation of a drunken hackney coachman were 'no legitimate subject for music in any shape'.[29]

   Yet for all the apparent conformity of the Crotches, the Horsleys, and the Bishops, as we know, it was the foreign not the English musicians who were generally favoured. For them were reserved the smiles and the gifts of the rich and the mighty. It was to hear the torrent-voiced Italian, Catalani, that the musical public paid a guinea apiece, leaving the likes of the sterling English composer and organist Samuel Wesley (1766–1837) to his own devices, reduced, in what the *London Magazine* described as 'very like a satire not to say a disgrace', to the small room of the Argyll Institution, supported by a 'committee of professors'.[30] Voluptuousness in a foreign language was, it seemed, safe from moral contamination, and consumers could comfort themselves at the same time with the knowledge that they were encouraging the acknowledged virtue of the age, 'free competition'. As for the dull and suddenly respectable English musician, why he was safely employed in their families as a teacher, where his moral qualities could be relied upon. Indeed, from the dissolute character of Locke and Campbell, the English musician had been transformed, it was claimed, into a proper custodian of family virtue. 'Seldom', after all, said 'An Observer', had the English musician forgotten, in his dealings with the softer sex, the duty he owed to honour, and it would be difficult to find another class of men 'among whom aberrations from the path of integrity have been less frequent'.[31] This was an extravagant claim to make, and was probably true, if at all, only at the

----

[27] Juvenus, 'Consideration of the Character of the English as a Musical People', *QMMR* iv (1822), 136.
[28] Review of, *QMMR* iii (1821), 248.
[29] Common Sense, 'On the Means of giving an Opera to the English', 160.
[30] *London Magazine*, iv (Aug. 1821), 204.
[31] An Observer, 'On the Present State of the English Musician', 436–7; ibid. 137.

higher levels of employment where a great deal was at stake—among the Dr Burneys or the Sir George Smarts. As we shall see, it was certainly not true of William Castell whose sexual morality was more likely to have justified the Bishop of Norwich's reservations of the previous generation about the moral quality of the profession. No more, he had mourned, were musicians qualified to perform the sacred role Agamemnon had once bestowed upon the unfortunate musician he had left behind to guard the morals of his wife, Clytemnestra. 'How different in those days', he had decided, 'must the character of a musician, and the use of music have been, from their character and use at present.'[32]

How different indeed. Had Dr Horne lived to read the *Quarterly* he might have revised his opinion. But in any case what these new claims to professional chastity signified was a passionate yearning on the part of educated, affluent music-lovers like Richard Mackenzie Bacon for English musicians to redeem by personal virtue what they apparently could not redeem by their music. It was as though, if the English musician could only behave like the most perfect ideal of a gentleman, he would suddenly find himself accepted in his own country by his fellow countrymen and women, who were only waiting for this transformation to occur before awarding him his due reward. There *was* of course, an élite corps of English musicians who sustained careers, in part, by maintaining an assiduous social conformity—the *beau idéal*, as we shall see below. But on a broader scale the problem of English failure had deeper and more complex roots.

Ironically foreign musicians had a poor reputation for morals, but it did not seem to matter. They had glamour. They bestowed status in a society consumed with status competition. Their manners, frequently gained as habits of obsequiousness and formed from long dependence upon aristocratic patrons on the Continent, flattered wealthy if not always the 'best bred' of English patrons—the parvenus, whom English musicians would have been quick to resent for the overt, insensitive attitudes of condescension often missing from the behaviour of the more established élite; the pretentious musical amateurs, the ones who so irritated Isaac Nathan, fancying themselves 'authorized to animadvert and dictate to professional men'.[33]

---

[32] The Right Revd George Horne, Bishop of Norwich, quoting Homer, *Odyssey* iii. 267, in *Works* (1809), i. 358.
[33] 'On the Character of Musicians', 286–7; Nathan, *Essay on the History and Theory of Music*, 34.

The dynastic crises of Europe at this time brought many foreign musicians to London, where, for the sake of forming 'connections' and much to the irritation of the locals, they often performed gratis in the houses of the rich. This made them particularly popular among the more parsimonious of society hosts and hostesses. English musicians, on the other hand, consistent with the ethos of a mercantile nation, expected payment. So too, on one occasion, did a French harpist, creating something of a *cause célèbre* in the courts. She lost her case, but won the plaudits of the *Quarterly*, who viewed it as scandalous that many of the 'grand musical assemblies' in private homes were no more than matters of mere trade—a means of furthering the financial interests of the already rich. Why should these 'poor rich people' it asked, take advantage of professional talent in order to make way for themselves?[34] It was perhaps this very English pragmatism that patrons sought to avoid by favouring foreign musicians. Such logic smacked of that French Jacobinism which England had spent twenty-two years defeating.

But it was probably also true that apart from the cream of the profession—apart from Cramer, Mori, Lindley, and Griesbach; apart from Holmes and Macintosh and Nicholson; the Philharmonic Society; the conductors, Greatorix and Smart, the organist Samuel Wesley, and the singers like Mrs Salmon, Miss Stephens, Braham, Vaughan, and the Knyvetts—standards among English musicians fell away fairly sharply and that among the 'million [who] sink and are little seen or known' there were many who were ill-trained and ordinary. Hundreds a year, according to 'Vetus' (R. M. Bacon), were attracted to the profession for the rewards they perceived were there, but these were for the most part only loosely and vaguely educated and many of them ended up sliding into 'the wretchedness of subordinates in every department'.[35] England still had no viable system of musical education compared to Continental countries like France, Germany, and Italy. And even after the establishment of the Royal Academy of Music in 1823, general musical education throughout the country was limited to small pockets of activity usually generated by individual enthusiasts, who tended in any case to be interested in music as a form of social work rather than for its own sake.[36]

---

[34] Honest Pride, remarks on 'Pallix vs Scudmore', *QMMR* iii (1822), 440–4.

[35] Vetus, 'On the Character of Musicians', 290.

[36] e.g., Robert Owen, under the educational influence of Pestalozzi, introduced music into his factory schools; Sarah Glover introduced new systems of teaching children psalmody. See Bernarr Rainbow, *The Land without Music. Musical Education in England 1800–1860 and its Continental Antecedents* (1967).

The beau idéal

Out of this general picture of gloom, there were of course success stories for English musicians. One of them was Sir George Smart—an associate of Castell's—who was highly successful not only as conductor of the Philharmonic Society but as a society musician and teacher. He played at soirées for Madame Catalani and at many other fashionable venues. Among his many clients was the Evangelical peer the first Earl of Harrowby, President of the Council, whose daughter he taught and by whose influence he was able to save a female felon from the gallows. The woman had been involved in a robbery of the musician's plate which, when displayed in the court, elicited the admiration of at least one by-stander, who was inspired to comment that 'these musicians live well'. The woman, to whom the soft-hearted Sir George had sent money in Newgate, was eventually transported to New South Wales.[37] His knighthood was an Irish one, conferred by the Duke of Richmond in 1811. It had cost him £66. 13s. 0d.—a fact he duly noted in his Journal.[38]

Although Smart was undoubtedly a very sound musician, there is no reason to believe that he was ever more than a scrupulously accurate technician with excellent manners and a good business sense. He was nevertheless much admired in his day. Not surprisingly, Richard Bacon, in his dedication to him of his *Elements of Vocal Science* in 1824, publicly declared himself an admirer of his 'knowledge, ability and integrity as a musician and as an instructor', and the singer Henry Phillips went to some pains almost half a century later to paint a flattering picture of him. 'A more rigid or methodical man of business I never met; we all knew that nothing would be wanting where he was conductor. He was certainly a Duke of Wellington amongst us, and I believe perfectly aware of the fact, for he always called us his *troops*, and under admirable discipline we were.'[39]

None of which apparently lessened the disgust felt for him by at least one contemporary musician. Perhaps representative of an 'old school' clique who felt themselves neglected, Isaac Nathan reckoned Smart had, no one knew how, 'crept into notice'. He played, acknowledged Nathan,

[37] H. Bertrum Cox and C. L. E. Cox, *Leaves from the Journal of Sir George Smart* (1907), 55.

[38] Ibid. 46.

[39] Henry Phillips, *Musical and Personal Recollections, during Half a Century* (1864), i. 213–14.

Sir George Smart.

11. Engraving from the portrait by J. Cawse. Ref. BM 1879–6–14–816.

accurately enough; but, he sneered, so could a schoolboy or an automaton. Sir George, he averred, was also a coward. Once, upon being 'called out', he had broken the gentlemanly code; 'and', accused Nathan, 'rather than risk his life, consented to make an apology'. This incident had occurred not long after Smart had been knighted in 1811, giving Nathan plenty of scope for scornful mockery. That he should have desired to wound the benignly rotund knight in print may simply have been a reflection of Nathan's own combative and vitriolic spirit, but it was perhaps unleashed by umbrage that favour had been bestowed upon respectability rather than upon talent—presumably his own.

The kind of fashionable success that Smart enjoyed may be judged by his being chosen to superintend the music for the funeral of George IV and the coronation of William IV. In 1838 he was paid £300 to perform as organist at the coronation of Queen Victoria, and was appointed organist for her wedding in 1840.[40] Perhaps this was the last straw for Isaac Nathan, who, having himself once enjoyed the patronage of the royal family,[41] emigrated to Australia in the following year.

As it turned out, Nathan's 1823 attack, originally included as part of his *An Essay on the History and Theory of Music*, but apparently suppressed,[42] probably did him more harm than it ever did Sir George. The *Quarterly* (i.e. his friend Richard Mackenzie Bacon) naturally leapt to his defence, dismissing the charge of cowardice and pointing out that he had risen to eminence 'by gentlemanly manners, by skill in his profession, and by honour and integrity in its exercise'.[43] And while Sir George went on to end his days in the bosom of the musical establishment, Nathan ended up in Sydney, where after a chequered but on the whole unsuccessful career he fell victim to a Pitt Street tramcar in 1864.

Indeed Smart became what was to be the epitome of the successful English musician—the cautiously acquisitive man of business, the astute juggler of engagements who gave value for money in a competitive world with his own interests securely at heart but who, above all else, carried

---

[40] Cox, *Leaves from the Journal of Sir George Smart*, 292–3.

[41] He was musical historian to George IV and music instructor to the Princess Charlotte of Wales. *DNB* (1922) [Nathan].

[42] Nathan's attack was printed and criticized in *QMMR* v (1823), 367, in a review of Nathan's *Essay*. It is not to be found in the British Library's 1823 copy, presumably the first and only edition; the 'calling out' incident referred to was probably the altercation between Smart and Catalani's husband, Monsieur Valabrègue, referred to in Cox, *Leaves from the Journal of Sir George Smart*, 46. In this version, a challenge was expected, but instead, M. Valabrègue sent Smart a snuff-box inscribed with the words, 'Un gage de paix'.

[43] Review of Nathan's *Essay*, 367.

himself with the deportment of a gentleman. However, his success cannot simply be dismissed in Nathan's terms. It can hardly be said that he 'crept into notice', since having been educated by Dr Ayrton at the Chapel Royal he was already marked out for success. Indeed he worked tirelessly at the Philharmonic Society, at concert series, at the Lenten Oratorios, as musical director at Covent Garden, as conductor at provincial festivals, as organist to the Chapel Royal, as private concert impresario, as accompanist, and as teacher. Apart from which, as Cyril Ehrlich remarks, he carried on a brisk trade in piano sales commissions. Unlike more conservative colleagues, like William Crotch and R. J. S. Stevens, for example, Smart was not averse to working in the theatre— for high-status academic and church musicians still an institution of dubious credentials in spite of its financial attractions. Indeed, he demonstrated a lively flexibility and an enthusiastic willingness to tackle any musical challenge that presented itself. He may not have intuitively understood the later works of Beethoven or of Weber, but it appears that he did justice to what was actually written in the scores as they were presented to him. And this cannot always have been easy.[44]

Part of the truth must be, though, that he was lucky. In his personality and attainments he was well situated to take advantage of both aristocratic and middle-class patronage in an age in which it was dangerous to rely exclusively upon either. Like Bishop he came from a commercial family, but unlike Bishop he had an early introduction through the Chapel Royal to aristocratic patronage. He had the careful mentality of a burgher but the manners of a courtier. He knew how to keep his books as well as any successful shopkeeper, but he also knew the value of largess. To Carl Maria von Weber (1786–1826), who died in Smart's house in London in 1826, he was an amiable and solicitous host.[45] Above all he had a reputation for integrity and no breath of scandal ever touched him.

But as a paragon of English virtue, he also exhibited traits that were representative of English limitations. Rossini, in acknowledging the professional skill of English musicians, had no respect for their motives. They would, he said, 'do anything to make money. I have witnessed there', he said, 'queer things . . .'.[46] Even Mendelssohn, who was to

---

[44] See *DNB*; Grove; Cox, *Leaves from the Journal of Sir George Smart*; Ehrlich, *Music Profession in Britain*, 38–42.

[45] He had a statue of Weber built in Leipzig. *DNB* (1922) [Smart].

[46] Rossini talking to Hiller, in Ferdinand Hiller, *Aus dem Tonleben unserer Zeit*, quoted in Engel, *Musical Myths and Facts*, ii. 73.

become almost an honorary Englishman himself, admitted that in England music was treated like a business. 'It is calculated,' he said, 'paid for and bargained over, and much indeed is lacking.' Tempering his criticism he observed, however, that 'however greedy of gain they may be ... [they] are always gentlemen, otherwise they could not retain their places in good society'. And he rather enjoyed, he said, their ideological philistinism, finding it a relief after the eternal German preoccupation with such matters.[47]

Economic balancing act

Part of the problem for the English musician was doubtless the tightrope act required to be performed in seeking both aristocratic and bourgeois patronage—walking the fine line between two sets of antipathetic values. The idea that musicians in the early nineteenth century suddenly transferred from aristocratic to middle-class patronage—from individual service to mass audience—is not borne out. The transitional period was a protracted one in England, where, unlike on the Continent, as Rohr points out, the influence of the aristocracy remained socially potent well into the second half of the century. In 1865, for example, we find Hélène Stoepel, the mint-new widow of William Vincent Wallace, thrown back upon her own professional resources, feeling the necessity to use the name of the Dowager Duchess of Sutherland in order to procure pupils.[48] It is arguably the case, then, that musicians like Nathan, relying significantly on the aristocracy, were left perilously exposed when the aristocracy failed them, which in the case of Nathan occurred with the deaths of his patrons. With his friendship with Byron and the disreputable Lady Caroline Lamb, and with his close associations with the dissolute and unpopular court of George IV, he was, perhaps, rather like Castell, too closely identified with the old norms and values to make the transition into the world of middle-class Evangelical piety, 'refinement', and professional discipline. *The Times* obituary of George IV rather sums up the altered mood of educated society, or at least of the reading public. Referring to him as the 'Leviathan of the *haut ton*', as an 'inveterate voluptuary' and guilty of 'artificiality and selfishness', it declared categorically that 'There never was an individual less regretted

---

[47] F. Mendelssohn, correspondence, in Elkin, *Royal Philharmonic*, 31.
[48] Rohr, 'Profession of Artisans', 77–8; Mrs Wallace's ad, *The Orchestra*, v (9 Dec. 1865), 1, and subsequent numbers.

by his fellow creatures. . . . What eye has wept for him? What heart has heaved one sob of unnecessary sorrow?'[49]

But even so, this new bright world of sensibility, taste, and righteousness was not quite able to sweep all before it, not least because significant parts of it still sought aristocratic sanction and pandered to aristocratic prejudices. Middle-class audiences were tentative and unreliable, constantly seeking social approval. In 1819, Sir George Smart inaugurated a series of concerts in the City which boldly sought to break the cultural monopoly of the West End, and thus, by extension, of aristocratic dominance of the musical scene. It had plenty of support from the *Quarterly*, which endorsed the idea that wealth should seek cultural refinement and that the 'solid acquirements of the city' should cease to be transferred to the 'mockery of the court'. In the mingling of the two, it believed, society would best find its equilibrium and refinement would be more broadly shared. The *London Magazine* was also very positive.[50] But the venture failed after a few seasons. The aristocracy declined to descend into the City, and where the aristocracy would not go, their emulators could see no point in going—indeed, would not dare go, for 'fear of appearing to be of an inferior order'.[51] The Empire of the West End was not ready to give way just yet and things would get worse before they would get better. Its position, if anything, appeared to consolidate.

In 1822, amid much hopeful speculation, the revived Concentores Society, prominent in which was Sir George Smart, as well as Henry Bishop, launched the British Concert, a last-ditch effort to galvanize support for native music and musicians. But among the names of two hundred subscribers, no more than eight were titled and only one of those was a member of the peerage.[52] It lasted one season. In the *Quarterly*, 'An Observer' poured scorn upon what he termed the supineness of the profession itself—upon its lack of commitment to projects which it was in its own best interests to support. It would seem that no members of the Concentores Society could be found who had the leisure to undertake further management of the concern.[53] But once again it was a question of class. The aristocracy was determined to

[49] *The Times*, 16 July 1830, p. 2b.
[50] 'A Slight Sketch of the Present State of Music in London', *QMMR* i (1819), 404; *London Magazine*, i (May 1820), 579 for commentary on the 6th concert of the series, 13 Apr.
[51] 'The City Concerts', *QMMR* iii (1821), 65.
[52] 'The British Concert', *QMMR* iv (1823), 245.
[53] An Observer, 'On the Present State of the English Musician', 291.

remain aloof. The Italian Opera and the Ancient Concerts were the only two 'public' venues which they graced, both of which effectively isolated them from contact with the rest of society.

Prince Pückler-Miskau remarked of England in the 1820s that the coarseness and uproariousness of the audiences at the English theatres in London had driven polite society to the Italian Opera.[54] Such an accusation could hardly be levelled at the heavily screened audiences at Philharmonic Society Concerts, yet not even these events, by now acknowledged as musically the most rewarding in London, could tempt them. This curious denial of pleasure served to show, said the *Quarterly*, 'with what scrupulous exactitude the distinctions of condition are kept up even against the attraction of the highest enjoyments art can offer'.[55]

By 1825, the only regular series of 'public' concerts still operating were those of the Philharmonic Society, with not even a dozen titled persons in the list of subscribers, and the aristocratically exclusive Ancient Concert.[56] The aristocracy and their wealthy emulators had actually resorted to the practice of holding their own private concerts, at which they could all the better select their company. The causes for this, as the *Quarterly* pointed out, had nothing to do with music but rather with a passion for exclusion, starting at the top and working its way down through the social layers. Hence nothing that was open to the public at large could afford temptation to rank and wealth, but was held in contempt. 'To sit in the pit at the Opera, or in the body of the Argyll Rooms, [was] somewhat allied to a sense of degradation.'[57]

One of the effects of this transfer of musical resources from public to private venues upon musicians themselves was to sustain the old need for private patronage; thus delaying entrepreneurial development even further.

In the short term, though, it is possible to imagine that many musicians gained by this process. It meant that wealth was being spread around quite extravagantly. Private concerts were often full-scale affairs, with orchestras, singers, and even whole ballet companies being engaged. While, at one extreme, the very deaf Duke of Devonshire might entertain his guests with a concert at which not one native musician was

---

[54] *Tour in England, Ireland and France* (1833), 249–53, in A. M. Nagler, *A Sourcebook in Theatrical History* (2nd edn., 1959).
[55] 'Sketch of the State of Music in England, May 1822', 252.
[56] 'State of Music in London', *QMMR* vii (1825), 210.
[57] Ibid.

employed, not one piece performed by an English composer, nor even one word of English sung,[58] others, like Sir George Warrender, although the programme might be all Italian, would at least employ Sir George Smart to superintend it.[59] Fees were often lucrative, especially for singers, many of whom were regularly (if not uniformly) paid twenty-five guineas a night.[60] Such a situation of course, also gave 'impresarios' like Sir George Smart a power of patronage in their own right, being no doubt importuned by eager candidates for employment. How far down the scale this wealth and influence extended is open to question. Rank-and-file professional musicians may indeed have seen little improvement in their general standard of living. Nathan's comment that they were as often as not 'labouring', amid all the trappings of affluence, 'under all the pressure of poverty, rendered doubly irksome by the necessity of keeping up an appearance of comfort and hilarity', would suggest that this was so.[61] But it must have created at least an aura of vitality in which money circulated and in which musicians felt the potential for material advantage. So much so in fact that the ever-vigilant *Quarterly* warned in 1824 that musicians were too much absorbed by their private interests 'to be able or willing to unite in the successful prosecution of any scheme, which has for its immediate object, the general advancement of art and of our national fame in art'.[62]

'Private interests' for musicians, however, were not confined to private engagements in the houses of the wealthy. Sir George Smart, for one, had other irons in the fire. From 1822 he was the musical director at Covent Garden and also managed one of the Lenten Oratorio series, arguably one of the first forms of mass musical entertainment. They evolved out of the legal requirement for theatres to cease stage performances during Lent and originally, as the name implies, were limited to the performances of religious works. By the 1820s the two London majors, Drury Lane and Covent Garden, were the chief venues. By 1822, however, it was noted that they suffered from the 'vilest spirit of retail traffic'.[63] This was the year that Smart and Bishop had the management of them in competition with each other. Failing to realize a profit, in

    [58] 'Sketch of the State of Music in London, May 1823', *QMMR* v (1823), 256.

    [59] 'Private Concerts in London', *QMMR* vi (1824), 227.

    [60] Ibid. 232. See also Ehrlich, *Music Profession in Britain*, 41 on the amounts Sir George Smart negotiated for performers, e.g. £42 for an evening's performance by Signor Velluti, last of the Italian castrati, in 1825.

    [61] Nathan, *Essay*, 34.

    [62] 'Public Establishments for Music in London', *QMMR* vi (1824), 44.

    [63] 'Mozart's accompaniments to Handel', *QMMR* iv (1822), 139.

1824 they passed to Bochsa, who took over both theatres, closing down one to create a viable monopoly. He invested heavily, improved variety and standards of performance, and seemed to have succeeded in establishing them as the best and cheapest concerts in London.[64] But they were wrecked by the exclusive King's Theatre opening up in direct competition with their *Concerts Spirituels* in 1824, headed by no less a celebrity than Rossini and with attractions like Madame Catalani and other leading members of the Italian Opera. The *Quarterly,* temporarily converted from its more usual free-market approach, deplored this 'injurious and uncalled for' competition and pronounced it against the 'public interest'. But in spite of their cheapness, quality, variety, and open access, the fact was that Oratorio Concerts just could not match the Italian Opera in social status. Bochsa's dilemma demonstrated once again the complex social environment of this period which persistently conspired to frustrate even the most daring and inventive of musical entrepreneurs. The harvest of these years of economic uncertainty was not to be reaped till the 1840s, when the Frenchman Louis Jullien cast aside much of the accumulated social impedimenta of polite 'taste' and wooed the greater musical public with a directness that was to appal the squeamish.

In the meantime, apart from busking in the street or working for tips on the river-boats, the only other entrepreneurial avenue for the individual musician was the benefit concert. These were one-off affairs, usually at the end of the season (although sometimes at the beginning), intended to exploit whatever popularity a performer might have gained. As with the benefit nights at the theatre, it was presumed that audiences would be undemanding and indulgent, having come to support a favourite rather than to get their money's worth.

But by the 1820s the system seems to have got out of hand, with more hopefuls than the public could or would sustain. They came to include not only recognized personalities but also obscure musicians hoping to promote their talents or to pick up pupils. The cost of putting on such concerts, according to the *Quarterly,* could not be less than £100 to £140, so that only the better-known performers or those with rare talent could ever hope to recoup such an amount.[65] But rather than stifling the explosion, these economic facts seemed only to have led to abuses. Popular singers and instrumentalists were often announced as appearing who either turned up late, or, owing to other engagements, not at all,

---

[64] 'The Lent Oratorios and the Concerts Spirituels', *QMMR* vi (1824), 72–4.
[65] 'Sketch of the State of Music in London, May 1823', 251.

with the result that the public was 'deluded' and 'insulted'. Even more fraudulently, there were instances where the names of the great were sometimes advertised without their consent.[66] Indeed it becomes difficult to distinguish between genuine benefit concerts and those which the *Quarterly* referred to as the efforts of 'incompetent speculators', citing the case of Mr William Cutler, Bachelor of Music, who put on a concert at the King's Theatre on Whitsun Eve in 1824 incurring a loss of £150.[67] Two years later William Castell would mount a similar assault against the indifference of the world, with similar results.

Evidently there was an awareness of a potential public for music performance outside of the old subscription system and the private concert, but the logistics were proving difficult to establish. Would-be entrepreneurs were still unable to find the magic formula which would unleash 'take-off' into 'self-sustaining growth'.

From the 1790s, as we have seen, music had been developing as a mass entertainment, and new industrial techniques were producing musical instruments as mass consumer products. Closely followed in popularity by the flute and harp, piano forte playing had become virtually universal throughout the country, 'and the daughters of Mechanics', noted A. Burgh in his *Anecdotes of Music* in 1814, 'even in humble Stations, would fancy themselves extremely ill-treated, were they debarred the indulgence of a piano-forte'. The price of a square piano had fallen from £50 in 1760 to approximately £18. 3s. 0d. in 1815. Piano production in Britain was fast becoming a major consumer industry. Music publishing also boomed. Everybody writes, said the *Quarterly*, everybody publishes—'what a figure we make as manufacturers of divertimentos, &c. &c. &c. for the piano forte, harp and flute!'[68]

The demand for instruction was also great, but it was noted with regret that, as with publishing, there was little discrimination by the public and anyone without the least pretension to taste or excellence

[66] 'Sketch of the State of Music in London, June 1821', *QMMR* iii (1821), 396.

[67] 'Private Concerts in London', 234.

[68] A. Burgh, *Anecdotes of Music* (1814), pp. v–vi; *QMMR*, review article, iv (1822), 94, on the 'universality of piano-forte playing in England'; ibid. 86–7, on the growth of harp playing; Prices, see Milligan, *Concerto and London's Musical Culture*, 16; Jane Austen bought a superior piano-forte in 1808 for 30 guineas. See Austen, *Letters*, letter to her sister Cassandra, 27 Dec. 1808; as a consumer industry, see George Dodd, *Days at the Factories. The Manufacturing Industry of Great Britain Described* (1843), 388; music publishing, see Charles Humphries and William C. Smith, *Music Publishing in the British Isles from the Beginning until the Middle of the Nineteenth Century* (2nd edn., 1970); An Observer, 'On the Present State of the English Musician', 290.

could set themselves up as a teacher.[69] Largely for social rather than musical reasons, playing the piano or harp had become *de rigueur* for women in middle-class families where it was perceived more as an indulgence than as a discipline; or in some quarters as an 'antidote to the poison insidiously administered by the innumerable licentious Novels which are hourly sapping the foundations of every moral and religious principle'.[70] Serious musicians like Thomas Worgan were appalled. His 'manly art' had become no more than an 'effeminate gewjaw'. He was writing, he said, for men, but had to live, like so many other professors, by teaching women.[71]

Indeed women in music had never had an integrated place. Often not welcome in church choirs, they were still banished from the cathedrals; a fact still complained of by John Hullah in 1855 and to this day a continuing taboo. They could not qualify for a university degree and most musical instruments, except the pianoforte and harp, were considered offensive to delicacy when played by women. Typical of the accepted attitude was the oboist W. T. Parke's comment on the occasion of attending a performance by the violinist Mme Gautherot, that 'the ear . . . was more gratified than the eye by this lady's masculine effort'. There were no women in the orchestras and the RSM did not admit women until 1866. Apprenticeships in music for women were rare and usually limited to the daughters or sisters of professional musicians. At the Royal Academy of Music in 1823, women were taught only singing, piano, and harp, and were given only an hour on Wednesdays for harmony and composition. When the boys were allocated music-copying as an evening chore, the girls were allocated needlework. Women composers were so few as to be almost invisible and their work was exclusively small in scale.[72] Is it any wonder Worgan called it a 'manly art'?

For the bulk of women, then, there was little thought of music as a profession and little interest on the part of professional musicians in altering the status quo. This reluctance and lack of seriousness in approaching what was virtually a mass female market was probably the reason why the teaching was so bad, as the School Enquiry Commission of 1868 confirmed.[73] And ultimately it did not benefit the profession

[69] An Observer, 'On the Present State of the English Musician', 437.
[70] Burgh, *Anecdotes of Music*, p. vii.   [71] Worgan, *Musical Reformer*, 33–6.
[72] John Hullah, *Music in the Parish Church* (1855), 23–4; Parke, *Musical Memoirs*, i. 120, and *QMMR* ii (1820), 390 f., comments on the prejudice against women playing the violin; RAM timetable, in *QMMR* vii (1825), 146–7; also *QMMR* iv (1822), 519. In 1825 Lucy Anderson, the pianist, was the only female 'professor' at the Academy.
[73] Mackerness, *Social History of English Music*, 173–4.

since many of these ill-taught women became teachers themselves, undercutting professionals of both sexes and failing to enhance public understanding or discrimination.

The *Quarterly* in 1819 maintained that it was easy to find numbers of 'British ladies' who were excellent musical executors, and who studied harmony and composition,[74] and certainly the *Quarterly* occasionally printed patronizingly friendly reviews of slight publications composed by women, but with the benefit of hindsight it is hard to be reconciled to this view. The same journal also commended the introduction of numbers of female 'assistants' into teaching, considering it a 'striking improvement, both in the condition of the sex and of society'.[75] But, for the reasons outlined above, it was not to bring any striking improvement to English music itself nor to the status of the music profession.

Indeed it is hard to see how any one element of the great musical boom of this period had any significantly beneficial effect either upon the standard of living of the ordinary musician or upon the creative credibility of the English musical profession as a whole. It is within this context that we find William Joseph Castell, born into the profession and now about to confront his heritage.

CASTELL'S LONDON CAREER

On 5 June 1814, William Castell signed the Admission Book of the Royal Society of Musicians[76]—the first public affirmation we have of his professional commitment to music. He signed it in his neat and pretty hand with a flourish on the end which convinced the Society's present honorary archivist that his name was still Castelli.[77]

In his application, he had declared that he had studied and practised music for the required seven years and that he played the Piano Forte, violin, tenore [viola], and double-bass. He was then, he said, engaged as chorus-master and in the orchestra at the Surrey Theatre and was the deputy organist at St Mary's, Lambeth, and at St Catherine Cree, a small parish church in Leadenhall Street in the City.[78] Only two other musicians were admitted in 1814, Richard Clark and Charles Wodarch,

---

[74] In a review of Dr Crotch's new 'Rounds', *QMMR* i (1819), 108.

[75] Vetus, 'On the Character of Musicians', 286.

[76] RSM, MS Admission Book.

[77] As a result he is listed in the RSM's *List of Members* under Castelli, rather than Castell. As explained in conversation, 1987.

[78] His application—RSM, MS Members' Files.

the former educated as a chorister at Windsor and Eton and deputy to Mr Bartleman at the Chapel Royal, Mr Sale at St Paul's, and Mr J. B. Sale at Westminster Abbey. Wodarch had less elevated credentials but was engaged at the Theatres Royal, Drury Lane, and Lyceum.[79]

Castell's motive for joining the Society may have been to offer some protection to his family, which by then consisted of the two boys, William and Alfred. It is more likely, though, that considerations of prestige were uppermost. London-based, the Society attracted the cream of the capital's musicians and had done so from the time of Handel and J. C. Bach. Of the list of first violins of the Philharmonic Society in 1819, seven out of the eleven were members. In 1818, out of the seventeen known members of the Covent Garden orchestra, twelve were members, with membership dropping only at the lower end of the pay scale. Of those paid £140 (for 200 nights) down to £66, ten out of twelve were members. Of the five paid only £58, there was only one.[80]

Membership, while it did not guarantee professional success for individuals (indeed its records show just how many failed to win financial security through their work),[81] did provide not only a bulwark against absolute poverty when their careers were ended, but very plausibly a sense too of that legitimacy and social approval still awarded with such reluctance to musicians by society at large. The Society of itself conferred no status. Nor is it easy to see how its existence raised public consciousness as to the intrinsic worth of musicians, except perhaps by the annual contribution by members to the Festival of the Sons of the Clergy at St Paul's Cathedral—a musical and social event of great celebrity, to which members were expected to give their services free of charge.[82] Yet in the eyes of the profession it evidently did so. Susannah Castell certainly desired membership for her son William even though, as we shall see, she was highly critical—his father's membership having afforded her no more assistance in her time of hardship than a £5

[79] RSM, *List of Members*, 'Chronological List of Members'.

[80] BL Loan 48.9/1, Philharmonic Society, MS Account Book, 1813–1866, cross-referenced against RSM, *List of Members*; BL Add. MS 29.365, MS Memorandum of Agreements between the proprietors of the Theatre Royal, Covent Garden, and various musicians, Sept. 1818–Sept. 1820, Cross-referenced, ditto.

[81] Particularly the Members' Files. From these, Rohr, 'Profession of Artisans', has drawn many of her conclusions about the failure of musicians up to the middle of the nineteenth century to achieve, as a group, middle-class economic status.

[82] See Drummond, 'The Royal Society of Musicians in the Eighteenth Century'; also L. G. D. Sanders, 'The Festival of the Sons of the Clergy 1655–1955', *Musical Times*, xcvii (1956), 133–5; SEC makes an oblique reference to this event when she says in SEC–WJC, 10 June 1828, p. 4, 'I have contriv'd to exonerate you from the performance at St Pauls'.

Christmas gratuity.[83] The exclusivity of the Society was closely guarded, making membership desirable, it would seem, quite apart from any potential financial benefits. She writes to Castell in 1831: 'W^m's introduction to the Society is too precarious for <u>hope</u> none but a favor'd few can hope to gain admittance . . . and our recent circumstances are doubtless unfavourable to his reception.'[84] Augustine was also to become a member, and it is telling that it was not until 1841 that the family stopped paying Castell's annual subscription, ignorant of the fact that he had been dead for more than two years.[85]

On the basis of Castell's engagement at the Surrey, and discounting the two deputy's jobs, which, as we shall see, would probably not have brought in much money, and assuming at that time that he had no pupils, he was probably earning in 1814 rather less than the £200 that Rohr reckoned was a minimum income for a successful and respectable professional man.[86] In 1818, Covent Garden pay for a rank-and-file cellist was around 5s. 10d. a night, or £58 for a season of 200 nights.[87] Charles Wodarch at Covent Garden was paid 10s. 6d. a night, or £105 for 200 nights. It is unlikely that Castell at the Surrey would have been earning as much as the first-chair cellist at Covent Garden.

But it is impossible to gauge his income accurately. John Mackintosh, his next-door neighbour, earned £140 a year as first bassoon at Covent Garden. He was also a member of the Philharmonic Society, and in 1819, for example, was paid £28. 7s. 0d. for eight concerts and eight to ten rehearsals.[88] Not a lot. That was supposed to be a labour of love and supposedly of high prestige value. But he almost certainly performed at private concerts, where he may not have earned the £8 a night Sir George Smart procured for Lindley and Dragonetti, but would hardly have accepted less than £5 since he was a highly regarded musician.[89]

Castell was not a member of the Philharmonic Society, but in a climate

---

[83] SEC–WJC, 20 Oct. 1827, pp. 2–3; 31 Oct. 1827, pp. 4–5; 10 June 1828, pp. 3–4; Dec. 1830, pp. 3–4.

[84] Ibid. 3 Feb. 1831, p. 2.

[85] RSM, MS Members' Files, Correspondence, Augustine Humble to the Society's Collector, John Watts, 20 May 1841.

[86] Rohr, 'Profession of Artisans', 332.

[87] MS Memorandum of Agreements, Covent Garden; Rohr, 'Profession of Artisans', Table 7.3, p. 261.

[88] As per, MS Memorandum of Agreements, Covent Garden, and Philharmonic Society, Account Book, 1813–1866.

[89] Ehrlich, *Music Profession in Britain*, 41.

of growing social demand for music there should have been opportunities in the next level down for a competent musician to enhance his income. And he may have had other professional or social connections which helped him do just that. On the face of it, though, apart from the Surrey, there were just his two church engagements—both of which were deputyships to Charles Lockhart, the blind organist and composer, who had once lived next door at 20 Stangate Street.[90]

In 1813, Lockhart had been the incumbent at St Catherine Cree for forty-seven years, on account of which he was granted a gratuity of £15 on top of his normal annual salary of £35.[91] It may have been at this stage that Castell was engaged as deputy, possibly taking the extra £15 as his salary. As we know, church organists commonly held plural appointments, requiring the engagement of a deputy. Arrangements seem to have been conducted on a purely individual basis, with the official organist, who was himself paid the full fee by the parish, deciding what to pay his deputy. The parishes themselves did not usually object, arguably because it saved them having to pay an organist a living wage— what the deputy was paid was no official concern of theirs. The parish records of St Catherine Cree indicate that the pew-opener and organ-blower Mrs Mary Richardson was paid £15 a year, but there is no record of any payment to a deputy organist.[92] Neither did it follow that upon the death of the incumbent the post automatically went to the deputy. On Lockhart's death in 1815, a Mr John Cash was elected without too much fuss on a salary of £40 a year.[93]

Presumably this was a disappointment for Castell, since it prevented him from himself appointing a deputy on a 'beggarly stipend' and making himself available elsewhere. Neither was he any more fortunate at St Mary's, Lambeth, where the post went to William Henry Warren.[94] This was even more galling because Warren was paid £89. 5s. 0d. a year, which was £43. 12s. 0d. more than old Lockhart had been paid at the time of his death.[95] St Mary's, Lambeth, was rather more prestigious

[90] He was living there in 1794 according to [J. Doane], *A Musical Directory for the Year 1794*. He was then listed as 'Composer, Organ, Tenor, Orgst Lambeth & St Catherine Cree Church & Lock & Orange St Chapels'.
[91] GL MS 1196/2, Records of St Catherine Cree Church, Leadenhall Street, MS Vestry Minutes, 20 Apr., 1813; GL MS 1198/4, Churchwarden's Accounts, 4 Oct. 1814.
[92] Ibid. Churchwarden's Accounts, 8 Feb. 1815, for Mrs Richardson.
[93] Ibid. Vestry Minutes, 8 Feb. 1815.
[94] Probably the Member of RSM from 1777, died 1839. RSM, *List of Members*, 151.
[95] LAD, Brixton, Records of St Mary's Church, Lambeth, MS Churchwarden's Accounts, 1802–20, 30 May 1815.

than St Catherine Cree. It was an important parochial church and, perhaps because it was hard by Lambeth Palace, much given to raising the flag and bell-ringing.

The Vestry of St Mary's was, of course, the centre of local government. In the 1820s its hegemony was broken up, but before that time it was a powerful parish, getting up petitions in 1813–14 against both the Property Tax and the Corn Bill at a combined cost to the ratepayers of £125. 1s. 1d. It was altogether a more desirable engagement than the historically interesting but tiny St Catherine Cree, where in all probability Castell had performed most Sundays for Lockhart.[96] There is no evidence of course that he even applied for either post, but he probably did. As we shall see, Castell had not given up the idea of a London church appointment as late as 1825.

The position of church organist still carried with it status in the musical and social world. For reasons peculiar to England, and in spite of itself, the Church and its music kept alive in the breast of the English musician the dream of social acceptability through music, still denied in every other sphere of his activity. It was also a useful lever in the never-ending competition for pupils. The position of deputy, although not well paid, was thus seen, rightly or wrongly, as a step in the right direction, even if the trend was in fact away from the appointment of professionals. Evangelical pressure was inhibiting virtuosic display and placing more emphasis upon personal respectability than upon musical excellence in the appointment of church organists.[97] Either or both of these factors may have played a role in denying Castell career opportunities, at least in London, in the more prestigious field of the Church.

The theatre, as already suggested, was not an ideal route to social success for the rank-and-file musician. Nor, from an economic point of view, was it very secure. In July 1814 Elliston relinquished the Surrey to Dunn, Heywood & Branscombe for the duration of his lease, and it became once more a venue for equestrian display and other forms of athletic

---

[96] Ibid. for St Mary's Property Tax and Corn Bill. The building is today used as a garden museum. For St Catherine Cree see Joseph Miles, *Brief Notes on St Katherine Cree Church* ([London], 1913, reprint published by and currently available from the church). The present building, one of the six which survived the Fire of London, was dedicated by William Laud, then Bishop of London, 16 Jan. 1630, in a service which was used in evidence against him at his trial. The organ, dating from 1686 and built by Father Smith (Mr Bernard Schmidt), was played by Henry Purcell, who declared it to be a good instrument.

[97] Minimus [Edward Hodges], 'On Church Music', 39; also A Lover of the Organ, 'Organists, voluntaries and psalm-tune singing', *QMMR* vii (1825), 16.

spectacle,[98] and Castell probably found himself out of a job. But in 1815 he was almost certainly engaged at the 'Little Theatre' in the Haymarket as a double-bass player on £1. 16s. 0d. a week.[99] The Theatre Royal, Haymarket, usually ran in the summer months when the majors were closed and was at that time under the successful management of George Colman the younger.

At 6s. a night at the Haymarket, Castell, whose third child, Emily Angelina Jones, was born in August of that year, could hardly have been unaware that he was professionally obscure. The 18-year-old Nicholas Mori was at that time leader of the ballet orchestra at the King's Theatre. But Castell's career, although largely invisible to us now, was possibly viable enough, and he may already have been developing it along the pluralist lines which Mori himself would also embrace with his marriage to the widow of the musician and music-publisher Louis Lavenu. In 1815 he had the use of the income from his grandfather's estate until his brother Peter came of age, which may have led him into business pursuits of some kind. And in spite of Susannah's claim in 1830 that he was only then 'just entering into the theatre of life' and that hitherto his experience 'was very limited your knowledge of the world confined to crotchets and quavers',[100] almost certainly after 1820, as we shall see, he dabbled in some form of financial speculation.

Peter returned safely from his tour of duty on board the *Diomede*, but went to sea again in 1817 as fourth mate on board the East India Company's ship the *Herefordshire*, suggesting family access to some form of patronage.[101] He produced a daughter in 1819,[102] and must have come to some agreement over the estate with his elder brother.

---

[98] Brayley, *Historical and Descriptive Accounts of the Theatres of London*, 74.

[99] *Biog. Dict. Actors, Actresses. etc.* In an entry for Thomas Costellow, the compilers have mentioned a Mr Castello who played the double-bass at the Haymarket in 1815, suggesting that it may have been Costellow. But this seems unlikely since Costellow was active in an earlier period and was known as a singer rather than as a db player. And WJC himself mentions that he was once a db player at the Haymarket, WJC–SEC, 30 Jan. 1828, p. 5. Without knowing the *Biog. Dict.*'s sources for this, it is possible to surmise that the 'o' on the end of 'Castello' was merely the end-flourish to Castell's signature already mentioned.

[100] SEC–WJC, 26 Jan. 1830, p. 3.

[101] Charles Hardy, *A Register of Ships employed in the Service of the Hon. the United East India Company from the year 1760 to the conclusion of the commercial Charter* (1835), Season 1816–17, *Herefordshire*. 1200 tons. 2 voyages—Madras, Penang and China ... 4th mate, Peter Castell. Sailed Portsmouth, 14 Mar. 1817. Moorings, 4 June 1818; BL India Library, East India Records, MS Log of the *Herefordshire* for that period lists Mr P. Castell as 4th mate and awards him the prescribed Certificate of Good Conduct.

[102] GLRO Parish Records of St Mary's Church, Lambeth, Baptisms, 12 Mar. 1819. Rosa Sophia Jones Castell, daughter of Peter and Sophia Castell.

Presumably on the value of the lease of Stangate Street, it was valued by the Stamp Duty Office at £1,315. 1s. 8d., to be split equally between the two grandsons.[103] Susannah always harboured distinctly unfriendly feelings towards Peter Castell, who appears in later life to have vanished without trace—having at the time of his daughter's marriage in 1849 slipped even beyond the recollection of his name, the space for it being left vacant. All that apparently could be salvaged from memory was that he had once been a 'Mate in the East India Company Service'.[104] Rumour had it in 1828 that he had married the 'widow of a diamond merchant', after which Susannah's wish never to see him again seems to have been gratified.[105] Perhaps she subconsciously resented the fact that he survived the *Diomede* to come home and claim his patrimony.

ST ALBANS

But in the year that Peter set off for the East again on board the *Herefordshire*, William also altered his mode of existence. By Christmas 1817 he was organist at St Peter's Church, St Albans, Hertfordshire.

Today very much within the northern London commuter belt, St Albans is still famous for its Roman ruins and its medieval abbey as well as for its pleasant, quasi-rural setting. In 1817, it was barely a half-day's journey by coach from London, and it is almost certain, in spite of the fact that he kept the Stangate Street lease, that Castell fully intended to make it his home. Although he was only paid £25 a year (£6. 5s. 0d. a quarter),[106] it was obviously his intention to use his position to build up a teaching practice among the townsfolk and outlying gentry.

Castell took over the post from Thomas Fowler, who had been paid up to the Sunday after midsummer of 1817, with an extra £3. 18s. 0d. for a voluntary, 'as per bill', in October.[107] It is possible that Castell may have performed his duties up till Christmas time gratis, perhaps having learned something from Continental musicians in London. The job entailed, as well as conducting the music of the Sunday services, teaching the boys (probably from the local charity school) to sing psalms. Unlike

---

[103] PRO I.R. 26/173, PCC Stamp Office. Stamp Duty, Estate of William Jones, 15 July 1811.

[104] GRO, Marriage, 1 Jan. 1849, Charles Henry Davis to Rosa Sophia Castell.

[105] SEC to WJC, 10 July 1828, p. 6.

[106] HRO, D/P 93, 5/4. Records of St Peter's Church, St Albans, MS Churchwarden's Accounts, 1787–1825, 1 Jan. 1817.

[107] Ibid. 11 Oct. 1817.

Fowler, he does not seem to have been required to write voluntaries—not at least any for which the Parish were prepared to pay him.

The family lived in a house just out of town in the New Road, near an inn, and perhaps next to the wheelwright, William Jones.[108] It was probably the house noted in the Rate Book for the first time in 1819 as occupied by Henry Castell (an error?) at a rateable value of £10.[109] In the early stages, Castell seems to have been quite successful. He was then, as Susannah later said, 'a man of property'.[110] His teaching clientele may not have been of the social calibre of a Sir George Smart, who indeed may have had a stake in the area,[111] but may have included some of those new-rich farmers of whom Cobbett so heartily disapproved, who took to drinking wine and having their daughters taught to play musical instruments.[112] It certainly did include tradespeople of the town like the coal-merchant James Nicholls and, somewhat further up the social scale, Isaac Piggot, attorney, coroner, chamberlain, and, in 1821, Town Clerk.[113] Initially, one of his clients (if not pupil) may also have been John Horner Rumball (1793–1879), land-surveyor and cartographer of St Albans, although it is more likely that this connection was made before Castell went to St Albans. Indeed, it may have been Rumball who was instrumental in organizing his entrée into the area.

Both the Rumball brothers, Horner and James, seem in fact to have been long-standing family acquaintances, perhaps through Susannah, since their mother, the formidable 'Mrs H.' of Susannah's letters, had been Marie Guinlie of Paris, the daughter of a medical officer in the French army.[114] 'Horner' Rumball, as Susannah called him, founded a

---

[108] SEC–WJC, 9 June 1829, p. 4. SEC mentions that she watched Betsy only twenty yards from home, soliciting a hostler from an inn opposite; the MS map of St Peter's Parish by T. Godman and J. H. Rumball (1826) shows William Jones at least owning property close by, and Pigot's *Directory* indicates that the wheelwright William Jones had his premises in the New Road. It is doubtful that they were related.

[109] HRO, D/P 93, 4/1. Records of St Peter's Church, St Albans, Church Rate, 1804–1819. Unfortunately the records between 1819 and 1828 are not extant, making it impossible to check for a later correction.

[110] SEC–WJC, May 1828, p. 4.

[111] Sir George Smart seems to have been among Castell's professional associates in St Albans. SEC refers to him in this light in SEC–WJC, 18 Oct. 1828, p. 9.

[112] Cobbett's *Register*, 18 June 1823, in William Smart, *Economic Annals of the Nineteenth Century, 1821–1830* (1917), 2.

[113] Nicholls is referred to in SEC–WJC, 31 July 1828, pp. 4–5; the Piggot in SEC–WJC, ibid. 3, is probably the Isaac Piggot in Pigot's *Directory* in which Nicholls also appears.

[114] Christine Shepperson, 'Out on Business', *St Albans Review*, 30 July 1987, p. 32. An article on J. H. Rumball as the founder of the St Albans firm Rumball Sedgwick, copy supplied by Rumball Sedgwick and other genealogical information by Christine Shepperson.

successful land-surveying firm which is still in existence today, and lived to become very much entrenched in the social and political establishment of St Albans. He was Mayor in 1840 and 1846,[115] and a person for whom Susannah expressed the deepest antipathy; although for his brother James, probably James Quilter Rumball, the surgeon and private lunatic asylum keeper, her feelings were quite different.[116]

But if the new life in St Albans held out professional promise for Castell, it presented its dangers as well. Whereas in London the social and domestic behaviour of a musician might, even in the new moral age, have escaped attention, in St Albans it was bound to be of greater interest. And it was.

Castell appears to have flung himself with much zest into the social life of the area and to have been the host of many dinners and parties from which, it would appear, Susannah had been excluded. Perhaps not surprisingly, then, she referred to his circle of friends there in rather unflattering terms as a public she 'detested', as 'Vanity Fair' and as 'unprincipled sycophants' who, while they had feasted at his table in the good times, when he crashed, she later claimed, had deemed him 'a most ridiculous man'.[117]

As we have seen, the 'chasm' between Castell and Susannah had already opened before they had left London, with Castell's behaviour before and after the birth of Alfred. Now, in rural St Albans, it widened even further due to his waywardness in the matter of a certain Miss Silvers—one of his pupils whose career he proceeded to foster with more zeal than propriety and whose 'sole happiness' became his chief preoccupation. Five shillings of her weekly earnings, he had said, would amply recompense him for his efforts and for the wreckage of his own financial prospects. Such was the 'visible attention paid to her apparent comforts', said Susannah, that the 'public' became indignant and complete strangers began to take sides, while at home she was 'cruelly and personally ill treated' and her family neglected.[118] Miss Silvers was obviously under some professional obligation to Castell by which he was entitled, as was usual in such circumstances, to a percentage of her earnings. But he was obviously not one of those who made the system of

[115] Ibid.

[116] The information on James Rumball was supplied by Brenda Harrison who is currently compiling a history of the Rumball family; SEC's comments on James are very warm and he was to remain a close confidant and adviser throughout the period of the correspondence.

[117] SEC–WJC, 4 June 1829, p. 5.

[118] Ibid. 2; May 1828, pp. 4–5.

articles or 'bonding' disreputable by minimum attention and maximum exploitation.[119] Like Dick Daly, his exploitation of Miss Silvers was of a kind which quite evidently transcended mere pecuniary considerations; but without, presumably, the overtones of ruthless coercion which had made Daly's name so infamous.

Then, with a Shelleyan abandon of all convention that would have made even Dick Daly gasp, and whose effect upon a rural society may well be imagined, he installed Miss Silvers in his house to become his wife's 'companion' and 'instructress' of his 'female children'—suggesting perhaps that Miss Silvers was no longer, for whatever the reason, in a position to earn for him even the five shillings a week that had previously so contented him. Susannah later recalled the response of outraged respectability; her own included.

I need not remind you of the commotion at St Albans caused by this imprudent connexion, your professional pursuits now began to flag, and those that were on the eve of making arrangements for your future attendance [presumably as music master] altogether declined. Upon one occasion, I remember your addressing me (for a few minutes only) but in a Strain very different to your usual 'costume' in which you imploringly wished me to copy a letter of yours as coming from myself. I then told you that in any other way you might command me but in such an affair I could not subscribe to my own dishonor, after that I was requested to copy a letter to Mrs Fitch [presumably a patron or client] in which it was intended I should say 'that all circumstances as concerned with Miss Silver's never cost me a sigh'. In this instance I could not comply, experience had taught me and my agonized feelings needed no prompter to return a negative reply . . . neither did the evil here rest—the servant 'Betsy' (to whom I also objected) and of notorious bad character was likewise to be introduced as my domestic.[120]

Nor was this all. Susannah speaks of what she calls 'a host of Menial houseless and unprincipled female dependents' in the house at St Albans, all conspiring to cause trouble between man and wife, among whom, presumably, was 'that strumpet Betsy' who was not embarrassed to be seen receiving her master's kisses in the presence of his children.[121] Betsy was to be a continuing source of domestic disquiet for some time. But it was the Miss Silvers affair which apparently continued to offend public morality, and Castell's failed attempt to head off scandal by requesting Susannah to provide a moral alibi was further undermined by her peremptory return to London, leaving him unchaperoned among his female 'dependents'; a situation which could hardly have helped to

[119] See *QMMR* iv (1822), 2 for abuses of the articling or bonding system.
[120] SEC–WJC, 27 Mar. 1829, p. 3.   [121] Ibid.

sanitize his position. It would seem that Castell was one musician who did not subscribe to the newly established *Quarterly Musical Magazine and Review*, or to any of its tenets either.

In April 1820, the Castells' last child, Susan, was born[122] and it was some time not long after this event that this particular marital crisis seems to have occurred. Castell followed Susannah to London, stripped the house almost bare, and returned again to St Albans with all the children except the infant, Susan. Tempers were evidently frayed. Young Alfred had remonstrated with his father for leaving Susannah with 'nothing but odd teacups to use', to which his father had replied, 'D—— the B—— anything is good enough for her.'[123] The removal of the children back to St Albans may have served, or at least been an attempt, to justify the continued employment of his female 'dependents' and thus to prevent raising provincial eyebrows even further. The damage to his reputation had apparently already been great—but without Susannah's physical presence as security for his reputation he probably needed some semblance of domestic normality to prevent a total collapse of his social credibility.

Susannah later claimed that she had been instructed not to darken his doors at St Albans on pain of having the London house shut up for good.[124] But matters did not rest there. On receiving a letter from young William, then about 8, written in blacking and in utmost secrecy, complaining bitterly of neglect and horsewhipping, Susannah had descended on St Albans with all the righteousness of outraged motherhood. 'Such things by a <u>mother</u>', she said, 'could not be borne.'[125] Her reception had been cool, to say the least, but it seems that connubial relations were actually resumed and that some kind of domestic stability was regained. Perhaps Castell was actually relieved. Her presence perhaps would stop the neighbourhood tongues from clucking. If it did, her sudden departure six weeks later must have set them going again, terminally. This was a blow that Castell's fragile reputation apparently could not sustain. He called it 'premature' and the 'act of a MANIAC', and he declared that it had indeed been Susannah who had caused his ruin in St Albans.[126]

The reasons for this final departure are unclear. On the one hand, Susannah claimed that owing to the children's 'filthy regimen' at St Albans, she was unable to keep them in a proper state of care—'free of

---

[122] Date recorded, W Jones C–WJC, 13 May 1828.
[123] SEC–WJC, 4 June 1829, p. 5.   [124] Ibid. 8 Aug. 1829, p. 5.
[125] Ibid. 4 June 1829, p. 6.   [126] Ibid. 8 Aug. 1829, p. 5; 4 June 1829, p. 3.

disease' as she put it. They suffered from what seems to have been some kind of parasitic, scabies-like infestation, the successful combating of which the amenities at St Albans were apparently not equal to. From Susannah's account, Castell kept an alarmingly disorderly establishment. The house, she said, was the work 'Of a madman'. But there were evidently other problems as well. Susannah's status in the household probably remained questionable. Her relations with the housekeeper were obviously not happy. The woman had greeted her arrival with discourtesy and a threat of giving in her notice. And then there was Betsy, whose behaviour towards her had, with Castell's own tacit approval, continued to be offensive. Indeed she acted in collusion with Castell, according to Susannah, not only in performing as her 'guard' but in intercepting letters to her from Augustine, who at that time was still living in London in the Stangate Street house. Only Augustine's arrival at St Albans to enquire into the lack of communication had revealed the truth. So, she said, she had decided to flee 'a nest of hornets' and return, with all the children, to London.[127]

From this point to the culminating events of 1826, family fortunes followed a downward path. In the short term, it led to a violent nocturnal altercation at 19 Stangate Street and Castell's subsequent absence from home. In the long term it led to financial ruin.

When Susannah arrived in London, probably at the approach of winter in 1820, she found the house boarded up, with the despicable Peter Castell (who had played some kind of predictably treacherous role in relation to Augustine's departure) in sole possession. Relations between William and Augustine had been deteriorating, it would seem, for some time; and unbeknown to Susannah he, with his brother's connivance, had obviously effected his removal. Now with Susannah's return, Augustine was instrumental in assisting her to regain entry to the house. The scenes that followed were less than edifying and, we may imagine, contributed to the family's reputation in the neighbourhood as being 'famous in fight'.[128]

Castell, evidently in hot pursuit of Susannah, had gone to 'Prison Hall' (presumably the police office in Union Street) to get an order against Augustine but had failed, since, according to Susannah, the magistrates recognized his vindictive motives. Knowledge of the proceedings quickly

---

[127] Disease, SEC–WJC, 8 Aug. 1829, p. 6; house the work of a 'madman', ditto, p. 5; housekeeper's reception, ditto, p. 5; Betsy, 9 June 1829, p. 6; 'nest of Hornets', ditto, p. 5.
[128] SEC–WJC quoting WJC, 4 June 1829, pp. 3–4.

became public. Susannah, though, it seems, was only later informed of them by one McCalla (there was a cellist of that name performing at the Surrey Theatre in 1827), who declared himself to be 'disgusted'. At the time, however, Susannah was unaware of Castell's presence in London, and had requested Augustine (who had gone to work in the orchestra at Astley's for the evening) to return afterwards to sleep. In the meantime, Castell arrived in no good humour and took himself to bed—with young William. Faced with a dilemma in relation to Augustine, who at 1 a.m. had nowhere else to go, Susannah let him in by the parlour window and then tried to reorganize sleeping arrangements to accommodate him. Her strategy, not a good one as it turned out, involved moving young William and attempting to join Castell. It was this that precipitated the ultimate crisis. Castell 'violently spurned' her and eventually struck her several blows in the dark, by which, she said, her eye was blackened for nearly three weeks; 'and other injury's I receiv'd,' she went on, 'being thrown down stairs and for a few minutes after I had no recollection whatever. The first object that presented was the stars shining through the parlour window.' She did not see him again for many months, during which time he managed, she said, to throw away his fortune and reduce himself (at least relatively we must assume) to the level of a beggar.[129]

THE DESCENT

In 1820, the new king, George IV, was similarly troubled with domestic turmoil. His hated wife, Princess Caroline of Brunswick, having declined an offer of £50,000 a year to stay out of the country and forgo her right to the crown, had instead returned to stir up public emotion on her behalf and against the king. One imagines that Castell's sympathies, if he had had any to spare from his own woes, would have been firmly with his sovereign.

Other events of 1820 were equally disquieting. In February, the Cato Street conspiracy had created a convenient sensation for the government in what was an election year. Arthur Thistlewood and his Spencean confederates were discovered in the nick of time plotting to blow up the entire English Cabinet in retaliation for the deaths the previous year at 'Peterloo', caused when crowds being addressed by the radical orator Henry Hunt had been attacked by the local mounted yeomanry in a decidedly over-zealous defence of King and Country. The trial of the

---

[129] Peter Castell, ibid. 9 June 1829, p. 5; Prison Hall, 8 Aug. 1829, p. 2; McCalla, ibid., and GL, Surrey Theatre Playbill for *Der Freischutz*, 15 Dec. 1827; black eye and other injuries, SEC–WJC, 9 June 1829, pp. 6–7; beggary, 9 June 1829, p. 7.

conspirators and the hanging of five of them in May had transfixed public attention.

Another five were transported to New South Wales, where Governor Macquarie was creating official dissatisfaction by adopting a policy of positive discrimination towards convicts, thus threatening to damage the capacity of English courts to terrorize an increasingly dangerous population with the threat of transportation. Commissioner John Thomas Bigge on board the *John Barry* had already arrived in Sydney the previous September to conduct his investigation into the situation.[130]

If life seemed perilous and uncertain, it was no less so in the world of theatre and music. An unguarded word or two by Edmund Waters, the manager of the King's Theatre, to his banker had led to the seizure of the house and a financial crisis in August, which left the members of the orchestra without pay. Performances were cancelled amid much public displeasure and speculation.[131] At the Surrey, Thomas Dibdin had ruined himself with debts, it was said, of £37,000. And the newly rebuilt Argyll Rooms, a fashionable venue for music performances, financed in a speculative venture by prominent London musicians, proved an economic disaster; in connection with which, the new music publishing initiative under the patronage of the Prince Regent, the Regent's Harmonic Institution (a rare example of royal support for local music and musicians), created unwelcome, and, as it turned out, terminal public hostility with charges of 'monopoly'.[132]

---

[130] See John Ritchie, *Punishment and Profit* (1970), especially pp. 23–4 for Home Office attitudes to NSW. Three of the Cato Street conspirators who were transported nevertheless did reasonably well. Therry records that Strange, Wilson, and Harrison were given tickets of leave and by 1830 had become 'reformed and useful men'. Strange became the Chief Constable of the Bathurst area and the 'terror of bushrangers'. Wilson became a constable under Strange and Harrison, 'of feeble intellect', ended up Bathurst's principal baker. Therry, *Reminiscences of Thirty Years Residence in New South Wales and Victoria* (2nd edn., 1863), 96–8.

[131] William Charles Smith, *The Italian Opera and Contemporary Ballet in London 1789–1820* (1955), 163, also *London Magazine*, i (Sept. 1820), 326–7.

[132] Dibdin ref. in Brayley, *Historical and Descriptive Accounts of the Theatres of London*, 74; Argyll Rooms disaster probably being referred to obliquely in 'Sketch of the State of Music in London, April 1820', *QMMR* ii (1820), 375, describing the inevitability of the failure of musical speculation due to excessive competition of venue; see also *London Magazine*, i (Mar. 1820), 307, for Regent's Harmonic Institution prospectus, and Cruikshank's cartoon, 'The Regent's Harmonica or—Monopoly a catch for 21 voices with a Royal Base', Print Room BM, DG 13692, and annotation in M. D. George, *Catalogue of Political and Personal Satire in the Prints and Drawings Department of the British Museum* (London, 1954). Retrospectively the *Harmonicon* (vii, 1829, p. 217) recorded that of the 21 professors who had become involved in the speculation only two escaped without loss, with many losing approximately £1,700.

Castell's own financial disaster at this time is clouded in mystery. He had apparently divested himself of whatever property (other than the lease on Stangate Street) that he possessed and had had an auction of his effects at some stage at Holloway—an affair concerning which Susannah had later made the caustic remark that the only person to benefit had been Horner Rumball, who, she said, had 'partly furnished his house at the expense of your own'.[133] It is very possible that, thus armed with cash, he made an assault upon some speculative project which failed. It may have been what Susannah termed the 'Leicester Square Affair', which, she later claimed, had it not been for Augustine, would have led them all to the 'Great House' (i.e. the Poorhouse) in Lambeth.[134] But this may in fact have been a later speculative excursion, a form of activity towards which, in obvious desperation to achieve financial independence, he seems to have been inexorably drawn. Of that early period, Susannah only refers generally to 'ruinous sums of money' and 'unnecessary expenditure', which, she said, had brought on 'a long term of misery'.[135]

Nor did his eventual return to his family, as 'a begar', effect any change of attitude in him. He was unbowed and unrepentant, re-engaging 'that strumpet Betsy', whom he permitted to assume the airs of a mistress and to spy upon Susannah. With his usual peremptoriness and in response to Susannah's ultimatum that either Betsy went or she did, he had declared, 'Then it shall be you.'[136] He was evidently in no mood for conciliation.

At this time, though, Castell must still have had some connection with St Albans, since he sustained his position at St Peter's till 1823, as well as a number of pupils, from whom in 1826 Susannah was to be keen to exact outstanding fees. He may indeed have divided his time between London and St Albans, with perhaps James Nicholls, the coal-merchant, who later took over the St Peter's organist's job,[137] deputizing for him on Sundays.

In London, the Surrey had reopened in 1822 under the proprietorship of Williams of the Globe Tavern, Fleet Street, and in June a company was

[133] SEC–WJC, 31 July 1828, p. 4; May 1828, p. 5.
[134] Ibid. 10 Apr. 1829, p. 1.
[135] Ibid. 9 June 1829, p. 7.   [136] Ibid. 8.
[137] St Peter's Church, St Albans, MS Churchwarden's Accounts. From 27 Sept. 1820, Castell had been paid £7. 10s. 0d. a quarter, but the 22 Mar. 1823 entry dropped it to £5. 0s. 0d. An entry for 26 Apr. 1823, in paying the balance of £2. 10s. 0d., refers to him as the 'late organist'. James Nicholls first enters the records as organist when he was paid £15 for a half year on 4 Nov. 1823. He also supplied the church with coals.

performing the *Fortunes of Nigel* with an overture and music by Mr Erskine and songs sung by Mr Phillips.[138] It is very possible that Castell procured an engagement in the orchestra. He was probably also struggling to gain pupils, and although Susannah complained of his wild and impracticable schemes, which she admitted she could not support,[139] he was probably dogged enough in pursuit of employment within his purely professional sphere. In December 1825, he applied for the organist's position at St Stephen Walbrook in the City—the parish church of the Lord Mayor of London just behind Mansion House. An attractive Wren-designed church, its Vestry thought it an important enough position to advertise publicly in three morning papers for applicants to submit to the 'ordeal of a competition', the judges of which were to remain undisclosed, presumably for fear of unwelcome pressure or in anticipation of accusations of corruption.[140]

There were twenty-five applicants for this position, including four women and one 15-year-old youth, from which eleven were selected on the basis of their testimonials to take part in the competition. Castell was not one of them, and it would probably have been of no consolation had he known that neither was the 15-year-old Samuel Sebastian Wesley. But on 14 December, in the presence of the inhabitants of the parish and the judge, the Revd W. Latrobe,[141] the competition took place, the choice falling to three contenders, Eliza Kingston Probyn, John Emmett, and Edward Sturgess, who had yet to undergo a final election by the 'inhabitants'. The eventual victor was the 45-year-old Miss Probyn with 45 votes out of a possible 56. Thus duly elected, Miss Probyn was (officially at least) obliged to forgo the services of all deputies unless prevented by illness, or unless leave was granted by the churchwarden— an obvious if unsuccessful attempt to cut across traditional professional practice. The appointment of a woman organist was still relatively rare and it is very possible, in spite of the 'public' nature of the competition, that the church authorities, in line with the trend, were opting for conformity and respectability rather than professional skill; although it

---

[138] Brayley, *Historical and Descriptive Accounts of the Theatres of London*, 74; BL Playbills 311–13, Playbill for Surrey Theatre, 28 June 1822.

[139] SEC–WJC, 31 Oct. 1827, p. 3.

[140] GL MS 595/4, Records of St Stephen Walbrook Church, London, MS Vestry Minutes 1775–1843. 16 Nov. 1825.

[141] It is possible that the Revd W. Latrobe may have been related to Christian Ignatius Latrobe (1758–1836), superintendent of the Moravian Brethren in London and composer, who vied with Novello in presenting Continental models of ecclesiastical music to the London *cognoscenti*. At least two of his sons took orders in the Church of England, John Antes Latrobe (1799–1878), and Peter Latrobe. See *Grove*.

should be said of Miss Probyn (later Mrs George Cooper) that she was no amateur, having already been appointed organist at St Bartholomew the Less, in May, on a salary of £25 a year, a position she held until 1863.[142] For Castell in any case, the Church in London still excluded him from a career choice which he evidently desired.

The preceding couple of years had seen boom conditions in the national economy. Many hundreds of joint-stock companies had been formed to soak up what was an embarrassment of riches—with the promise of even greater wealth. Esoteric prospectuses, like the one which promised to drain the Red Sea to recover the treasures of the Egyptians lost in the biblical story, blossomed alongside the more banal, and by April 1824 Parliament had handled some 250 private Bills for Companies requiring special help from Government to realize their potential. One of these was the Australian Agricultural Company, which requested and obtained a million acres in New South Wales for the purpose of 'improving the growth of wool'. On many of these companies, a 5 per cent part payment could yield an eight fold return almost immediately. Speculation quickly became a national pastime among those with any capital at their disposal. Intelligent discrimination went by the board in the rush to be part of the gamble, and men and women of all the middling conditions 'hastened', as the *Annual Register* for 1824 commented, 'to venture some portion of their property in schemes of which scarcely anything was known, except name'.[143]

Could Castell have resisted such temptation? Events would suggest not. In the inevitable crash that followed in December 1825, numerous country banks failed: London bankers stopped payments and panic spread quickly, causing a knock-on effect in every form of commercial enterprise. As a result, quite legitimate firms failed and depression set in in many manufacturing districts. And although the panic was virtually over by February 1826, the collapse left in its wake a record number of bankruptcies and widespread distress.[144] In March 1826 Castell was in prison—presumably for debt. It is possible that he had borrowed in order to make part payment on shares and then with the crash been unable to realize a profit with which to repay the loan.

[142] See Donovan Dawe, *Organists of the City of London 1666–1850* (1983), 34; ibid. 135.
[143] Smart, *Economic Annals*, 186–90; *Annual Register for 1824*, 3; ibid.
[144] William Hone, *The Everyday Book and Table Book*, ii (1831), 27–8; Smart, *Economic Annals*, 324.

For some, such a situation may have been the end of the road. Incarceration for debt was all too common, and for many rehabilitation was impossible. But Castell was lucky—he was to be spared for one more spin of the wheel of fortune. For reasons unknown he seems to have been able to make some kind of deal with Raper, his creditor, and was released. Susannah understood that the debt had somehow been cleared. But this, as it turned out, was not the case.[145] Almost immediately, though, he must have begun preparations for his last desperate gamble.

Back in Stangate Street, things stumbled on. Susannah had at last got rid of the pernicious Betsy, but only because Betsy declared that the work of the household was too much and because Castell 'persuaded' Susannah, against all her principles to give the girl a 'character'. Susannah was convinced that Betsy was in fact a prostitute, but even so passed her on to Mr Bennett's school nearby at Carlisle House, where she was sure she would act more as a 'decoy' than as a servant. But Betsy's departure did not bring a return to the connubial bliss that Susannah had hoped for. On the contrary, Castell was even more secretive, cold, and provocative, made frequent allusions to her already being a 'widow', and was much absent from home. Her life was rendered burdensome, and her only remedy, she said, was to close her heart 'against all future invasions'. Such was the situation when the final blow fell.[146]

It seems fairly certain that at this time Castell was working at the Surrey Theatre. Susannah obliquely confirms that this was so.[147] Roger Therry says he was leader of the orchestra of a theatre on the 'Surrey side' of London—presumably the Surrey—just prior to his departure.[148] But there is no reason to believe that he held such a post. Playbills for June 1826 show that the leader of the Surrey band was Mr Erskine, the musical director J. Whitaker, and the leader of the choruses Mrs Aris. Castell may have been the first double-bass or cello.[149]

Since Easter 1825, the Surrey, now named the 'New Surrey', had been managed by Charles Dibdin the younger (1768–1833). It featured many of Dibdin's own 'operas' composed by his director of music and friend John Whitaker (?1776–1847)—twenty-one of which were performed in the first twenty-eight weeks, 'chiefly three Acts each, eight of which were

145 SEC–Raper & Jones, 27 Mar. 1827.
146 SEC–WJC, 8 Aug. 1829, pp. 3–4; 9 June 1829, pp. 8–9.
147 Ibid. 25 June 1828, p. 1.
148 Therry, *Reminiscences*, 114.
149 BL Playbills, Surrey Theatre Playbill, 5 June 1826. In 1839 S. C. Walton suggested that he may have been with the Sadler's Wells orchestra (SCNSW/PD 968/1: Walton to Manning, 30 Jan. 1839), but I have been unable to substantiate this.

grounded in French plots and the remainder British manufacture'.[150] The great single attraction, however, was the nightly appearance of Monsieur Gouffe, the 'man-ape', who stunned audiences by his startling prehensile and gymnastic feats.[151]

A fairly typical evening at the Surrey would have followed much the pattern of that of 5 June 1826. It began with a 'popular new melodrama', written by C. Dibdin with the vocal and action music by Mr Whitaker, called *The Terrible Peak, or a Mother's Sorrows*, during which Mr Beckwith introduced a ballad written by himself and composed by Mr Nathan. Also included in the piece were 'several Grand and terrific Combats'. This was followed by a favourite Musical Extravaganza written by Mr Dibdin called *A Cheap Bargain*; and the night's entertainment concluded with a 'Pantomimic Ballet of Action', produced by Mr C. Dibdin, called, *The Isolate & the Ape, or, the Pirate of the Straits*, the ape being played by Monsieur Gouffe, who, in the course of the piece, exhibited his 'unparalleled Gymnastic performances' and concluded 'by running round the front of the Gallery sustained only by the thread-like mouldings'.[152]

To this might be added several ballets, a 'Grand Pas de Quatre' or an 'Indian Pas de trois' composed (i.e. choreographed) by Mrs Searle and performed by her troupe of twenty juvenile performers (the same immortalized in Thackeray's *Pendennis* by Fanny Bolton's mother, who had once been the 'thirteenth of Mrs Searle's forty pupils').[153] The band, 'sufficiently effective in Talent', said Dibdin, 'for either of the principal theatres',[154] worked very hard indeed. Performances began at 6.30 p.m. and frequently did not end till one in the morning.

Castell was no longer a young man. At 37 the idea of continuing in such employment must have palled. He had pupils certainly and perhaps other business interests—but also debts, a growing family, and an

---

[150] Charles Dibdin, *Professional and Literary Memoirs of Charles Dibdin the Younger* (1956), 148.

[151] Monsieur Gouffe, real name variously thought to have been Gaff, Vale, Sam Todd, and—according to his employer, Charles Dibdin—John Hornshaw, was a continuing phenomenon in theatrical circles as the 'man-monkey'. Almost illiterate, he apparently possessed an ape-like physiognomy as well as acrobatic skills. He made his début in America in Boston, 29 Nov. 1831. Refs. in Dibdin, *Professional and Literary Memoirs*; Frost, *Old Showmen*; W. J. Lawrence, Miscellaneous Papers, i. 24–5, collected various newspaper snippets on him. He was supposed, after having made a fortune, to have ended his life in the workhouse.

[152] Surrey Theatre Playbill, 5 June 1826.

[153] W. M. Thackeray, *Pendennis* (1849), ii. 34.

[154] Dibdin, *Professional and Literary Memoirs*, 150.

NEW SURREY THEATRE.

Acting-Manager, Mr. C. DIBDIN.　　　　　Stage-Manager, Mr. GALLOTT.

New Musical Extravaganza;—New Ballet;—The Jew of Wilna at Half-Price.

Composer and Leader of the Band, Mr. ERSKINE.　　　　Ballet Master, Mr. RIDGWAY.

Monday, September 12th, 1825, and During the Week,

First Time, a New Musical Extravaganza, in Two Acts, *(written by Mr. C. Dibdin,)* Called,

THE OLD BEAR;

Or, BOUND OVER TO THE PEACE.

The Overture and Music, *excepting the Pieces specified, by* Mr. ERSKINE.—The Scenery by Mr. TOMKINS and Mr. MAXWELL.
Principal Characters, Music Brigade, *a testy old Officer,* Mr. T. B. CLIFFORD.
Young Brigade, his Son, Mr. J. JONES, *(from the English Opera House,)* his First Appearance here these Seven Years.
Bolstay, *a superannuated Boatswain, turned Farmer,* Mr. GALLOTT.　　　Platoon, *a superannuated Lieutenant, turned Farmer,* Mr. CLIFFORD.
Harry Habeas, a Lawyer's Clerk, Nephew to Bolstay, Mr. FITZWILLIAM.　　　Swearby Hang, a Village Publican, Mr. VALE.
Ned Grumer, *an Independent Booby,* Mr. HENNING.　　　Clerk, Servant to the Major, Mr. SMITH.　　　Crowdie, of the Village, Mr. LLOYD.
First Farmer, Mr. P. WHITE.　　　Second Ditto, Mr. SHAW.　　　Sa线, Footman to Mrs. Brigade, Mr. TURNER.
Countryman, Mr. COUGH.　　　Farmers, Countrymen, &c. &c.
Mrs. Brigade,　*(an Admiral's Widow, and Sister to the Major,)* FOR A FEW NIGHTS ONLY,　Mrs. KENNEDY,
From the Theatre Royal, Covent Garden.
Jessy Brigade, her Daughter, Madame SIMON.　　　Patty Platoon, *Daughter of the Lieutenant,* Miss TUNSTALL.
VOCAL MUSIC IN THE PIECE.
A BALLAD, (the Music composed by himself,) Mr. J. JONES.　　　A SEA SONG, (Music by Whitaker,) Mr. GALLOTT.
Introduced.—"MY BEAUTIFUL MAID," Braham, (from Mr. T. Dibdin's Opera, the Cabinet,) Mr. J. JONES.
"DOCTOR BROWN," (Music by Reeve, from Mr. C. Dibdin's Opera, the Farmer's Wife,) Mr. VALE.
DUET, "PRETTY MAID," (Hora,) Mr. J. JONES and Miss TUNSTALL.
Duet, "WHILE GREAT LORDS AND LADIES," (Haunted Tower,) Mr. FITZWILLIAM and Miss TUNSTALL.

After which, a New Ballet, composed by Mr. RIDGWAY, Called, The

OLD COMMODORE;

OR, CROSS PURPOSES.

With a New Overture and Music, by Mr. Erskine.
The Old Commodore, Mr. HENNING.　　　Doctor, Mr. RIDGWAY.　　　Chief, Mr. RIDGWAY.　　　Nomp, Mr. T. RIDGWAY.
Apothecary, Mr. BOULANGER.　　　Squire Stump, Mr. G. RIDGWAY.
Julia, *Daughter of the Commodore,* Miss SEARLE.　　　Her Confidante, Miss FAIRBROTHER.
In the Course of the Ballet, among other incidental Dances, are the following.
A New Scotch Pas de Deux, by Mons. Simon and Mrs. Searle, to the favorite Caledonian Melodies, *Charley is my Darling and the Soldier Laddie.*
The Music arranged by Music Simon.
A Highland Medley and Fling, by Mr. Ridgway and Mrs. Searle, the Music by Mr. Erskine.
A Scotch Strathspey and Reel, by Misses Ricky, Billing, Foster, and Phillips, (Pupils of Mrs. Searle.)
A Grotesque Melange, by Messrs. T. and G. Ridgway.　　　A Pas de Deux, by Misses Fairbrother and Rountree.
Grand Finale,—The LANCERS' QUADRILLE, by the Principals and the whole Corps de Ballet, including
Miss A. FAIRBROTHER, LANCASTER, MANNING, MERIT, &c.　　　Messrs. TURNER, GRIFFIN, COUGH, SHAW, &c.

MONSIEUR GOUFFE,

WHOSE EXTRAORDINARY PERFORMANCES IN THE

ISLAND APE

Will, in that Piece, renew his admirable Efforts which have excited such an unusual Sensation through every Circle;
Including his Extraordinary Leaps,—Features of Agility and Gymnastic Displays,
HORIZONTAL BALANCINGS,
Supporting a Boy on his Shoulders, never attempted by any Man but himself;
TO CONCLUDE WITH HIS
Running round the Fronts of the Boxes and Gallery, supported only by the Thread-like Mouldings.

The Entertainments to conclude with the popular Melo-Drama, (written by Mr. C. Dibdin,) Called, The

JEW OF WILNA;

Or, Bravery and Gratitude.

Laban, the Jew of Wilna, Mr. HUNTLEY.　　　Dupré, a French Colonel, Mr. MORTIMER.　　　Lancelot Bull, English Servant to Laban, Mr. VALE,
Who will introduce the Popular Song, (by Mr. C. Dibdin, the Music by Mr. Whitaker,) called, "THE OLD BACHELOR."
Teddy O'Monaghan, Irish Servant to the Jew, Mr. BRYANT.　　　French Soldier, Miss LLOYD & TURNER.　　　Bandits, Mess. HENNING & COUGH.
Rachael, the Jew's Daughter, Miss LOUIS.　　　Katherine, a Russian Girl, Rachael's Maid, Madame SIMON.
Soldiers and Bandits, Messrs. SHAW, GRIFFIN, &c. &c. &c.
The Scenery (New) by Mr. Tomkins.
Will exhibit Interiors of the Jew's House,—his Garden,—and an adjoining Wild, by Moonlight.
The Chorusses got up by Mrs. Aris.　　　The Dresses by Mr. Lyons & Miss Freelove.　　　The Decorations by Mr. Maxwell.　　　The Machinery by Mr. Keys.

MR. ROWBOTHAM IS ENGAGED, AND WILL SHORTLY APPEAR.

Boxes 4s. Pit 2s. Gal. 1s.　　　Doors open at Half-past 5, and begin at Half-past Six.　　　Second Price at Half-past 8.
Places and Private Boxes (which have been splendidly decorated and newly furnished) may be engaged by the Night or Season, on Application to
Mr. PARKER, Box Book-keeper, at the Box Office, from 11 till 4; or of Mr. SAMS, Royal Library, St. James's Street.
Free Admissions for the Season, transferable, or not transferable, may be purchased by Application to Mr. G. Lewis, Treasurer, at the Treasury of the Theatre.
The Public are most respectfully informed, that Mr. Marsh's Coach calls Every Evening at Hoseman's Coffee House, to convey
Passengers to Deptford and Greenwich.　　　[T. Romney, Printer, Lambeth.]

12. Playbill, New Surrey Theatre, 12 Sept. 1825. Ref. LAD. 3/951.

unsatisfactory marriage. Perhaps all of this, plus his experiences in prison, may have unbalanced him—or brought out in him a recklessness and an instability that had always been there. His friends would later say, 'The man was mad', and perhaps in a way he was. But in his madness he did at least find a resolution of sorts.

On 10 June 1826, an advertisement appeared in *The Times* announcing that Master Castell's concert, 'this season', would take place in the Great Room at the Horns Tavern, Kennington, on Friday, 16 June. Heading the bill was Mme Caradori Allen of the Italian Opera—quite a coup. Miss Love was also to appear, as well as the two Miss Cawses—and the declining but still much admired Mrs Bland. Signori Curioni and Pellegrini of the Italian Opera headed the male singing list, which also boasted Mr C. Bland, son of the 'sweet melodist' herself, and Henry Phillips, one of the most promising English baritones of the day and, if we recall, late of the Surrey Theatre's 1822 *Fortunes of Nigel*. The band was to be led by the prodigious Mr Mori and enhanced by the celebrated cellist Lindley, and the harpist Mr Chatterton of the Royal Academy of Music. The conductor was to be the much admired, if once chastized composer and professor of piano-forte, Pio Cianchettini. The star, however, was to be the 14-year-old William Jones Castell, son of William Castell the elder. Tickets were to be had of Master Castell at No. 19 Stangate Street, Lambeth, and all the principal music shops.[155]

There is a temptation to dismiss the whole affair as a fantasy or at least as a con. It does not seem believable that singers of the calibre and public esteem of Caradori Allen (1800–65), on £500 a season at the King's Theatre, or Alberico Curioni (1785–1875), on £800,[156] would have bothered to perform on a Friday night at Kennington on behalf of an unknown child. Or that Mori, then principal violinist at Covent Garden and prominent member of the Philharmonic Society, would likewise condescend, let alone the almost legendary Robert Lindley (1776–1855) of the King's Theatre and Philharmonic Society. Scepticism is reinforced by the knowledge that Curioni and Pellegrini both appeared on the same night, 16 June, at a benefit concert at Covent Garden supported by the full strength of the Italian Opera Company.[157] But of course, as we already know, artists did indulge in multiple engagements. And is such scepticism justified?

[155] *The Times*, 10 June 1826, p. 1b.
[156] 'Kings Theatre', *QMMR* vi (1824), 521.
[157] *The Times*, 17 June 1826, p. 3.

THE "HORNS" TAVERN, KENNINGTON, IN 1820.

13. Originally published in E. Walford, *Old and New London. A Narrative of its History, its People, and its Places* . . .

Castell was certainly not one of London's leading musicians—certainly not in any public sense—and yet it is impossible for us now to judge what may have been his credentials among those who were. Among the performers at the concert, only one, John Balsir Chatterton (1805–71), can be established through the documents we have as a close friend of Castell's,[158] yet it is entirely possible that his social and professional contacts were widespread. Through his mother and his grandfather, and even perhaps through Susannah's connections through Maximilian Humble, he had several generations of musical association to draw upon in what is known to have been a very closed and intimate professional community, especially close perhaps among those who, like himself, were first- or second-generation children of Continental forebears. He may have enjoyed a rather higher standing in that community than our limited knowledge of him suggests. A Jewess, Mrs Bland herself had been born Maria Theresa Romanzini and had, after all,

---

[158] SEC–WJC, 31 Feb. 1828, p. 2; ibid. 25 June 1829, p. 7. Probably also WJC's 'Hampshire friend', of 8 Aug. 1829, p. 10 and 20 Oct. 1829, p. 5.

as we have already seen, appeared way back in 1784 on the Irish stage on the same bill with Monsieur Castelli and the 'CELEBRATED DOGS FROM PARIS'. And the strong contingent from the Italian Opera may have been due to the fact that Signora Castelli was among the performers there in 1824, 1825, and subsequently in the 1830s.

In any case, the concert certainly did take place. Susannah tells us that it was Dean, the second-hand music dealer near Waterloo Bridge who moved the piano from Stangate Street to the Horns Tavern for the occasion.[159] And there is no question about its ultimate failure, which hurried him to the extremes, Castell later said, 'of blowing my brain to atoms—or leaving the country, or being confin'd some months in prison—by which I would lose all my employments'.[160] He was left owing over £300.[161]

It would have been little satisfaction to him to know that the benefit at Covent Garden on the same night at which Curioni and Pellegrini had appeared had also been a signal failure; 'Lenten encouragement to the management of theatres in general', lamented *The Times*.[162] The unfortunate fact was that times were very bad for public entertainments of all kinds. The aristocracy and the wealthy, as already noted, had virtually withdrawn into their own exclusive realm, and what activity remained was unpredictable. Not even Weber had made out of the fabled wealth of London anything like the amount he had anticipated. His opera *Oberon*, written expressly for Covent Garden, was hailed as a triumph but failed in raw box-office appeal.[163] His benefit concert in the Argyll Rooms on 26 May 1826 netted £96. 11s. 0d., while on the same night the private concert of Signor Begrez at the home of the Duke of St Albans made 400 guineas.[164]

Weber's death on 5 June and burial on the 21st probably cast a further pall. The benefit for his widow at Covent Garden, on which account, in respect for the great German master, Drury Lane closed its doors, raised barely enough to cover expenses.[165] Would such unhappy facts have lightened the burden of gloom for the desperate entrepreneur of the Kennington Concert Rooms? No more, one imagines, than the less

---

[159] SEC–WJC, 16 May 1832, p. 2.
[160] Quoted by SEC in SEC–WJC, 14 Jan. 1828, p. 3.
[161] SEC–WJC, 18 Oct. 1828, p. 7.
[162] *The Times*, 17 June 1826, p. 3.
[163] George Hogarth, *Memoirs of the Musical Drama* (1838), ii. 455.
[164] Cox, *Leaves from the Journal of Sir George Smart*; Julius Benedict, *Weber* (1881), both in *Weber in London* (1976), 35.
[165] Hogarth, *Memoirs of the Musical Drama*, 455.

unhappy fact, if he had known it, that in Sydney, on 7 June 1826, the first of a series of eleven amateur concerts took place at the Freemason's Tavern which may be said to have established the European concert tradition in the Antipodes. Susannah claims the date of Castell's departure as 3 July—Monday;[166] Therry says it was a Sunday and that he took a passage in a *chasse marée* that sailed from Gravesend to St Malo. The previous night, Saturday, he had appeared at his usual place in the orchestra and was seen there as late as ten. Therry reconstructs the final scenes:

On that evening he wore a new hat, inside which his name and address were written in very legible letters. On his way home, Devenish [Therry's pseudonym for Cavendish, by which name he later knew him] had to pass over Waterloo Bridge. In passing over it, he threw his hat over the parapet of the bridge, in order that it might be supposed he had thrown himself over with it. The stratagem succeeded. The hat was picked up the next morning close to the bridge; the owner was nowhere to be found, the river ineffectually searched, and the supposition prevailed that he was drowned.[167]

We need not place too much faith in the details of Therry's exposition. He was reconstructing the scene from hearsay and gossip forty years after the event. One small detail is obviously an error. Castell could not have been coming home from any theatre on the 'Surrey side', over Waterloo Bridge, since Stangate Street was already on the 'Surrey side', and close by Westminster Bridge. More likely he was hurrying *from* home, perhaps on his way to the Golden Cross coaching-house in Charing Cross to catch some form of conveyance to Gravesend, or perhaps he was on his way to Beale's Wharf at Queenhithe. Nor did he go directly to St Malo. He went first to Portsmouth, to his friend Chatterton.[168] Certainly, though, some identifiable object was found, and it was presumably his hat.[169] Whether or not he actually intended the suicide hoax is another matter.

The summer of 1826 was a warm one. Perhaps burdened with his luggage and made careless by the heat, the hat was an inadvertent loss. Perhaps not. Perhaps in tossing it into the breeze over the parapet, he was making a spontaneous gesture of exorcism—casting off, as it were, his old world and his old self, and making, perhaps, a salute to the new.

[166] SEC–WJC, 31 July 1828, p. 5.
[167] Therry, *Reminiscences*, 114–15.
[168] SEC–WJC, 31 Feb. 1828, p. 2; ibid. 25 June 1829, p. 7.
[169] SEC–Watmore, 22 Nov. 1827, p. 1.

5

'A Nest of Butterfly's', 1827–1830

If that you deceive me in the present instance, depend that
you will never prosper.

SEC to WJC, 11 Apr. 1828

IN LIMBO: JULY 1826–AUGUST 1827

THE England that Castell had left was a nation committed, whether it
knew it or not, to industrial civilization. But the view of the future was
obscured by the great conflict of interests that accompanied the
fundamental communal changes that were taking place. In London, for
centuries in such a constant process of adaptation as to make change
itself look unchanging, the impact was not so noticeable—except
perhaps as it was filtered through and reflected in the arts and fashion. In
the soirées and the drawing-rooms, primitivism and the early Romantic
ideal survived only as a polite aesthetic. The *Irish Melodies* of Tom
Moore, and the discreet but sanitized passion for native airs, were among
the few vestigial remains. The three great spirits of English nineteenth-
century Romanticism, Keats, Shelley and Byron, were already dead. The
intellectual rebellion against industrialism and its values had been lost.
The nation's energies were now to be turned to containing the massive
economic, social, and political problems that industrialism had created
so far, and would continue to create throughout the century, and to
manufacturing a new culture based upon the work ethic, secular
individualism, and competition.

In the intervening historical moment, it would seem, from our
perspective, that the vacuum that was thus created by these great changes
was filled on the one hand by bourgeois materialism strained through the
sieve of conformist Evangelicalism, and on the other by working-class
radicalism, often enough strained through the sieve of Methodism. If the
mix was potentially volatile, its elements were nevertheless not always

entirely antithetical. But at the time this was not apparent, and for the next three decades England was to be, from time to time, a turbulent and frightening place. Susannah was left to confront it alone with her four children, the eldest of whom, in 1826, was 14 and the youngest, 6.

With her deep resentments and anxieties, her prideful social isolation, siege mentality, limited means, combative spirit, and powerful material ambitions, she was a sort of human sluice-gate, a narrow, rigid, yet living and feeling channel, through which the waters of the new order rushed. But she would have laughed to scorn any idea that the painful pressures she endured helped to turn the great cog of national ambition. As far as she was concerned she was merely a fractured atom, smashed and wasted, while all others, excepting her own children, simply profited by her unending sufferings.

Crisis conditions prevailed from the very start. In a state of frantic confusion she had ordered the river to be searched, and the drags were out. Augustine led the search since Susannah was not prepared to place her trust in outsiders, and especially not in the watermen whose only interest was in profit. As it was, it cost her a guinea a day and, unknown to herself, Augustine had offered a reward of £5 for the discovery of the body. Handbills were distributed and pasted—again, though, by the family only since Susannah would not 'Suffer One to escape [her]'. Understandably she was very distressed. Indeed, her mental state was such, she said, 'that no one ventured to approach her', adding in the next breath that she was dunned by creditors and the false reports of watermen who, for purely mercenary motives, daily lacerated her feelings.[1]

A professional associate, Tate ('that ill-principled fellow'), had meaningfully suggested to Susannah that Castell had received a large sum of money the night before his disappearance, but this she did not believe.[2] But it would seem that no one really believed that Castell had drowned except Susannah. Tate's insinuation was to be only the first. Certainly there was no sensitivity on the part of Castell's creditors. M. Cazzi's note was presented as the drags were out and as Susannah paced the floor wearing threadbare 'an entire new p^r of shoes which before night was worn into holes for I never ceased walking during the whole of that succeeding day'.[3]

---

[1] SEC–WJC, Dec. 1827, pp. 5–6.
[2] Ibid.   [3] Ibid. 10 Apr. 1829, p. 2.

Susannah's position was made even more precarious by her total ignorance of the extent of the debts and by fear of the powers that her husband's creditors might possibly exercise over her own security. Nor did the uncertainty surrounding his disappearance assist matters. Should the authorities declare him dead, she feared that she would lose all—bed and home. If alive, she feared that a number of creditors could jointly begin a bankruptcy proceeding which would produce the same result. She managed to prevent the former,[4] but was alarmed at the activities of Castell's erstwhile friend, Hatton.[5] She heard that his intentions were decidedly hostile and so removed all her best furniture and effects out of the house in order to forestall him, moving them back only when she perceived the storm had blown over—a dangerous and exhausting manoeuvre.[6] Indeed her position remained critical for some time. Her heart, she said, had 'Sunk from its socket', in contemplating her threatening difficulties. 'My brain at times <u>has turn'd</u>—in contemplating how I <u>could possibly</u> go on—and my Nights were spent in fev'rish dozings without the refreshment of rest. <u>You</u> had left <u>all</u> behind While I, (as a woman), had to contend with the most severe of trials—I heard that you had been seen at Portsmouth. <u>I believ'd it not</u>, I could not suppose that <u>you</u> were capable of such dissimulation . . .'[7]

On 10 July, at the Surrey, Dibdin, winding up his management, produced the second of his Hogarth 'operas', a piece called *The Rake's Progress*, which incorporated twenty vocal pieces and ran for many nights, 'to gratified audiences'.[8] Dibdin was a dab hand at extempore works and topical subjects, but perhaps he was too kind-hearted to make his audiences laugh at the expense of his 'drowned' double-bass player, the rake of Stangate Street.

It was about this time that a body was in fact found in the Thames and reported to Susannah, doubtless by the heartless watermen, as William's.

The Garden was <u>too small</u> to contain me—my screams were heard in the streets and the inhabitants were at their windows and doors to ascertain the cause— Augustine was Sent for from the theatre and James Rumball from his home who 'like a child' wept over me—<u>Those were feelings</u> that can <u>never</u> (under any circumstances) be felt more <u>than once</u> . . . <u>another such trial</u> would in all likelihood have <u>ended my sufferings</u>.[9]

    [4] SEC–WJC, Dec. 1827, pp. 9–10.
    [5] Probably Richard Hatton, the cellist. Member of the RSM and Philharmonic Society. Born 19 Apr. 1804.   [6] SEC–WJC, Dec. 1827, pp. 5–6.
    [7] Ibid.   [8] Dibdin, *Professional and Literary Memoirs*, 153.
    [9] SEC–WJC, Dec. 1827, p. 8.

As it turned out, the body belonged to a young man who had gone bathing the evening before.[10]

This melancholy incident had a shocking sequel, at least so far as Susannah was concerned. One Sunday in early August she had gone up to St Albans to attempt to recover some outstanding debts, presumably owed to William, and to consult with Horner Rumball on the subject. She arrived in the evening, having previously given notice of her intention to dine. It was church time and Horner was taking Communion at nearby St Peter's.[11] When he eventually returned, conversation turned to the recent discovery and Susannah was appalled to hear Horner, in the presence of his mother, the redoubtable Mrs H., suggest that Susannah should have claimed the body as her husband's in order the better to make claims on his 'friends'. She was, she said, speechless. 'Oh Horner what, take a false Oath?' his mother exclaimed, at which Horner simply made reference to the 'four children in the case'. The future Mayor of St Albans had, in Susannah's eyes, placed himself almost beyond redemption.

I cannot say whether or not I should have felt so <u>horror struck</u> at his remark, but what the more heighten'd it, he had but that instant return'd from the Communion table at St Peter's Church and the <u>flavor</u> of the sacramental wine must have been <u>fresh</u> on his palate. The setting aside religion, there was something so immoral and revolting in the Act—that my blood ran cold—and I considered his hypocracy of the vilest description—I never told his brother or <u>ever shall</u> and none but my own family, and yourself know of it (his mother excepted).[12]

The reasoning behind Horner's blasphemous suggestion seems rather fatuous, since Susannah probably had less to gain from William's debtor 'friends' in the event of his death, and perhaps even more to lose from his creditors. She had already perceived this when she acted to prevent the law administering as in the event of death. Indeed Susannah may have summed up the balance herself when faced with the macabre choice, and decided that the truth was her best option.

Dead or not, Castell had nevertheless plunged her into painful difficulties. Cut off from society by her sense of humiliation, her

[10] Ibid.

[11] Shepperson, 'Out on Business'. From her research into the firm of Rumball Sidgwick, Mrs Shepperson has identified the original office of J. Horner Rumball and the site of his house in the 1820s, both of which were close by the church of St Peter's in St Peter's Street, St Albans.

[12] SEC–WJC, 31 July 1828, pp. 2–3.

unwillingness to hear Castell's name disparaged, and by the suspicions of some that she was a knowing conspirator, she became, she says, 'an exile under my own roof'.[13] Even more disturbing, though, was the threat of destitution. To Castell's major creditors, Messrs Raper & Jones, she expressed her deepest anxieties: 'nothing short of the duty I owed my four dear little children could have possibly supported me under the heavy weight of my trials which have rapidly pressed upon me', pleading that if they pursued their claim it would 'end in my total ruin, and render our misery complete'.[14]

Less pressing but perhaps more embarrassing were her difficulties in relation to the local tax gatherers—Mr Steare, the poor's-rate collector, Mr Massy, the window-tax collector, and others, concerning whom she had written to the vestry clerk, Mr Watmore, requesting their names and addresses, as 'gentlemen who may have it in their power to relieve me from the payment on the enclosed demands which I am totally unable to meet'.[15] Parish records confirm that on 11 April 1827 a charge of non-payment of the Poor's Rate was heard at Vestry Hall against the householder 'William Castell', and again on 12 September. It was, however, declared to have been paid at the session of 22 December.[16]

At the time that Susannah was writing to Raper & Jones in March 1827, a report had prevailed that Castell was 'domesticated with a female companion' in the neighbourhood of Kennington, barely a mile or two away from Stangate Street. Susannah, as she had done Tate's story, refused to believe it.[17] But almost certainly by then she could no longer have sustained her belief that he was dead.

In August 1827, thirteen months after his disappearance, she received from him a long, apparently valedictory and not very gratifying poem accompanied by a short formal note,[18] neither of which revealed his whereabouts. Susannah replied in her letter of 24 August 1827, as

---

[13] SEC–WJC, 13 Jan. 1829, p. 5; 4 June 1829, p. 3; Dec. 1827, p. 10.

[14] SEC–Raper & Jones, 27 Mar. 1827.

[15] SEC mentions Mr Steare quite often in her correspondence in relation to money demands. Parish records identify him as Thomas Lamb Steare, collector of Poor's Rate. GLRO MRY/1. Records of St Mary's Church, Lambeth, MS Register of persons summoned for arrears of Poor Rate; Massey, SEC–WJC, 13 May 1830, p. 3; Watmore, LAD, Records of St Mary's Church, Lambeth, MS Churchwarden's Accounts 1819 ff.; SEC–Watmore, 22 Nov. 1827.

[16] GLRO MRY1/160, p. 85 ff. St Mary's Church, Lambeth, MS Marsh and Wall, 2nd Part. Register of persons summoned for arrears of Poor Rate . . . May 1824–May 1831.

[17] SEC–WJC, 20 Oct. 1827, p. 3.

[18] Ibid., Dec. 1827, p. 1.

requested, '(under cover) to Capt Cameron', but received no reply.[19] It would seem that he had regretted his lapse, for he contrived, although through what medium we do not know, to give Susannah the impression that he had 'gone to Rio'.[20]

CASTELL IN FRANCE, 1826–1829

The truth was that he had set himself up as a music master in St Servan in France and was rather precipitously, if perhaps predictably, involved in an *affaire de cœur* with one of his young pupils, a Miss Ellen Jones. It was these facts that were discovered by Nicholas Mori (or perhaps by his wife),[21] and brought back to London for the delectation of friends and foes alike. 'I frequently think', commented Susannah later, 'that had it not been for Mori's discovery I should never have heard from you.'[22]

The Moris, it would seem, had stirred up something of a storm for Castell in St Servan, which, just as a similar storm had once done in St Albans, threatened his professional credibility. A testament perhaps to the ease of communication within the musical community for which, it would seem, the English Channel presented no barrier. As in the case of Miss Silvers, Castell once again turned to Susannah for an alibi. It had been two months since he had sent her his poem. Now once more he broke his silence. His letter, when it came, 'bewilder'd' her imagination.[23] It unfolded that Ellen's father, Thomas Jones, was making life in St Servan very difficult for Castell on account of his having slighted his daughter's love (so he said), and he had written to Susannah requesting that she co-operate in defusing what had become an uncomfortable situation. Castell's request was that Susannah support him in his claim that he was not a married man, or at least should refrain from supplying any evidence that he was. This was certainly a new approach. In return, we may assume that Castell assured Susannah that his relationship with Miss Jones was entirely innocent. 'I hope and trust', she had said to him, 'that I may firmly rely on the <u>real</u> truth of your statement—as on the conviction of that, I continue to act.'[24]

But she was understandably cynical about his claim that Mr Jones was pursuing him for '<u>slighting his daughter's love</u>', and expressed a wish to see certain letters which had passed between himself and Miss Jones as

[19] Ibid. 20 Oct. 1827, p. 1.
[20] Ibid. 25 June 1829, p. 8.
[21] Ibid. 14 Feb. 1829, p. 3.
[22] Ibid. 10 July 1828, p. 2.
[23] Ibid. 31 Oct. 1827, p. 1.
[24] Ibid. 5 Nov. 1827, p. 1.

evidence of his good faith.[25] We may imagine what other more urgent and melodramatic arguments Castell employed on his behalf from at least one reference to suicide, Susannah having felt obliged, at one stage, to pronounce such thoughts as 'weak', 'ignoble', and 'grovelling'.[26] Reluctantly, she nevertheless acquiesced in his scheme. 'For your sake and yours alone,' she said, 'I shall attend to your instructions to the best of my ability but a more painfull task could never have been impos'd on a woman, knowingly consenting to her own disgrace.'[27] But she exhorted him to total ingenuousness in his correspondence with her. Anything less, she declared, would be as impolitic as deceiving 'our doctors'. 'Only endeavour', she went on, 'to merit my love and my Heart and Arms shall be at all times ready to receive you.'[28]

Even so, when the expected letter from Jones finally came, Susannah found its contents difficult to swallow. It obviously put a somewhat different slant on proceedings in St Servan. 'He is here now', Jones began,

presenting a very advantageous line, that of music master under the assumed name of Cavendish—the son of a colonel—a man of Great family and connected with a lady, the descendent of Henry IV of France, whom he has been oblig'd to quit from her in furious temper. Under this guise he has partly ruined the happiness of my family by corrupting the mind of my daughter. If you have any wish to reclaim him you ought to come over as his Wife . . . he denies all acknowledgment of his being a married man . . .[29]

It plunged her 'in deep distress'. She acknowledged that 'on the face of it' Jones's account seemed honest and accurate and that his source for some parts of the letter could only have been Castell himself. Once again his 'dreadful vice' (incontinence), she said, was causing trouble and misfortune.[30] More galling still, the news of his denial of marriage was already abroad in London, and Mori had already dispatched Brooks (the cellist) to her neighbour Mackintosh (the bassoonist), so that the information might be 'delicately' conveyed to her.[31]

But she was committed to seeing it through. Apart from her emotional attachment to William, doubtless she also perceived it to be in her own interest to assist him. If he was ever to be in a position to aid her, she had little choice. The will to survive was strong. 'I have had to encounter and surmount a hundred times more difficulty's and real trouble for these last 16 months', she had remonstrated to Castell, 'than you ever did in your

[25] SEC–WJC, 31 Oct. 1827, p. 1; 5 Nov., p. 2.   [26] Ibid. 27 Nov., pp. 4–5.
[27] Ibid. 31 Oct. 1827, p. 3.   [28] Ibid. 5 Nov. 1827, p. 2.
[29] THJ–SEC copy, sent with SEC–WJC, 27 Nov. 1827.
[30] SEC–WJC, 27 Nov. 1827, p. 3.   [31] Ibid. 2.

whole life and my heart at times has appear'd to throb with aching, but am still alive and for the sake of our children hope I shall remain so.'[32]

Castell had not been idle, then, in the thirteen months since his disappearance. Portsmouth had evidently been a useful first stage from where he could make emergency exits to either Jersey or France, or reconnoitring excursions back to London. There was probably some truth in the tale of his having been at Kennington, although it is unlikely that he would have stayed very long for fear of being discovered and consigned to the debtors' prison. But, as we have seen, it was to St Servan, just around the bay from the fortress port of St Malo, that he eventually went, and where he stayed (for most of the time) until he finally left Europe.

The area, on the coast of Brittany, was, if we accept the authority of Victor Hugo, a haven for all kinds of castaways and criminals awaiting suitably unscrupulous sea-captains to transport either themselves or their ill-gotten gains, or both, to the safety of more distant ports. At that time, according to Hugo, St Malo was a town of narrow streets and dubious low-fronted inns at whose tables many nefarious deeds were plotted. The sea then came up to the gates of Saint Vincent and Dinan, and the communication between St Malo and St Servan was maintained at low tide by carts and other vehicles which plied backwards and forwards among the debris of vessels left high and dry by the tide. Even coaches used this method and drove their horses over sands that six hours later 'were overspread by foaming billows'. As if to reinforce the sinister aspect of the place, Hugo adds a touch of the macabre. 'On these same sands formerly wandered the twenty-four porter dogs of St Malo, until they were suppressed, owing to their having, in a mistaken excess of zeal, eaten a naval officer in 1770, and their nocturnal barking is now no longer heard between the great and little Talard.'[33]

But somewhere Castell had found a 'Happy arbor' where, like Count Gramont, he had surrounded himself with a 'train of ladies', who flattered him with their 'adoration',[34] not least of whom must have been the very youthful Ellen Jones. It is not surprising, then, that he was so loath to answer Susannah's first letter of August 1827 and that he conspired to have her think he had gone to Rio.

This letter of Susannah's and subsequent ones he appears to have embellished and amended with ticks, crosses, grammatical corrections,

[32] Ibid. 6.   [33] Victor Hugo, *Toilers of the Sea* (1866), 74.
[34] SEC–WJC, 10 July 1828, p. 2; p. 1; 3 Nov. 1828, p. 5.

and pencil alterations, forming an eerily silent dialogue the intention of which, when not defensive, was derisory. Her 'Our Love had receiv'd a shock which was of too <u>pure</u> a nature to admit so gross a rival, indifference followed' he made, for example, read, 'as indifference followed': her 'our home' he made 'my home'. Prefaced to her statement, 'But I forgive thee <u>All</u> thank God!', is a bold cross in red.[35] Sometimes there appears a tick in pencil accompanied by a cross in red, or vice versa, and this seems to suggest a third voice, conceivably that of Miss Jones, who, as Susannah later discovered to her chagrin, had read her correspondence.[36] It is not hard to imagine the two in their 'Happy arbor', entertaining themselves in this diverting manner.

It is possible that Ellen's father had actually encouraged the match, believing Castell's story about his non-legitimate 'attachment' to Susannah, the descendant of kings, and other flattering tales about his own lineage. Castell had initially cautioned Ellen about revealing her feelings to her parents,[37] but this may simply have been his normal way of operating. He was a man who enjoyed secrets. Jones himself says that he had treated Castell with 'marked attention', and the 'black ingratitude'[38] of which he now complained may only have become apparent to him through the revelation, by Mori, of his marital status. Ironically Castell's deception cut both ways. In London it had the effect of creating doubts as to Susannah's married status as well.[39]

In December 1827, Susannah received from Castell, as a token, we suppose, of his ingenuousness, the file of letters from Ellen Jones to himself. It provoked her into a massive epistle that she did not finally complete till 19 February 1828.[40] Her anger is evident in the wild scrawl of her handwriting. The letters confirmed all that she was expected to believe had never happened—all that she was expected to deny to the world. Worse even than this, however, she hears the pathetic voice of Miss Jones calling her to account as the Fiend—the Tiger—who had driven William into exile.

'Even now', cries Ellen, 'my heart <u>swells with indignation</u> at the fury who forc'd you to abandon your home and country.'[41] Susannah could endure, even while she blamed, William's sexual frailties. The letters, after all, proved that it had been he, not Ellen, who had initiated the

[35] SEC–WJC, 24 Aug. 1828, p. 3; p. 2; p. 3.   [36] Ibid., Dec. 1827, p. 16.
[37] EJ–WJC quoted in SEC–WJC, Dec. 1827, p. 3.
[38] THJ–SEC, 25 May 1828, copy in SEC–WJC, 10 June 1828, p. 1.
[39] SEC–WJC, 27 Mar. 1829, p. 5.   [40] Ibid., letter dated Dec. 1827.
[41] Quoted in ibid., Dec. 1827, p. 4.

affair and that he had enjoined her to a deceitful silence. What she could not endure was that she, Susannah, should be the subject of blame.

The titles she has so lavishly bestow'd upon me are the <u>least</u>—<u>Tigers</u> and <u>fury</u> are far beneath <u>my</u> notice, but why should she or (anyone) arrogate to themselves (and as a stranger) the privelege of arraigning <u>my</u> conduct, and Why, Should <u>Her</u> heart swell with indignation at the <u>Fury</u> who forc'd you to abandon your <u>Home</u> and Country—If that She <u>has</u> Succeeded in making a conquest or obtaining <u>your</u> good wishes—<u>that</u> ought to suffice, the <u>indignity</u> of being regarded in the light of <u>your mistress</u> is in <u>itself</u> degrading without these <u>uncall'd</u> for injury's and <u>that too</u> in a <u>foreign</u> country, where I cannot defend myself—The cause for leaving your home is particularly apply'd to 'my tempers' [a red tick is inserted here] Could you have <u>safely</u> remain'd 24 <u>hours</u> after your departure? NO . . .[42]

Yet even in the teeth of so much ignominy and palpable deceit, she did not draw back from her undertaking to follow his humiliating instructions. The 'fev'rish feelings'[43] stirred by Miss Jones's protestations did not, it seems, interfere with her surer instincts.

This sordid little tale of seduction amongst the 'foreign' English at St Servan did not go unnoticed by the gods, however, and in this petty *Aeneid*, Neptune, perhaps at war with Venus, delivering a *coup de main* of his own, lent tragedy to farce.

Unfortunately the victim was an innocent bystander. Poor Miss Murray, daughter of a well-known Jersey family, returning home from a mission of consolation to Miss Jones in St Servan, was drowned when on 1 January 1828 the sloop *La Fanny* foundered and went down within sight of Jersey Harbour. What actually happened, according to a report in *The Times*, was that because there was not enough water in the harbour, the vessel had to tack off and wait for the tide.

... soon after, a sudden and almost tremendous hurricane arose; they immediately let go both anchors, which did not hold, and the vessel drifted on the rocks, about one mile from the shore. ... In the number ascertained to have perished are—Lord Harley, Captain and Mrs Fitzgerald, with an adopted child, Miss Murray, Mrs Duval, and Master Collins . . .[44]

But Miss Murray, according to Castell, was culpable. Her mind having been prejudiced by Mr Jones, she had 'contaminated' all her acquaintance, and 'spread my name from one end of the Island [presumably

[42] Ibid. 5.
[43] Ibid. 11 Apr. 1828, p. 2.
[44] *The Times*, 8 Jan. 1828, p. 3c.

14. Extract from letter, WJC–SEC, 30 Jan. 1828, on the death of Miss Murray.

Jersey] to the other'. His own version of the disaster has about it rather less of the detachment of *The Times*' report.

. . . they were overtaken by a storm at 2 O Clock the same day, and were wreck'd within half a mile of Jersey Pier, where the rocks are most terrific, and in sight of Mr Murray's house . . . The storm was the most tremendous I ever remember, it was impossible to walk against the wind in the streets, and the slates flew about like hail. Only 4 of the bodies have been found, which were so devoured by the crabs and congar eels, that they were only known by part of their dress remaining. One lady was recognized by a ring on her finger bone, for all the flesh had been eaten away. £40 has been offered for the body of Miss Murray, by her distracted father, but neither <u>her</u> or her trunks have yet been discover'd.[45]

Even after her death, though, Miss Murray's influence was still at work, which perhaps explains some of his relish: 'The <u>wretches</u> here say, that <u>I</u> was the cause of her death, for if Miss Jones had not been so miserable, she would not have come over to visit her. They might as well say that I was the cause of the Wind. But to return to your letter . . .'[46]

Of course he was right. He himself was one day to be the inexplicable victim of the elements in similarly capricious mood. But it says something of his standing in St Servan that he should have been the victim of so patent an irrationality.

In the meantime, back in London, Susannah continued her holding operation. In early April 1828 she was bandying words with Mr Jones's agent, 'a very stout man with a red face—dressed in shabby black clothes', who she was certain was a lawyer from the probing scrutiny of his questions. 'I never in my life', she told Castell, 'underwent such a trying scene and the circumspection necessary to be observ'd in giving indirect answers was to me a difficulty more arduous than I had conceived.'[47] He had brought with him another letter from Thomas Jones, which repeated that Castell was masquerading as a single man under the name of Cavendish and that she ought to go and claim him, as he was 'well able not only to render you assistance but were you here to support you and his family very comfortably'.[48]

Her reply, apparently not her first, was an embarrassed mixture of levity and dedicated evasion, garnished with a dash of passionate self-defence. She had not, she said, expected to become 'so popular in France'

[45] SEC–WJC, 30 Jan. 1828, p. 2.
[46] Ibid.
[47] Ibid. 11 Apr. 1828, p. 2.
[48] THJ–SEC [n.d.], copy in SEC–WJC, 11 Apr. 1828, p. 3.

and was highly indignant to learn of the rumour there that she had once been an actress on the stage. This she solemnly denied. She had also learned, she went on, that Mr C.'s professional pursuits in St Servan had been much injured by 'many unpleasant discussions'. Her opinion of his integrity, she claimed, remained unaltered and she was convinced that he would never marry 'your daughter or any other lady'.[49]

But perhaps the worst was over for Castell in St Servan, at least on this score. In May, Mr Jones wrote Susannah another letter, which, in its desperate invective, had the ring of defeat.

Madam,
You said your worthy husband W. J. Castell would do nothing dishonourable. Bred in such a demoralizing school as a theatre it is no wonder at his being capable of fits of the blackest dissimulation. That I have reason to persecute him, every parent will allow that knows of his villainy. A married man (if you are his wife which I must doubt) paying himself out to gain the affections of a female of 16 years of age and under his charge as a music master and his black ingratitude towards a person who treated him with marked attention, ignorant of what a scoundrel he would turn out. He is nothing dishonourable? His manner of leaving his family, his denying his wife, to crown all going out to the Isle of France leaving his family to their fate. But I have not done with him yet.
    Yrs etc
       Thos. H. Jones[50]

Certainly it does not seem that Castell was at that time about to depart for the Isle of France (Mauritius) as Jones had suggested, although something must have provoked what was to turn out to be an accurate prediction.

In May 1828, Susannah was cautiously optimistic about his prospects in a mercantile venture, which, if successful, would afford her, she said, 'an additional pleasure to hear of your removal from a nest of butterfly's in whose society flattery holds her court—and folly revels at her carnivals'.[51] By October, she could even congratulate him on the 'occasion of your late ventures'.[52] But her pessimistic view of human nature as universally founded on self-interest, and her ingrained suspicion of the entire French nation, 'at best but Butterfly's and not to be depended upon',[53] tempered her enthusiasm. And she was still uneasy at his insistence on wearing the mask of a single man. Nothing could be

[49] Copy in SEC–WJC, 11 Apr. 1828, p. 4.
[50] THJ–SEC, 25 May 1828, copy in SEC–WJC, 10 June 1828, p. 1.
[51] SEC–WJC, 8 May 1828, p. 1.   [52] Ibid. 18 Oct. 1828, p. 2.
[53] Self-interest, ibid.; French character, 10 July 1828, p. 3.

achieved of real substance while such duplicity was maintained. He would live, she told him, 'in jeopardy and fix eternal disgrace on your self by plunging deeper and deeper into hypocracy'.[54]

But she was confident enough, at least, to employ herself arranging Castell's accounts in preparation for his return. They represented a 'frightful catalogue', amounting in all to about £300.[55] She argued against Castell's plan of offering his creditors interest on the debts in return for a further six months' credit. It would have cost, she said, £15 a year and some of the debts had already been due for three years. Instead of discharging his debts, she reasoned, he would be accumulating them, and in any case some were 'unworthy objects'. She would be happy, she said, to see everyone receive their respective demands. More they could not expect. Besides times were perilous. A war might break out between England and France and then all would be done for. Their children were still young, and what thanks would Castell get in any case for his honourable gesture? The gentlemen in question would not esteem him a whit the better and in a short time they would forget that there ever existed in the world a person of Castell's name.[56]

Such hard-headed realism had little to do with 'honour' in gentle-manly terms, and was doubtless formed out of the hardship she had already endured, and out of an instinctive grasp of essential priorities. But one wonders who out of the extensive list of his creditors was 'unworthy' of the benefit of Castell's laudable motives. Sir George Smart of the despised St Albans set who was owed £10? Or Broadwoods the piano manufacturer, owed £22? George Strange the tailor,[57] owed £8. 11s. 11d.? Hann the local baker,[58] owed £14. 5s. 6d.? Or Williams, perhaps the proprietor of the Surrey Theatre in 1822–4,[59] owed £9. 0s. 0d.? Or Goulding, presumably the music publisher Goulding D'Almaine of Soho Square, owed £10. 8s. 0d.? Or Howson, perhaps Francis Howson, music teacher,[60] owed £11. 8s. 0d.? Or Lavenu,

[54] Ibid. 4.   [55] Ibid. 18 Oct. 1828, p. 7.
[56] Ibid. 7–8.   [57] SEC describes him as such, SEC–WJC, 26 Jan. 1830, p. 5.
[58] See SEC–WJC, 10 Apr. 1829, p. 11. SEC's text could read 'Harn', but St Mary's, Lambeth, MS Poor Rate Books, 1809 ff. establish that Robert Hann lived in Stangate Street. His shop was probably No. 3 Stangate Street, at the St Thomas's Hospital end. *Horwood's Plan of London*, also *Survey of London*, xxiii, pl. 59, shows it to be the only shop-front in the street.
[59] Brayley, *Historical and Descriptive Accounts of the Theatres of London*, 74–5.
[60] James D. Brown and Stephen S. Stratton, *British Musical Biography* (1897). The entry for the Howson brothers, Frank and John, who were prominent opera singers in Australia in mid-nineteenth-century Australia, gives as their father, Francis Howson, a music teacher of London.

presumably Louis Henry of the music publishers Mori and Lavenu of Bond Street, owed £5. 11s. 3d.? Alphinstone, owed £25. 19s. 10d.? Was Castell's friend Hatton considered unworthy? He was owed a substantial £26. 10s. 0d. but had given Susannah not a little unquiet. The debt to Raper of £75. 6s. 4d., by its very magnitude was probably treated with more respect. James Rumball, always a close adviser, eventually suggested to Susannah that Castell's best option was to offer 3s. in the pound, 'with the explanation that your own friends are willing to advance so much to enable him to return again to his family'.[61]

There was certainly hope in the air of his return. A semblance of family normality was even introduced by Castell, who bestowed gifts upon his children. To Emily, evidently a favourite, he sent a miniature portrait of himself and to his sons he sent the two bows which young William had requested: a violin bow for Alfred and a cello bow for himself.[62]

They were not, however, received with the joy that Castell may have considered they warranted. Susannah accused him of insensitivity and favouritism in sending the miniature to one child only, and further suggested that it had been commissioned not for Emily but for some other 'lady'.[63] As for the bows, Susannah commented that the French bows selling in London, although expensive, were very superior, and tactfully offered that Castell had been the victim of a fraud—a substitution. Later Susannah was to give much less tactful vent to her opinion of the bows.[64] The controversy about the portrait did not die quietly either, and charge and counter-charge sallied back and forth across the Channel for some time.

The venture from which so much was hoped was yet another speculation. Susannah well knew the risks. It involved a Captain O.,[65] about whom Susannah was characteristically sceptical. He could, she reasoned, be intending merely to use Castell as a front and as a scapegoat in the event of failure. 'You will at once see the necessity', she warned, 'of being constantly on your guard as I do not yet conceive you are a match for the artifices of mankind.'[66] Nor was she any more sanguine about the Cornish tin miners who, it seems, were to be recruited to work some

[61] J. J. Rumball–SEC [n.d.], copy in SEC–WJC, 31 Nov. 1828, p. 1.

[62] W Jones C–WJC, 13 May 1828, p. 1.

[63] SEC–WJC, 14 Feb. 1829, p. 4; 18 Oct. 1828, p. 2; 14 Feb. 1829, p. 5; 27 Mar. 1829, p. 6.

[64] Ibid. 3 Nov. 1828, p. 2; see ibid. 15 Dec. 1828, p. 5; 26 Jan. 1830, p. 6.

[65] In another reference, presumably to the same person, SEC refers to what looks like Captain D. see SEC–WJC, 26 Jan. 1830, p. 3.

[66] SEC–WJC, 3 Nov. 1828, p. 3.

foreign mining El Dorado. They were proverbial, she said, for their lies and cunning, and for their always acting together, a trait which in a country 'likely to answer any bad purpose' could only be exacerbated. 'And they are likewise the most superstitious beings imaginable.'[67] The capital involved was £22, an amount which Susannah could not refrain from observing 'would more infinitely serve me than twice that sum two years hence'.[68]

William's life in St Servan during these years was probably easier, financially and socially, than Susannah's in London, but for all that it must have presented its difficulties. In spite of his 'Happy arbor' and his pleasant female companions (presumably his pupils), he was in all likelihood prey to anxiety about his future and to regret at his London failures. Nor would his emotional entanglement with Ellen Jones have made his life simpler, involving as it did her father's quasi-vendetta against him. We may even perhaps imagine him as a rather pathetic and lonely figure for all his apparent bombast to Susannah about women, and his boast of wearing constantly his 'bosom friends', as he termed his pistols. About the latter, Susannah was crushingly dismissive. 'I should naturally suppose them', she said, 'an inconvenient appendage to dress—I cannot judge of the [?French] fashions but this I do know that were an Englishman to be discover'd so habited he would be accus'd as a madman or suspected of assassination'; and the morbid fantasy that he would use them on himself as a way out of his difficulties had also provoked, as we have seen, an unsympathetic and therefore unsatisfactory response.[69]

But hardly anything in Susannah's imagination could have been further from her norm of English, middle-class, ordered decency, to which she was so attached, than this sleazy little corner of post-Revolutionary France.[70] With that emphatic, narrow patriotism perhaps characteristic of the children of foreigners, she knew only that the French were butterflies—vain weathercocks—and without a proper moral sense;[71] beyond that she could not go.

In his precarious isolation, though, Castell seems to have needed this contact—no matter how exasperating and self-righteous. His long poem

---

[67] Ibid. 2.
[68] Ibid. 4–5.
[69] 'Bosom friends', ibid. 27 Nov. 1827, p. 4; suicide, ibid. 4–5.
[70] See André Lespagnol, *Histoire de Saint-Malo et du Pays Malouin* (Toulouse, 1984), 215–34. The region was then in decline.
[71] SEC–WJC, 10 July 1828, p. 3; 16 May 1832, p. 1.

of August 1827 had probably been some months in gestation. Its content was not conciliatory—'Every line breathed the most vindictive rancour that could possess the human heart'[72]—but its intent had been to communicate, albeit negatively. Certainly there was that hiatus immediately following, when he had tried to pretend he had gone to Rio, but the intensity of the correspondence, once begun, rather suggests its inevitability. What did he want from it? An anchor in an uncertain world? Or perhaps a solid surface against which he could bounce his identity and be reassured of its continued existence and of its power to command and punish? Only fragments of his side of the correspondence survive and we are frequently only able to interpret his motives through Susannah's own responses to the contents of his letters. Her motives are clear enough. She desired to set down the record and exonerate herself from blame. She also wanted him back, a desire which evidence suggests was not mutually felt. It is hardly surprising, then, that the correspondence was unpredictable and often less than cordial; never less so than when dealing with the Miss Jones affair, which in February 1829 took another strange turn.

It would seem that Castell desired in some way to legitimize Miss Jones's position in France, where she was suffering, he told Susannah, 'the mockery of a cruel and curious world', and being unkindly referred to as his whore.[73] In his by now predictably ingenuous or predictably insensitive fashion, he requested Susannah's assistance. The nature of this assistance is, however, obscure because Susannah's language becomes veiled and impenetrable in reference to it. But it is certain that whatever was requested of Susannah was in no way to her advantage. Mysterious documents were sent for her examination which apparently contained an account of certain transactions—possibly of a marriage of some kind between Castell and Ellen Jones, to achieve which one or both of the parties may have become Roman Catholic. Susannah's oblique reference to 'proselytism' and later talk of conversion[74] suggest this as a strong possibility. Perhaps, taking his cue from the Prince of Wales's morganatic Roman Catholic marriage to Mrs Fitzherbert in the previous generation, he had hoped, in similar mode, to bestow the blessings of legitimacy upon Miss Jones. But even a Catholic marriage in Catholic France would have required legal safeguards. These Susannah may have

---

[72] SEC–WJC, 13 Jan. 1829, p. 5.
[73] Ibid. 14 Feb. 1829, pp. 3–4. I am assuming that in this context, SEC's 'xxx' equals 'whore'.
[74] Ibid. 2; 10 Apr. 1829, p. 11; 9 June 1829, p. 10.

been asked to supply by relinquishing any claim to Castell, at least in France.

There is also a possibility that he may already have been attempting to claim French patrimony, perhaps through his father, who as already suggested may once have held a commission in the French Army. In 1828 he had requested Susannah to send him his father's 'commission', his miniature, and his uniform.[75] She may have suspected his intentions on that occasion. This time, however, his intentions, whatever they specifically entailed, were made painfully clear to her. But it was one thing to play ducks and drakes with Mr Jones's man in black about her precise relationship to William, and another to countenance any legitimizing of his relationship with a rival; and this, whatever were the exact proposals, was the essence of Castell's request to Susannah. And it would seem that this time he had stretched her credulity as well as her perception of her own interest too far. Her refusal was couched not in outrage but in calm moral argument:

I need not tell you that it is not only my duty & interest to serve you, but also my inclination, but in doing which, my honor and integrity must remain inviolate and (by this time) I hope that you are fully aware that I cannot consistently (with those rules) comply in the performance of your wishes—To myself only (in such a case) am I ameanable for my actions—but believe me, that the tribunal of your own conscience are of more considerable importance than all the judiciary proceedings in the world beside—you will, so far, do justice to my opinion when I say that wrong is not right—Command me in any way whatever, and where I may be of real service to you & I will carry it into effect—but here 'tis morally impossible for me to become party in the affair you wish me.[76]

After consultation with James Rumball, and upon his advice, she burned the documents, the contents of which, she said, had 'frightened' him.[77]

Thus, if Susannah had thought William was to be free from the 'nest of butterfly's', she had been sorely disappointed. But she was not wholly dismayed. She preserved yet a wifely equanimity. She spoke now in almost placid tones of the miniature Castell had sent to Emily, which she considered had left its subject 'in arrears with time', and she criticized, as she doubtless felt entitled to, the 'close lock over the forehead'. It was, she said, 'a costume that we have been unaccustom'd to see in the original', and she continued affectionately, 'It may perhaps be some consolation to know that with my left hand I at present hold that impression which I have just press'd to my lips.'[78]

[75] Ibid. 30 Jan. 1828; 11 Feb. 1828, p. 1.
[76] Ibid. 14 Feb. 1829, pp. 1–2.   [77] Ibid. 5.   [78] Ibid.

In March 1829 a rumour circulated that Castell was in London, which seems to have been the case. He had been there for some weeks and had probably already gone before Susannah heard of it and declared she would not believe it. Later, however, she seems to have acknowledged its truth,[79] although there is no evidence that the two met at that time. The event seems to have stirred passions in the neighbourhood. Mrs Alphinstone had apparently descended upon Hann's and, in a public performance for which the baker later felt obliged to apologize to Susannah, had relieved herself of several 'infamous falsehoods': 'First that you had left me with £10 and sold your business to a young man (an acquaintance of her son's) for £70 and was possessed of property and had turned Roman Catholic to blind the world.'[80] Susannah offered Mr Hann certain proofs of the inaccuracy of Mrs A.'s assertions, although precisely which ones is not clear.[81] The last of them, however, seems to have been true. Susannah conceded as much in a later letter: 'I believe there was something in that . . . for I wonder'd myself at the Catholic subjects brought home in the shape of books . . .'[82] And by August of the same year, we hear her accuse him of having changed his religion, 'for the sake of escaping your taxes'.[83]

The year 1829 saw the passing of the Catholic Emancipation Act. Susannah herself makes what seems to be an innocent enough allusion to it in a March letter,[84] although exactly how Castell proposed to save his taxes we do not discover. It is much more likely that if he did change his religion he did so in order to marry Ellen Jones, and the possibility that this is what happened is reinforced at a much later date by his taunting of Susannah that he had 'two wives'.[85]

SUSANNAH'S BELEAGUERED KINGDOM: THE YEARS OF STRUGGLE

Throughout all of this period, from Castell's departure in July 1826 to this latest complexity, Susannah, in London, had been very much pre-occupied with the mechanics of simple survival. That, at least, was the impression she gave. She had been particularly angry when she learned that Castell had told Miss Jones and his other female 'confederates' that

[79] SEC-WJC, 27 Mar. 1828, p. 9; ibid. 10 Apr. 1829, p. 11; 9 June 1829, p. 11.
[80] Ibid. 4 Apr. 1829, pp. 11–12.   [81] Ibid. 12.
[82] Ibid. 9 June 1829, p. 11. I assume she is referring to the period prior to July 1826, not to that of his recent visit.   [83] Ibid. 8 Aug. 1829, p. 9.
[84] Ibid. 27 Mar. 1829, p. 10.   [85] Ibid. 3 Feb. 1831, p. 1.

15. Detail of the drawing by B. Shawcross (Fig. 7) of the front door and pediment to No. 19 Stangate Street.

he had left her with a well-furnished house and a 'competent income to support respectability'.[86] The truth was that it was only with difficulty that she had been able, she said, to keep a roof over their heads, and any benefit they enjoyed came not from Castell but from their own, unaided exertions.[87] Augustine, still playing at the Amphitheatre, had become resident again in Stangate Street in order to offer as much assistance as possible, and young William by May 1828 at the age of 16 was engaged as double-bass at the Surrey Theatre. Their combined salary was £2. 10s. 0d.[88]

From the very beginning the lease on the house had been in jeopardy because it had required Castell's signature and, as we have already seen, because she had had difficulty paying her rates and taxes, quite apart from the £5. 7s. 0d. ground rent for Mr Chisholm. In September 1827,

[86] Ibid. 8 May 1828, p. 3.   [87] Ibid. 20 Oct. 1827, p. 1; 8 May 1828, p. 3.
[88] Augustine, ibid. 18 Oct. 1828, p. 4; William, 22 May 1828, p. 3; salary, 18 Oct. 1828, p. 4.

only the intervention of Mr Knight of Bloomsbury, who seems to have had some connection in matters of real estate, had prevented, she said, their peremptory eviction. The very nature of Castell's departure had also alienated people who might have helped them, and had it not been for Augustine they might have been starving and homeless. From the time of Castell's departure up to June 1828, the house alone had cost Susannah 'not much less than £36',[89] all of which had had to be found from their very limited resources.

Some of Castell's erstwhile customers, like Mrs Dearmer of St Albans, had paid their outstanding accounts promptly into Susannah's hands, thus saving her from certain destitution, she said, but others refused outright or prevaricated. Nicholls, 'the Brute', who had taken over Castell's organist's position at St Peter's, and like so many others 'had avail'd themselves of the advantage of [her] misfortune', had been offensive, and had counter-claimed against the Castells for coals which he said he had supplied to them at St Albans, eight years previously.[90] Edward Tate, pianoforte manufacturer and music seller,[91] had owed Castell £12 which Susannah could not recover because he himself had become an insolvent debtor in the King's Bench Prison, and she had no officially recognized proof of the debt to present to the court.[92]

Susannah had a particular disrelish for Tate, probably because it had been he who had first implied that Castell's drowning had been a fake. She evinced absolutely no sympathy for his plight and could only consider that he had taken advantage of hers. He was a 'bad unprincipl'd man', who had already spent £2,000 of his wife's money on a wine cellar, which Susannah of course had predicted would fail, and 'has been spending ours too . . .'. Tate, she posited, 'exactly knew my situation and it was cruel in him to withhold my claim. He said in my parlour, on the morning after your departure that you had a larger sum of money in your pocket—the previous evening—his real meaning requires no comment . . .'.

Eventually Tate tried to palm off two old instruments on her. She at

[89] Signature, SEC–WJC, 10 June 1828, p. 2; ground rent, Dec. 1827, p. 9; eviction, 10 June 1828, p. 3; alienation, 10 July 1828, p. 2; house costs, 10 June 1828, p. 3.

[90] Mrs Dearmer, ibid. 31 July 1828, p. 4; Nicholls, May 1828, pp. 3–4.

[91] 'Edward Robert Tate, formerly of Doncaster Yorkshire, afterwards Prospect Place, St George's, Southwark, afterwards Bridge House Place, Newington Causeway and later of London Road all in Surrey, Piano-Forte manufacturer and music-seller . . . before the Court for Relief of Insolvent Debtors; Court House in Portugal Street, Lincoln's Inn Fields, Monday 2 June, 1828.' London Gazette, 9 May 1828, p. 914.

[92] SEC–WJC, 24 Aug. 1827, p. 5; 10 June 1828, p. 4.

first declined such 'lumber', but when it became clear that no cash would be forthcoming she accepted. Too late. The instruments had been disposed of. He then sent her on a wild-goose chase to a Mr Wallace who seems to have had some form of liability in the matter. But this gentleman, feigning a desire to be of service, nevertheless assured her, falsely as it later transpired, that he had no part in the business. Such were the almost insurmountable obstacles that Susannah faced in her quest for justice. But Wallace too, she noted, ended up in the Bench.[93]

But of course, while she was hounding Tate and Nicholls and others, she in her turn was being hounded also. It was Tate in fact who had told her of Hatton's sinister intentions,[94] and ominous rumblings had come from St Albans, where Sir George Smart was not sparing in his criticisms of Castell's behaviour.[95] Sir George, rather in contrast to Castell, was a man much given to keeping strict account and his lost £10 doubtless rankled with him, but in the event he took no action. Petty litigation, it would seem, he had no interest in, and, as we have already noticed, his kind heart extended even to a convicted felon, although he had on that occasion at least recovered his property.

There seemed to have been a general sense, however, that Castell had let people down and that his irresponsible actions in putting on the Kennington concert without capital or connection[96] had put his friends as well as himself at risk. The cellist Richard Hatton was a young man, and the £26. 10s. owed him was probably critical compared to the £10 owed such an established figure as Sir George Smart. And it would seem that he owed other money as well to his musical friends which did not appear on Susannah's list, some of whom, she said, 'are not so generously disposed as you have imagined'.[97]

As we have already heard her say, she cut herself off from the world. With the exception of James Rumball she would see no one, and her only solace was her own dear family—the four deserted little orphans, for whose sake alone she struggled against the world. Guileless and morally untainted, Susannah challenged all England to find 'better dispos'd children'. A united family—a happy fireside—a mother, surrounded by happy smiling faces—such an ideal admitted of 'no SECOND ancillary', as far as Susannah was concerned.[98]

[93] Tate, ibid., May 1828, pp. 2–3; Wallace, Dec. 1827, pp. 6–7.
[94] Ibid., Dec. 1827, p. 9.   [95] Ibid. 18 Oct. 1828, p. 9.
[96] SEC–Raper & Jones, 27 Mar. 1827, p. 2.   [97] SEC–WJC, 8 Oct. 1828, p. 9.
[98] James Rumball, ibid. 4 June 1829, p. 3; orphans, SEC–Raper & Jones, 27 Mar. 1827, p. 1; Dec. 1827, p. 8; 24 Aug. 1827, p. 4; 20 Oct. 1827, p. 1; untainted, SEC–WJC, 13 Jan. 1829, p. 2; no second ancillary, 13 Jan. 1829, p. 3.

This image became for Susannah not only an aim to be achieved, not only a solace in her trials, but a vindication in the eyes of the world, a world which she perceived to be hostile towards her, a world which in many respects was synonymous with Castell's own hostility towards her; so that it is not surprising that it is for his ears that she proclaims her achievements in this field.

But in fact the world was much closer to her own views than she imagined, and the world that Castell represented—of moral ambiguity, not to say laxity, and of intellectual cynicism, not to say opportunism—was fast being overtaken by the neo-Puritan culture of middle-class Evangelicalism. The family, as opposed to the coffee house and the club, was about to become the cradle not only of English freedoms but of English virtues. At least in theory.

Susannah was, in fact, moving quite firmly in step with respectable opinion, which execrated slavery as well as drunkenness, and extolled free enterprise and the family, Sunday observance, the discipline of work, and the containment of sex within marriage—all of which comprised the Evangelical inheritance which was to become within the next twenty years the backbone of Victorian cultural values.[99] Its inspiration, declared William Howitt in 1838, had not been Methodism, as was often proposed, but the original Puritanism of Geneva and the Solemn League and Covenant from Scotland, which had once and for all denounced the carnality of Antichrist and the rags of the scarlet woman. 'And what has been the course of England since?' he went on, 'One ever-widening and ascending course of mighty wars, expanding commerce, vast colonization, and the growth of science, literature, and general knowledge. We are no longer a nation of feudal combatants, of piping shepherds, and thoughtless peasantry—but of busy, scheming, money-collecting, family-creating men.'[100] And as for happiness, 'of which the people, however unwisely, are always in quest', it did not, he believed, consist 'in booths and garlands, drums and horns, or in capering round a May-pole. Happiness', he ascertained, was 'a fireside thing.'[101]

Susannah would doubtless have agreed with the last remark, but might have found herself quibbling with Howitt's nation of 'family-creating men'. In her equation it was women not men who created families. It was towards the habits of the mother that the children 'will naturally <u>lean</u>'. Much depended on her '<u>felt</u>' sense of duty, her love of

---

[99] See G. M. Young, *Portrait of an Age. Victorian England* (1977), 21 ff.
[100] William Howitt, *The Rural Life of England* (3rd edn., 1844), 418.
[101] Ibid. 420.

home and domestic pursuits—her instinctive belief in home as 'the resort of <u>all</u> her earthly comforts'. Indeed all devolved upon the woman. Men on the other hand had merely their professional calling, and to that and that alone they dedicated their talents and energy. In contrast to this luxury of specificity, 'A woman's work is never done', she said.[102]

Only one thing clouded the shining image of the cheerful hearth and the ring of smiling faces, and that was the nagging question, 'How are we to pay?'[103] Next to her pride in motherhood was her pride in her independence and respectability; and when misfortune had reduced her to the point of seeking redress from those with power to assist her, she did so in characteristic style, declaring her virtue rather than her need as the obligating factor.

Nay <u>paupers</u> receive Parochial assistance—who are unworthy Members and whose imaginary privations are emblazon'd and credited, but are <u>not real</u> objects of charity and like bounty received from their friends is soon transferred to the publican whilst the modest housekeeper still struggling with the spirit of independence shrinks from the <u>last</u> and most dreadful necessity's—but to which—he has <u>first</u> claim.[104]

Theodore Zeldin has suggested that the French middle class or bourgeoisie was identifiable not so much by considerations of wealth as by style of life and aspiration,[105] and to a large extent this was true also of the English middle class. The obligation to keep up appearances so as to avoid identification with the 'masses' by means of prescribed formulas of behaviour and dress was certainly a feature of nineteenth-century English town life. As with his French counterpart, the English bourgeois' home required its parlour, in which could be displayed the artefacts of status even if the rest of the house were bare: the musical instruments, the paintings, the clocks, the bibelots and bric-à-brac, 'to show that he possessed a surplus of wealth dedicated to cultural living beyond the basic necessities'.[106]

In Susannah's parlour, we know, there was at least one portrait (of her son William), and most probably the organ, which even in her direst necessity, and even though unplayable, she refused to part with.[107] It was presumably in her parlour that she 'gave audience' to Mr Jones's shabby agent, and it was perhaps due to its powerful symbolism that she was

---

[102] SEC–WJC, 13 Jan. 1829, pp. 2–3.
[103] Ibid. 3.   [104] SEC–Watmore, 22 Nov. 1827, p. 2.
[105] Theodore Zeldin, *France 1848–1945. Ambition & Love* (1979), 15–16.
[106] Ibid. 15.   [107] SEC–WJC, 22 May 1828, p. 3; 12 Nov. 1829, p. 6.

able to muster the necessary reserves of self-respect and resolve to see the thing through.

She too, like Zeldin's bourgeois, had a high regard for education and regretted her inability to provide her children with more of it. For the first twelve months of her desertion, by her own report her days of most 'threatening danger', it transpired that she had paid to send the two girls to a 'cheap school', but withdrew them, not because of lack of funds but because, she said, the association with the other children—'for the most part . . . of hardworking industrious parents'—threatened to taint them with modes of expression that were 'ill-adapted' to her views. Since then they had remained 'solely under my wing', thus preserved not only from glottal stops and dropped aitches but from what she termed 'savage ignorance'.[108]

The education of male children was of higher priority, and it was at some sacrifice that she later hired for Alfred a private tutor. This was Mr Catherby from Carlisle House, who 'at present' did not reject 'respectable day scholars'. She could afford, however, only those basics which would allow him to 'pass the world over'. These she considered to be writing, arithmetic, orthography, and grammar.[109] In this she betrayed, however, a social ambiguity. Such an education would not have distinguished him from an assiduous mechanic—albeit a mechanic with ideas above his station.[110] For all her middle-class pretensions, then, Susannah remained to some extent contained within the social expectations of an artisan or 'middling' rather than a middle class. Several times in her correspondence she claimed that she wished her sons had been apprenticed to trades rather than brought up to music, even while reviling the sharp practice of tradesmen in general.[111] One cannot imagine Zeldin's bourgeois entertaining such a thought.

However, in the first decades of the nineteenth century, social stratification, below the level of absolute 'independence' from any need to work, was very fluid. As R. S. Neale has argued, the Ricardian model of landowner, capitalist, and labourer (or aristocracy, middle class, and

[108] Regret, SEC–WJC, 27 Mar. 1829, p. 8; 'threatening danger', 20 Oct. 1827, p. 1; 'cheap school', 3 Nov. 1828, p. 5; 'savage ignorance', ibid.

[109] Ibid. 27 Mar. 1829, p. 8. The 13th-century Carlisle House was a famous Lambeth landmark. In our period it was a boarding-school run by Richard Bennett. It was demolished in 1827. (SEC–WJC, 21 Aug. 1828; see also Walford, *Old and New London*, vi. 417–18.) SEC mentions a fee of one guinea a quarter for Mr Catherby's services, SEC–WJC, 27 Mar. 1829, p. 8.

[110] See Llewellyn Woodward, *The Age of Reform, 1815–1870* (1962), ch. 11, 'Education, 1815–1870'.

[111] SEC–WJC, 16 May 1832, p. 3; 2 June 1832, p. 2.

working class) was an abstraction that was not reflected in reality. There were no categories in it for 'self-employed shop-keepers and artisans, peasant farmers, industrial labour, and the expanding professions, or for women except as adjuncts to husbands and fathers . . .'.[112] There was certainly no category in it for Susannah. Within his argument for a five- rather than a three-class model, Neale basically defines class, as opposed to economic stratification, as conflict groups, the formation of which depended not only on collective identity of interest but upon 'relation- ships of authority and subjection as felt and experienced',[113] within, that is, the imposed power structures of society itself.

Susannah demonstrated that she had an acute sense of class and considered herself to have been of the 'middling order'. 'In England', she wrote, in 1829, 'the distresses of the working classes are great but the <u>real</u> sufferers [meaning herself and family] are those of the middling order and which if things do not wear a better aspect soon will become extinct.' She excluded, however, from this gloomy scenario 'those who has fortu- nately laid by a store for future wants, or the fraudulent tradesman—who exacts from his customers, "cent p^r cent" and which is <u>often</u> proved to be the case'.[114]

What Susannah meant by 'middling order' is of course imprecise; but she was probably referring to a relative position akin to Neale's own perception of a 'middling class' rather than to a 'middle class' in Zeldin's meaning of the term. Her own sense of identification was tinged with an anger and a bitterness not so much against the top class, the aristocracy, whose frailties and natural selfishness she accepted almost with com- placency,[115] but against members of the more 'satisfied' classes[116] just above her, who possessed authority which she resented, and for whom she felt no deference, only an impotent defiance. The management of the Surrey Theatre was a case in point. The Royal Society of Musicians was another. First, the theatre.

Young William had been appointed first bass at the Surrey, a fairly rapid rise in status, even if the salary was only £1. 5s. 0d. a week. He was

---

[112] R. S. Neale, *Class and Ideology in the Nineteenth Century* (1972), 4–5.
[113] Ibid. 19. 'Social classes, however, are really conflict groups arising out of the authority structure of imperatively co-ordinated associations.' Neale defines an im- peratively co-ordinated association as: 'any group of people in which authority is unequally distributed and in which those in dominant positions exercise legitimate authority. The state and industrial enterprises are examples of such associations.'
[114] SEC–WJC, 28 Nov. 1829, p. 2.   [115] Ibid. 27 Nov. 1827, p. 3.
[116] J. S. Mill's term, used in Neale, *Class and Ideology*, 5.

obviously talented. But Susannah harboured a deep resentment against that 'amiable trio', as she sardonically called Elliston, Blewitt, and Erskine, who together superintended the 'discipline' of the orchestra, the latter two, according to Susannah, opposing each other in everything, 'except their mastery over their humiliated band'.[117]

Jonathan Blewitt (Susannah calls him Blewett) was the musical director of the Surrey Theatre under the management of Elliston, who had taken over the Surrey in July 1827 after his financial collapse at Drury Lane. Blewitt was a London organist, composer, and conductor who had spent many years in Ireland as private organist to Lord Cahir and, from 1813, as musical director at The Crow Street theatre. He had returned to London in about 1824.[118] Erskine (a violinist), as he had been under Dibdin, was the leader of the band. It was Blewitt however who was the particular target of Susannah's ire. She told Castell in December 1828 that she had written to him respecting the ill treatment of 'one of my family'—presumably William. She received no reply, which irked her. 'He is mighty high and of great importance . . . I suppose he considered it derogatory towards his dignity for such plebeians as ourselves to address him. He hinted to Mr Brooks something about an apology, but that he will never receive of me.'[119]

Her chagrin was complete, however, when William was summarily demoted to second bass at a salary of only £1. 1s. 0d. 'Mr Pom Poms [presumably a term for Elliston] fool Mr Blewett' had done it to make way for 'one of his sycophants'. She considered that her son had not only been humiliated but professionally injured. She had had the opportunity at Easter, she said, of placing him elsewhere but had not done so precisely because she thought his status as first bass at the Surrey, in spite of the low pay, 'would ultimately be of service to him'. Blewitt's only response by way of excuse had been the evasive *non sequitur* 'Age before honesty'. Susannah knew she was powerless to resist 'such treatment'. 'The fellow', she said, 'knows our situation and takes advantage of it.'[120] She would not forget this insult and injury to her 'poor deserving boy', and would eventually take her own petty revenge.

[117] SEC–WJC, 10 Apr. 1829, p. 9.
[118] Boydell, 'Music, 1700–1850' in T. W. Moody and W. E. Vaughan (eds.), *A New History of Ireland. IV: Eighteenth-Century Ireland 1691–1800* (Oxford, 1986), 602. In his third letter on the state of music in London (10 May 1829), the French critic F.-J. Fétis especially noted Blewitt's comic glees as performed at the Society of Melodists, which he thought were of 'a very piquant character'. Reprinted *Harmonicon*, vii (1829), 184–6.
[119] SEC–WJC, 15 Dec. 1828, p. 3.
[120] Ibid. 9 June 1829, p. 11; ibid. 12; ibid. 25 June 1829, p. 11.

Susannah certainly sensed and felt her subjection within the imposed power structure of the theatre and chafed against the limitations inflicted by it upon the professional development of her son. In broad social terms, Neale suggests that the intensity of conflict was heightened in the early nineteenth century 'by the existence of upwardly mobile men with high need for achievement but with subordinate positions'.[121] Obviously there were upwardly mobile women too. In Susannah's particular case the conflict was probably even more intense because she had actually regressed from an earlier state of some privilege and had to catch up before she could progress further. But she was isolated, firstly as a woman, and secondly because the profession itself had created no effective tools for changing the ground rules.

Susannah's contact with the Royal Society of Musicians was not so direct, but once again an imposed authority became a limiting factor and inspired a resentful defiance. The Society represented the musical establishment whose role, as Susannah saw it, was to sit in judgement upon the more unfortunate members of its own profession. Her neighbour John Mackintosh, a 'guardian' of the society, had procured for her £5 as a Christmas gratuity in 1826, but otherwise the Society declared her ineligible for assistance.[122] This was probably because of the dubious circumstances surrounding Castell's disappearance, and the suspicion that Susannah may have been acting in collusion. It had considered itself an interested party concerning the rumours that were circulating in London in 1827 that Castell was denying his marriage to Susannah. It fell to Mackintosh as a 'guardian', presumably, to seek from Susannah an assurance of her genuine status.[123] Susannah's response was predictable. She had not begged anything from them. The £5 was completely Mackintosh's own solicitation, not hers. They need have no fear that her family would ever become 'burthensome to <u>Them</u>, and if ever in my power will return them their <u>generous gift</u> in appropriate answer with <u>many thanks</u>!!!' Furthermore she was entirely suspicious of the nature of the Society's charity. As with other public institutions, she feared that 'there is more ostentation than real charity'.[124] With the passage of time her position hardened even further.

[121] Neale, *Class and Ideology*, 9.

[122] SEC–WJC, 3 Feb. 1831, p. 2. The term 'guardian' is not one that the Society recognizes today, but it may have been a term used for quasi-official inspectors—those who inquired into the legitimacy of claims perhaps. The term is more familiar in association with the workings of the New Poor Law; SEC–WJC, 20 Oct. 1827, pp. 2–3.

[123] Ibid. 27 Mar. 1829, p. 5; 3 Feb. 1831, p. 2.

[124] Ibid. 31 Oct. 1827, pp. 4–5; 10 June 1828, p. 4.

In 1830, when the nation was facing severe crisis and possible revolution, Susannah was scathing that the Royal Society would accept no general responsibility for its membership. This was of course naïve, but to Susannah it was just another indication that they had become 'a most illiberal set', motivated by pure ostentation, 'and merely to say Theirs is a charitable Institution'.

If a widow (for instance) after her Husband's death apply'd for her merited stipend, her feelings are harrow'd up by the cabals of the 'professional members' raking up and gathering all the bad qualities and propensity's of her late husband, grudging her that which is unquestionably her right, on the petty grounds that He was a drunkard—or anything else will do . . .[125]

Poor Veale, as she said, had had his stipend 'curtailed' merely because his father, they discovered, had left him, 'a trifle'.[126]

Susannah, it might be argued, was merely a disappointed and disgruntled individual at the lower end of the middle-class spectrum. But if this was so, she nevertheless expressed much of her resentment by way of the public institutions of the musical profession, and there is a sense in her writing not only of individual gripe but of a collective discontent (identified with the Veales of the profession rather than the Macintoshes). She is to an extent, then, echoing a consensus opinion. Indeed there were many other disappointed and disgruntled people in roughly similar circumstances, not only musicians, who chafed at their powerlessness and who, like Susannah, did not necessarily identify with those middle-class individuals or institutions which did possess power.

Edward Gibbon Wakefield called them the 'uneasy class'—lesser professional men, cut out of affluence by fierce competition, and whose interests were not identical at all with those of their more successful brethren. To quote Neale:

Whatever the real reasons for the frustration of the ambitions of these people, they came to believe that a very important one was the weight of ancient restriction and aristocratic and oligarchic privilege. What was additionally galling were the attitudes of superiority adopted by people who were regarded by the petit bourgeois and literates, i.e. the 'uneasies', as inferior to themselves, at least in terms of usefulness and intellect.[127]

A large majority of musicians, whose existence cannot be doubted simply because so few of their voices survive, could be considered to belong to

125 SEC–WJC, Dec. 1830, p. 4.
126 Ibid. 3 Feb. 1831, p. 2.
127 In Neale, *Class and Ideology*, 23–34.

such a class. To the extent that they were, Susannah's voice, which against so many odds did survive, is representative rather than merely neurotic.

Musicians ('literates' rather than 'petit bourgeois' within this taxonomy), as we have already seen, were perceiving their social and economic progress blocked not only by old prejudices but by new economic factors, by over-supply which outstripped even the burgeoning demand of the period, but especially by increased foreign competition.

Neale believes that both the 'petit bourgeois' (that is, small-scale producers, retailers, and tradesmen) and 'a class of professional men' had proliferated in the early stages of industrialism in Britain, and that their children had 'flooded the grammar school systems only to turn out half-educated, half-gentlemen unfitted for industrial employment'.[128] These are Neale's 'literates', who, accustomed to relatively affluent circumstances but without capital or connection, and because of the competition for respectable employment which their own numbers produced, faced a decline once more into the 'mass'. Such an analysis might easily apply to musicians. We have already noted the burgeoning of musical consumption in England in the late eighteenth century which brought with it new levels of affluence for some musicians—especially fashionable teachers. Instrumental performers also reached peaks of affluence that were not to be sustained, except in exceptional circumstances, in the nineteenth century.[129] It is instructive to note that salary scales for members of the Philharmonic Society remained fairly static throughout the first forty years of the nineteenth century, and in some cases actually declined.[130] Both Susannah and William Castell were almost certainly products of this late eighteenth century boom, and their expectations of comfort and even gentility were thus likely to have been correspondingly high, making their decline all the more appalling.

Susannah's background aside, Castell's pretensions to higher things probably originated with his grandfather, the trumpeter William Jones, who had contrived to make himself comfortable enough and had educated his daughter Sophia and probably his grandsons as well. But while other professional groups like doctors, apothecaries, and lawyers managed to shore up their defences and make substantial inroads into

[128] Ibid. 22.
[129] See McVeigh, 'Felice Giardini', 170–1; Rohr, 'Profession of Artisans', ch. 8; Richard D. Leppert, 'Music Teachers of Upper-Class Amateur Musicians in Eighteenth-Century England', in Allan W. Atlas (ed.), Music in the Classic Period (1985), 154.
[130] BL MS Loan 48/9, Philharmonic Society Accounts.

the established middle class, musicians, as Rohr has shown, did not. Neither did successful musicians like Sir George Smart, Henry Bishop, or even Jonathan Blewitt, who may have considered themselves safely entrenched, offer leadership in any practical or political sense to the members of the profession as a whole. The best they seemed to be able to do was to demonstrate an individual possibility, and/or dispense charity through such organizations as the Royal Society of Musicians. Even the Royal Academy of Music, as we have already noted, was not really within the sphere of their direct influence, and served only to introduce a new strand into the profession which added, at least at first, even more tension and competition for established musicians.

Thus Susannah's response of bitterness and cynicism towards the upper echelons of the profession is understandable, especially so since they seemed even to conspire to obstruct her rehabilitation and progress. The family was indeed struggling desperately to maintain their foothold in respectable society, and had it not been for Augustine, declared Susannah, 'we could not keep our position in society one month longer'.[131]

The fear of sliding back into the amorphous anonymity of the 'mass' was certainly real enough for Susannah, for whom the difference between 15s. and a guinea a week seemed to constitute a firm enough demarcation line. Commenting on the general decline in opportunities for musicians in 1830, she commented that 'Good performers are playing at the rate of 15/- p^r week—so that you may suppose the grade of society they belong to'.[132] William at that time was earning a guinea.

Indeed, the grand image of the glowing hearth-fire and the ring of happy smiling faces—the glory of the family itself—had no meaning or relevance unless it could exist in respectable society, and the grand aim of the 'middling order' was to make sure that it did. To this extent, certainly, the middling and the middle classes shared a common understanding, and a common aspiration.

It should not surprise, then, given the circumstances in which the family found itself, that Susannah's entire existence should have been devoted to this objective and that it produced a dourness and a bitterness that in the end seemed completely to submerge the ardent spirit of the early letters. Susannah in fact seemed to have surprised herself by her own determination and competence in worldly affairs. When Castell had been

---

[131] SEC–WJC, 2 June 1832, p. 1.   [132] Ibid. 25 May 1830, p. 3.

head of the family she had been deprived of effective control of the household. She had not been consulted in its running—in the hiring and firing of servants—any more than she had been involved in or consulted about Castell's business affairs. Now everything devolved upon her. As she said to Castell, 'You had left all behind while I, as a woman, had to contend with the most severe trials.'[133] She had had to confront obstacles which in her own mind she felt few women could have surmounted; not least in having to compromise the truth before the inquisition of the shabby man in black—a truly 'masculine undertaking', in the execution of which even her inquisitor had complimented her. Notwithstanding, she said, 'I hope & trust that my manners and deportment are truly feminine.'[134]

Susannah's efforts, however, were largely concentrated in avoiding confrontation with Castell's creditors, maintaining her lease on the house, collecting moneys owed from Castell's 'book' (presumably his accounts), keeping the tax collectors at bay, protecting her son William's interests at the Surrey Theatre, and generally husbanding the family's combined resources, so as to maintain a general appearance of respectability. In the latter she seems to have had too much success, since she eventually complained that she could get little sympathy as it was generally thought that they were doing well.[135]

For all her association with the less practical professions, Susannah does not seem to have been without those instincts of practical self-help and respect for material assets that were part of her Huguenot heritage. It was her, 'pride', she said, that she repelled meanness,[136] but in her dealings with others she demonstrated a canny enough self-interest. She had been negotiating for the renewal of the lease almost from the beginning and had availed herself of the services of the Edwards, father and son, who, at some pains, had carried the papers to France and back in order to get Castell's signature. It was evident that she trusted them, yet at one stage she wrote to Castell concerning some unspecified object, and told him not to return it to Mr Edwards, since 'property is allways best in our own hands—and you may now if you please, pay me instead of him'.[137] In all business dealings, she said, there were 'two' principal points to be adhered to, 'INTEGRITY PROMPTNESS . . . ELOQUENCE and last 'tho not least SECURITY'.[138]

133 Ibid., Dec. 1827, p. 10.   134 Ibid. 11 Apr. 1828, p. 5.
135 Ibid. 12 Nov. 1829, p. 6.   136 Ibid. 18 Oct. 1828, p. 4.
137 Ibid. 10 June 1828, p. 5.   138 Ibid. 18 Oct. 1828, p. 2.

ARENA of ASTLEY's AMPHITHEATRE, SURREY ROAD.

Little in her past, it would seem, had prepared Susannah for the events which had followed Castell's defection, when 'nothing, upon this earth except my affection and duty I owe my dear little ones . . . could possibly have supported me';[139] nothing, that is, except her natural financial instincts, which, it would seem, Castell, to his cost, had never utilized. Every shilling of the family's income passed through her hands.[140] According to Susannah, they had no business, and no teaching—nothing but the two orchestras, the Surrey and the Amphitheatre, to support six.[141] This represented a combined income of £2. 10s. 0d., and, after William's demotion, 4 shillings less. Nor was this income always to be relied upon. In Augustine's case at least, sometimes his salary would be held by his employers for months at a time. And William seldom brought home his full salary from the Surrey.[142] Then there were overheads too, like porterage.

It is very possible that Susannah exaggerated the extent of her hardships in London in order to gain Castell's sympathy or perhaps to reinforce the legitimacy of her financial claim upon him. There is some evidence from Castell's cryptic ticks and crosses, as well as from some of the defensive responses he drew from Susannah,[143] that he thought that she did. Susannah does not mention porterage till 1832, but then it is in the same breath as deputies' fees,[144] which would suggest that one or both of the breadwinners had a second job which was never mentioned in her letters. For musicians the transport of instruments was (and still is) a problem, especially with such large, ungainly, yet fragile ones as double-basses. Nor was it seemly to be seen lugging your own about the streets of London. Thus a porter would have to be hired for the purpose—a species of manual worker ubiquitous but fairly well regulated at that time. If, as Susannah claimed, both the 'boys' had only one job each, their instruments would not have required the relatively expensive services of a specialist porter, but remained at their respective theatres. Nor would a

[139] SEC–Raper & Jones, 27 Mar. 1827, p. 1.
[140] SEC–WJC, 2 June 1832, p. 1.
[141] Ibid. 8 Aug. 1829, p. 4.   [142] Ibid. 2 June 1832, p. 2; 9 June 1829, p. 10.
[143] See SEC–WJC, 26 Jan. 1830, pp. 1–2.   [144] SEC–WJC, 2 June 1832, p. 2.

16. (*Opposite*) Engraving after George Jones, 1815, showing some details of the orchestra. Note the bowing technique of the strings, the seeming redundancy of the music, and the fact that the orchestra is not seated. The double-bass player, far left, could conceivably have been a young Augustine Humble. Ref. GLRO. Lambeth D 17451.

deputy have to be hired unless they were performing elsewhere. But notwithstanding the possibility of a petty deception or two, Susannah would seem to have received very little in the way of material support from Castell. In 1830, she claimed that she had received from him in four years no more than £10, four of which had gone to pay his subscription to the Royal Society of Musicians.[145] And there can be little doubt that, in the early days at least, things had been critical.

The first domestic priority in the Stangate Street household was evidently suitable clothing for the two breadwinners, Augustine and William. Business had to be attended to in respectable attire, and, as Susannah pointed out, William's clothing had become as expensive as his father's. Indeed this supports Cyril Ehrlich's point that clothing for musicians was a greater financial consideration than musical instruments, which were then (except for exceptionally fine examples) still relatively cheap; representing a neat inversion of the economic priorities of the musician of today.[146] The two girls and poor Alfred might become almost prisoners for lack of decent clothing, said Susannah, but the two 'senior males' must slave over their double-basses well turned out in tie and tails. Decorum required nothing less than that the musician give no offence to his 'patrons' by appearing scruffily or inappropriately dressed, even if he had, often enough, to endure much less than polite decorum from them—especially from theatre audiences. Expensive clothes, porterage, deputies' fees, and managerial forfeits constituted the routine overheads of the theatre musician's day-to-day business. It was well for him that at least his instrument did not have to cost him a year's earnings.

But clothes were important not only for William and Augustine—the lack of them, said Susannah, greatly retarded the girls' progress in life,[147] even more, it would seem, than their lack of education. The moral principles which she had inculcated in them might stand in the stead of formal education, but nothing could stand in the stead of the horsehair petticoats, ribbons, and stays in that style of 'rapturous buoyancy' that had ousted the simpler romantic elegance of the Revolutionary period. Gigot sleeves, whip waists, and elaborately bouffant skirts must have seemed almost a conspiracy against striving mothers on slender means.[148]

[145] SEC–WJC, 13 Oct. 1830, p. 1.
[146] Ibid. 18 Oct. 1828, p. 4; 12 Nov. 1829, p. 8; 12 Nov. 1829, p. 8; Cyril Ehrlich, 'Market Themes', Journal of the Royal Musical Association, 114 (1989), 2–5.
[147] SEC–WJC, 12 Nov. 1829, p. 6.
[148] Cunningham, Handbook of English Costume, 383–400.

Food came a poor second. If we are to judge from Susannah's account, bread was the staple. Nine loaves were consumed each week. This was because, explained Susannah, the children did not particularly relish, *yet*, the homely quality of the food that economy forced her to provide. This seems to have consisted at least in part of potatoes—six of which were consumed daily. In 1830, the weekly bill for bread alone was 8 and sometimes 9 shillings. But by then she seems to have had some success with her homely offerings and claimed to be able to feed six for 8*d*.: pease at 6*d*. and bones at 2*d*.[149] Presumably these were for pea and ham soup—something to stick to the ribs in the extremely cold weather of January and February when the Thames came close to freezing.[150] And this made with her own hands in her own kitchen—presumably without the aid of any servant. Doubtless, though, the two girls, Emily and Susan, assisted their mother, perhaps while Alfred worked at his lessons or practised the violin, and William attended his daily rehearsals at the theatre.

THE CHILDREN: HEIRS OF CONFLICT

All four, Susannah declared, were the children of Genius, and if Castell could have seen them he would have had to agree that she had 'not been deficient' in her duty towards them.[151] Apart from Augustine and of course Susannah herself, the family circle was completed by the cat and a number of goldfish. Such was Susannah's 'state and belov'd subjects',[152] over whom she ruled in amity, peace, and openness. Or so she said.

It is unlikely that Susannah would have sent across to France anything but a glowing picture of the family scene. Indeed in terms of their relationship there seemed to have been much currency in this. Castell may have had his 'nest of butterfly's', but she knew she had what really mattered—the living, breathing, status-creating family. Understanding the nature and implications of this posture, Castell accused her of preventing communication between himself and his children—of turning them against him.[153] To these accusations she replied with indignation

---

[149] Nine loaves, SEC–WJC, 11 Feb. 1828, p. 2; homely food, 12 Nov. 1829, p. 8; potatoes, 11 Feb. 1828, p. 2; bread bill, Dec. 1830, p. 3; pease and bones, 20 Feb. 1830, p. 1.   [150] Ibid. 26 Jan. 1830, p. 1.
[151] SEC–WJC, 3 Feb. 1831, p. 4.   [152] Ibid. 14 Jan. 1828, p. 3.
[153] WJC–SEC, 30 Jan. 1828, p. 4; SEC–WJC, 10 July 1828, p. 6; ibid. 13 Jan. 1829, p. 4; 25 June 1829, p. 4; 20 Oct. 1829, p. 3.

and sometimes with anger, but a letter from William or Alfred, or a note from the girls, was sometimes the result—as proof, since it was deemed necessary, of her good faith.

William, the eldest, born 18 April 1812, seemed to have been held in special regard by both his parents. He had been the offspring of love, and 'cast in beautious mould'. His birth had so entranced his father, as we have already seen, that Susannah had feared a transfer of affection. At almost 17, his features, said Susannah, were becoming manly, 'but they are still as lovely as ever'.[154] He was everything she could wish for or desire. She had, she said, at all times 'taken infinite pains in forming his principles (as being the eldest of the family) and now reap the pleasure and consolation in feeling that my exertions were not lost'.[155] At about this time he was about 5′ 5½″ tall,[156] and employed at the Surrey, possibly in his father's old position as first bass, on a salary of £1. 5s. 0d. a week. Susannah might complain about this rate of pay, yet it was evidently as much as Augustine was getting at the Amphitheatre if what she said was true and their total income was then £2. 10s. 0d.: and Augustine was fifteen years William's senior. From this we could deduce that either Augustine was a very ordinary performer or William an exceptional one; but this would not be taking into account the narrowness of opportunity at this level within the profession, where the best chance for material advancement was in having jobs in two (or more) orchestras rather than hoping for promotion on merit, or even age, in one. It was plain, though, that young William was a proficient performer.

Almost certainly his father's pupil, he was evidently given a thorough grounding in music. In his early childhood—probably at St Albans—'practice' was considered by his father to have been of more importance than what Susannah called 'education'. That commodity, he considered, could be acquired at any later period of life, and days of William's schooling, Susannah had complained, had been missed while he remained at home and practised.[157] It had not been a happy time, it would seem, especially after Susannah had returned to London because of family dissension, and he and Alfred had been left to the tender mercies of their father's horsewhipping servant—probably the infamous Betsy—when 'blood ran down Alfred's fingers'.[158] It was then that he had written to his mother, secretly and in blacking, begging her to come back. As we have seen, the results were significant.

---

[154] SEC–WJC, 13 Jan. 1829, p. 7.   [155] Ibid. 18 Oct. 1828, p. 4.
[156] Ibid. 15 Dec. 1828, p. 4; 14 Feb. 1829, p. 6.
[157] Ibid. 27 Mar. 1829, p. 8; 25 June 1829, p. 5.   [158] Ibid.

William, however, seems to have had a natural aptitude for music. He played the pianoforte 'above mediocrity', took pleasure in playing the organ, or would have, if it had been playable, and made 'wonderful' progress on the cello under the desultory instruction of Brooks from 1828.[159] The double-bass it would appear inspired no special interest and was probably considered no more than a means of gaining employment in an orchestra. Domenico Dragonetti (1763–1846) was the foremost exponent of the instrument in London at the time and his performances made him a celebrity, but on the whole the instrument was considered to have few advantages and certainly presented few opportunities for displays of virtuosity. It was hard work too. Susannah drew a vivid enough picture of her son 'working to the "Horses" till he has not a dry thread on his back, he cannot sit down from 6 till 12 at night'. The cello on the other hand, while it might not pay any more, would 'undoubtedly relieve him from much exertion'.[160]

William's relations with his father, if we may judge from the letters he sent to him, usually under duress from Susannah, were reserved to the point of coolness. His very first had a sting in its tailpiece: 'This is but the second letter I ever wrote the first was done in blacking.' A reference to the bad old horsewhipping days in St Albans. One can detect almost a sullenness in his deadpan statements about the 'improvements' of which he had obviously been instructed to inform his father: the new building developments behind Stangate Street and in the West End; and his summation of domestic affairs is almost absurd in its reticence.

The cat is still alive the fish are dead and I go on with my practice on the Piano Forte and Alfred his violin but receives instruction from a friend of Augustine's. Susan and I ina are very well   Mr Sulsh is dead Mrs Daws over the way and Mrs Cooper of Pratt St and Mr Kusunder.

Without endearment or any formal embellishments of respect, it is signed 'W J'. The note about the blacking letter was an afterthought, as were the full names of the other three children appended beneath.[161] Hardly what Castell had had in mind when he had exhorted Susannah to let him write 'his own ideas'.[162]

His next letter, in May 1828, was slightly more expansive. Castell had evidently asked what 'authors' he played from, suggesting a fatherly as well as a professional concern, to which the boy replied with what must

---

[159] Piano, ibid. 26 Jan. 1830, p. 5; organ, 12 Nov. 1829, p. 6; cello, 18 Oct. 1828, p. 6.
[160] Ibid. 25 May 1830, p. 5; 26 Jan. 1830, p. 6.
[161] W Jones C–WJC, 19 Feb. 1828, p. 1.   [162] WJC–SEC, 30 Jan. 1830, p. 4.

have been an aggravating obtuseness, 'They are those whose works we have in the house or anything we can get.' Then he informed his father of all their ages, requested the bows for himself and Alfred as well as some foreign music, and ended with the following flourish:

I have nothing particular to communicate as I suppose mother writes what is necessary—our garden begins to smile 'tho the weather has been very indifferent. I will send our heights in my next since I last wrote James Mackintosh has died.
    I remain
        Dutifully yours

                                                    W

The deaths of neighbours seemed to preoccupy him. On 15 July 1828, by comparison, he wrote in almost epic terms. But Susannah made several amendments to this letter as well as emphatic additions which suggest something less than a spontaneous effort. And one senses that he was happy enough simply to be a vehicle for his mother's sentiments, for there is in this letter little that is boyish—even boyishly gauche. He had by then started working at the Surrey, but this hardly accounts for such a marked alteration in style.

I have scarce an hour to myself my whole time is so taken up with daily rehearsals that my practice is neglected except what I get by stealth. I am with Mr Erskine and hardly contrive to see our street before One in the morning [This heavily underscored by Susannah] ... London swarms with teachers so terms and business in general is very bad—Alfred will not be able to do anything of consequence for these two years to come he may then perhaps be so fortunate as to acquire 25/- pr week in bad company his appearance will also be against [him] as he very slowly ...

Here Susannah actively intervened, crossing out a whole line of William's attempt to describe Alfred's problems, and substituting simply the word 'grows'. The last three sentences, however, have a ring of authenticity.

Buildings rapidly proceed in our neighbourhood we shall be shut out of our prospect we are all well but Alfred has a breaking out at the back of his neck. The weather is very dreadful tremendous showers. since I last wrote Mr & Mrs Daws have died Maria Cook Susan Knight and the Archbishop of Canterbury on Monday last.

                                                    WJC

On 30 July 1828, he sent what appears to have been his last chilly little missive, thanking his father for a present of some music, suggesting how the bows might be packed, and enquiring into the likelihood of additional duties that might be charged on them in England. It ends:

The weather is very cold and miserable. I am commissioned to inform you that you will receive in a few days after this, an answer to yours

W

No one, it seems, had died.

Castell appears to have been less than content with these filial efforts, or at least complained of their infrequency, and Susannah was often at pains to assure him that William's reasons for not writing were not sinister—he was just so busy attending rehearsals, practising, studying the cello, and attending nightly performances at the theatre. 'His most valued hours', she explained, were 'devoted to the caprice of others', that is, in the gaining of a livelihood. This might appear strange to Castell, she suggested, 'but William's time is completely occupied'.[163]

In about May 1828, Castell suggested that William should visit him in France. Susannah declined to permit this. He had been, she said, a long time in training and his engagement at the Surrey was at last serviceable and the needs of the family were pressing. He might lose his place. There were plenty ready and willing to fill it. It would be imprudent to break the chain. These, she declared, were her only reasons. It was not that she did not trust him to keep his word to return the boy to England, for, in any case, she knew that William would not stay away from her.[164]

Susannah may have convinced herself if not Castell of the honesty of these arguments. Years later, though, she revealed the nature of the suspicions which were more likely to have influenced her decision. She had suspected that William was to be introduced to Miss Jones, in order to bring about an 'Eclaircissement'.[165] William would have been peculiarly insensitive had he not recognized his position in relation to his warring parents, both of whom evidently needed to claim him as their victory.

Not long after this altercation, the victory having conclusively gone to Susannah, she told Castell of an event that had occurred in St Albans in 1826, just a month after his departure, on the occasion when Horner Rumball had so affronted her with his blasphemous suggestion. Castell's own bed had somehow come to repose in Horner's house (as a result, presumably, of the auction at Holloway), and that night, she said, she had insisted that both she as well as her son 'partake of it'. She had known at the time that Mrs H. had thought him too old to do so with propriety, but she had left them to their musings and had had her way. It

[163] SEC–WJC, 14 Dec. 1828, p. 4; 10 July 1828, pp. 5–6.
[164] Ibid. 22 May 1828, p. 3.   [165] Ibid. 8 Feb. 1831, p. 4.

was, she said, 'the last time he has slept by <u>my</u> side in the <u>same</u> bed and I think it more than probable that he never again will . . . I may say that my repose <u>did not</u> suffer from the idea of <u>our having slept under the same canopy</u>.'[166] In the currency of Susannah and Castell's relationship it is difficult to know the value of this little story and what effect it sought to achieve.

William's relationship to Susannah herself is unclear. It may have been just as intransigent and reserved as his letters suggest it was with his father. We have only Susannah's word that it was not. Susannah had once remarked that in one respect at least their children were more fortunate than their parents had been, 'being early initiated into life with a heavy cloud hanging over their brow—this has not only made them <u>feel</u>—but they will <u>seek</u> independence . . .'.[167] For William this seems to have been true enough. He was, said Susannah, 'indefatigable & gets on',[168] and his later career, though (as far as we know) undistinguished, was to achieve for him the material success that had so eluded his parents.

Alfred, as we have already seen, had had a dubious start. He had not quite escaped, as we know, the 'direfull results' of his father's 'incontinence', although what those results were was never elaborated upon. His aptitude for music, however, was not pronounced and Susannah despaired of his ever making a living by it.[169] He would seem also to have suffered, as William's letter suggested, from some sort of growth retardation.

He was born 8 February 1814[170] and seems to have been quite a different proposition to his elder brother, the cool, competent William. We first find him in about 1820 remonstrating with his father about leaving Susannah in the Stangate Street house with odd teacups, and this alone would suggest a sympathetic disposition. Whereas William's role in domestic politics was that of moral trophy, Alfred's role seems to have been that of inducer of guilt. His very birth was closely associated with Castell's irregularities. Later, Susannah recalled that it was when she had tried to stop him once from 'running and mixing with a set of blagards to see a fire near Waterloo Bridge' that Castell had struck her for the first time.[171] And it had been Alfred's fingers that had run with blood from the horsewhip, applied in circumstances associated with Susannah's

[166] SEC–WJC, 31 July 1828, p. 3.   [167] Ibid. 18 Oct. 1828, p. 4.
[168] Ibid. 26 Jan. 1830, p. 6.
[169] Ibid. p. 5; 16 May 1832, p. 3; 3 Feb. 1831, p. 3.
[170] W Jones C–WJC, 13 May 1828, p. 1.   [171] SEC–WJC, 8 Aug. 1829, p. 6.

humiliation and Castell's waywardness at St Albans. Indeed, whenever Susannah mentions Alfred it is almost always to remark some limitation or set of circumstances that are of concern to her and which carry an implicit remonstrance. Poor Alfred had been, said Susannah in 1829, for a long time 'a dead weight on my mind',[172] and doubtless Castell knew what she meant by that.

He was certainly quite tiny. In February 1829, at the age of 15, he was only 4′ 6½″ tall—one-and-a-half inches shorter than Emily who was sixteen months his junior, and nearly a foot shorter than William.[173] But there is no evidence that he had other, more serious, disabilities. His first letter to his father of 30 July 1828 demonstrates a warmth and charm not evident in William's letters. Indeed the contrast between them is quite stark.

This is the first letter I ever wrote so that I hope you will look over all mistakes I have a favour to request but not till it is perfectly convenient which is some violin music for there is a dearth of this at home, there are some Spohr's which are almost too difficult I am tired of Corelli's Solos and now want a little variety The cat is well but growing old the last Gold fish died Jan 28th 1827. Our garden is fill'd with flowe[r]s and looks very pretty. We have a verandah reaching to the little wall and supported by a light frame with a handsome front. We have 52 bunches of grapes which look very pretty, the neighbours are completely shut out by the vine. On Mackintosh's side we have a lattice work above the wall 2 feet high. We are all in tolerable health and hoping that you are the same.

                                                                                           A

Susannah's misgivings about Alfred, regardless of their domestic implications, were born no doubt out of genuine maternal solicitude, and there can be little argument that she was seriously concerned about his ultimate welfare. Her affection is evident enough in the pride she took in his progress under Mr Catherby.

Should an opportunity occur I will send you Alfred's next school letter which I expect previous to the vacation—you will then judge of the improvement he is making—I consider that he has rapidly advanced in Arithmetic & has just enter'd into the rule of three and all since Lady Day [25 March]—he was then desparately ignorant for the little he had been acquainted with was entirely forgotten.[174]

But his musical career she despaired of, particularly in the light of the increased competition from those 'half taught and worse educated

[172] Ibid. 27 Mar. 1829, p. 8.
[173] Ibid. 14 Feb. 1829, p. 6.   [174] Ibid. 28 Nov. 1829, p. 5.

youths' from the Royal Academy of Music with their automatic access to patronage. He would never, she feared, be able to acquire an existence by music and he was now too old to learn a trade even if she had had the ability to pay a premium. She had not even the funds, she said, to provide him with clothes for the duration of an apprenticeship.[175] So music it continued to be.

The violin seems to have been Alfred's only instrument. There is no mention of his ever having learnt or played the pianoforte or organ, keyboard instruments of great importance to professional musicians. This may have been because of his size or perhaps because he showed no aptitude. But even so, his instruction on the violin seems to have been sporadic and insufficient. Susannah remarked in November 1829 that he was making 'but small progress and has practised by himself for the past twelve months', admitting later, though, that 'with a master [he] would play the violin very well'.[176]

To what extent Alfred was aware of these maternal anxieties on his behalf we do not know. He seemed blithely unconcerned enough on his seventeenth birthday on 8 February 1831, when he sent his father a little piece of verbal whimsy, probably not of his own invention, about the German doctor and his horse—'Rund away or sdolen or vas sdrayed'—a popular strain of chauvinistic humour which may have had a particular attraction for English musicians at the time, who were then confronting yet another wave of German competition.

He holts up his head and looks gaily, and ven he has been frighten he joomps apout like everything in the vorld. He vill ride mit a saddle or a chaise or a kart, or he vill go by himself without nopoddy but a pag on his pack & a poy on it. He is not very old, and ven he valks or runs his head goes first and his dail stays pehind, only when he gets mad and turns round, then his dail come first . . .[177]

Castell received this effort at the French port of Le Havre as he was awaiting his departure from Europe. Did it make him smile? The previous week Alfred had provided him with other happy *morceaux* as well.

We have lost a troublesome neighbour Mrs Wadham has been dead about three months was in her 87th year. Our old cat is gone we were obliged to drown her, owing to her dirty habits, she had worn to a skeleton, and about 2 inches of her

[175] SEC–WJC, 3 Feb. 1831, p. 3.
[176] Ibid. 12 Nov. 1829, p. 5; 25 May 1830, p. 3.
[177] Unsigned; presume AJC–WJC; prefaces SEC–WJC, 8 Feb. 1831, p. 1.

tail we keep suspended from the kitchen ceiling to perpetuate her memory. She was buried in a coffin at the top of the garden under the Ivy.

AHJ Castel[178]

Perhaps it was the recollection of such friendly offerings from his second son that motivated Castell to suggest, years later, that Alfred might join him in New South Wales, an idea, however, which, according to Susannah, he rejected. 'I read to him the subject of your letter as related to him (but without comment) but he adheres to remaining in England to the chance of sailing to a country from whence he might never return.'[179]

For all Susannah's fears about Alfred's lack of ability on the violin, he does, however, appear to have been launched into a musical career, albeit a short one. In 1834 he was 'at present' without an engagement, and in 1835, at 'past 21', was not earning a farthing.[180]

It was the two girls, however, Emily and Susan, over whose fate Susannah felt the least repose. Boys, she said, could somehow buffet with the world—not so her two dear female children. Tenderly bred, neither, she believed, was capable of earning a living. Who, she asked their absent father, would protect them?[181]

The elder, Emily Angelina, also called 'Lina', was born 15 August 1815. As Castell's first daughter, she seems to have been something of a favourite. It was to Emily that the contentious portrait was sent in 1828, and in 1830 came an invitation to visit him in France, apparently in response to a remark of Susannah's that the child had of late been 'rather drooping'.[182] The invitation was declined. She had merely had a cold which Susannah had thought rather too protracted, but in any case, even if Emily had been ill, sending her to France would have been considered an unlikely remedy. She could hardly prevail upon herself, she said, to consign her child to the guardianship of strangers in a foreign country. To whom could Emily look, she argued, when on a bed of sickness, for that maternal tenderness so congenial to her feelings? And for all their good intentions, men were not always the best judges in such matters. But in any case, Emily herself had firmly rejected the offer and she, Susannah, could confidently assert that no accusation of improper motive or feeling whatever could be made.[183] Another victory to Susannah.

Susannah described Emily in May 1830 as 'uncommonly tall', being

178 With SEC–WJC 3 Feb. 1831, p. 6.
179 SEC–WJC, 28 May 1834, p. 2.   180 Ibid. 4 May 1835 [No. 2], p. 3.
181 Ibid. 28 May 1834, p. 1; 4 May 1835 [No. 1], pp. 2–3; 28 May 1834, p. 1.
182 Ibid. 25 May 1830, p. 3.   183 Ibid. 16 June 1830, p. 2.

an inch and a half taller than Alfred, but this had been true in February
1829 when she was 4′ 8″ and Alfred 4′ 6½″,[184] so that in all likelihood she
was still under five foot fifteen months later at nearly fifteen years of
age—surely not all that tall, especially since we know that Alfred himself
was underdeveloped for his age. But perhaps maternal pride was not
altogether rational upon such points. Earlier, Susannah informed Castell
that 'Emily's limbs are very passable the defects must be looked for',[185] so
we are in little doubt that Emily was the subject of some gratification to
her mother. Indeed, it is perhaps notable that the one and only recorded
occasion where the hearth was forsaken for a place of public amusement
was when Susannah was prevailed upon to take Emily, probably for her
birthday in August 1828, to Vauxhall. Susannah does not recall whether
Emily enjoyed the experience but she certainly did not.

I accompany'd Emily to Vauxhall on Wednesday evening and have not since
recover'd the fatigue. She had never been there before and I was induced to
remain on my legs for nearly eight hours. The Gardens (in my opinion) have lost
their celebrity, worse company I never saw or anything so bad—the incessant
rains have induced the proprietors to a new trade of attracting their visitors by
advertising lottery drawings consisting of presents of wine and even suppers. The
Rotunda, that had formerly been a elegant lounge, is metamorphos'd into a
would-be theatre. My evening's amusement was to me a degree superior to a
culprit sentenced to run the gauntlet.[186]

Such was Susannah's exhaustion on account of this indulgence that
she subsequently made a mistake in addressing a letter to Castell which
she found intensely embarrassing. 'You can have no idea how this
mistake has agitated me.' The reason for her 'apparent stupidity', she
said, was not only the trip to Vauxhall but a case of 'the "state grows too
large for the head" and we have no security in our establishment but our
own weak brains—State ministers have no more all beside is performed
by underlings'.[187] But Emily had had her treat.

Apart from her name appended to William's letter of 19 February
1828, Emily's communication with her father was limited to one brief
and inconsequential note.

I have nothing particular to communicate but when this you see, remember ME
    Emily Angelina[188]

    [184] SEC–WJC, 25 May 1830, p. 3; 14 Feb. 1829, p. 6.
    [185] Ibid. 27 Mar. 1829, p. 10.   [186] Ibid. 23 Aug. 1828, p. 2.
    [187] Ibid.   [188] With SEC–WJC, 8 Feb. 1831, p. 6.

The rhyming element was evidently a kind of standard autograph of the day. In 1829 a convict, William Vincent, had written to his family in Sussex from Australia,

> When this you See
> Remember me,
> And banish all trouble away from thee.[189]

Perhaps the last line had been the convict's own inspiration, for that wish had not been extended from Emily to her father.

Susan, the second daughter and youngest child, was born 25 April 1820, just as the marriage had reached one of its critical turning-points. She had been too young for her father to cope with at St Albans when he had taken all the children there and left Susannah in Stangate Street. Susannah's response had been to name the child after herself, and thus, she said, 'she became doubly dear by adoption'.[190] But of all the children she is the least mentioned. In 1828 Susannah speaks of her with great affection: 'All I pray for is that my life may be spared for the sake of my two girls, my dear little NAMELY (register'd Susanna) is a very pretty little girl and already plays the Egyptian Rondo.'[191] But she seldom enters into the debate about either the past or the future, not specifically in any case. This may have been because, of all the children, Susan was the least known to Castell. After 1820 he appears to have spent a great deal of time away from home, and perhaps her having been 'adopted' by Susannah reduced his own regard for her in proportion as it had doubled Susannah's.

The formal education of the 'dear girls', had been, as we have seen, rather a question of preserving them from 'savage ignorance', as well as from the savage influences of the local vernacular. Susannah also had firm ideas, however, on the importance of moral values, and we can be certain that her girls received from her own lips those precepts by which she considered their lives should be shaped. In her view, one of the greatest dangers to females was in their leaving the nursery prematurely, presumably before the process of moulding their minds was complete.[192] The spectacle of Castell's 'nest of butterfly's', some barely in their sixteenth year, behaving, as described by Castell, with apparent forwardness and impropriety, appalled her as a parent. She sincerely felt 'compassion for their posterity'.

---

[189] In Hughes, *Fatal Shore*, p. 316.
[191] Ibid. 3 Nov. 1828, pp. 5–6.
[190] SEC–WJC, 25 June 1829, p. 4.
[192] Ibid. 8 May 1828, p. 3.

In England she was certain that things were managed differently. There a man felt nothing but disgust at such female conduct, and if a marriage actually resulted, the woman would be reduced to obsequious servility while the husband, having given her the boon of marriage as a reward, would rule like a Turk. After all, what complaint could she justly make? Nor would it end there, for, self-mortified, the woman would seek a new lover, 'the consequences of which are but too obvious to require more explanation necessary'.[193] But she was sure in any case that true English femininity would never run such terrible risks, and her general opinion of French manners and morals was so low that nothing in all this surprised her. 'The Manners of the French Nation I *detest*.'

France would be the last place I would wish a daughter of mine educated at— they acquire such manners as are most disgusting to Englishmen who unite in opinion that there are no other such wives and mothers in the world as their own countrywomen—a french education is sufficient to ruin any female and were I unfortunately destin'd to spend my days in France, I would certainly send my daughters to an Establishment in England.[194]

From the other side of the Channel the view of English womanhood and female education was rather different. Flora Tristan considered that the innate qualities of English women were 'stifled by an education system based on false principles, and by the atmosphere of hypocrisy, prejudice and vice which permeates their lives'.

Although it has been fashionable for a long time to praise this country [England] for its freedom, it is the home of the most dreadful tyranny, and woman is subjected by prejudice and by law to the most revolting inequalities! She can inherit only if she has no brother. She is deprived of civil and political rights, and the law has made her in every way a slave to her husband. She is trained to be hypocritical, and made to bear alone the heavy yoke of public opinion. Everything that her awakening senses perceive, everything that develops her faculties, everything that she has to endure, inevitably result in materializing her tastes, hardening her heart, and numbing her soul.[195]

Susannah's own attitude to the rights and duties of women is extremely ambivalent. She herself, as we have already seen, was brought up in an atmosphere of at least some intellectual liberation, and she contests the idea that a wife should be the echo of all her husband's ideas and opinions, and rejects that she should become 'subservient to all his

---

[193] SEC–WJC, 8 May 1828, pp. 2–3.   [194] Ibid. 10 July 1828, p. 3.
[195] Flora Tristan, *London Journal, A Survey of London Life in the 1830s* (1980), 191.

desires'.[196] There are even times, she thought, when women 'should not act under the influence of their husbands'. There were good and bad of both sexes, 'but when the female is prudent, her counsels ought not to be rejected for they are sincere'.[197] Ultimately, though, all depended on the male. It was he who defined the nature of the partnership between man and wife. If the woman was not to be a slave, it depended on the disposition of the man and the value he attached to the alliance. But by the same token, as we have already seen, any errors on the part of the female may be traced, 'out of "nine cases in Ten"', to the 'misconduct of their husbands', or 'injudicious treatment'.[198]

Susannah, who had probably absorbed some elements of the late eighteenth-century feminist debate, seems to say,—although this is not altogether clear from her rather muddled syntax—that although He furnished the female with 'intellectual reason', she did not think, 'or ever shall, that the Almighty out of the Greatness and Supremacy and equatable distribution of his Mercy's when he first made Male & Female ... gave Her the same distinguishing faculty's as Man'. In this view Susannah would not have been especially reactionary. Even the redoubtable Caroline Norton, née Sheridan (1808–77), who in the 1830s took on her husband and the legal establishment (unsuccessfully) over the custody of her children, declared that ideas about women's intellectual equality with men were 'wild and stupid theories'. Nor would a Rousseauesque education have altered Susannah's conventional thinking on this issue, as Mary Wollstonecraft was at pains to establish.[199]

Within a general framework of inequality and dependence then, Susannah suggests that woman's essential goodness ought to be acknowledged—and that she ought to be both protected and respected by men and granted even some occasional moments of independent judgement, provided her case was demonstrably 'prudent' and 'sincere'. One soon discovers, however, that Susannah when expostulating upon such subjects is not really generalizing at all, but is talking only about herself. Her opinion of most other women was not very high at all: 'to some men, love is a trade—but it is the ordinary occupation of women as

[196] SEC–WJC, Dec. 1827, p. 12; p. 14.
[197] Ibid. 27 Mar. 1829, p. 9.   [198] Ibid., Dec. 1830, p. 2.
[199] Ibid., Dec. 1827, p. 13; Mrs Norton quoted in Dorothy Marshall, *Industrial England 1776–1851* (2nd edn., 1982), 137–8; see Mary Wollstonecraft's criticisms of Rousseau's attitudes to women in *A Vindication of the Rights of Women*; for a useful overview of 18th-century feminist thought, see Alice Browne, *The Eighteenth Century Feminist Mind* (1987).

most of their pursuits are of a sedentary nature and their minds contaminated by flattery . . .'.[200] The insults she received from Miss Jones were nothing to her, as she pointed out, since they came from 'the pen of a <u>mere</u> woman only'. And as she once informed Castell, 'I am totally distinct from any <u>other female</u>.'[201]

Out of this peculiar amalgam of prideful individualism and collective abnegation we may only conjecture what she distilled and passed on to her two daughters as her contribution to their moral equipment. When she tells us, though, that her daughters were 'tenderly bred and incapable of earning a living', we may presume to guess that tacked on to Susannah's own moral priorities were those of the middle-class culture to which she aspired, which increasingly reduced the role of the woman in society from active partner to childlike appendage and passive and powerless symbol of all the virtues which men admired as civilized but could not afford to practise. Humility, tenderness, delicacy, duty, chastity, fidelity, and selflessness were all the female virtues to be expressed by women with an emotionless reserve that marked them as the true daughters of Albion. Spontaneity and will—passion and power—like the natural vigour of Shakespearian English, became, in women, an affront to refined sensibilities.

On the subject of Miss Paton, the *Quarterly* pondered:

how much diminished are the effects of our most distinguished vocalists by the constraint or coldness of manner. In this indeed our singers are truly national— their reserve accords with English notions of feminine manners, and we would not, for any consideration, trespass upon an opinion which is perhaps one of the great conservators of our morals and our happiness. At the same time we have that confidence in the natural temperament of our females, both constitutional and intellectual, that we stedfastly believe they might indulge the display of their sensibilities in art to a much greater extent with perfect safety.[202]

But 'perfect safety' could never be really guaranteed for women unless they could demonstrate conformity and procure male protection. Susannah was probably acutely aware of this and was aware also that her two daughters had the marriage dice loaded against them because of their impoverished condition, yet she seems to have opted to improve their chances in that field by reducing their ultimate potential for financial independence. From what evidence we have, it does not appear

[200] SEC–WJC, 4 June 1829, pp. 2–3.
[201] Ibid., Dec. 1827, p. 16; 10 Apr. 1829, p. 5.
[202] 'Miss Paton', *QMMR* v (1823), 192.

as if the gamble paid off. Of Susan's fate nothing is known, but Emily died unmarried at the age of 33.[203]

REVOLUTIONS

Predictably, Castell had not been pleased by Susannah's rejection of his proposals regarding the rehabilitation of Miss Jones's social status in France,[204] and resented her soliciting advice from James Rumball on the subject. Her own judgement, he thought, 'might have been sufficient'.[205] But Susannah stressed that her 'noncompliance arose from motives of pure zeal toward you', and that as usual, 'you impute blame to me, whose only object was to be of real service—if that I have done wrong in this affair it was the farthest from my intention. I have yet one consolation left—an approving conscience.'[206]

Castell had obviously taken the opportunity for a comprehensive offensive against Susannah for her deficiencies in regard to him, past and present, including what Susannah described as a 'flowing account in describing the Amiable duty of a wife' (which he subsequently corrected, altering the word 'wife' to read 'female').[207] Very pretty reading for some, she declared; too bad, though, that 'during the course of our Union no opportunity was ever afforded me of evincing and convincing you that I am capable of those qualities (tho without fascinations) for in a female that is studied hypocracy . . .'[208] (Castell altered the word 'Union' to 'acquaintance'). He had also accused her of viewing him 'in the light of a "younger brother"'. 'Believe me,' she reassured him, 'under similar cases, my conduct would have been the same towards a man older than myself.'[209]

As regards Miss Jones, he continued to defend his conduct, suggesting that he had only told Miss Jones of his fiery connection with Susannah to 'alienate her feelings' at a period when 'her light and life was in [his] keeping'. Susannah was highly sceptical of this line of argument and critical of his remark that 'she still pretends to love me as you do'. Such a remark she considered 'both ill-timed and worse placed'. She had no desire, she said, 'to take an active part in the drama of the "Rival Queens" [in which] you have thought proper to class us'.[210] Indeed, one

[203] GRO, Deaths, 28 May 1849.
[205] Quoted in ibid. 27 Mar. 1829, p. 1.
[207] Ibid. 3; p. 3 n.
[209] Ibid. 7.
[204] SEC–WJC, 10 Apr. 1829, p. 1.
[206] SEC–WJC, 10 Apr. 1829, p. 2.
[208] Ibid.
[210] Ibid. 4; 5.

can understand her annoyance at such an allusion. If she were to be the raging Roxana and Miss Jones the disappointed Statira, the two competing wives, this left Castell as the tragic hero Alexander, the ultimate victim of female passions.[211] If there was to be a victim, it was to be Susannah, not Castell. Already his behaviour towards her had taken its toll.

... remember what I have often predicted may prove true 'That you will (in a double sense) love me in the grave' my health was never in such a state as at present. I do not calculate from the disappearance of the 'rose on my damask cheek' but something more formidable in appearance, which with long agitated state of mental sufferings have produced on my frame. I have this day (Thursday) consulted Mr White who says I have a a partial affection of the Liver, and my limits are affected by it, my left leg is bandaged from knee to ankle and it is at this moment supported by a chair, but 'heaven's will be done'.[212]

But Susannah had not yet despaired of the relationship. In June 1829, Castell sent a present of some money, which, although it would not cover all the parish rates and the window tax, then due, had been gratefully received.[213] It would seem, though, that the Jones affair had ended, and that Miss Jones was returning to London, possibly in some dudgeon, although specific details are not dwelt upon. Susannah declared herself ready to take on both father and daughter on Castell's behalf while expressing the hope that the whole unfortunate affair would 'prove a lasting lesson never to behave with more than slender kindness to any female',[214] and after reiterating some of the major causes of family discord—all attributed to Castell—she ended on a marked note of reconciliation: 'Notwithstanding all I say—my "anger is turned away—and my hand stretched out still".'[215] Another long letter quickly followed containing further analyses of past events and grievances and ending with this passionate declaration to her 'Dear William':

I love you most fervently and your unnatural treatment at times nearly drove me to distraction for my feelings as you know are strong—I do most sincerely forgive you and if my heart in its present state is worth your acceptance—it is yours—but keep it and do not again risk its loss . . . believe me you are not friendless and your memory lives in my heart as I think your last letters breathe contrition which is all

---

[211] Nathaniel Lee, *The Rival Queens: or the Death of Alexander*, prod. 1677. Revived in some splendour in 1795 with John Kemble as Alexander. There were also burlesques by C. Cibber in 1729 and Thomas Holcroft in 1794. *Biographica Dramatica*, iii. 211–12.
[212] SEC–WJC, 10 Apr. 1829, p. 9.   [213] Ibid. 4 June 1829, p. 1.
[214] Ibid. 2.   [215] Ibid. 6.

I expect as it is impossible to retrace our steps—now tell me candidly. <u>Do you,</u> <u>OR NOT, LOVE ME?</u> let us not deceive each other for much depends on your answer to this simple question.[216]

She was right, much did depend upon his answer to this 'simple question'. It was indeed to be the turning-point in their post-1826 relationship, after which nothing seemed more unlikely than that he would ever return.

To say that Susannah regretted her declaration and her question would hardly be to exaggerate. She knew, she said, it had been a mistake as soon as the letter was posted, but by then it was too late.[217] She had asked him to pass over her indulgences in silence, but no, such a treat was not to be missed, she said.

Castell had obviously taken the opportunity to compose another major assault in what Susannah referred to as his 'pamphlets', which, she said, displayed 'a total absense of common humanity or good feeling'.[218] He had evidently filled at least two sheets reproaching her for her 'deformity' in writing in 'affectionate terms', and accusing her of insanity; but at the same time he had demonstrated his own brand of perversity in including in those same sheets a 'composition' ('Oh Susanna'), which was meant to 'extort . . . or . . . <u>extract</u> from me a confession of the strong attachment I continued to possess for you'. Thus, she argued, it was he, not she, who was insane.[219] Neither was obviously insane, but Castell certainly seems to have enjoyed twisting the knife. And he did not let up: 'You have literally open'd a battery on me, and taken me by storm. Is not my forlorn <u>destitute</u> situation, <u>of itself</u> <u>sufficient</u> to allay your resentment, without grasping at every slender opportunity to destroy the few remaining hours of my life . . .'[220]

Not only had he directly attacked Susannah, but he had taken the opportunity to scatter his fire over a broader area as well—in the first instance directed towards Augustine, whom he accused of having been his 'greatest enemy',[221] a revelation which Susannah, obviously outraged, considered 'impolitic', to say the least.

His health, strength and <u>future</u> prospects in life are all blited in the cause of <u>your</u> family. You never had occasion to work for them as <u>he</u> has done and I am certain (tho their parent) <u>never</u> felt the anxious solicitude that he has evinc'd for their <u>future</u> welfare. Can you explain what it is not to enter a bed <u>four</u> successive nights

[216] Ibid. 9 June 1829, pp. 9–10.
[217] Ibid. 8 Aug. 1829, p. 8.
[218] Ibid.
[219] Ibid. 12 Nov. 1829, p. 3.
[220] Ibid. 20 Oct. 1829, p. 3.
[221] Ibid. 8 Aug. 1829, p. 4.

and attend to the hardest drudgery of an orchestra (Astley's)? and were you so intention'd would you do so for other children than your own? I think not.[222]

Neither did Susannah consider that he demonstrated much concern for his family in leaving them 'to the mercy of the wide world, depending for their support and existance to one whom he considers his greatest enemy'.[223]

It was also apparent from Castell's reference to flying 'from flower to flower'[224] that he was anxious to let Susannah know that he had no intention of reforming his ways. More distressing still, however, was his taunting of Susannah with a proposal to marry the daughter of a Dr Paddock for the £2,000 this gentleman had, he claimed, offered him—a proposal which he congratulated himself upon having declined, even though it would have meant being able to provide for Susannah and her family. Susannah's response to this was predictably unequivocal: 'and you thought it a meritorious act that you did not so conclude by paying off your debts with the lady's fortune and providing for a former wife and family. That under these conditions I would accept your bounty—NO! not while there is a great house at Lambeth would I partake of such bread or suffer my children to do so.'[225]

He had taken particular exception to her reference to 'stretching out her hand', as if by such means she had intended to destroy his 'serenity' on the other side of the Channel. He need have no fear on that score, she reassured him—her arm would not stretch across 'the fathomless gulph which lies between us. There is no danger of contamination by my touch', and, she went on with unwitting irony, 'common prudence would prevent me from seeking my death by sinking'.[226]

Indeed the whole tenor of Castell's response to Susannah's 'question' suggests a total rejection by him of all marital or emotional claims. He seems in fact to have been quite explicit that in the event of his returning, there would be no reconciliation, and that the marriage itself would somehow be conditional and that it would be up to the children to choose between their parents. None of which, as far as Susannah was concerned, was acceptable.

Our ever meeting again is uncertain and at present improbable; but in the event of such a circumstance, do you ever imagine that I will ever consent to your proposal as 'conditionally'? Or do you suppose that I will submit the cause of my

[222] SEC–WJC, 8 Aug. 1829, pp. 1–2.
[223] Ibid. 4.   [224] Ibid.
[225] Ibid. 7–8.   [226] Ibid. 25 June 1829, p. 6.

children to settle between us. NO! Not if I were certain of dying this night and without seeing YOUR FACE AGAIN. Because you think I am sufficiently humiliated, this fresh proof of degredation is intended, but from what I should expect of my children is that they would never undertake such an unpleasant office. If then, Ever we meet it must be as (MAN AND WIFE) and without restriction. If that cannot be accomplished 'AMEN'.[227]

Susannah never quite recovered from this overwhelming rejection, and maintained from then on, with only a few minor lapses, a reasonably consistent coolness. At first it was somewhat contrived and self-conscious: 'You must [not] feel surprised that I do not address you in more affectionate terms—or otherways I could not answer your letters . . . as you have taken occasion to severely reprove me for so doing.'[228] But it later became more genuinely habitual, no doubt in response to Castell's continuing recriminations. One thing at least had been achieved by this event, according to Susannah: 'Your reproaches have now lost their sting. You have had your say and I defy you to exceed it.'[229]

It was not until November 1829, while the two were still engaged in the closing stages of this bitter episode, that Susannah finally gained possession of her final five-year lease, duly signed by Castell and lodged with the appropriate authorities. 'The thing has passed,' he said, speaking rather like a potentate reluctantly handing out a gratuity, 'and you have your lease.'[230] There was a new sharpness in Susannah's response. 'Done but what use can I make of it if that I cannot keep a roof over my head? for the tiles are falling in abundance and I am cautious in keeping the children within doors to prevent accidents. The kitchen stairs too are in such a dilapidated state that the man who brings our weekly stipend of coals (one bushell) on Saturday last hesitated to descend with his light burden—I deem it necessary else I could ennumerate a score of such like inconveniences.'[231]

Shaken out of whatever dream she had entertained of his return, the world suddenly seemed to impinge upon her reality with even greater harshness than before. Tax collectors had left an unprecedented bill for the payment of a new charge—£1. 4s. 0d. for lighting and watch rate. Gas pipes had recently been laid down in the Marsh, and the new 'watch' was not more than five or six weeks old. On top of this the poor rates were becoming excessive. Alfred's lessons with Mr Catherby would have to end.[232] Castell sent her £5. She was grateful, but he had painted such a

[227] Ibid. 8 Aug. 1829, p. 10.   [228] Ibid. 20 Oct. 1829, p. 5.
[229] Ibid. 8 Aug. 1829, p. 1.   [230] Quoted in ibid. 12 Nov. 1829, p. 1.
[231] SEC–WJC, ibid.   [232] Ibid. 7.

gloomy picture of his own situation that she said she could view his act of generosity 'in no other light than a mere transfer of misfortune and privation'.[233] But her tone softened, and her subject-matter turned from family politics to world politics. 'Our London newspapers team with the dissatisfaction manifested abroad and the bad feelings which actuates the proceedings of Cabinet Ministers which more or less disturbs the natural tranquility of the Subject as far as regards his liberty or interest.' She did not require, she said, the assistance of the 'bas bleu' (bluestockings) to contemplate the significance of passing events. She herself had already predicted them.[234]

Compared to the period immediately following the end of the Napoleonic Wars, the 1820s had been relatively tranquil, 'a prosperous plateau of social peace', as Edward Thompson called them.[235] The widespread agitations, and political demonstrations led by such radicals as William Cobbett, Henry 'Orator' Hunt, and the publisher Richard Carlile, which had provoked the government of the day into the suspension of Habeas Corpus (from March till 1 July 1817), had culminated in the bloody events of 'Peterloo' (16 August 1819) and the Draconian measures of the Six Acts of 1819, only to move into a less volatile phase in the 1820s. But by the end of the decade, widely felt economic hardships led to renewed unrest. The harvests of 1828 and 1829 had been poor, exacerbating already appalling conditions for agricultural workers, especially in southern England, and heightening resentment against farmers using job-destroying machinery.[236] In other areas of the economy things were little better: 'with abundance of capital—with great energy—with unwearied industry—with foreign commerce pouring upon us from all quarters—with all the circumstances which are generally quoted as proofs of prosperity of a country—we are in a state of general calamity and distress.'[237]

In May 1829 there was rioting in the Manchester area with looms being broken, webs cut to pieces, factories set on fire, and bakers' shops looted. A mob in Rochdale set upon the military force that had been sent to disperse them, resulting in several civilian deaths. In Barnsley, a

---

[233] SEC–WJC, 28 Nov. 1829, p. 1.

[234] Ibid. 1–2. The reference to the 'bas bleu' may have been a response to a remark by Castell, who perhaps perceived Susannah in this light. The term of course came to refer generally to women who had educated opinions and carried its own rebuke.

[235] Thompson, *The Making*, 781.

[236] E. J. Hobsbawm and George Rudé, *Captain Swing* (1969), 85–91.

[237] Lord Western, quoted in Smart, *Economic Annals*, 466.

threatened reduction in pay caused a strike. Things had settled down by the end of the year,[238] but by the summer of 1830 the 'Swing' campaign among rural workers in the south-east began creating panic in establishment quarters and in the Press which was fanned by the disturbing portent of the July Revolution in Paris of that year.

A seemingly organized pattern of rick burnings and machinery smashings by large bodies of agricultural labourers, often accompanied by threatening letters signed 'Swing', created general apprehension and provoked savage repression. There was no loss of life or personal injury sustained, but nineteen men were hanged and 481 were transported to Australia.[239] At this time, there was a great deal of talk about 'redundant' population apropos of 'supply and demand' economics and of the need to use mass emigration as a means of solving the country's demographic embarrassment. The year 1829 saw the publication of Edward Gibbon Wakefield's *Letter from Sydney*.

Susannah's concerns in November 1829, apart from the new watch and lighting taxes and the increasing Poor Rate, embraced, however, cultural as well as political matters.

Our Arts and Sciences are degenerating for want of capital and encouragement and literary pursuits are becoming a far more weighty concern on the <u>heart</u> than head, for in proportion to our intellects we judge & <u>feel</u>—These national difficulty's do not here stop. Our Theatres are becoming a matter for speculation (only) to the manager for either the tastes of their audience or the trash of their authors are so vitiated that nothing short of novelty will 'go down' with the public.[240]

She was appalled that the proprietors of the Adelphi Theatre were paying £2,000 for an elephant from Paris for one hundred nights. 'A <u>new</u> stage has been made capable of bearing his weight & an entrance <u>expressly</u> built (for this "<u>living wonder</u>") in Maiden lane.'[241]

It was to the Adelphi in the Strand that young William had finally made his escape from the Surrey. Augustine had been there 'for years & thro his interest ... attain'd a reception for Wᵐ'.[242] She had taken particular pleasure in having arranged the transfer months before he actually quit the Surrey and in his having left without giving any notice. As it happened, the event coincided with another altercation with the

238 Smart, *Economic Annals*, 472–3.
239 Hobsbawm and Rudé, *Captain Swing*, 263.
240 SEC–WJC, 28 Nov. 1829, p. 2.
241 Ibid. 2–3.   242 Ibid. 3.

Surrey management, thus affording Susannah particular pleasure. Indeed, in her own words, she 'exalted at leaving them in the lurch for we managed the affair with such secrecy that it could not be believed that he had quitted ('Tho the Bass was gone) & was actualy fined at the time he was performing at the other theatre—so far I am quits with Mr Blewett . . .'.[243]

The final conflict arose over Blewitt selecting William to be his 'apprentice', his having been recommended as a 'very [clever] lad in his orchestra'. Susannah seems to have acquiesced, sending Augustine along in some sort of capacity, but, as she crowed to Castell, she had had no intention of 'depriving [William] of his liberty and means of serving himself & relatives for such a being as Mr B—whose sole intention was, to relieve himself of the drudgery of his profession'.[244] William accordingly played for Mr Blewett, and Susannah subsequently earned the ire of his 'holiness' by then ignoring the matter. Her 'want of good manners' was apparently remarked upon, at which the orchestra, she said, 'laugh'd at the fool's expression presuming to such a lad for an apprentice'.[245] (A fair comment on the low status that musical apprenticeships had by then acquired.) Then Platts, the first bass, left and William was placed in his stead, but without a raise in salary. Susannah naturally protested, through the post, but again, as in the earlier instance, received no reply, except that William was discharged. Being a minor, though, it would seem he was protected, and Brooks (presumably the cellist and William's teacher) took his part and threatened to 'expose' such practices. In this hectic climate it was then that the clandestine removal to the Adelphi took place, and Susannah had her revenge. Her only concern now, however, was the elephant from Paris. 'All I fervently hope is, that he will not feel disposed to take a peep into the "Orchestra", for there I have much at stake, my two Sons are the Basses.'[246]

The winter of 1829–30 was extremely harsh. The snow at Dover, said Susannah, had been 'upwards of 5 feet in depth'.[247] Never before had the family been without a cellar of coals. Augustine had only just paid for the coals from the previous winter, for which he had been threatened with a 'lawyer's process'. No sooner had it been paid than the same merchant offered to supply more, but Augustine declined. As usual, she said, the harpies of trade would make the needy suffer.[248]

From France, the news from Castell was bad. He had been forced to forfeit 240 francs, as a 'debt of honor' to the merchant; apparently on a

[243] Ibid.   [244] Ibid. 3–4.   [245] Ibid. 4.
[246] Ibid. 3.   [247] Ibid. 26 Jan. 1830, p. 1.   [248] Ibid.

technical point of some kind, which Susannah could see in no other light than as a needless waste of resources. 'Such a Sum under my present exigency's would be a little estate and partly clothe my family.'[249] Captain O. had turned out to be all that Susannah expected. Her longer experience of life had taught her to be always on the look-out for such scoundrels. She told Castell that he was 'but just entering into the theatre of life', and that hitherto his knowledge had been 'confined to crotchets and quavers'[250]—observations which could hardly have failed to irritate him. She had suspected the man all along as a fraud and probably a criminal and was sure that no government had ever commissioned him to explore countries in search of ore. 'Very often have I felt a disposition to write my opinion & sentiments on this subject but felt no disposition to receive in return your censures "for throwing cold water on all your procedings". The affair has pass'd & "Time has shown".'[251]

Her own position, she insisted, was still deplorable. None of the children except William were capable of earning a shilling. Alfred's prospects were almost nil. To get 25s. a week it was necessary to be a 'confirm'd good player', which Alfred obviously was not. Pianoforte teachers swarmed and the very highest fee for a lesson even in respectable families was no more than 2s. 6d. and mostly only 1s. But in any case neither Augustine nor William had a single pupil, although both played 'above mediocrity'.[252] Furthermore, the house was 'literally falling about our ears'.[253] The roof, stairs, and rails were all in a dilapidated state, the privy less than adequate, the window sashes decaying for want of paint, and the coal-cellar arch had given way. She was paying ground rent of £5. 4s. 9d.; '£3 odd' for the Poor Rate; window tax (£4 for 3 years); the 'new police' rate, one bill for which alone was £1. 14s. 0d., and no one knew how often these charges would be levied—and all on a house which was 'barely tenantable and such a one as I know not what to do with or without'.[254]

Susannah's disappointment in Castell was obviously extreme, and perhaps nowhere did she express it more caustically, if indirectly, than in her final denunciation of the cello bow he had once been so generous as to send his son William.

Mr B. [Brooks] has procured a bow & for which I am allowed the liberty to pay for at my leisure. The price is £1—as the one you sent was entirely useless—you were impos'd upon neither did we think France could produce its like—it being

[249] Ibid. 2.   [250] Ibid. 3.   [251] Ibid. 4.
[252] Ibid. 5.   [253] Ibid. 20 Feb. 1830, p. 2.   [254] Ibid. 3–4.

manufactur'd in point of workmanship equal tho not superior to the Dutch toys which are sent over to us. You paid a very fair price (that is to say for England) for W^m was playing with one that cost only 6/6 and much better.[255]

Perhaps not surprisingly, Castell complained of an unwell stomach.[256]

Catastrophes, however, were not limited to the El Dorado tin mines of Castell's nefarious Captain O. In London, fires had destroyed two major musical venues: the Argyll Rooms and the English Opera House (the Lyceum). Platts, former first double-bass player at the Surrey, had lost a valuable double-bass in the latter, as had a Frenchman whom Laporte had brought over 'to perform at his French plays'. About the Frenchman Susannah was equivocal in her sympathy. She felt 'neither glad nor sorry, and under existing circumstances it would not become me to use a harsher expression but heaven knows we have not sufficient for more than half the applicants for admission to our orchestras'. Even for the greats there were unwelcome surprises:

M. L [Laporte] brought over last year a 1st bassoon^st for the Italian Opera. Consequently our neighbour [Mackintosh] was compelled to retire and the orchestra was stripped of its principal hero's—the absentees were Spagnioletti, the Lindleys—father and son—Mack and about six more of the principals whose names I have forgotten. Dragonetti was included this season I understand that the Lindleys are re engaged—Dragonetti, the leader, and some others[.] Mack is out & I think will remain so. He may consider himself fortunate in being able to do without it as his income is yet very considerable.[257]

Pierre François Laporte was not a popular figure with many musicians in England, nor with some theatre patrons. His high-handed, not to say unscrupulous, methods of filling the King's Theatre earned a stern rebuke from *The Times* in April 1828,[258] notwithstanding which he became the first foreigner, in 1832, to assume the management of Covent Garden Theatre, an event which probably led, even in that bastion of Englishness, to a more Gallic configuration of the orchestra and perhaps to an attempt to eradicate some of the strange practices which were endemic to London orchestras, like the hiring of deputies.[259]

Even, or perhaps particularly, at fashionable Almack's, the quadrille parties of the nobility were taken over by French players, who, said Susannah, because they were foreign, were paid two guineas a night. They then paid the equally competent English musicians 18s. to perform

[255] SEC–WJC, 26 Jan. 1830, p. 6. [256] Ibid. 7.
[257] Ibid. 20 Feb. 1830, pp. 4–5. [258] *The Times*, 25 Apr. 1828, pp. 3 f.
[259] Rosenthal, *Two Centuries of Opera at Covent Garden*, 42.

for the evening and pocketed £1. 4s. 0d.[260] The French players, apparently picking up the deputizing habit from the natives, must have worked more than one orchestra a night, for Susannah assured Castell that a certain French double-bass player, who visited every year, was able to live in his own country for nine months out of the proceeds of three months' work in England.[261]

But foreigners were not the only threat to the English musician's livelihood. In May 1830, after a 'tedious' Lent, during which the theatres were required to close, the king, George IV, was in the last stages of his mortal illness and daily expected to die, a prospect which threatened an obligatory fortnight's closure of the theatres. Susannah's anticipation of the event was rather less than patriotically deferential: 'public performers may well <u>shout</u> our national anthem, "<u>May the King Live for ever</u>"—for I suppose the same ridiculous custom will be repeated as on former occasion of closing the Theatres for a fortnight—which after a tedious "lent"—cannot fail of producing much inconvenience to many.'[262]

Yet another instance of hierarchical obstruction of Susannah's legitimate pretensions. That the rituals surrounding the death of kings (not to mention Christ, the 'King of Kings') should be viewed by Susannah as just so much unnecessary harassment might be laid at the feet of her Calvinistic background—as a puritanical aversion to popish ritual and kingly pomp. But one suspects that it stemmed from no ideology other than an increasingly cranky notion of what was due to her and her deserving sons. When Mrs Brooks, the cellist's wife, became seriously ill in early 1830, her response was strictly pragmatic: 'I hope she may recover', she wrote to Castell, 'for it is through her means W^m is instructed.'[263]

Events continued, however, to challenge even Susannah's determined endomorphosis, and, by November 1830, to provoke her comment. Discontent and even sedition, she declared, were paving the way in England for a revolution such as the French had so recently experienced. The plight of the peasantry and labourers, she conceded, was 'heart-rending', a plight 'aggravated by the universal resort to machinery in lieu of manual labour—Oppressive taxation and reform in parliament is clamourously insisted upon'.[264]

In Susannah's view, though, there was another cause almost as pressing—Peel's 'new police'—which she herself could obviously

[260] SEC–WJC, 25 May 1830, p. 5.
[261] Ibid.
[262] Ibid. 1–2.
[263] Ibid. 26 Jan. 1830, p. 6.
[264] Ibid. 12 Nov. 1830, p. 1.

identify with. Not only the lower classes were in revolt over this gendarmes-style imposition, she said, but the inhabitants of all the parishes.[265] Her own antipathy towards the 'new police' was of course financial, but it was probably heightened by the fact that Strange the tailor, who had made William repay Castell's debt in pianoforte lessons to his daughters, was one of the 'new police' collectors.[266] But in any case, things were so tense in the capital, that the new king, William IV, and Queen Adelaide were forced to cancel their attendance at the civic feast at the Guildhall, creating a scandal that Susannah seems to have taken to heart. It was her belief that never had a monarch been so enthusiastically greeted by his people as William IV. The event was anticipated, with its 'rare and magnificent procession', with excitement, reminiscent of the 'former coronation [presumably of George IV] but without its galling sting'. Thus the consternation was universal. 'Thousands having been expected on the occasion. The Dinner all cooked with the exception of a warming up, having been the business of three days preparation.'[267]

Susannah gave Castell several versions of current speculation concerning the affair, her own conclusion being that the blame lay not with the king but with his self-serving and cowardly ministers. 'They are responsible for rendering the king's conduct such as to provide fuel for such a trio as "Hunt, Cobbett and Carlisle" who nightly harangue the mob at the "rotunda" Blackfriar's Bridge for the small charge of 2ᵈ— which after quitting proceed toward the parliament house and wait for our noble premier and his colleague Mr Peel who are happy to evade their pursuers "hiding their diminished heads"—the aspect of affairs are truly woeful . . .'[268]

Cobbett she singled out as a 'wretch' and blamed him for the rick burnings in the south-east[269]—a routine accusation which she doubtless imbibed with her reading of the daily press. Ironically, however, she may inadvertently have derived some of her own ideas from Cobbett himself. In May she had written to Castell describing how 'some of our peasantry have resorted for temporary support to the degrading situation of yoking themselves—and performing the duty of horses drawing the farmers waggons'.[270] Cobbett in his *Political Register* of 27 November printed the same story, having in all likelihood used it well before it appeared in print in his 'harangues' at the Rotunda. Neither was her basic position

[265] SEC–WJC, 12 Nov. 1830, p. 1.
[266] Ibid. 26 Jan. 1830, p. 5; 20 Feb. 1830, p. 3.   [267] Ibid. 12 Nov. 1830, p. 2.
[268] Ibid. 3.   [269] Ibid., Dec. 1830, p. 5.   [270] Ibid. 25 May 1830, p. 1.

that far from Cobbett's own. 'The root cause of the evil', she believed, lay with 'such men as Mr Yardley and the Tythe holders . . .'.[271] Whoever Mr Yardley was, Susannah's tythe holders were one and the same as Cobbett's 'tythe-eaters'. Perhaps Mr Yardley was one of Cobbett's 'tax-eaters'.[272]

Susannah's horror of Cobbett stemmed from her belief that he was actively promoting violent revolution, and not unnaturally she feared the outcome of any such revolution, even while she might understand and even sympathize with its underlying causes. There was nothing inconsistent therefore in Susannah's position. Her supreme concern was for herself and her family, and while she hoped that wrongs might be redressed she hoped even more that calm and order would prevail.

With judicious treatment the storm may float or disappear which God grant it may, for in the event of internal commotion all professional engagements will be suspended. My family's necessity's are but ill supplied from the produce of a theatre. It is not an existance for more than One. What then is to become of me and my little ones—we cannot obtain bread from the point of a cannon ball . . .[273]

Meanwhile, in France, Castell was confronting troubles of his own. The July Revolution does not seem to have caused him a great deal of alarm, but whether or not he shared the same enthusiasm for it as his friend Linton [or Linden] writing to him of it from Paris at the time,[274] we do not know. Probably not. There is no indication that Castell ever embraced the liberal principles that Englishmen were held by many on the Continent to have possessed so naturally. Nevertheless, his English-ness may have been of some use to him since, according to Linton, 'we are all well and have not been insulted on account of being English—on the contrary, all the English have been receiv'd as friends of the people, and the English on their part have assisted them in every way in their power, some were seen fighting with the people against the troops'.[275]

Linton, himself a musician and evidently a St Servan acquaintance, considered that staying in St Servan would have been more hazardous than being in Paris, for at least there they were not attached to—or, as he put it, 'at the mercy of'—a local family, or their 'dependencies', which would, he considered, have been 'equally miserable and base'. Whether

---

[271] Ibid., Dec. 1830, p. 5.

[272] *The Political Register*, 27 Nov. 1830, in Christopher Hampton (ed.), *A Radical Reader. The Struggle for Change in England, 1381–1914* (Harmondsworth, Middx., 1984), 451.   [273] SEC–WJC, 12 Nov. 1930, p. 4.

[274] M. Linton [or Linden]–WJC, Paris, 2 Aug. 1830.   [275] Ibid.

Castell was so situated 'at the mercy' of a local family at that time is unknown. The scandal of his liaison with Miss Jones may have effectively preserved him from such a fate, although in June he had written requesting that William write out a fugue for him, which would suggest a continuing professional involvement.[276]

But by early August it was clear that the tin-mining venture had been a disaster, that his time at St Servan was running out, and that he was pondering his next evacuation. The United States was evidently being canvassed. Susannah was non-committal, restricting her remarks to a bare minimum. 'America', she said, was 'a large field—but debts are cognizable in the United States consequently deliberation is necessary previous to so deciding a step'.[277]

Nor was his personal life apparently any more tranquil. He was still trying to push Susannah into a renunciation of her marriage claims. This time he sent an envoy in the form of a Captain Hyde, to whom Susannah was meant to 'boldly state' that she was Castell's mother. Susannah did not feel that she could comply. How could she, she said, 'become my own victim by a guilty conivance and at once rendering myself odious in my own eyes as well as others'. In any case, plain logic made nonsense of such an idea. 'If it were <u>possible</u> to call me by the title you suggest—the probability is that I ought to have been married to your father at the age of 13—but such marriages are very rare in England and I should think illegal.'[278] She made no other comment in a letter which, like others of this period, was remarkable for its brevity.

Rather incongruously, Castell had also made persistent requests for her to scour London for a mysterious commodity that seems to have been cobalt ceramic glaze. His reasons for such a request were not revealed. Without much grace and accompanied by complaint, Susannah went through the motions and established that it was to be had at Apothecary's Hall for 15s. an ounce. The matter was not alluded to again, except for Susannah's saying that 'under <u>Existing</u> circumstances you could not avail yourself of any beneficial results'.[279] Perhaps he was contemplating some new financial venture—or, as Susannah may have suspected, simply obliging the whim of yet another female admirer. Rather ominously, from October, he began to write to her through a third party, to which she objected on the grounds that it created unnecessary embarrassment and that the party in question was not a

---

[276] SEC–WJC, 16 June 1830, p. 1.
[277] Ibid. 3 Aug. 1830, p. 1.   [278] Ibid. 1–2.
[279] Ibid. 16 June 1830, p. 1; 3 Aug. 1830, p. 1; Ibid. 2.

willing intermediary.[280] What it probably indicated to Susannah was that he was hiding her existence in order to preserve his image as a single man, for reasons she had ample reason to suspect, especially, perhaps, since the Captain Hyde episode. At about this time he also wrote to Susannah accusing her of expecting him, by 'violent exertion calculated to inspire despair', to provide for her; a charge which she denied. Ten pounds in four years she did not consider an excessive contribution.[281]

By November it was evident that he had determined to leave Europe, although he was still giving Susannah false leads. He wrote instructing her not to write again, since 'before you hear from [me I will] have quitted Europe', but then disclaimed it, saying he had merely been going to Madame Gallien's—a cryptic message that probably held the seed of some deeper meaning. Madame Gallien is a new player in the game, although Susannah evidently knew to whom he was referring. 'Sometime since,' she remarked, 'you inform'd me that Madame G had quitted France for three years.'[282] She remains a mystery to us, but, as we shall be discussing in Chapter 6, she may have been the wife of the French naval captain with whom, according to Therry, Castell eventually eloped.[283] 'Why not state the truth,' exhorted Susannah, adding equally cryptically, 'perhaps xxx could explain it.'[284]

The reason for Castell's equivocation was probably the fear that Susannah might yet descend upon him in the guise of bringing the children to Jersey for a last farewell.

. . . would it not have been more natural to solicit an interview with objects both near and dear before taking so decided a step. They might for instance have met you in Jersey had you been inclined to meet the expenses of the journey, One only obstacle remaining—I must have accompany'd them—For where they go, I go and which you probably might not relish—'tis about a thousand to one, you may ever again be blessed or gratified by so propitious an opportunity. You will think of this by and by, and to a feeling and reflecting mind [it] might afford some sort of consideration should the blackened cloud and foaming wave arrest the mariner's progress, your thoughts will be wildly employ'd—on absent objects.[285]

Neither did he probably enjoy her renewed insistence on his duties as a breadwinner to his family. 'Those who have FIRST CLAIM—ought to alarm your peculiar thinking', she warned him. He might also have

[280] Ibid. 13 Oct. 1830, p. 2; 12 Nov. 1830, p. 5.
[281] Quoted in ibid. 13 Oct. 1830, p. 1.
[282] Ibid., Dec. 1830, p. 6.   [283] Therry, *Reminiscences*, 115.
[284] SEC–WJC, Dec. 1830, p. 6.   [285] Ibid. 16 Nov. 1830, p. 1.

panicked in detecting a slight relapse into those expressions of devotion which, coming from Susannah, he found so repugnant to his sense of decency. 'If my wishes for your health hapiness & prosperity could avail,' she had dared to utter, 'you have them undivided.'[286]

The year 1830 had certainly been an eventful one, with the death of George IV in England, the forcible removal in France of Charles X, perceptions of a threatened revolution in England and its reflex of harsh repression, and of course, for Castell, the failure of his 'bubble' mining company. As well, his normally 'robust constitution'[287] failed him. The stomach complaint of January was followed in May by what Susannah diagnosed as either scarlet fever or measles.[288] This was probably indicative of a high level of stress, caused no doubt by his precarious situation and financial failures. It is very likely, also, that he had embarked on yet another romantic alliance, which would have taken its toll of his resources, especially if he was still having to lie about his marital status. He lived also with the constant threat of Susannah's love for him waiting just across the Channel, and perhaps with a residual guilt about his children, who, finally, he was about to forsake.

Back in London in November, Susannah was aggravated by the news of the death of a distant relative—the 95-year-old apothecary John Milward, who had left an estate of about £140,000. To her disgust, almost half of it had been left to charity. She was particularly chagrined that the newspapers had implied that he had amassed his fortune through his profession, which had been, she said, but a 'mere avocation from ennui'. He had inherited it through his mother, who had brought over to England, presumably from France, a substantial fortune. As if anticipating censure from Castell for being behindhand in approaching this now lost source of possible financial assistance, she forestalled it by declaring that he had always been rudely unsympathetic to those members of the family who had done so, and was sure, in any case, that he was ashamed of the poverty of his distant relations. He had, after all, she said, sold them all for three guineas![289]

In December, Susannah, still uncertain of Castell's plans, lectured him upon the meaning of a woman's love, the meanness of the Royal Society, the detrimental nature of the Royal Academy of Music, and the

---

[286] SEC–WJC, 3 Aug. 1830, p. 2.
[287] Ibid. 20 Oct. 1829, p. 3.   [288] Ibid. 25 May 1830, pp. 2, 5.
[289] SEC, 12 Nov. 1830, p. 6; *The Times*, 8 Nov. 1830, p. 3b; PRO PROB. 11 1777/612, will of John Milward of Artillery Place, City Road.

parsimony of farmers whose inadequate wages, supplemented by parish rates, reduced working men to pauperism. (The flaws of the Speenhamland system had obviously not escaped her notice.)[290] She warned him also of the Swan River speculation and others like it, citing the case of Sir William Adams the oculist who lost all of his fortune on overseas ventures.[291] Such broad-ranging perceptions were probably all lost on Castell, however, whose mind was doubtless preoccupied with thoughts of his imminent departure.

[290] A system originally introduced in 1795 in a single shire as an emergency measure to alleviate poverty among the lowly paid by making up a living wage from the Poor Rate based on the price of bread. However it became institutionalized and gave official sanction to farmers to pay labourers less than a living wage, the balance to be made up by the parish. It meant effectively that a labourer could not earn over the parish rate, no matter how hard he worked. What had begun as an act of charity became a tool of Malthusian economics, designed to maintain a bare subsistence wage for a superfluous commodity in order to keep down prices while deterring matrimony and procreation among the working class. See Hobsbawm and Rudé, *Captain Swing*, 47–8; Perkin, *Origins*, 185–7; Thompson, *The Making*, 242–8.

[291] SEC–WJC, Dec. 1830, pp. 1–6.

6

The Speculative Voyager: Mauritius and Australia, 1831–1839

'You have become the sole arbitrator of your future fate'.

SEC to WJC, 16 Nov. 1830

DEPARTURE FROM EUROPE

CONSIDERING that by mid-March 1831 Castell was *en route* for Mauritius, it seems unlikely that at the end of January, even as he waited in the port of Le Havre for departure, he would not have known his destination. Yet he was then still telling Susannah that he planned to go to India.[1] Mauritius was certainly in the right direction, but that he did not plan to go on to India from there is suggested by his declaration at Port Louis, at the outset, that his intention was indeed to settle in the ex-French colony.[2] Quite likely he was simply keeping Susannah in the dark—for him a fairly normal reflex. She could not, she said, fathom his motive for going to India. He had never hinted at such a thing before, but she felt no surprise or disappointment since, as she said, 'your practice with me has invariably been to "keep your own council" '.[3]

Neither had he (perhaps to forestall any emotional recidivism on her part) softened in his attitude toward Susannah. Indeed he had, as she said, once again 'Thrown the Glove', and she had been quick enough to pick it up, retaliating in sardonic vein, and with some verve.

. . . as well as you I know that what has transpired is of little consequence now. I thank you for the compliment you bestow upon me by remarking how 'welcome

---

[1] SEC–WJC, 3 Feb. 1831, p. 4.
[2] MA Z2D6/102, p. 159, typescript, Return of passengers on the French ship *Indus* . . . arrived from Le Havre on 15 July 1831.
[3] SEC–WJC, 8 Feb. 1831, p. 2.

and <u>edifying</u>' my replys were—now as I never keep a copy of my letters I feel somewhat at a loss to conjecture the particular subject you allude to, neither am I conscious of any offence offer'd you much less 'taunts' as you express it—I am equally depriv'd the means of an indication as regards the '37th verse of your poem' or till now did I know it contain'd <u>so many lines</u>.[4]

Castell rejected the proposal she had earlier made that they should all meet in Jersey prior to his departure, on the grounds, it would seem, of the cost of Susannah's attendance upon the children, bringing home to her his determined rejection.

My chief and <u>only</u> reason for suggesting a meeting at Jersey arose from an idea that you would feel gratified <u>once more</u> beholding your family by which I do not mean to include myself. I merely considered my attendance <u>on them</u> as an <u>indispensible</u> appendage to their safety—and should feel sorry and grieved to be the cause of unnecessary expense to one who would desire neither satisfaction or pleasure from the result; for in no other light do I conceive you view me than as a cast-off mistress.[5]

Nevertheless, Susannah still clung to the idea that the family itself had the power to command Castell's ultimate allegiance.

<u>Remember remember</u> your children. They are a credit to <u>you</u> as they are to myself . . . 'Tis now 9 O'clock. The eldest is at the theatre and the three Junrs are at this present moment employing themselves at the <u>same</u> table with me, writing and arithmetic—If this sheet of paper could speak it would inform you and 'tis possible for it to convey more <u>domestic</u> information than a <u>volume</u> could contain. It might rivet your affections to those [in] whom they ought <u>solely to be placed</u> . . . Marr not their future prospects in life by any imprudent act of yours.[6]

She was acknowledging in effect that her own power over him was gone. Yet she could not restrain what she still saw as her legitimate right to candour: her right to tell him those things which no one else but she would dare to, and which she believed he ought to know. In this voice, she warns him:

<u>You</u> are not a young man or a very old one but few amongst us, I believe is born without a <u>natural</u> propensity to <u>something</u>—yours (and I mean no offence) is highly tinged with vanity and a desire of pleasing <u>on any terms</u>. To a disposition so framed, it is seldom ungratified—'tis your lot <u>particularly</u> to associate with females, members of which carry on a considerable commerce in that article they call <u>love</u>. The supplication is not infrequently <u>pleasing</u> to a '<u>Married ear</u>' or vice versa.[7]

[4] Ibid. 3 Feb. 1831, p. 1.   [5] Ibid. 3.

[6] Ibid. 4–5.   [7] Ibid. 5.

Nor was her advice constrained only to his personal conduct—or to the sealed portion of her letters. On the outside of one, she offers him the observation that she would have preferred America to India, since there 'debts are not cognizable', and proclaimed that in her opinion it was 'madness to proceed without a <u>certain</u> prospect of success'. Should he fail it would be too late, and for want of funds he might starve.[8]

But underlying all her anxiety about his departure was the understandable fear of his loss as a future economic support to her family. 'You ought to make a <u>will</u>,' she warned him, 'for were you to <u>now</u> die, your creditors would strip me of bed and home';[9] and she admonished him, 'You ought to remember your family in all that you do, and unless a prospect offers short of <u>Independence</u> I pronounce your journey <u>Rash</u>.' And what, she asked, would happen to her children should she suddenly be taken from them. The Parish would not take them in. 'They are too old, and of an <u>Age</u> to get their living . . .'.[10]

She reminded him too of the deplorable state of music in England, and its attendant difficulties for native performers. 'We are not', she told him, 'of the <u>favor'd race</u>.' Even Their Majesties had a French band. She feared that Alfred would never be able 'to acquire an existance by music', that William would never be accepted into the Royal Society of Musicians ('none but a favor'd few can hope to gain admittance'), and that the Royal Academy of Music was the agent of privilege and unfair competition.

> The Regency (that was) has changed its name to the 'Queens Theatre' and the orchestra entirely filled with 'Academy boys' Ld Berghersh is a 'would be' composer he lately brought out an opera (a very indifferent one) <u>he</u> was the first to patronise the Academy at its rise, and has never lost sight of the object—the boys <u>can</u> well afford the time to practise his music—and their teachers whose interest it is, drills them desires no small share of the benefit . . . hence the patronage afforded to these half taught and worse educated youths.[11]

Neither had the political situation improved. The burnings and disorder were far from being quelled and the clashing of interests of 'all ranks and description of persons' would end only heaven knew where. 'All is uncertainty,' she warned meaningfully.[12] The success of his new venture was important to them all, then, and it would depend ultimately, she was sure, upon Castell's own deportment. She thus exhorted him not

---

[8] Ibid. 7.
[9] Ibid. 5.
[10] Ibid. 8 Feb. 1831, pp. 2–3.
[11] Ibid. 3 Feb. 1831, p. 2.
[12] Ibid. 8 Feb. 1831, p. 3.

to allow passion to delude and devour him and recalled the difficulties of the past which had been caused by one thing only—'incontinence'[13]— which brought her directly to the penultimate point.

Without wishing to wilfully offend him, and assuring Castell that she had never in her life been better disposed, she offered that none of the children—not even the boys—would ever countenance any 'unhallow'd engagement' he might be imprudent enough to form. 'No female, whatever her <u>pretensions</u> will', she assured him, '<u>ever succeed</u> in supplanting their <u>mother</u>.'[14] It is doubtful whether Susannah had anyone particularly in mind when she penned this unequivocal challenge, yet her last words to Castell before his final departure from Europe declare that she was still troubled by at least one nagging possibility. 'You do not say what is become of Miss Jones,' she queries. 'I hope she is not your companion.'[15]

MAURITIUS, 1831–1832

On about 19 March 1831,[16] Castell departed from Le Havre on the French ship the *Indus* for Mauritius. With him was a Mrs M. Cecil, officially designated his sister.[17] Equinoctial gales accompanied them, beating them back for a month into the English Channel, creating much frustration and, it would seem, certain tensions on board among the ship's company[18]—altogether eleven passengers and two stowaways.

All were either French or French Mauritian; except, that is, for Castell and his 'sister', an Indian servant called Figaro, and the slave Louis, who was 'recused by Madame Colonia' and on arrival duly noted at the Custom House as unwanted merchandise.[19] Apart from Castell and Mrs Cecil, there were only three other prospective settlers, all of whom, upon arrival, were 'desired to petition' to stay. Not so Castell and his 'sister'. Officially listed as Mr Cavendish, an 'artist' of 36 years of age, Castell was 'recommended' by a Captain Royer, as was Mrs Cecil, about whom, however, no details were provided.

The island's administration, legally British since the Treaty of Paris in 1814, was thus exercising a certain amount of surveillance over new arrivals. The 'Return of Passengers' document for the *Indus* was required

[13] Ibid.
[14] Ibid. 4.
[15] Ibid. 6.
[16] Ibid. 28 May 1831, p. 1.
[17] Return of Passengers, *Indus*.
[18] SEC–WJC, 28 May 1831, p. 1.
[19] Return of Passengers, *Indus*.

to be signed by the Chief Commissary of Police. That this was so was doubtless due, at least partially, to the political turmoil in which the island was plunged over the volatile issue of slavery, which had effectively split the two non-slave communities, French and British, into warring factions. It was a situation that would ultimately have serious repercussions for Castell.

Mauritius, or the Isle of France as it was then sometimes called, lies in the Indian Ocean east of Madagascar and 1,200 miles from the African coast. About 35 miles in length, 28 in breadth, and 95 in circumference, its capital, Port Louis, nestles beneath imposing volcanic peaks which, while creating a striking backdrop, effectively cut off the prevailing north-east to south-east winds, making it excessively hot and humid in the long summer months from November to May, and, throughout the nineteenth century, assisted by poor public hygiene, prone to outbreaks of plague and cholera.

No indigenous human population is known to have existed on the island. Early settlements by the Dutch had failed. The Dodo became extinct. But sugar, produced from estates worked by French planters using slave labour from Africa and Madagascar, eventually triumphed. When the British took over the administration they added to the racial composition by importing Indian convicts to work on the creation of roads, particularly the road to Mahébourg, which in seven years made into a pleasant morning's drive the route that British troops had had to hack their way through in 1810 in order to take the island. And in 1829 the 'coolie' trade commenced, with labourers systematically indented from India.

Robert Townsend Farquhar, the first British Commander-in-Chief of the island (1810–23), had had little initial trouble appeasing the French inhabitants, maintaining the French legal system, casting a blind eye to the unpleasant details of the slave economy, and creating easy access to English credit. By 1831, however, things were very different. Pressure from public opinion and parliamentary faction in England had rendered slavery moral anathema and finally forced the British government to ban not only the trade but slavery itself in 1833. In Mauritius in 1831, the writing was on the wall, and the British authorities there were actively attempting to suppress slave-trading by the French planters, to their great resentment, not least because it coincided with a world sugar glut and falling prices. The planters' spokesman, the lawyer Adrien d'Epinay was indeed in London in 1831, seeking assurances from the Secretary of State

17. The rocky outcrop left of centre is 'Le Pouce'. Lithograph from T. Bradshaw originally published in his *Views in the Mauritius . . .* (1832). Ref. BL 562 e. 14.

for War and the Colonies, Lord Goderich, which would allay fears and raise the island 'from the depth of despair into which it had been plunged'.[20] In November he returned to Mauritius with some concessions, including provisions for a free press, which was to become a powerful weapon for the planters in the lively battle that still lay ahead.[21]

It is unlikely that Castell would have been aware of the depth of these complexities when he made his decision to go to Mauritius. As a musician he would surely have known the profound effect that political dissension and civil unrest could have upon the economic viability of his profession, and to have consciously exposed himself to such vulnerabilities would have been a folly of major proportions. He should have known, however, that the island was in the grip of severe economic recession. But then, as Susannah had commented often enough, he was strangely innocent when it came to matters of economics. His decision may have been influenced by an altogether different criterion: his father's old regiment, the 87th, was due for a tour of duty there from New South Wales (Hobartown) in December 1831[22] and it is possible that he may have been friendly with or have had some communication with its bandmaster, Smith.

The society that he found at Mauritius, when he arrived there on 15 July 1831, was not only seriously divided—between the French majority who owned most of the land and ran the majority of businesses, and the British minority, some traders, but mostly employed in the administration—it was also a society preoccupied by the fact that the total European population of about 8,000 dominated a slave and free black population of over 80,000;[23] what T. Bradshaw termed a 'fearful majority'.[24] In Port Louis, where there were 7,511 free blacks and 15,717 slaves,[25] it was nevertheless possible for the 2,387 whites to carry on with some conviction, the cultural paraphernalia of European civilization.

---

[20] *The Times*, 22 Feb. 1832, p. 3f, extract from letter from Port Louis dated 3 Nov. 1831.

[21] Sources for the above, except where otherwise stated, are P. J. Barnwell and A. Toussaint, *A Short History of Mauritius* (1949); T. Bradshaw, *Views in the Mauritius . . . with a Memoir of the Island, and a Description of each View* (1832); Lindsay Riviere, *Historical Dictionary of Mauritius* (1982).

[22] PRO WO 17/456, 87th Royal Irish Fusiliers, Monthly Return, 1 Jan. 1832.

[23] Barnwell and Toussaint, *Short History of Mauritius*, 255, Appendix 3, population in 1830: 8,135 European, 18,018 free blacks, 64,919 slaves; the *London Magazine*, i (Feb. 1820), 217, gives a somewhat contrary but probably less accurate figure for 1820 of 25,000 whites, 80,000 slaves, 105,000 total. For 1817, Barnwell and Toussaint give a figure of 7,375 for whites, 10,979 for free blacks and 79,493 for slaves: a total of 97,847.

[24] Bradshaw, *Views in the Mauritius*, 3.   [25] Ibid. 4.

There was a plain behind the town, called the Champs de Mars, which performed the function of a promenade, where in the cool of the evening, along the circular drive, would rendezvous the white citizenry, either in open carriages or on horseback, while upon the turf pedestrians scattered themselves in idle groups. The French ladies, who, according to Bradshaw, hermetically sealed themselves in their houses during the whole day, would now venture forth 'to inhale the evening breeze, and [would] frequently continue their moonlight promenade till a late hour, when they [would] retire to conclude the evening with music and dancing'.[26] Bradshaw, writing probably in late 1830 or early 1831, noted that there was little social fraternizing between English and French resident families, except at the annual ball at Government House in honour of the king's birthday, a situation, he declared, that had not originated with the French, whom he found to be 'uniformly hospitable'.[27]

In Mauritius absentee-landlordism was rare. Small estates were usually directly supervised by their owners and worked by the owners' slaves.[28] This did not preclude though, strong, even passionate, links with French traditions and modes of life, which were indeed conspicuously maintained. The theatre in Port Louis saw performances of the latest French plays.[29] There were libraries, bookshops, and literary clubs.[30] At the Royal College, the sons of the well-to-do were prepared for future study at the Sorbonne in Paris, and there was no shortage in the French community of well-educated and urbane leaders in social and political affairs. Powerful families like the d'Epinays, the Raffrays, and the de Spévilles were socially and intellectually more than a match for successive British administrators, who, except for Ralph Darling in 1819, did not challenge them.

The slave-based economy, however, according to observers like James Backhouse, although not as cruel as in the West Indies, produced widespread personal profligacy and public callousness. White men eschewed marriage in favour of concubinage with slave women, with the cruel result that their progeny, although free, frequently found themselves in the position of buying and selling their own mothers, brothers, or

[26] Ibid. 5.   [27] Ibid.
[28] PRO CO 167/161, Colville to Goderich No. 51, 5 June 1832, in B. M. Howell, 'Mauritius, 1832–1849: A Study of a Sugar Colony', Ph.D. thesis (London, 1950), 7.
[29] A Lady [Mrs Bartrum], *Recollections of Seven Years Residence at the Mauritius . . .* (1830), 71. In Howell, 'Mauritius, 1832–1849', 7.
[30] C. Pridham, *England's Colonial Empire* (London, 1846), i. 201, in Howell, 'Mauritius, 1832–1849'.

18. In the mid-foreground is the Champs de Mars. Details as for Fig. 17.

sisters.[31] The caste system *vis-à-vis* blacks and whites was rigid. In labour as well as in love segregation was the official norm. All manual labour, including (at least till 1827) transport and cartage, was performed by blacks.[32] Marriage between whites and blacks was forbidden by French law, and the prohibition not revoked (in principle) by the British till 1829;[33] while in the streets petty rituals of racial paranoia required blacks to bow before any white man however lowly. By 1830, while many free blacks had managed to acquire land and educate their children,[34] the progress towards general amelioration of both free blacks and slaves remained powerfully obstructed by French planters aided by the French judiciary, and by lack of any real commitment by successive British governors. From the very start of his administration in June 1828, Sir Charles Colville had openly identified himself with the interests of the French planters, even to the point, in 1832, of helping many of them to avoid the legitimate claims of their London creditors.[35]

The town of Port Louis, the port and administrative and commercial capital, for all the natural beauty of its surroundings was notoriously unsalubrious. Roads were almost always in a state of disrepair, and drainage and sanitation virtually non-existent. In 1819 a cholera epidemic had killed between 6,000 and 20,000 people,[36] and the crowded and filthy state of the town's two coloured quarters posed a constant threat to the health of black and white alike. The town nevertheless possessed a permanent theatre. Recently rebuilt in stone, it replaced an earlier wooden building damaged in a hurricane. But by the time Castell arrived, its resident company had failed and by late 1829 had departed,[37] and the question only remained whether to sell it or to demolish it for building materials. The issue was not settled until 1832, until when no performances apparently took place.[38] Ultimately it was sold by the government in February 1832 to one Le Compte Fisicat in collaboration with Jean Desbleds, and reopened its doors on 3 May of

---

[31] PRO CO 167/208, James Backhouse to Thomas Buxton. Report on Mauritius Society, 14 May 1836. Sent to Colonial Office, in Howell, 'Mauritius, 1832–1849', 9.
[32] E. Stirling, *Cursory Notes on the Isle of France made in 1827* (Calcutta, 1833), in Howell, 'Mauritius, 1832–1849', 4.
[33] Howell, 'Mauritius, 1832–1849', 5.
[34] Ibid. 6.   [35] Ibid. 43; 46.
[36] Ibid. 4.
[37] Bradshaw, *Views in the Mauritius*, 6.
[38] MA, typescript extract from Antoine Chelin, *Le Théâtre à L'Ile Maurice, son origine et son développement*, 37–8.

that year, with a company comprised of the residue of the previous one.[39] It was not a spectacular success, and apart from the appearance of the acrobat Georgino Idalgo, neither was it memorable.[40] Under normal circumstances it might have been expected that Castell, with his undisputed skills and experience, would have featured prominently in the orchestra pit; but circumstances almost certainly intervened.

At the time that the theatre was reopening, the Mauritians were in fact awaiting the arrival of John Jeremie (1795–1841), the official sent by the British government to superintend the provisions of the 1829 Order in Council meant to improve the status and working conditions of the slaves, and to reform the obstructionist machinery of Mauritian law,[41] neither of which was welcomed by the island's inhabitants. Jeremie, it was soon broadcast, had well-known anti-slavery views and a reputation not only for uncompromising zealotry but for his 'morose character and harsh manners'.[42] Passions among the French were soon high, and animosity towards their English masters unequivocal. As an Englishman, Castell had almost certainly been boycotted by the French theatre manager, Fisicat, as a representative of the by now hated enemy.

It may have been as a result of this enforced leisure that Castell found the time to keep a kind of political 'register', and in September 1832 was moved to send a 15-page report to the Colonial Secretary in London, Lord Goderich, concerning the remarkable events which accompanied the arrival of Jeremie in Port Louis. The report, he offered, 'may contain information that could reach you through no other channel, of the disgraceful circumstances & scenes, which have blotted the escutcheon of this beautiful Island'.[43]

The trouble, he observed, had begun as early as March, when a private letter from London to Messrs Chapman & Co., outlining the principle 'heads' of the Order in Council relating to slave property in Mauritius, had been widely circulated. Then, by 'the natural incaution & want of reflection in the French by their unguarded conversations', the news

---

[39] MA, typescript extracts from Seymour Hitié, *Le Théâtre à Maurice depuis son origine jusqu'à nos jours 1788–1914* (*impressions, souvenirs, incidents, anecdotes*), 5, and Pierre Renaud and Gaëtan Raynal, *Histoires et légendes d'un théâtre*, 7.

[40] Chelin, *Le Théâtre à L'Ile Maurice*.

[41] Printed in PP 1831–2, XLVI, pp. 93–138 and sent out to all Crown Colonies, 5 Nov. 1831, arriving Mauritius end March 1832. These details from Howell, 'Mauritius, 1832–1849', 48.

[42] *Memorial presented by the Inhabitants of Mauritius, in support of their Petition to His Majesty . . . and containing a brief Narrative of the Events which have taken place in the Colony during the Months of June and July, 1832* (1833), 22.

[43] PRO CO 167/167, Cavendish de Castell to Goderich, 12 Sept. 1832, p. 1.

reached the slave population and fears of an uprising became wide-spread, with reports of risings circulated 'for the avowed purpose of alarming the government'. From then on, according to Castell, panic and agitation were orchestrated, and a Colonial Committee formed, 'which created itself despotic director of public affairs, & seized with gigantic grasp the public mind'.[44] Vigilante groups of armed men roamed the streets, and the Governor was prevailed upon to endorse the formation of an armed civic guard of nine companies of a hundred men each. Not even the Governor had apparently bargained for the results of this error. 'They met,' wrote Castell, 'elected their own officers, assumed a military form, armed themselves with good muskets & swords, and appointed M^{ons} Adam (one of Napoleon's Legion of Honour) Colonel, who issued his orders for adopting the uniform of the National Guard of France.'[45] From this point onwards, according to Castell, a carefully organized plan of civil disobedience was put into practice, notably with a refusal to pay taxes and rents. Heightened tension was also maintained through publication in the press of extracts from the pamphlet on slavery by Jeremie,[46] who was known by then to be on his way to implement the Order in Council. 'Had the purport of this gentleman's journey been to inoculate the islanders with the hydraphobia, or to introduce among them the yellow fever,' said Castell, 'the consternation could not have been greater.'[47]

By the time Jeremie arrived on board the Ganges in the evening of 3 June 1832, Colonel Adam's Civic Guard was rumoured to be 7,200 strong in the Port Louis area alone, and excitement was at fever pitch. He did not disembark that evening, but remained on board. From the following day, however, all normal activities of the town ceased. Castell described the scene in self-consciously elegant prose:

Every species of labor instantly ceased, the shops were immediately closed, the boats and barges in the harbor refused to ply, carts and waggons on the wharfs were driven home, Contractors with the government refused to fulfil their engagements, the slave-gangs were recalled by the proprietors, merchants ceased to purchase, tradesmen to sell, the college-youths were sent home, the colonial committee assembled & usurped the direction of public affairs & so perfect was the system of its power, that, like the Spanish Inquisition, the whole population either from choice or fear bowed & trembled before its banner. It had been pre-determined to receive Mr Jeremie in the most sombre manner & the theatre, courts of justice, public baths & shops closed, the total absence of activity &

---

[44] Ibid. 3.   [45] Ibid. 4.
[46] J. Jeremie, *Essays on Colonial Slavery* (1831).
[47] Cavendish de Castell to Goderich, p. 5.

labor joined to the tranquility of the air, the water & the light, threw a gloom over the town, as dreary and deep as for a good king's death; & all was mournful & mute as the City of Sleep.[48]

When Jeremie finally did disembark at 7 a.m. on the 5th, he did so with an escort of marines and gunboats and was met on shore by two companies of the 99th Regiment, from which time, however, he was virtually a prisoner at Government House, to which all entrances save one were sealed, and that one guarded by cannon. Gunboats armed with seven pounders cruised close to shore, with every man on board armed with a brace of pistols and a cutlass.[49]

Violence attended Jeremie's first failed attempt at being sworn in as Procureur-Générale. Public meetings led by such notables as Adrien d'Epinay demanded Jeremie's removal and fanned French resentments against British rule. These meetings of the 'Notables' had in fact been convened by Colville himself, as a last-ditch attempt to reach consensus, but, skilfully organized, they became yet another powerful force against Jeremie.[50]

On 20 July, Jeremie, threatened by a mob, was forced to fire upon them. Colville ordered Jeremie to leave at once, which he did on 29 July 1832 on board the *Emma*. The French colonists believed themselves delivered from a monstrous tyranny, and celebrated long into the night. The situation, however, remained tense and uncertain. On arrival in London, predictably, Jeremie was instructed to return immediately, suitably supported by military force.

Castell's account of these events was, on the surface, accurate enough and can be compared factually, for example, with the account given by the French planters in their own *Memorial* to the King or with the sober and seemingly balanced account by an anonymous correspondent published in *Blackwood's Magazine* in January 1833.[51] But the tone is odd, and the function of the report is questionable indeed. On one level it is decidedly anti-French. He speaks not only of the 'natural incaution & want of reflection in the French', a prejudice that Susannah might have been proud of, but lays the blame for the entire fracas at the feet of the leaders of the French judiciary, 'men of the courts of law', who had the most to lose by the reforms that Jeremie had come to put in place. Every-

[48] Cavendish de Castell to Goderich, pp. 6–7.
[49] Ibid. 8.   [50] Ibid. 15–20.
[51] *Memorial*; An Inhabitant of the Island, 'A short statement on the causes that have produced the late disturbances in the colony of Mauritius', *Blackwood's Magazine*, xxxiii (Jan. 1833), 199–205.

body knew, he said, how five dollars could purchase the decision of the Courts. He also defended Jeremie in his final use of firearms against the mob, since, although he had already 'run the gauntlet' and appeared safe when he fired, it was the intention of the mob, Castell reckoned, to have seized his horse's head and to have 'dragged him out & trampled him to death. It was determined to send him to Fort blanc (the burial ground) had he remained.' This exonerates both Jeremie for firing and Colville for insisting that he leave. It perhaps supports Colville's own claim that he had sent Jeremie away after this event in order 'to save the subjects of Mauritius from fire and sword and the horrors of internal warfare'.[52]

But, on the other hand, there is also implied criticism of the governor himself; especially of his allowing the French to form their own civic guard, supposedly in response to threatened insurrection of the slaves and largely fabricated reports of the breaking open of houses. He had been 'ill-advised', thought Castell, and 'many reflecting English' thought so too. The speed with which the newly established body armed itself and the secrecy with which it drilled was alarming, and it was from that point, he claimed, that the proprietors were emboldened to refuse to pay their taxes.[53] He also let it be known that while the English merchants did not go along with the notorious Colonial Committee in its more extreme demands, they too desired the government to remove Jeremie from the Colony.[54]

So what lay behind this report? Was it, after all, a piece of surveillance work requested by the Mauritian administration? It certainly supplied enough names—almost exclusively of the French leaders of the disturbances; and Castell seemed well placed to gather information, quoting from the proceedings of meetings at which he may even have been present. Or was it forwarded in the hope of gaining remuneration as a government spy, a role he may have conceivably have been familiar with in France? Certainly in his last paragraphs we hear the voice of what seems to have been the professionally dispassionate observer.

Here he criticized aspects of the British administration. The taxation policy was ill-thought-out, confusing and inconsistent. The institution of a Protector for the slaves created more mischief than it avoided. The government in thus taking to itself sole powers of coercion, he said, produced unfairness for the slave-owner, who, if he took a slave for a judgement, would either suffer the indignity of a ridiculously light

[52] Cavendish de Castell to Goderich, p. 21; p. 19; p. 21; PRO CO 167/167, Colville to Goderich (private), 12 July 1832, in Howell, 'Mauritius, 1832–1849', 61.
[53] Cavendish de Castell to Goderich, p. 4.   [54] Ibid. 13.

sentence being given, or the inconvenience of a heavy one, being then denied the services of his slave for a prolonged period. Besides, in the country areas, where supervision was most required, the Protector was completely impotent and his rulings ignored. The corruption of the courts and the weakness of the government, he concluded, made sure that this was so.

He also criticized the leniency of entry to the colony. Too many French were allowed in, he said, who were likely always to stir up trouble. There were also too many Lascars who had become rich, owning many ships and much property, with the result that British trade and British wealth were damaged. Besides which, all the Lascars, he reckoned, had French hearts. The Chinese, he thought, were also of limited use to British commerce. Their economic habits precluded their ever paying taxes to the government and this disadvantaged the honest trader who did. Besides, their consumption, he observed, was limited to rice. It would be better if their place could be filled by consumers of Cape and Sydney produce. Finally he turned his attention to the Malabars, who, he proclaimed, were so poor in manners and circumstances as to be unable to enrich or improve any country in which they might settle. Their presence, furthermore, occupied ground which a 'few enterprizing english would take up & render profitable to themselves & productive to the government'.

But it was his parting comment which seems to confirm that at least he had not been commissioned in his report by the Governor or the administration of Mauritius. There were many causes, he said, which tended towards the impoverishment of the Colony. And these causes, he went on, the Governor could not possibly rectify because they were 'studiously kept from him'. Hardly a vote of confidence in Colville and his officers. Indeed, in the end, it is most unlikely that any one group in the Colony would have thanked Castell for his efforts, or that Lord Goderich or any of his officers in London, even if they had admired the prose, would have found it a particularly helpful document. But one thing can at least be said: he certainly demonstrated that not all musicians were the 'mutilated eunuchs' of Emerson's stinging criticism, who scraped and tooted in happy abandon, indifferent to the troubles of the world.

Although Castell did not arrive in Mauritius till July 1831, he managed to get a letter back to Susannah before 28 May in which he apparently extolled the virtues of his choice of destination. Susannah agreed that he would do well to settle there, or at the Cape, 'whichever place profits most—both are flourishing and well govern'd'.[55] But she had reason to fear that he might have been seduced into joining the dreaded Swan River settlement, or even into going to Van Diemen's Land. 'I particularly warn you', she wrote, 'from attending to every account you hear respecting "Swan River" etc.—for were you to read our newspapers you would be of a different opinion. I speak from knowledge of others, who <u>have</u> severely suffer'd from emigration, for neither the former or Van Dieman's Land are yet sufficiently established for the introduction of arts and sciences.' They, she considered, were for '<u>after</u> consideration, and not before a country becomes independent'.[56] And with her familiar resigned pessimism about Castell's unworldliness and vulnerability, she cautioned him against siren voices:

you write an account of a '<u>young</u> gentleman' lately returned from 'Swan River' who describes the settlement as consisting of 5000 persons, but I should like to know how many labourers and other description of menial dependents form part of these 5000 for we must not suppose their <u>half</u> consist of '<u>Ladys and Gentlemen!</u>' and I verily believe that a professional man would find it difficult to procure six pupils out of their united classes for <u>ornamental</u> instruction.

For Susannah, long hardened to the stern realities of life in the city which was already the mercantile capital of the world, music, if it had ever once been a 'flow of soul', had evidently ceased to be anything but a luxury product available to those who could afford to buy it, and with no higher function than to provide the means by which she and her expensive family might somehow sustain a decent respectability. And she added with that scepticism born of bitter experience of the human heart: ''Tis natural for your informant to paint a country in its fairest light when his representations are made to a speculative voyager, for by so doing <u>one more</u> might be added to their number.' And as to Castell's hopeful boast that money there was 'too plentiful', she enjoined, with her customary insight into such matters: 'It plainly shews that they cannot profitably make use of it and what they <u>do</u> expend will never be enjoyed by <u>themselves.</u>'[57]

Susannah's instincts—or prejudices—about Swan River were to be vindicated. The first English settlement on the western coast of Australia, founded on the principles of free capital rather than unfree convict labour, through a combination of land greed, poor planning, and bad luck, was to be saved in the end only by the introduction in 1849 of the

[55] SEC–WJC, 28 May 1831, p. 1.   [56] Ibid. 2.   [57] Ibid. 2–3.

despised system of convict transportation so spurned at the outset. At that time the colony's population was still only about 6,000 and in 1830 had dropped from something like 4,000 to 1,500.[58] But in the same period Van Diemen's Land was enjoying boom conditions. Indeed on 1 July 1830 *The Times* published a letter from a Hobart correspondent who boasted of a lively market for musical talent there. He reckoned that his own music teacher, whom he paid £200 per annum with a cottage and all expenses found for him and his family, could do much better than remain with him. 'He has only to teach from ten till one, and from three till six every day. Many I should think would gladly accept such liberal offers. In fact there is ample employment in the Island for three music masters, two dancing, two French and one drawing master.' Susannah had evidently not read this report, or remained unconvinced. Her view remained pessimistic. If such places were to have their day, as D. H. Lawrence was to remark of Australia almost exactly one hundred years later, it would not be *her* day. 'Tho children unborn will call them good people but not before thousands are ruined which was the case in America and all new settlements.'[59]

Castell did not receive this letter from Susannah till 12 October, by which time he must have realized something of the nature of the crisis confronting Mauritius and the limited prospects the place offered for his material advancement. Its exotic quality, however, could not have escaped him. Sweltering beneath the dramatic backdrop of volcanic rock out of which reared the crooked, thumb-like peak called 'Le Pouce', how remote and unreal must have seemed Susannah's talk of Belgian revolutions and the political vagaries of dynastic Europe—

the affairs of Belgium are not yet adjusted on which so much appears to depend. The French people are again uneasy at something, they are forever a restless set. Their king appears not so popular among them as formerly, himself and family are making a tour thro' France in order, as is supposed to court popularity. So much for royalty. I envy them not for their palaces—£300 pr ann. and a choice of residence is worth them all

—or of the street arch at 19 Stangate Street, which had given way 'just under the scraper'.

[58] For the Western Australian colony of Swan River, see A. Wyatt Tilby, *The English People Overseas. V: Australasia 1688–1911* (London, 1912), 104–5.

[59] SEC–WJC, 28 May 1831, p. 3.

I begin to feel uneasy, but hope that we shall escape all accidents it will be a most disagreeable and expensive affair and a mortifying circumstance to repair it and nearly the [?end] of the lease . . .[60]

Nor would he have welcomed her insensitive prognostications about his future prospects:

With you, the affair has become serious another five years (and the most vigilant period of your life) has past—a blank. In the course of ten more you will find yourself comparatively an old man for age creeps on so imperceptably that it takes us by surprise, and yourself will require that aid which you now design for others—promptness, with judgement, are now become indispensables, for such an undertaking—you ought to abandon all projects unconnected with your profession—you are not adapted for undertakings of that sort—the privileg'd few (only) are in the grand secret of getting money without working for it. You lose the little you get. I forsaw the breaking of the 'Mining bubble' from its commencement, but I made up my mind to keep silence otherways you would have reproached me with spoiling the concern. You will excuse my plainess of style, but remember more years have passed over my head than yours and [I] have all my life been a watchfull observer of passing events, which to a reflecting mind, act as so many lessons of experience.

He doodled cryptic, half-formed messages in pencil over the front of this particular letter, the odd decipherable words suggesting that he was uncomfortable in the heat, that the price of vegetables was dear, that he had been evicted from his cottage more than once, and that the idea of Van Diemen's Land was still preoccupying him, as was Sydney.[61]

In December he wrote full of description of the place, its customs and manners, which failed to enthral Susannah, and evidently outlined some of the social and political problems caused by the activities of the French colonists which did not surprise her. As she said in her reply of 16 May 1832: 'My opinion of the French character remains unalterable. They are mere butterflies and weathercocks ever changing viciously virtuous and virtuously vicious but never inclined to leave well alone.'[62]

Castell, however, seems to have gone along with the French arguments for the retention of slavery on the grounds that the negro slave was physically better off than the 'English peasantry'. Susannah's response to this was adamant and presumably not very original. Unlike Castell, she said, she rejected slavery on the grounds that it was 'inconsistent with religion and reason'.

---

[60] Ibid. 4.   [61] Ibid., front.   [62] Ibid. 16 May 1832, p. 1.

As well as you, I am aware that our English peasantry are worst fed and badly cloth'd, their family's in a state of starvation, but not one amongst their numerous tribe would be found willing to bear the yoke of bondage, like their black brethren. If foreign luxuries <u>cannot</u> be obtained without such inhuman practices, how much better to altogether abstain from them. If a 'washerwoman' cannot proceed with her daily occupation without the assistance of Tea from China, and sugar from Jamaica it would be worse than useless to argue against the system of slavery! That it produces an enormous revenue is undeniable—but who is better for it? and does not the consumer pay for <u>All</u>.[63]

Susannah had had, of course, no direct experience of the system Castell was defending, but she had absorbed the prevailing attitude of the British middle classes in what was the great moral question of the day,[64] and had no need of it. She had the authority of conviction supported by popular endorsement. And she evidently rather enjoyed her position of moral superiority as she communicated to Castell her sentiments on that subject, a position which overflowed into others she touched upon as well. That 'impudent fellow' Paganini had earned, she reckoned, £20,000 by his recent tour, 'and will scarcely condescend to lend his body as a return for their money and applause bestow'd on him'.[65] The state of music in London, she assured him, was deplorable. It was the old story: foreign music and musicians were usurping the place of native musicians. The German operas were patronized by the Queen, and the nobility would have nothing but French music. In June she reported that Laporte had taken over Covent Garden. William had been unemployed for the winter season.[66] At the English Opera, the first violinist was paid £1. 5s. 1d. 'so much for bringing up children to music'.[67]

It would be useful to them, she suggested to Castell, if he would supply them with '<u>original</u> and <u>choice</u> national airs, and adapt them for quadrilles, Waltzes etc. . . . as the rage for <u>novelty</u> required in that line is in such request, that compositions of some of our finest authors are pulled to pieces bit by bit to furnish passages—endeavour to collect

---

[63] SEC–WJC, 16 May 1832, pp. 1–2.

[64] Since the abolition of the slave trade in 1807 and the association with the cause of such essentially conservative figures as William Wilberforce, the continuing crusade for total abolition had much middle class and Evangelical support. See John Pollock, *Wilberforce* (London, 1977). It should be noted though, in relation to Mauritius, that in 1819 quite a stir had been created over the then Major-General Sir Ralph Darling's treatment of Mauritian planters. Following the letter of the law regarding the slave trade, and obviously distrusting the Mauritian judiciary, he had several sent back to London for trial, an act which outraged sections of British liberal opinion. See e.g. *London Magazine*, i (Feb. 1820), 217.   [65] SEC–WJC, 16 May 1832, pp. 2–3.

[66] Ibid. 16 May 1832, p. 3; 2 June 1832, p. 2.   [67] Ibid. 2 June 1832, p. 2.

Indian, Russian or any other whether outlandish or otherways and endeavour to compose some yourself, adapted to the figures'.[68] She thought he might contrive to rule the five lines on writing-paper and 'by a close connection of the notes (tho plain)' send them as letters. What they wanted from such productions was 'prompt payments', as things were very difficult, with Augustine scarcely managing to prise a trifle of his salary out of his employers.[69] And at any time she expected the country to explode in a civil war.

On 16 May she had written: 'I dread the consequences of the rejection of our Minister's as regards the upper house, of the reform Bill, so long pending. Earl Grey and his colleagues have tender'd their resignation to the King which has been accepted to the no small discomfiture of the People.' Everywhere, she said, the people were rising. Householders were withholding rates 'untill their just demands [are] complied with'. There were numerous public meetings 'and Tens of Thousands ready to shed their blood in the grand cause of reform and have it they will'. She had, she said, seen a great deal in her lifetime of an infuriated London mob, but this time their rage would beggar description, 'for we have men of property and the flower of the Kingdom to lead them on'. The French may well be so foolish as to court revolution, 'But it is for such as us, poor unprotected beings [Mothers] with a family of Boys and GIRLS that contemplate this approaching scene with all the horror of parental agony, what scenes may I not be subject to, or my family of Five for oftentimes soldiers are monsters in the shape of men'.[70] And from a musical point of view it was all disastrous, since 'the great folks have been so much engaged in political squabbles that they will not meet each other in their houses'.[71]

Beside all this dangerous ferment at home, the civil war in far-off Madagascar that Castell had presumed to mention in his letter looked pale indeed. Events did not justify Susannah's fears, but from her perspective she may be excused for her alarm. There had been cause enough for revolution, fed over decades of resentment, and England did not develop the complacent certainty that as a nation she was exempt from such things till much later.

Unbeknown to Susannah of course, events in Mauritius, even as she was penning these fears, were reaching fever pitch, with the imminent arrival of Jeremie, the 'Great Liberator', feeding talk of revolution from more quarters than one.

[68] Ibid. 1.   [69] Ibid. 2.
[70] Ibid. 16 May 1832, p. 5.   [71] Ibid. 2 June 1832, pp. 2–3.

The exact nature of Castell's employment or the conditions in which he lived in Mauritius are unknown. He informed Susannah that he was barely able to live, which may have been true enough. It appears though that he could not leave because he was under some kind of 'engagement', probably to his sponsor Captain Royer.[72] That it was musical is suggested by his requesting Susannah to make enquiries from Lincoln, the Holborn organ-builder, about a seraphine,[73] which he evidently wished to procure—hardly a minor investment at 42 guineas.[74] An early type of harmonium, the seraphine might seem a little inappropriate to the musical requirements of a tiny tropical island about to lose its livelihood and tear itself apart, but perhaps by its very novelty Castell may have hoped, even under these difficult circumstances, to realize a profit on his investment.

His social life is no less obscured, but there is some evidence that, notwithstanding the presence of his 'sister' Mrs Cecil, he worked his way into the same complex involvements with his female acquaintances there as he had done in St Albans and at St Servan. He seems to have thrived upon sexual intrigue. In his December letter it would appear that he had already entered into certain transactions, requesting Susannah's co-operation in regard to an unnamed 'Lady at Kensington', who had recently returned to London from Mauritius, having apparently fallen under his spell there. But Susannah, in a tone of genuine indifference to her husband's apparently unending search for true love, replied that she could not summon the energy, having exhausted all she had on the Miss Jones affair.[75] More to the point, she queried his not altogether new practice of addressing his letters to third parties, this time to William rather than to herself.

I understood from you when [you] left France that your intention was to make mention of your family when you landed in the Isle of France. Who now have you got to be afraid of, and who is the existing cause of this scrupulous secrecy. Is there anything so dishonourable in being a married man, and the father of four children. Is it not a common occurrence for men to leave their family's to try to better their situation in life if so understood and I feel assured that you would not be less respected on that account—you may believe me I am not so ambitious of external honours as you may imagine, but the thing looks bad and unaccounted for.[76]

---

72 SEC–WJC, 16 May 1832, p. 2.
73 Ibid. 3.   74 Ibid. 6.
75 Ibid. 5.   76 Ibid. 3.

Up till the time of Jeremie's first departure in July 1832, it would seem that there were few, if any, public music performances at Port Louis as a result of all the agitation. But in August Messrs Philip and Olivier Fils gave a 'Soirée Musicale' at the 'Loge de la Paix', performing piano pieces by Rode, assisted by an amateur who sang several songs.[77] M. Philip and 'sa jeune demoiselle', Mlle Philip, had recently arrived from the Grand-Théâtre, Bordeaux, where M. Philip had been principal violinist.[78]

But apart from such visiting celebrities, it would seem that the island possessed quite a reservoir of talent. Not only was the colony rich in actors, said *Le Cernéen* in September 1832, it was also rich in musicians, and good ones at that. It possessed an orchestral philharmonic society, which had successfully joined forces with Monsieur James in that month to present a major musical event, utilizing much of this talent. M. James was a violinist, apparently of quite accomplished stature; M. Widet, a bassoonist; M. Lacarriére, a flautist; and Mme Chardon, a singer. They performed works by Boildieu, Berbiguier, Fontaine, and Mayseder.[79] At another concert in October, M. Crispin impressed with a performance of a clarinet concerto by Weber.[80] Later in October, another 'soirée musicale' was given by Monsieur and Mademoiselle Philip.[81] And on the 23 October it was noted that M. Bellerive would conduct an orchestra in yet another concert featuring four overtures never before heard in Mauritius: 'L'ouverture d'*Anacréon* de Cherubini, celle de *L'Agnese* de Paër, celle de la *Cenerentola* de Rossini, et celle de *Fra-Diavolo* d'Auber'.[82]

It was evident, then, that not only was there quite a developed audience for music in Mauritius, but public performance of music was dominated by the French. It was against this background that Castell prepared for yet another musical venture—the first, as far as we know, since the débâcle at the Horns Tavern in Kennington in 1826. It was to be a concert in the *Salle de Spectacle* in partnership with Mr Smith, bandmaster (*chef de la musique*) to the 87th Regiment. But the omens were not good.

On 16 November 1832, even before the concert was advertised, *Le Cernéen* rather mischievously published a letter, the authorship of which

[77] MA, typescript of advertisement in *Le Cernéen* (Port Louis), 7 Aug. 1832, p. 6a. (Note that all subsequent references to *Le Cernéen* are from MA typescript extracts.)
[78] 'Soirée Musicale', *Le Cernéen*, 2 Oct. 1832, p. 3a.
[79] 'Concert', *Le Cernéen*, 11 Sept. 1832.
[80] 'Soirée Musicale', *Le Cernéen*, 2 Oct. 1832, p. 3b.
[81] 'Seconde Soirée Musicale par Monsieur et Mademoiselle Philip', *Le Cernéen*, 9 Oct. 1832, p. 4a.   [82] 'Concert', *Le Cernéen*, 23 Oct. 1832, p. 4a.

it claimed not to know, containing assertions that the paper could not guarantee were true, which indeed it thought too absurd to be true, but which it felt obliged to publish nevertheless as a public duty, since in the present climate it felt it should show concern even if others didn't.[83]

The facts, as reported by their correspondent, were that Messrs Smith and Cavendish were putting it about that their concert would not only be extraordinarily fashionable and *distingué*, but that it was to 'have all the English, none but English'.[84] The correspondent followed up this assertion with loud protestations and barely veiled threats. 'I tell Mssrs Smith and Cavendish that if they expect a full house on such terms they must persuade the officers of the Garrison, their "patrons", to march at the head of their soldiers into the *salle de spectacle*.'[85] A further cause for contention seems to have been that the officers of the 87th Regiment had joined their patronage with that of Lady Colville, 'a lady justly esteemed and beloved by the inhabitants of Port Louis, as well as for uniform and habitual condescension as for her connection with him, whom they consider "the saviour of the colony"'. The correspondent went on to ask: 'Do these officers think that [the] Lady needs their support when she pleases to associate herself with intelligent people in enjoying one of their greatest and most refined pleasures—does she need the aid of swords and bayonets to be welcome whenever she appears in public ...?'[86] The writer also asked whether Messrs Smith and Cavendish feared the professional judgement of their betters. There is a reference to certain 'female musicians who have brought with them a well learned reputation in larger if not better judging communities', but the scrambled syntax makes it unclear whether these persons were being indulged by Messrs Smith and Cavendish or were feared by them. Possibly the former. Intimations of Susannah's 'nest of butterfly's' in St Servan. But this was a diversion—the main thrust was political and the tone distinctly threatening.

'A beggarly return of empty boxes' unless military influence be employed. Be it so—Let Mssrs Smith & Co. entertain their gentlemen masters, and their indulgent patroness at their mess table and when they have finished their claret let them repair to the Theatre to enjoy a *row*—and make themselves agreeable to a people just recovering from a fearful agitation, and longing to reconcile themselves to a government too indifferent to their interests, too heedless to their rights.

[83] 'To the Editor', *Le Cernéen*, 16 Nov. 1832, p. 1b.
[84] Ibid. 1b–2a.   [85] Ibid.   [86] Ibid.

I compliment them sincerely upon the good feeling, good taste and promised enjoyment of their national Reunion. The inhabitants of Port Louis will know how to show their contempt, as well as their energy when occasions require.[87]

The letter was written in English and signed, probably falsely, 'An Englishman'.

Although Smith and Cavendish's advertisement in *Le Cernéen*, when it appeared on 16 November, was in French and was completely unexceptionable except perhaps that it claimed the patronage of Lady Colville, the damage was done. It was a total failure.

Le Cernéen published Cavendish's reply to his accusers on the 23rd, an indulgence which the paper thought warranted a lengthy explanation, arguing that it had agreed to do so out of a strong belief in the principle of 'defense' no matter who was involved, and would honour its pledge in spite of what it considered 'Sieur' Cavendish's abuse of the privilege, and in spite of the fact that as an individual he was not worthy of affection or esteem.[88]

It was a long letter which bore all the marks of anger, bitterness, and bombast. He still did not know who his attacker was and thrashed about in rather an orgy of vituperation. Whoever he was though, he was assured that 'Like the viper in the fable, he may gnaw the file until his lips are bloody, but he will get very little good by nibbling at me, who on occasions, can bite iron and steel'.[89] His attacker, he went on, had he 'consulted the opinion of some prudent reflecting friend', might have escaped the 'chain of mortifications which he may still be required to sustain and suffer, and quietly have *rotted upon the dung-hill from which he sprung*'.[90] He was no Englishman and no patriot. His accusations had been entirely false. What professor, Castell quite reasonably argued, would have been so incautious as to so risk that public opinion upon which so much depended? And as to the patronage question, no Englishman would have mistaken it for anything else than what it was—a matter of etiquette, with which his friend, as a military man, could not dispense. His calumniator, he said, had done nothing to assist in closing the 'yawning breach' between the two societies, which ought to be the aim of any man wishing to see the establishment of harmony and peace, and must indeed have been happy, he added, to know that his triumph had been complete. The concert had been a failure. They had been deserted

---

[87] Ibid.
[88] *Le Cernéen*, 23 Nov. 1832, p. 2b (translated from the original French).
[89] Ibid., 'To the Editor', 23 Nov. 1832, pp. 2b, 3a, 4a.   [90] Ibid.

by nearly all of the amateurs, 'which rendered our position one of peculiar distress'. But he would have it known that on the subject of his disappointment, 'I hope my friends will be silent, and I shall know how to make my enemies so'.

He did not blame the public, who had been plunged into error by his traducer, who from the 'general tenor and vulgar style' of his letter could have 'no claim whatever to the country of which he signs himself a native, and whoever bestowed upon him the title of an *Englishman* paid him a compliment as high as it was unmerited'. Slightly ironically (for an Englishman), he signed his own letter, 'W. J. Cavendish de Castel'.

Le Cernéen ended the debate with the observation that to those who had rented them the *Salle de Spectacle* and who had provided the lighting, Cavendish owed the sum of 60 piastres which he was unable to pay, adding, with a sarcasm that was distinctly hostile, that for a man so keen to balance his account, here was a fine opportunity which it urged him to profit by.[91]

Nineteen days later, on 12 December 1832, the ship *Sovereign* carrying a cargo of sugar departed from Mauritius. On board, in the steerage, were Mr Cavendish and his 'sister' Mary.

SYDNEY, 1833–1839

A cultural vacuum

On 20 January 1833, just over five weeks after departing from Mauritius, the Cavendishes, as we shall now call them—for indeed Mary, having ceased to be Mrs Cecil, became immediately known as Miss Cavendish—arrived in the port of Sydney after an apparently uneventful, non-stop voyage.[92]

Cavendish may still have been intending to go on to Hobartown, where he had had reports, probably through Smith, that a musician by the name of 'Dean' had settled[93]—John Philip Deane (1796–1849), in later times, in contention with the ghost of Isaac Nathan, called the father of Australian music. After the exotic physical beauty of Mauritius, Sydney, for all the impressiveness of its many-armed deep-water harbour and villa-embossed peninsulas, may have seemed ordinary even in the

[91] *Le Cernéen*, 'To the Editor', 23 Nov. 1832, pp. 2b, 3a, 4a.
[92] NSWSA 4/5204, COD 26, Shipping Lists. Report of Arrival, *Sovereign*.
[93] SEC–WJC, 16 May 1832, p. 2.

intense light and sub-tropical heat of high summer. But the musician, fresh from scenes of high communal drama, may have been more impressed with aspects of the colony other than sheer physical effect. Even then, Sydney had all the outward appearance of a tranquilly prosperous English town. As one observer remarked in October 1833:

Were you to stand on some of the higher parts of the town, whence you might see both the town and some of these [outer] residences, you would be highly gratified with the European feature which Sydney wears; and that which is of much higher importance, and more astonishing, is the strong proofs of wealth and comfort that every where present themselves.[94]

The population of Sydney was about 16,200, almost all white, Anglo-Saxon; only 2,770—surprisingly, considering the penal function of the place—were actually convicts,[95] and, according to the above report, there were not many more than 40 Aborigines in the area: 'perfect and complete objects of human wretchedness'.[96] Such unchallenged British ness, after his recent experiences was probably in its own right a compelling factor.

It would not have taken him long to uncover the schisms within Sydney society: between the freed (i.e. the emancipists or fully freed convicts, as well as those convicts who, with tickets-of-leave, lived as free men and women) and the free settlers; between Currency (native-born) and Merino (i.e. the land-owning, status-quo-supporting, self-styled gentry); between Currency and New Chum (i.e. free immigrant); or between Protestant and Catholic; between the Revd Dr J. D. Lang and the establishment, the theatre, the papists, and vice; between the declining oligarch John Macarthur and almost everyone; but even so, there was still land to be had and a developing pastoral economy that offered not only the chance of some return for even modest speculation, but high wages, and a growing economic and cultural infrastructure. Sydney, after all, had a theatre, which by the time Cavendish arrived was almost fully operational and which, unlike that of Port Louis, was founded on solid English traditions, and likely to afford him at least some opportunity for employment. But its very existence, proclaiming, on the face of it, a cultural normality, had emerged from what had only recently been a situation of considerable abnormality.

[94] Grandfather, 'Letters from New South Wales to my grandson No. 1', *New South Wales Magazine*, i (Dec. 1833), 318.
[95] 'Abstract from Census, 2nd Sept. 1833', *New South Wales Magazine*, ii (Jan. 1834), 64.
[96] Grandfather, 'Letters from New South Wales', 316.

Whereas in Mauritius the theatre, for the French, had been a natural social phenomenon, it had not been so in Sydney. A slave colony and a convict colony, in this respect at least, were quite different. Whereas in the former, organized social spectacle was deemed a cultural necessity, in the latter it was viewed as a threat to order. The reason for this was quite clear. In Port Louis the theatre was the adjunct of a fairly homogeneous élite, while in Sydney it was to serve a majority of the population which, while it was free, had not always been so, or if born free was the progeny of the unfree. In many ways, given the intellectual parameters which guided middle- and upper-class opinion on such matters as the inveterate nature of the 'criminal classes',[97] this posed a much more complex set of problems. Confusion of aims regarding the convicts themselves had been evident since Macquarie's time.

Well over a decade earlier, the Bigge Report had aimed to reinforce the basic founding principles of the colony as a tool of judicial terror, but the gradual infiltration of free settlers and the emergence to maturity of the first generations of the convicts' own free children, and the growing power of the emancipists, made it increasingly difficult to draw hard and fast lines. In the late twenties and early thirties the theatre had in fact become a battleground upon which disparate interest groups thrashed out their arguments and prejudices. It had begun when Barnet Levey, himself the brother of one of Sydney's most successful emancipists, Solomon Levey, built a theatre inside his Royal Hotel in George Street but had been denied a permit to operate it by the then Governor, Sir Ralph Darling.

It was probably a less significant battle than that waged by the press on its own behalf against Darling's rigidly uncompromising views on colonial discipline. Darling, who in Mauritius in 1819 had claimed that the laws of England were the only suitable tools with which to discipline recalcitrant French slave-owners, maintained in Sydney that the same laws 'were not made for convicts' and that free settlers ought 'to conform to such rules as the peculiar nature of the community . . . may render necessary for the public good'.[98] But the fight was taken up by both sides in the press and elsewhere with almost equal fervour. Roughly speaking, the executive, the Church, the Merinos, and the *Sydney Gazette* stood on

[97] Jeremy Bentham's 'set of *animae viles*, a sort of excrementitious mass', quoted in Hughes, *Fatal Shore*, 2, from *Panopticon Versus New South Wales* (1812), 7; Portia Robinson, *The Hatch and Brood of Time* (1985), esp. p. 52.

[98] Quoted in A. G. L. Shaw, *Heroes and Villains in History. Governors Darling and Bourke in New South Wales* (1966), 22.

19. View of George Street, Sydney, showing the Royal Hotel which housed Levey's Theatre Royal. Ref. State Library of New South Wales.

one side; while the Currency, the emancipists, William Wentworth's *Australian*, and Richard Hall's *Monitor* stood on the other. Major Thomas Mitchell expressed a little more than just a patrician exasperation in his comment on the controversy: 'I have just been called on by two clergymen to sign a petition *against a theatre* which has been erected, on the plea that the people are too bad and that the theatre will make them worse. Who would live in such a country.'[99] The full story of the conflict has been told admirably by Eric Irvin in his *Theatre Comes to Australia*.[100]

Cavendish arrived in Sydney just as the furore was dying down. On 22 December 1832, Levey had finally been granted his licence by the new governor, Richard Bourke, a Whig appointment who had brought to Australia a whiff of the new liberalism which in England had paved the way for the passing of the Reform Bill that June. Levey had opened in the

[99] Mitchell Library. MS Papers of T. L. Mitchell, vol. iii, 1820–9, quoted in R. Thorne, *Theatre Buildings in Australia to 1905* (1971), 343.
[100] E. Irvin, *Theatre Comes to Australia* (1971).

Saloon of the theatre on 26 December with the nautical drama that Elliston had produced at the Surrey with such success during his last management in the late 1820s, Douglas Jerrold's *Black Eyed Susan*, along with the farce, *Monsieur Tonson*. The debate, however, was far from over. It had merely shifted its ground. For the next five years until his death, poor Barnet Levey would be lectured and vilified in turn, but rarely extolled, and even in death would be the victim of unrelenting spite. The *Gazette* printed a letter on that occasion from one William Kerr, claiming that he 'should congratulate himself on having had a hand in freeing the world of the late Mr Levey'.[101]

Yet from its very inception, the theatre became an integral part of the Sydney social scene, even if it seldom seemed able to sustain the allegiance of any prominent faction for very long. After having supported its creation, newspapers like the *Australian* and the *Monitor* often seemed over-willing to add their voices to the chorus of censure and criticism. Almost universally, among the literate members of society, the demand was that the theatre, if it was to exist at all, must be an agent for 'improvement' rather than simple entertainment. The hope had already been expressed that the theatre would become a tool for moral education: 'This institution if rightly understood will be of incalculable advantage to the rising generation of the colony. It will make them conversant with the "ways of the world" and teach them that while justice may slumber a while, vice will never fail to be punished, nor virtue rewarded . . .'[102] But the theatre and its company were made of mere clay and much prone to the very failings that it was meant to redress. Rowdy, belligerent, undisciplined, materialist, and not always sober might describe both the broad Sydney community as well as the *corps dramatique* of the Sydney theatre.

The unreasonable demands made of the theatre were the expressions of an anxiety which was quite pronounced in the booming thirties, that the unmitigated pursuit of mammon would inherently and permanently corrupt what many already perceived to be a nation in the making.[103] Everybody knew that the great aim of any immigrant was to amass a fortune if he could. Why else would he have left the comforts and security of his native land? Susannah, with her unerring insights into the mechanisms of self-interest, had made this very point to Cavendish. 'Few persons', she had written, 'would be found willing to quit their native

    [101] In *Aust.* 27 Oct. 1837.   [102] *Currency Lad*, 26 Jan. 1833.
    [103] See George Nadel, *Australia's Colonial Culture* (1957), ch. 3, 'Colonizing and Culture'; Crauford D. W. Goodwin, *The Image of Australia* (1974), 11–22.

land with property, merely to settle in either place [Swan River or Van Diemen's Land]. No, none but the necessitous entrepreneurs.'[104] How, then, to counter the scenario that Wakefield had drawn from his imagination in his *Letter from Sydney*?

We are in barbarous condition, like that of every people scattered over a territory immense in proportion to their numbers; every man is obliged to occupy himself with questions of daily bread; there is neither leisure nor reward for investigation of abstract truth; money-getting is the universal object; taste, science, morals, manners, abstract politics are subjects of little interest unless they bear on the wool question . . .[105]

Into this cultural vacuum was thrust the infant theatre, to be found instantly wanting. Nevertheless, this very sense of disappointment fed the desire for cultural improvement in the colony and offered to someone like Cavendish, speculative voyager as well as musician, a chance of survival and even of material security that would probably have been highly unlikely even three years previously, and would be so again in the financially rocky forties. Indeed it appears that, almost effortlessly, he slipped into a niche that circumstances had already created for him.

Yet, musically, Sydney was nowhere near the relatively advanced state in which he had found it in Mauritius. Amateurs among the establishment and Merino 'classes' tinkered on their pianos in their elegant houses, and evidently purchased musical instruments if we are to judge from the quite early existence of retailers in this field.[106] And a cluster of music teachers advertised their services.[107] But on a public scale little activity could be discerned. In 1826 Levey had featured in the Sydney Amateur Society's series of concerts at the Freemason's Tavern. And from about mid-1829, while the battle raged over Levey's theatre, concerts and 'at homes' were substituted for plays there. Apart from the military bands in the barrack square, neither was music al fresco welcomed in the colony. A Mr Naylor, like Levey, was rendered insolvent by the government's refusal to permit him to operate his 'Cherry Gardens' on Parramatta Road, which with banquets, music, and lights had been meant to imitate London's

---

[104] SEC–WJC, 28 May 1831, p. 2.

[105] Quoted in Nadel, *Australia's Colonial Culture*, 36.

[106] Nov. 1824—Robert Campbell from Clementi & Co., London, 93 George Street, in James Hall, 'History of Music in Australia 1788–1843', *Canon*, a series of articles, Jan. 1951–June 1952; John Wood, his second music shop, 1826, noted in J. P. McGuanne, *Music and Song of Old Sydney* (Sydney, n.d.), 23.

[107] Mr H. R. Harvey taught 'polite dancing' as well as violin (*Mon.* 21 Aug. 1830); Mr Brunton taught dancing and probably music (*Mon.* 9 Jan. 1830).

Vauxhall Gardens. Yet another victim, as 'Vindex' in the *Australian* complained, 'of false morality and puritanical saintship'.[108]

Indeed it seems almost certain that music was tinged in Sydney, as it was in England, with similar kinds of puritan prejudices. Evangelical piety and commercial pragmatism had been early and strongly represented in the person of the Revd Samuel Marsden, the colony's most notable Anglican clergyman (known by the sobriquet of the 'flogging parson'); while Calvinist stringency was overtly demonstrated in the very public career of the Presbyterian leader, the Revd John Dunmore Lang, in the pages of whose newspaper, the *Colonist*, a constant war was waged against weakness and profligacy of all kinds and colours.

Cavendish seems to have early recognized a possible stumbling-block to his musical pretensions in the colony, and perhaps in consequence turned his energies within a couple of months to setting himself up as a dancing master. Colonial society in its first quest for culture seemed to have adopted something of the Locke–Chesterfield equation whereby the dancing master but not necessarily the musician was an essential cog in the educational machinery of the upper classes, or of those who had pretensions in that direction. As we shall see, dancing was taught at Lang's very own Australian College as well as at the Establishment opposition, the King's School in Parramatta.

Cavendish had not been the first in the field. In January 1830 a Mr Brunton, 'Professor of Dancing', felt obliged to advertise that he was 'under the necessity of giving notice, that every pupil that comes under his tuition must pay for the whole of the quarter, whether they attend or not'.[109] And in August 1830, H. R. Harvey advertised 'polite dancing' in the saloon of the Royal Hotel.[110] Yet in Cavendish we do see something new. His blatant and distinctly theatrical self-promotion was certainly intended to grab attention.

DANCING ACADEMY

Mr Cavendish de Castell, member of the Royal Academy and Conservatoire, Paris, respectfully announces that his 'Salle de Danse' will open for the season, at his residence, Macquarie-Place, on Tuesday 26th instant. Minuets, Gavots, Quadrilles, Swedish, Spanish, and Polish dances, Boleros, Muscovian and Circassian Circles, Galopodes, the Grand Polonaise and Gymnastic exercises.

Terms, including Soirées
Two Guineas per quarter[111]

---

[108] *Aust.* 28 Jan. 1831.   [109] *Mon.* 9 Jan. 1830.
[110] *Mon.* 21 Aug. 1830.   [111] *Currency Lad*, 16 Mar. 1833.

This ebullient announcement, less than accurate in its biographical detail, appeared in the press in mid-March, and marked the beginning of what was to become a lucrative business.

He did not, however, limit himself to this field. Music was obviously not without possibilities. In April yet another notice appeared, this time to announce the formation of a Philharmonic Society under the auspices of one 'Dr J. L.', presumably the Polish explorer, geologist, and collector of Aboriginal songs, Dr John Lhotsky. Cavendish was named as one of four participating musicians. The other three were Messrs Edwards, Sippe, and F. Wilson.[112]

Lhotsky had recommended the Society to the notice of the citizenry on the not altogether unchallenged grounds that 'Sciences and Arts are so closely connected', and congratulated the 'Lovers of musical science upon this opportunity to improve the minds of our fellow citizens'.[113] The improving impulse in evidence here in Dr Lhotsky's friendly 'puff' for the Philharmonic Society echoed the establishment earlier in the year of the first Mechanics Institute—an organization ostensibly dedicated to the propagation of useful knowledge which turned out not to be particularly friendly to the idea that music was an art that could effect the improvements so claimed.[114]

Dr Lhotsky had promised, that in a month or six weeks, 'friends' would be admitted to 'witness the proceedings of the society', but it was to be more than a year before we hear of its first concert (if indeed it was by then the same group). In the meantime, the society seems to have performed the role of orchestra to the theatre, with a mention of its work in this regard appearing in the *Monitor*'s review of the first night in the refurbished Theatre Royal on 5 October 1833; rather a flop by this account. It was Bishop's *The Miller and his Men*. The 'grand spectacle' of the burning of the mill failed altogether, and the music left much to be desired. Where the band of the garrison (presumably that of the 17th Regiment directed by Mr Lewis)[115] had previously made the walls

---

[112] *Gazette*, 27 Apr. 1833, p. 2. Born a Czech, John Lhotsky came to Australia in the hope of gaining official employment. Bitterly disappointed, he became a most trenchant critic of colonial government.

[113] Ibid.

[114] In 1841, the Prahan Mechanics' Institute, in a debate, affirmed that music was a greater evil than novel-reading. J. H. Furneaux, *Short History of the Prahan Mechanics' Institute as disclosed by the Minute Books* (Melbourne, 1930), in Nadel, *Australia's Colonial Culture*, 149–50.

[115] *Currency Lad*, 29 Dec. 1832, on the opening performances in the Saloon of the Theatre Royal.

vibrate, the 'phil-harmonic society's instruments were weak'.[116] Even so, they apparently drowned the choruses and songs.[117]

What role Cavendish took in all this is not known. Sippe was advertised as the principal cellist and Edwards the leader.[118] It is possible that at this time Cavendish, apart from any musical role, may actually have been stage-manager, in which case the débâcle of the immolation scene would have reflected rather badly on him.[119]

Family and friends

Perhaps surprisingly, Cavendish still maintained his links with his family in London. He wrote to Susannah in about September 1833, indicating his whereabouts. Her reply of 28 May 1834 was her first letter to him since June 1832 when she had asked him to provide them with the quadrilles from Mauritius, which she now regretted to inform him were 'a total failure both in style and quality'.[120] She was gratified, however, that his present employments enabled him 'not only to exist but something more in a state as you describe'.[121] She hoped something might be spared 'from the common stock' to be invested for the benefit of her two daughters, who for the past nine months had been afflicted with whooping-cough, and who, in the event of her death, or if business should fail, had no protection or support. Business, indeed, she informed him, was very bad already. Alfred had no engagement, and William was recovering from an attack of erysipelas.

She was full of scorn for the music festival that was to be held the following month at Westminster Abbey. The profits were partly to go to the Royal Academy of Music, which did not please her: 'boys with nothing but impudence to recommend them'. Neither did the rate being paid to participating musicians please her. 'They are liberal enough to offer 4 guineas for 4 rehearsals and 4 performances, each expected to last the whole day. Mr G. Smart, conductor and head of the mob—tickets 2 guineas each, scarcely one left a month ago—King Queen Bishops Lords and Commoners and a host of everything and nothing.'[122]

---

[116] This comparison is rather unfair since performances prior to this were held in the much smaller Saloon.

[117] *Mon.* 9 Oct. 1833, p. 3.   [118] *Mon.* 5 Oct. 1833.

[119] Cavendish is mentioned in this capacity in C. H. Bertie, *The Story of the Royal Hotel and Theatre Royal Sydney* (Sydney, 1927), p. 14.

[120] SEC–WJC, 28 May 1834, p. 1.

[121] Ibid.   [122] Ibid. 3.

For all Cavendish's talk of his apparent success in Sydney, it was clear that Susannah was still not enthusiastic about the Australian convict colonies. Indeed, she considered that if his going to New South Wales were to be generally known, it would 'form a precious thread for neighbour's gossip'.[123] Mauritius, even though a slave colony, and in spite of her professed antipathy to that immoral and irrational system, would seem to have had more to recommend it in her eyes than a convict colony, with its odious associations with criminality and the lower orders. As she remarked in a later letter, 'the major part of the population are a mass of thieves & the refuse of creation'. Perhaps she had picked up an old copy of *Blackwood's Magazine*, which in 1829 had published a description of the denizens of New South Wales as: 'the most rascally and villainous population that ever congregated on the surface of the globe . . . a sort of moral cloaca into which the very scum and refuse of society is periodically discharged.'[124] She should, she said, 'be afraid to close my eyes fearing to be murder'd by them in the night time'. Her interest in Castell's new environment was thus rather closer to that of a housewife discovering a dead sewer rat in her privy than to an expectant partner clamouring for information. She read in the English newspapers of the terrific exploits of the bushrangers, and in the Australian newspapers that Cavendish sent her of high food prices in Sydney. The combination made her feel sincerely grateful to be poverty-stricken where she was—rather than (by implication) affluent in such a place as he had now chosen as his home. In her letter of 4 May 1835 she finally requested him to send her no more Australian newspapers, 'for they are too expensive and very uninteresting. We paid 3.6 each packet—besides you had written your initials on some which subjects the receiver to pay a heavy fine, perhaps as much as 13ᵈ each paper.'[125]

She had more pressing demands upon her time and energy. The lease was finally up, and she had at last to move from Stangate Street. She feared that the owners would exact every penalty they could by the terms of the contract which he, Cavendish, had signed. If they could not get money, she reckoned, they would resort to other means, 'and seize on what they can lay hold on'.[126] Neither was finding somewhere else an easy matter. They could not do without four bedrooms, a sitting and

[123] Ibid.
[124] Ibid. 9 Oct. 1834, p. 2; T. Hamilton, 'Cunningham's N.S.W.', *Blackwood's Magazine*, xxii (1827), 603, in Goodwin, *Image of Australia*, 12.
[125] SEC–WJC, 4 May 1835, p. 2.
[126] Ibid. 9 Oct. 1834, p. 2.

practice room, a kitchen, '&c &c', which could not be procured, rates and taxes included, for under £40 a year.[127]

Even if she had room or opportunity, she could not write half of the harassing circumstances which crowded on her. But she contrived to send him the double bass-strings he had requested along with an assortment of oddments and mementoes: a pair of scissors with knives attached—a gold *petit d'or* pencil-case with a case of leaden points—2 small quadrille books—a copy of the *Messiah* (the vocal score)—3 Abbey festival bills—a shilling coin and a small china egg[128]—all in a deal box wrapped in brown paper and costing 15s. 6d. in postage. In contravention of the standard practice, she sent him the written authority separately by post, 'otherways', she argued, 'they would not only have the property but the security in their own hands'.[129] Susannah's basic distrust of the human heart showed little sign of having relented.

She continued to run his messages in London or at least tried to give the impression that she had attempted to, but these last letters of hers to Sydney seem to testify in their almost mechanical bitterness to a loss of any real hope that any part of the old relationship could ever be restored—even its combativeness. Perhaps Cavendish, when he received the last one, sent from London 4 May 1835, decided the effort was pointless on either side. Perhaps he was piqued by her continued suggestion that his venture in New South Wales was such a potential source of embarrassment to her. She was very glad, she had said, that a certain letter he sent to Mr Watmore had gone astray, 'for it would have occasion'd a great deal of unpleasant description and scoffings very much to our disadvantage when it became known that you had repair'd to Sydney . . .'.[130] It seems likely though, that he had declined to answer her very first letter to Sydney, the one in which she had demonstrated herself so ungrateful in the matter of the quadrilles.

In this last letter she gave him her new address at 8 North Terrace, Mount Gardens, near Marsh Gate, off Westminster Road, and made what was to be a final appeal.

You must be aware that I have a family and an expensive one too, we have struggled on for nearly nine years neither can you accuse me of incessantly importuning you for the support of a family grown to the state of Man and womanhood; Many privations we have suffered and [have] much more to endure and I regret to think that I have two daughters tenderly bred and incapable of

---

[127] SEC–WJC, 9 Oct. 1834, p. 2.   [128] Ibid. 1; 4 May 1835, p. 2.
[129] Ibid. 9 Oct. 1834, p. 1.   [130] Ibid. 4 May 1835 [No. 1], p. 1.

earning their living. Their health too is delicate . . . Alfred is past 21 Lena 20 next August and her sister 15—I should think something might be spared for us. I am getting [?on] in years and they are without friends—reflect on this and if possible, set about ameliorating our situation.[131]

With this letter the correspondence ends. Why? It is unlikely that Susannah, with so much at stake, would have simply ceased to write without some reason. When Augustine finally wrote to the Royal Society of Musicians in 1841 to cancel Castell's membership, he indicated that the family were 'entirely ignorant in what part of the world (if living) he may reside'.[132] This would suggest that Cavendish himself, at some stage, had given Susannah reason to think that he was no longer resident in Sydney.

Sydney was a small, acrimonious society, rather given to private scandal and public abuse. Cavendish may have felt, quite apart from any pique at Susannah's ingratitude and prejudice, that the continued link with her made his position less secure; more vulnerable perhaps to the curious pryings of the unfriendly or the jealous. At any time, he may have thought, Susannah could shatter his security—send someone looking for him—write a letter to the press—or simply excite, through her continued correspondence, the curiosity of his enemies. For in Sydney he was sure to have had a few—perhaps Sippe, or Edwards, or other dancing masters whose trading patch he had probably invaded. And as we shall discover, only about 60 miles away to the south, in Woollongong, there existed, indeed, real cause for anxiety. Mr S. C. Walton and his information, to be so readily supplied in 1839, would, if Cavendish had ever been aware of it, have induced in him considerable agitation and a desire for even greater secrecy.

He may have feared most of all exposure of the truth about his relationship to Mary Cavendish. There is no evidence that he had ever had a sister, and Susannah would have been the first person to appreciate such an anomaly. It was unlikely that he believed Susannah would purposely expose him—she had, after all, connived on his behalf in the Miss Jones affair and probably still remained loyal enough. But should anyone like Walton find it possible to contact her, he may have reasoned that she might inadvertently have become a conduit of damaging information. Quite apart from Susannah, though, as more and more free

[131] Ibid. 3.
[132] RSM, MS Members' Files. Augustine Humble to Watts, 20 May 1841.

immigrants poured into Sydney, the greater the personal links with London, and the greater the chance that such information might be siphoned back to Sydney.

Indeed, the tension of living in a town like Sydney in such a precarious relationship must have created strain and amplified whatever fears they both had. How were they to conduct themselves? Who could they tell? And how would each respond to interlopers when both were ostensibly single persons? With the chronic shortage of females in the colony, Mary may have found herself frequently importuned by hopeful wife-seekers. And having declared themselves brother and sister, how indeed, even if they became legally free, could they ever marry and remain in Sydney? The corner into which they had painted themselves may have seemed at times almost impossibly small and tight. And the anxiety on top of these pressures that Susannah might unwittingly lead to public questioning about the real identity of 'Mary Cavendish' doubtless preyed on their minds as well. But who was 'Mary Cavendish'?

According to Therry, she was the wife of a Captain C. of the French Navy.[133] His source for this allegation is unknown, but whoever she was, she was certainly the Mrs Mary Cecil who arrived with Cavendish and who was designated his 'sister'. She was also the person from whom (ostensibly) two letters survive,[134] one of which was written from Mauritius to her 'dearest brother' by way of third parties back to Europe, when in fact the 'dearest brother' had arrived with her in Mauritius on the same ship.

In these letters, she professes to have originated from Jersey and to have been employed with a family in France, presumably either as governess or companion. This family had travelled first to Palermo in Sicily via Tours and then via Marseilles to Mauritius in 1831, arriving at the Cape of Good Hope on 10 June and Port Louis on 19 July—these two dates closely paralleling those of the *Indus*. The first letter was written on the back of a letter to a Mrs Dominy and dated, presumably incorrectly, 29 September 1831. The second, like the first, without any direction or postmark, was dated 30 July 1831. It was in this letter that Mary wrote from Mauritius to tell her brother, supposedly still in Europe, the news of her marriage at the Cape to Mr Cecil and of their prospects in Mauritius.

Mr Cecil, the story went, was engaged as a junior clerk in a merchant's house on the small salary of £200 a year, a salary which

---

133 Therry, *Reminiscences*, 115.
134 Mary Cavendish to Mrs Dominy, 29 Sept. 1831 [wrongly dated—probably meant to have been 1830]; verso of which MC–WJC; Mary Cecil–WJC, 30 July 1831.

would by the third year be increased to £300 and upon his remaining longer to £540. They had, she said, a very pretty little pavilion, with two slaves to wait upon them, there being not a dozen English servants in the place. 'The little black children run about quite naked, the men have only a cloth tied round their waists which does not reach their knees, but the female slaves are often better dressed than their mistresses except that they are not allow'd to wear shoes and stockings.'[135] At first the 'musquitos' had bothered her, she said, but their effects were wearing off. She promised to try to send every month a letter which her husband would copy for her.

That both letters were fakes there can be little doubt. Apart from the descriptive passages, the only truth consciously contained in them was probably the reference to her 'husband' copying her letters, for the handwriting is uncannily like Cavendish's. It is impossible now to know who they were intended for or what the circumstances were that made them necessary; or whether it was a coincidence or part of the fiction that their final residence in Sydney at King Street East, three doors from George Street, was in a building called 'Cecil House'.

The name 'Cecil' itself, like 'Cavendish', is a prominent one in the genealogy of the great—arguably, the pair are simply too 'establishment' to be true. But by the time the couple had reached Sydney they were reduced to a single name and a less ambiguous set of titles. Whereas a Mrs Cecil may have had to be explained and re-explained, how could 'Miss' Cavendish, have been anything but a sister? One assumes at least that this was the reasoning.

She was officially at least eighteen years Cavendish's junior,[136] but apart from this nothing more is directly known about her, except that her profession at the time of her death was recorded as 'Teacher of Music'.[137] She may, of course, have assisted in the compilation of the two letters and some of the opinions advanced in them may indeed have been her own; in which case she emerges as a rather conventionally xenophobic member of the English lower middle class. Writing to Mrs Dominy she is given these happy lines:

I have seen mountains three miles high and living lions and tigers, I have travelled by land and sea, and seen people of all nations, black and white and can safely

---

[135] Ibid. 2–3.
[136] At the time of their deaths he was recorded as being 48 and she 32. He was actually 50, and she could have been younger. Christchurch St Lawrence, Sydney, Record of Burials, 1839, William Joseph Cavendish and Mary Cavendish, Nos. 21 & 22.
[137] Christchurch St Lawrence, Sydney. Record of Burials.

declare that no persons I have known are equal to my own country, and if I were not with those I esteem, I should certainly regret leaving England.[138]

There is also the lingering but remote possibility that she may have been Ellen Jones, married off perhaps by her father to the Frenchman, Captain C., to save face. When Cavendish first knew Ellen in St Servan in about 1827, she was probably 16.[139] At the time of Mary Cavendish's death, she was meant to have been 32, yielding a discrepancy of only about four years, by no means a barrier to the possibility that she could have been Ellen Jones.

However, it seems more likely that she was indeed the mysterious Madame Gallien to whom Susannah had obliquely referred in her December letter of 1830: 'I cannot close this without noticing your very strange conduct in prohibiting me from writing to you, alleging as a reason "that before you <u>could</u> hear from me you would have quitted <u>Europe</u>". Your next account pretends to explain it by saying you were <u>merely going to Madame Gallien's</u>. Why not state the <u>truth</u> perhaps xxx can explain it —— If "<u>mystery</u>" does exist—'tis my province to complain not <u>yours</u> —— —— some time <u>since</u> you inform'd me that Mme G <u>had</u> quitted France for <u>three years</u>.'[140]

Madame Gallien, in Cavendish's little joke, being not in 'Europe' was probably in Jersey, which, as we have seen from her 'letters', was the home of 'Mary Cecil'. And like 'Mary Cecil', Madame Gallien too had recently 'quitted France'. 'Mary' writes to her 'brother' ostensibly from Palermo in the erroneously dated letter of 29 September 1831.

It is so long since I wrote that I forget the date, but I believe it is since I left Jersey. I have receiv'd a great deal of friendship from Mrs Dominy, which I hope, I shall never forget, I have written to her from this place, in which I have given her a short history of my journey. We have travelled a great deal since we left France, and have seen much and I can safely say that I have known but one good foreigner. The family I am with is very amiable and as they are going to leave Europe, I think it likely I shall go with them.

The most likely possibility, then, given the known facts, is that Therry's 'Captain C.' was printed in error for 'Captain G.' and that his errant wife was indeed Madame Gallien-cum-Mary Cecil-cum-Cavendish. But whoever the unfortunate woman was, it must have been no mere amorous whim, no momentary girlish infatuation which led her to follow such a

---

[138] Mary Cavendish to Mrs Dominy, p. 1.
[139] THJ–SEC, 25 May 1828. Copy with SEC–WJC, 10 June 1828, p. 1.
[140] SEC–WJC, Dec. 1830, p. 6.

precarious star as Cavendish's and to live such a precarious lie. It was either love, or fear, or madness.

Musical life in Sydney in the thirties was quite suddenly transformed in 1836 by two sets of new arrivals. A sea change in the economy of Van Diemen's Land brought the musical family of John Phillip Deane to Sydney, prior to which a youthful and then almost unknown William Vincent Wallace[141] had descended, literally out of the blue, along with his father, wife, sister, and brother, all musicians. Susannah would have been surprised indeed had she heard of such a concentration of artistic excess in such a new and barbaric setting. Not only surprised, she would probably have been quite alarmed as well. But it is unlikely that she ever did. Whether this musical inundation surprised, alarmed, or delighted Cavendish and the other resident musicians is not known. Feelings were probably rather mixed. Certainly the arrival of another refugee from Hobartown, Mrs Chester, created hostilities in the theatre, where the ascendancy of Maria Taylor, the colony's favourite 'warbler', was distinctly threatened, causing the *Monitor* to be fiercely defensive of the old and the *Australian* blithely euphoric about the new.[142]

Neither Mrs Chester nor Wallace were shy of self-promotion. She was 'late of Drury Lane and Covent Garden', while he was 'Leader of the Anacreontic Society, and Professor of composition at the Royal Academy'.[143] In Wallace's case, neither claim was correct, but, like Cavendish's claims, neither could they easily be disproved, although at that time the aristocratic Anacreontic Society (at least in London) had been defunct for years. The Deanes were more low-key.

John Phillip Deane had come to Hobart in 1822, apparently on a commercial venture with a cousin, who unfortunately drowned, leaving Deane without legal claim to their merchandise. That at least was the story that came down through the family.[144] He then turned to music,

[141] William Vincent Wallace (1812–65), ex-leader of the Theatre Royal orchestra, Dublin, virtuoso violinist and pianist, world traveller, eccentric, and composer of English operas, notably *Maritana* in 1845, which established him in the forefront of English composers for the theatre of his day. (See Grove.)
    There seems absolutely no substance to the romantic notion circulated on his death that he 'went bush' out on the Darling River 'near the place afterwards crossed by Burke and Wills' and was only inveigled into appearing at a few concerts in Sydney. See for example his obituary in *The Orchestra*, v (28 Oct. 1865), 68. The confusion may have been due to the fact that there was another William Wallace, a squatter, in New South Wales at the time, or due to Wallace's own story-telling, to which he seems to have been rather addicted.
[142] *Mon.* 3 Oct. 1835; *Aust.* 2 Oct. 1835.   [143] *Aust.* 2 Feb. 1836.
[144] This was the story according to John Philip Deane's descendant, Mr W. H. Deane, with whom I spoke in Sydney in 1976. See also *ADB*.

becoming organist at St David's church in Hobart in 1825 and later setting up Hobart's first theatre in the Argyle Rooms in 1834.[145] In this capacity he shared similar difficulties to those of Levey in Sydney, particularly in 1834 when the rebel actor Mackie from the Sydney theatre created mayhem there as well. Mackie had insulted the Sydney audience in declaring many of their number to be 'ticket men'.[146] In Hobartown he had insulted Mr Deane and his family and had been discharged—as usual going before the public to state his case and ending his performance with a display of fisticuffs.[147] And the nature of the insult? Was Deane too one of the despised class? Or was his wife?

Deane claimed to have been a member of the Philharmonic Society in London,[148] but there is no evidence of this. Neither was he the gentleman who Susannah had suggested had been the second-hand music seller by Waterloo Bridge who had moved the piano from Stangate Street to the Horns Tavern for young William's ill-fated concert in 1826.[149] That was the only 'Dean' she knew in London in musical circles, she said. Cavendish had mentioned the name to her in 1832 in connection with Van Diemen's Land—enough perhaps to elicit a negative response, but it is certainly true that the name does not occur in any of the major London sources: neither in the records of the Philharmonic Society, nor the RSM, nor the Company of Musicians, nor in Doane's 1794 *Musical Directory*, nor in Donovan Dawe's *Organists of the City of London 1666–1850*. But this does not preclude the possibility that he had been a professional musician before going to Hobart, if not in London then perhaps in a provincial town; if not under the name Deane, then perhaps under another. Certainly he followed the traditional pattern of the music profession by training his children in the art. His three sons, John, Edward, and Charles, were string players, and his very talented but ill-fated daughter Rosalie was a pianist and singer.[150] All were quite young when they arrived in Sydney. Rosalie at 14 was probably the eldest, followed by Edward who was 10.[151] John was probably the next, while Charles Muzio would have to wait till he was 5, in 1838, before leading the orchestra 'in a set of quadrilles'.[152]

---

[145] See *ADB*; W. Arundel Orchard, *Music in Australia* (1952), 12–13; M. Roe, *A History of the Theatre Royal, Hobart from 1834* [n.d.], 3.

[146] During *Castle Spectre*, 18 Feb. 1833; *Mon.* 20 Feb. 1833.

[147] *The True Colonist*, 16 Sept. 1834, in *Mon.* 1 Oct. 1834, p. 2.

[148] *Aust.* 13 May 1836, notice for Deane's concert of 18 May and subsequently.

[149] SEC–WJC, 16 May 1832, p. 2.

[150] Her public career was ended by early blindness.

[151] *SH* 19 May 1836.   [152] *Aust.* 21 Sept. 1838.

20. William Vincent Wallace, water-colour by J. Hanshew, 1853, detail. Ref. National Gallery of Ireland, cat. no. 2511.

The Wallace family were somewhat more mature. William, himself already a composer and virtuoso violinist and pianist, was 24. His brother, the flautist Stephen Wellington, was probably also in his twenties, and his sister Eliza, for whom it was correctly predicted that she would become 'the first singer in this hemisphere',[153] was about 16. She was taught singing not by Wallace but by his wife, Isabella (née Kelly), who was also to take her place on the Sydney stage, if not so

[153] *Aust.* 3 June 1836, p. 2.

conspicuously as her sister-in-law. Of the elder Mr Wallace, once a
military bandmaster and bassoonist, almost nothing is heard, although
he may have slipped quietly into a niche in the theatre orchestra. He may,
however, have been the same Mr Wallace who in 1827 had so deceived
Susannah in the Tate affair of the disputed musical instruments. If so, it
was possible that he knew and recognized Cavendish. The world was
becoming decidedly smaller, even then.

Cavendish, of course, was guilty of no actual crime, nor was he living,
in a technical sense, bigamously. However, it may have been this musical
invasion which prompted him to forestall any further communications
from Susannah, for, had the truth been discovered, a technical nicety
would probably not have spared him from social ostracism and
professional ruin. Sydney was a town of closets full of dark personal
secrets, and for this reason it was not good form to be inquisitive about
the past, which certainly offered some security against exposure. The
anxiety, however, would have remained.

Sydney's collective moral conscience was a rather bizarre, hybrid beast
though. It could sustain most truths, no matter how unpalatable,
provided they did not get in the way of profit. This was very evident in
the case of one John Thomas Wilson, whose story might as well be told
briefly here since he was to become Cavendish's most intimate friend,
and in the year 1836 featured rather prominently in Sydney's demono-
logy for the first, but not the last, time.

As the Wallaces, the Deanes, and Mrs Chester were dazzling Sydney's
musical dilettanti, John Thomas Wilson was outraging accepted norms
of decency by blatantly consorting with Mrs Maria Taylor of the Theatre
Royal, and, not content with 'showing off in the streets accompanied by
his dashing Cyprian in a curricle and pair', threatened to buy up the lease
of the theatre and place the whole establishment under the direction of
his 'chere amie'. This proved his undoing, as Dr Lang's *Colonist* took up
the defence of public morality in its inimitably direct fashion. Before
fleeing the colony, leaving his creditors empty-handed (one, at least, to
the tune of £36,000), Wilson added one more insult to offended decency
by publicly horsewhipping his detractor, the Revd Dr Lang.[154]

Yet remarkably, and unabashed, Wilson returned from London, where
he had barely escaped imprisonment, and set up again in Sydney as an

[154] The foregoing story, except where specified, is based on an article in *Aust.* 24 Oct.
1839, p. 2, reprinted from the *Gazette*. The horsewhipping incident is recounted in Irvin,
Theatre Comes to Australia, 192–4; see also the entry for Wilson in the *Australian Dictionary of Biography* (Melbourne, 1966), vol. ii.

auctioneer. Business flowed in and he diversified into shipping and property speculation. Cavendish did not live to see his final crash, which, when it came in late 1839, precipitated by massive borrowing, and crowned by a brazen flight from under the very noses of his creditors, took some £50,000 with it. The *Australian* was to be scathing of the selfish stupidity of the creditors; after the event, of course.

... if a man comes amongst them with a tolerable stock of impudence and assumes the appearance of being in easy circumstances, they become his dupes without any hesitation.

Let such a man as friend Wilson only set up his carriage, drink his champagne, and talk of the best way of investing money and he will find in Sydney plenty of easy merchants who will send him goods on credit and endorse his bills to any amount.

'John Thomas, you know he is all right. He must make a capital thing out of those steamers you know' ...[155]

It was only after this second and final defection that it was evidently thought safe to publish what many must already have known. His real name was James Abbot, of 'stout build, portly frame [and] ... insinuating address'—an abductor and seducer—with a wife and four children left destitute in England—his entire career one of deception and betrayal—a libertine who not only caroused with the 'dashing Cyprian' of the theatre, but, finally, with one Mrs Peacock, the wife of a Special convict at Port Macquarie[156] who like the rest had been 'bilked' by her gallant lover and would soon be a mother.[157]

Whether by 1836 Cavendish had already been drawn into Wilson's world of conspicuous display, easy credit, and amorous adventure, we do not know, but certainly by the time of his death there was evidence that he had.

Music as politics: concert, theatre, and oratorio

However, while Wilson was demonstrating in 1836 those very evils of unfettered materialism that it was hoped the introduction of culture would, if not eradicate, then at least temper, the improvers of the Press

---

[155] *Aust.* 24 Oct. 1839, p. 2, reprinted from the *Gazette*.

[156] The term 'special' referred to educated convicts with class origins higher than the norm. They were usually kept apart from other convicts, not for their own comfort but because they were considered dangerous to discipline. Port Macquarie was a convict settlement which had a high proportion of 'specials'. See Hughes, *Fatal Shore*, 349–51; ibid. 438–9.

[157] *Aust.* 24 Oct. 1839.

were full of the prospect of refinement on offer from the sudden advent of so much musical talent in the colony. It offered at last a viable alternative to the levelling experiences of the theatre—the possibility of an exclusively polite audience enjoying the cultural fruits which were not only the social reward of the self-styled middle, or 'respectable', class but its inherited entitlement, an entitlement which no autocratic oligarchy of exclusivists could now fail to appreciate. As the *Monitor* pointed out in reviewing yet another Wallace concert in 1836:

if any one doubt whether the people of this colony are getting powerful some criterion might be formed from the great numbers of most respectable persons both male and female, (very few of whom were known to us, though old colonists) as were congregated at this concert. The efforts of our small band of Tories will be in vain.[158]

The *Herald* considered that the concerts had given the community an opportunity to demonstrate its 'nascent taste, refinement and liberal spirit'. The journal went so far as to suggest that to these events might one day be traced the foundation of 'future schools of art that may flourish in this land when the Institutions of the older nations of Europe (the sun of whose fame has probably already passed its zenith) may be dying . . .'.[159]

Perhaps surprisingly, the musical profession in Sydney, instead of dividing into jealous faction, seems to have recognized the potential advantage of co-operation. Even Mrs Chester and Mrs Taylor put their differences to one side. They gave a concert together as early as March 1836, at which Mr Wallace lent his assistance, although the *Australian* mischievously admitted that it could not help thinking that 'the ladies have paid rather too dear for his whistle'.[160]

Wallace's programme for his first concert of 12 February 1836, reproduced below, established the general pattern of the many concerts which followed.

PART I

Overture—Guillaume Tell (Rossini)
Glee—The Forresters (Bishop)
Variations brilliantes—pianoforte, sur le trio favori du *Pré aux Clercs* with
    orchestral accompaniment.   William Wallace
Song 'Should he upbraid' (Bishop)   Mrs Chester

[158] *Mon.* 4 June 1836, p. 3.
[159] *SH* 9 June 1836.
[160] *Aust.* 18 Mar. 1836, p. 2.

Pot-pourri—flute (Nicholson) Mr Josephson
Glee 'Merrily goes the bark'
Song 'Savourneen Deelish' Mrs Chester
Concerto—violin (Mayseder) William Wallace

PART II

Overture—*Gustavus* (Auber)
Glee 'Who is Silvia'
Solo—clarionet (Gambaro) Mr Lewis
Song 'Glory from the battle plain' from *Rosina* (Shield) Mrs Chester
Grand Duett—pianoforte (Herz) on the favourite march in
  William Tell William Wallace
    and Mr Josephson
Song 'Where the Aspens quiver' (Lee) Mrs Chester
Fantasia di Bravura—violin—dedicated to Paganini in
  which he will introduce the 'Last Rose of Summer'. William Wallace[161]

Most of the concerts of this period, even more than this one, utilized all available musical resources and offered local musicians a rare enough opportunity to be heard in 'glittering' social contexts, in which the Governor himself, and therefore the 'establishment', featured prominently. To what extent musicians benefited financially, however, is another matter, and there is no evidence to suggest that any musician could have sustained himself in Sydney from public performance alone, even if audiences had remained willing captors, which of course they did not.

Even the talents of Wallace, so closely modelled on Paganini, were soon to attract criticism, and what we might term consumer resistance. The *Monitor*'s correspondent was soon complaining of mechanism and of Wallace's being too much a 'slave of the trade' to resist 'galloping up and down the gamut'. He was sure that such bell-like tones on a violin had never been heard before in the colony, but deplored the over-ornamentation of his style. The same criticism was levelled at Mrs Chester and Miss Wallace, who he would rather have heard singing 'Auld Robin Gray' or the 'Soldier's Tear' with pathos and judgement than 'all the tweedledums of Rossini'.[162] By December 1836 the gilt had definitely become somewhat tarnished, with the *Monitor* confident that Wallace was just the man to 'give us the false German taste'; for, while he was an exquisite artist, he was no musician. 'He handles the violin with the legerdemain of a conjurer; he touches it with exquisite manual delicacy,

[161] *Aust.* 12 Feb. 1836.
[162] *Mon.* 4 June 1836.

but that is all . . . music he does not seem to understand . . . in short he is a good watch-maker.'[163] How much of this was genuine criticism, how much the self-conscious demonstration of the 'taste, refinement and liberal spirit' of the community, how much the bloody-minded cutting down of tall poppies, it is difficult to say.

Cavendish's involvement in this cultural explosion seems to have come rather late. It was not until May 1836, at Deane's first Sydney concert on the 18th, that he is noted as appearing. It was a concert to which many Sydney musicians made contributions, including Mrs Chester, Mr Sippe, and Mr Wilson, but, perhaps significantly from Cavendish's point of view, none of the Wallaces. The orchestral pieces were performed by the Band of the King's Own 4th Regiment, but the occasion was not graced, as Wallace's début had been, by vice-regal patronage. Cavendish performed in a piece described as a Septette, 'in which will be introduced Haydn's Surprise', presumably an arrangement of part of Haydn's Symphony in G Major, No. 94, written in London in 1791 and considered to be the first piece of 'chamber music' publicly performed in Australia, by which was possibly meant that it was the first time that an intimate string sound had been heard, in contrast to the wind and brass of the military bands so much a part of public music-making in Sydney at this time. This particular arrangement utilized eight players: from the order in which they were listed, and from the players' own known areas of instrumental expertise, perhaps two forte pianos were played by Miss Deane and Mr Cavendish, the flute by Mr Stubbs, violins by Messrs Wilson and Deane, and (?viola) and cello by Masters John and Edward Deane respectively.[164] It appears to have been carried off with great success, exceeding in brilliancy, said the *Australian*, 'the expectations of the most sanguine'.[165]

However, this was not by any means Cavendish's first appearance at a Sydney concert. Before the arrival of the Deanes and the Wallaces, there had been several notable musical events outside the theatre in which he had taken an active part. He had probably participated in, and may even have organized, the first concerts of the Philharmonic Society between July and September 1834, perhaps accompanying the nervous Mrs Boatright and other amateurs who, along with the band of the 17th Regiment, seemed to take a prominent part in proceedings. These were

163 *Mon.* 21 Dec. 1836.
164 *Aust.* 13 May 1836.
165 *Aust.* 20 May 1836.

subscription concerts in the exclusive tradition of the London Philharmonic Society. At 7s. 6d. per ticket, paid for in advance and hand-delivered by the management,[166] the subscription list was evidently intended to keep out not just the economically undesirable elements of Sydney society. The first of these events was hailed by the *Australian* as the birth of classical music in Australia,[167] probably more in hope than in truth, for musically there seems very little basis for such a claim.[168]

It was in response to this event that that newspaper made the remarkable claim for music that 'among the whole prison population that have arrived in Australia, there never was a *professor of music*'. And, in a tone rather reminiscent of Richard Mackenzie Bacon's *Quarterly Musical Magazine and Review*, it went on to declare that music 'affords to teachers an existence and to the amateur an employment that not only keeps him from actions that he should regret—but thoughts that would create a blush'; a defence of music which was not perhaps as loftily disinterested as it was meant to sound.[169] As suggested earlier, there was a hidden political dimension in this apparent embrace of cultural values which was to reach its apotheosis after 1836.

At the Philharmonic Society concert in September 1834, Mrs Boatright appeared again, also a Mrs Ellard, with Mr Lewis performing 'wonders' with the band of the 17th. But we learn more about the small but very élite audience on this occasion and even less about the performances.[170] Cavendish's involvement in these concerts is uncertain, but if what the 'Englishman' in Mauritius said about his penchant for exclusivity was true, then the Philharmonic concerts might be said to have borne his mark. Subsequent concerts in 1835 leave more certain traces of his involvement.

In January 1835 he organized a rather splendid affair at the Pulteney Hotel on behalf of a Polish refugee and amateur musician named Gordonovich. It involved a 'noble orchestra', the principal singers from the theatre, including Mrs Taylor and Conrad Knowles, the band of the 17th Regiment, and the 27 singers from the Roman Catholic chapel. It was attended by 300 persons, including the governor and his suite, with 'even the large gallery on the top of the room filled'.[171] Cavendish's name is not listed among the participants and if the *Monitor* had not credited

---

[166] *Mon.* 23 July 1834.   [167] *Aust.* 29 July 1834.

[168] The *Gazette* mentioned the ballad 'Young Lochinvar', a duet, 'I love thee', and an unspecified 'Solo on the Clarionet', while the *Australian* recorded that a gentleman amateur sang 'Mary Lee' and captivated his audience who sat in silence, 'as if the melody came from heaven'.   [169] *Aust.* 29 July 1834.

[170] *Aust.* 3 Sept. 1834, p. 3.   [171] *Aust.* 23 Jan. 1835.

him with the organization of the event[172] his involvement would not have been recorded at all. By all account it was a rather exuberant affair, with rowdy patriotic songs and glees, 'too coarse even for the taproom',[173] combining with, among other items, two Mozart overtures, Weber's 'Polacca', and a grand choral arrangement of Haydn's 'Hymn to the King'.[174]

Then, in March, he undertook the pianoforte accompaniment at Mrs Taylor's concert at the Pulteney on the occasion of her desertion of the theatre due (yet again)[175] to a disagreement with Mr Levey. This was a highly contentious event. The musical profession, except for Cavendish, appears to have been conspicuous by its lack of support, a point remarked upon by the *Monitor*,[176] leaving Mrs Taylor heavily dependent upon the amateurs, and the audience was not only thin, but hostile, with members of the *corps dramatique* punctuating the evening with hisses. But it was interesting as well as contentious because it was at this concert that Cavendish introduced what the *Herald* called a seraphine[177] and the *Australian* called a metalaphone, an instrument which that journal likened to the 'sostenuto attached to Motte's pianofortes', and which it noted with some dissatisfaction that Mr Cavendish was unable to play. Developed in England by John Green in the early 1830s (Ord-Hume says in 1833 or 1834 but obviously earlier), the seraphine, a prototype harmonium, or domestic organ, was described by its maker as 'a keyed instrument with sustained sounds' of five complete octaves which produced sound on the principle of 'vibration of metal acted upon by wind'. Compact (2′ 10″ high, 3′ 3″ wide, and of simple construction, and 1′ 7″ deep), it was considered to be particularly serviceable both for ships' cabins and warm climates.[178] This was the instrument he had requested Susannah to make enquiries about in London when he was still in Mauritius in December 1831. It had probably only just arrived, and it may have been his desire to try it out on a live audience that led him to agree to accompany Mrs Taylor at her controversial concert. It was only used to accompany her in one song, Rawlinson's 'Isle of Beauty', but it

---

[172] *Mon.* 24 Jan. 1835.

[173] *Mon.* 24 Jan. 1835.   [174] *Aust.* 23 Jan. 1835.

[175] There had been a similar desertion of the theatre by Mrs Taylor due to disagreements with Levey in May 1834.

[176] *Mon.* 25 Mar. 1835, p. 3.   [177] *SH* 26 Mar. 1835, p. 3.

[178] *Aust.* 27 Mar. 1835; *The Royal Seraphine. A New Musical Instrument*, by J. Green, 33, Soho Square (3 pp., [London, 1833]). Green quotes a notice of the instrument from the *Lady's Magazine*, Jan. 1831. See Arthur W. J. G. Ord-Hume, *Harmonium. The History of the Reed Organ and its Makers* (London, 1986), 22–6.

would seem that its initial impact was not quite as he would have wanted. He may also have agreed to perform because he had already become friendly with, and perhaps even financially dependent upon, J. T. Wilson, whose relationship with Mrs Taylor may already have become scandalous. In any case it was certainly another first. The harmonium, which was to become such a ubiquitous feature of Victorian musical life, was heard for the first time by Australian audiences somewhere in among Cavendish's inexpert squeaks, bumps, and wheezings and, more than likely, the hissings of the anti-Taylor claque from the Theatre Royal.

April brought yet another concert. This time for Mr Stubbs, the flautist, and again Cavendish's role appears to have been that of accompanist. This event introduced a new musical star, the singer Mrs Rust—an enigmatic figure, acclaimed as the most accomplished vocalist ever heard in the colony and declared to be a student of the Royal Academy of Music and member of the Philharmonic Society of Milan,[179] she was prominent in musical circles for a few years in Sydney, then apparently disappeared into the hinterland in about 1839.[180] Her charm for the Sydney dilettanti lay not only in her musical talents but in her unsullied respectability. At the time the *Monitor* thought her on a par with Miss Paton and Camporese,[181] hardly faint praise from the *Monitor*. Unlike Mrs Taylor, Mrs Rust was supported by a full complement of local professionals. Among the instrumentalists were Messrs Wilson, Cavendish, Sippe, Stubbs, Lewis, Coleman, Josephson, and the band of the 17th Regiment. Mrs Taylor, however, was not among the performers. Indeed there were few other females on the programme, but among them was the ever-game but nervous Mrs Boatright, whose emotional fragilities the *Australian* took note of in declaring that 'Mr Cavendish was not a good person to accompany a timid singer'.[182]

At the end of April 1835, the *Herald* stated that Mr Cavendish was about to give a concert of his own,[183] but if he did it was so exclusive as to have been completely invisible, for there was never any further mention of it in the Sydney press. He was at this time, however, also negotiating with the Theatre Royal, the outcome of which may have distracted him from such an undertaking. In early May 1835, it was announced that the lessees of the theatre had engaged all the 'first rate' musical talent in Sydney to form the orchestra. Twelve gentlemen were named. Mr Clarke

---

[179] *SH* 20 Apr. 1835.   [180] *SH* 20 Sept. 1839.
[181] *Mon.* 25 Apr. 1835.   [182] *Aust.* 24 Apr. 1835.
[183] Noted in *Aust.* 28 Apr. 1835.

was the leader; Messrs Spyers, Johnson, Dyer, and Scott, violins; Mr Stubbs, principal flute; Mr Cavendish, violoncello and grand pianoforte; Messrs Turner and Sharp, clarinets; Messrs Hoare and Ball, bassoons; Mr Pappin, bugle; Mr Vaughan, drums. All was to be under the direction of Mr Cavendish.[184]

It was the theatre of course which was the most constant source of music in Sydney. The Roman Catholic chapel, soon to become St Mary's cathedral, was probably its nearest competitor in this regard, apart perhaps from the town taverns, about whose musical activities at that time little is known but whose popular balladists and comic songsters were probably as familiar to Sydney's ordinary folk as Mrs Taylor or Mr Levey of the theatre.

The music of the Sydney theatre would have been very familiar to Cavendish from his days at the Surrey and other London theatres. In the first month of his new job, there were no fewer than four separate musical productions: Bishop's *Clari*, on 7 May, concerning which the *Monitor* noted that there had been a great improvement in the orchestra;[185] on the 11th, another probable Bishop work, his musical adaptation of Scott's novel, *The Heart of Midlothian*; on the 18th, the stock piece, Samuel Arnold's *The Mountaineers*; and on the 28th, a relatively new piece, Nathan's *Illustrious Stranger* (1827).

Audiences at the theatre were probably appreciative enough and, by and large, well enough behaved,[186] but the fact that they were predominantly composed of the lower orders was enough to discourage the sustained patronage of their betters. Many were the complaints about improper dress and other disaffecting improprieties committed by Sydney audiences, and, as the *Monitor* put it, 'Our *very first* class will never attend a theatre, be it ever so perfect.'[187]

Whereas in England the division of theatres into pit, box, and gallery effectively segregated audiences into classes, in Sydney this was not always possible to achieve—at least in ways which could easily be recognized by patrons used to the English model. This was partly because the old perceptions of social stratification were themselves already beginning to disintegrate under the pressure of changed realities. The 'very first' class may not have come to the theatre because it was a theatre, but the proprietor was obliged to sell, if not his boxes, then at least the pit benches to whoever could pay for them—to the patron who

---

[184] *Aust.* 5 May 1835.   [185] *Mon.* 9 May 1835.
[186] G. C. Mundy, *Our Antipodes* (2nd edn., 1852), ii. 51.
[187] *Mon.* 2 Nov. 1836.

had never worn evening dress in his life, nor ever would, and who might just as easily have been an emancipated convict on a nice wage, who in England might never have been affluent enough to have attended a theatre.

Such an individual, accompanied by his lady and very possibly their suckling infant too, was not necessarily rowdy or a threat to order or decency; on the contrary, he might even have been rather in awe and seeking to improve himself. He would, however, inevitably come dressed in inappropriate clothing which, according to the *Monitor*, drove the higher classes from the theatre.[188]

The brutal economic fact was that if the proprietor of the theatre refused such persons admission on the grounds of dress, he would have had no one in his theatre at all except the rabble—the half-price hooligans from Kent Street and the prostitutes. In the absence of a large, well-established middle and upper class, it was these unfortunate embarrassments to refined sensibilities that became the much-sought-after bread and butter of the theatre. This was a reality that nothing could change. Indeed, the *Monitor* in more sensible mood acknowledged that it was to what it termed 'our second and third classes' that the theatre must look for its audiences. Indeed they were, it believed, the classes who were the most certain, steady, and truly respectable.[189]

Whether the *Monitor*'s 'second and third classes' ideally included emancipists or not, is uncertain. The paper's 'liberal' principles ought to have ensured this, but in any case it was not always possible to know the origins of the otherwise orderly and unremarkable persons who attended the theatre—which remained, however, except on those exceptional occasions when the Governor was present, a low-status institution.

It remained so for other reasons as well. The performers, like the audiences, were also of questionable origin and quality. As 'A Friend to the Drama' remarked in 1838, Levey had got together to form his theatre a 'mass of ignorant, vulgar, and vicious materials'. Even among the 'stars' were those with vulgar pronunciations and gross ignorance of grammar. Theatrically, all were self-taught, and the only truly educated one among them had been Conrad Knowles, by early breeding a gentleman. But he had destroyed himself with drink in an effort to sustain himself in what became the impossible task of both managing the theatre and acting in it. Of the women, all again were theatrically untaught, and none had received much general education.

[188] *Mon.* 10 Jan. 1835.   [189] *Mon.* 2 Nov. 1836.

'Nothing', said this 'Friend to the Drama', 'in the provincial theatres of England, even the lowest of them, falls so short of discipline, management and industry, as what I have witnessed at the Sydney theatre.' He spoke of vulgar acting, miserable music, dirty pit, and continual 'gag' (that is, extempore and often vulgar substitutions or additions to the written text of plays). He personally had been willing to forgive such shortcomings because he had felt that it was at least a beginning and worth persisting in;[190] but in general such tolerance was not a feature of Sydney society.

It was not social kudos, then, that Cavendish was seeking in taking over the theatre orchestra, but for such a task we may assume that he was paid at least as much as the best paid actors, which, in 1834, had been £3. 3s. 0d. a week.[191] The theatre operated four nights a week, one more than was usual in English provincial theatres, but from the much-complained-of shortcomings of the Sydney actors in memorizing their parts and the high incidence of 'gagging', presumably there were fewer rehearsals, which would have left Cavendish with some time during the day, with Mary's assistance, to develop his dancing academy.

The arrival of the Wallaces and the Deanes and the inauguration of their concerts must certainly have changed not only the pace of professional life but its social profile. For the first time, as we have seen, the concert became a means for the town's 'respectability' to establish its claims to superior culture, and it was taken up with a vengeance, at least for a while. In many respects this class was a colonial extension of Wakefield's 'uneasy class'. Like its English equivalent, it was galled by what it considered the patronizing and authoritarian attitudes of a self-appointed 'Merino' oligarchy whose credentials to rule, it believed, were only equal, if not inferior, to its own. Its open challenge was a bold advance on the English model, but then was not this the proper function of colonies—to provide new space for those talents and abilities which in the homeland, by the very nature of things, were either cramped, suppressed, or thwarted? Thus it was to become imperative to the exiles from home, family, and civilization that the 'demon' of oligarchy, which had so soon found its way into the new colony, 'exciting all whom he possesses with sole regard to their own interests, and a desire to monopolize all power and dominion and dignity to themselves and families', be eradicated. Macquarie had felt its 'insidious and persever-

---

[190] A Friend to the Drama, 'The late Miss Douglas', Mon. 19 Jan. 1838, p. 3.
[191] Letter from Conrad Knowles, *Aust.* 24 Mar. 1834, p. 3.

ing' enmity in all his attempts at broad cultural improvement, just as Bourke still did, and it would still, if it could, 'trample alike on the neck of Governor and people'.[192]

Certainly that was the view of the newspaper proprietors Hall and Wentworth, and, one assumes, their readership. In first supporting the theatre and then embracing the new cultural assets provided by these two musical families, they were quite clearly claiming a cultural ascendancy over the puritanical philistinism of their enemies and reinforcing the sense of their own fitness to govern the colony. The theatre had proved something of a double-edged sword, but in the concert there was much less risk of disappointment and embarrassment. Not only was the standard of performance high beyond expectation, there was little chance of encountering in the audience the same uncouthness that was inevitably to be found at the theatre.

At 7s. 6d. a ticket, 3s. 6d. more than the cost of a box seat at the theatre, and even without a subscription list, a certain decorum could be relied upon, if not always guaranteed. It must have been rather disappointing that in June 1836 the *Monitor* had to admonish the rudeness of certain sections of a Sydney concert audience for 'pushing and thrusting to get to the head of the room in violation of the rights of other spectators'. In order to prevent concerts becoming indistinguishable from pot-house clubs, it demanded the appointment in future of a master of ceremonies.[193]

On the whole, however, the concert served its purpose, and in 1837 the *Australian* was happy enough to declare that '"the Wallaces," "The Deanes," &c, by whose performances we have been delighted, and by whose instructions we have been improved, are justly classed among the most valuable and respected additions to the number of our Fellow-Colonists'.[194]

Unfortunately it is impossible to establish how far such a statement reflected the musicians' actual social standing in Sydney or how far it was merely useful rhetoric on behalf of a larger political argument. We do not notice, say, in Therry's *Recollections* (and Therry was a man not only socially and professionally prominent at the time, not only a member of Bourke's 'liberal' administration, but a friend and patron of the arts), any personal association with Wallace or Deane. His only mention of musicians is impersonal and detached. Cavendish (Therry's 'Devenish') and Bushell[e] (who we meet soon) are no more than legal specimens, set

---

[192] *Aust.* 3 Oct. 1837, p. 2: 'Royal Exchange Company—their projected building'.
[193] *Mon.* 4 June 1836.   [194] *Aust.* 3 Oct. 1837, p. 2.

up rather like dwarfs and fat ladies at sideshows, to titillate his audience.[195] The rhetoric did, however, express the degree to which music itself temporarily held the social focus.

This was a rhetoric which, on the face of it, may seem rather surprising. The men who indulged in it, in spite of their protestations, were unlikely worshippers at the shrine of Apollo. Music, as we have seen in an earlier chapter, was the least likely art to receive the active protection of a striving middle class nurtured on the tenets of Locke and Adam Smith, whose heroes were more likely to be Oliver Cromwell, Warren Hastings, or Josiah Wedgwood than Henry Purcell, or even Handel. Yet for all its diminished reputation as a profession, as an abstract, indeed as idealized in the name of Handel, music was still possessed of a powerful symbolism which survived the rationalist Enlightenment to take its place as one of the cultural mediators of power.

Out of the Aristotelian and Platonic matrix of eighteenth-century thought had emerged the idea that music, if not as high an art as painting or poetry, was nevertheless rational and elegant, and perhaps even more than any other art, being the least necessary, demonstrated that man was framed by nature 'for something more than mere Existence'.[196] For a man of taste, according to Dr James Beattie, to appreciate music, in the full control of all the rules of the art, was to exercise a form of aesthetic judgement—to make, that is, those rational choices which distinguished true taste from mere sensibility and, by extension, man from nature.

When once he can attend to the progress, relations, and dependencies of the several parts: and remember the past, and anticipate the future, at the same time he perceives the present; so as to be sensible of the skill of the composer, and dexterity of the performer;—a regular concerto, well executed, will yield him high entertainment, even though its regularity be its principal recommendation. The pleasure which an untutored hearer derives from it, is far inferior.[197]

---

[195] Therry, *Reminiscences*, 113–16. Sir Roger Therry (1800–74), an Irishman and a Catholic, was appointed Commissioner of the Courts of Requests in New South Wales in 1829. Acting Attorney-General from Mar. 1841 to Aug. 1843, he was appointed resident judge at Port Phillip in Dec. 1844, from where he transferred in 1846 to the Supreme Court in Sydney. High in reputation within his profession, in 1856 he was a nominee member of the first New South Wales Legislative Council under responsible government. A passionate advocate for Catholic emancipation, he earned the unremitting enmity of the eventual Anglican Archbishop of Sydney, William Grant Broughton. He retired to England in 1859. See *ADB* for further details of his life and career.

[196] James Harris, 'A Discourse on Music, Painting and Poetry' (1744), in Edward A. Lippman (comp.), *Musical Aesthetics: A Historical Reader* (1986), i. 171.

[197] James Beattie, 'Essay on Poetry and Music as they Affect the Mind', in Lippman, *Musical Aesthetics*, ii. 230.

Music was, therefore, ultimately if properly considered, a metaphor for control and order. Furthermore, the Platonic fear of music's power to affect the emotions and hence, potentially, to demoralize men had been softened by the argument that music was incapable in itself of engendering any but socially virtuous affections. As Dr Beattie was at some pains to point out:

Music may inspire devotion, fortitude, compassion, benevolence, tranquility; it may infuse a gentle sorrow that softens, without wounding, the heart, or a sublime horror that expands, and elevates, while it astonishes, the imagination: but music has no expression for impiety, cowardice, cruelty, hatred, or discontent. For every essential rule of the art tends to produce pleasing combinations of sound; and it is difficult to conceive, how from these any painful or criminal affections should arise. I believe, however, it might be practicable, by means of harsh tones, irregular rhythm, and continual dissonance, to work the mind into a disagreeable state, and to produce horrible thoughts, and criminal propensity, as well as painful sensations. But this would not be music; nor can it ever be for the interest of any society to put such a villainous art in practice.[198]

Richard Leppert's recent study of eighteenth-century portraiture of the English 'at home' in India analyses the use to which musical imagery was put, in conjunction with other potent Graeco-Roman cultural images, in communicating the idea of order and harmony as civilizing achievements of British colonialism. Men made wealthy by ruthless exploitation required for their own sakes that posterity perceive them not only in the enjoyment of their wealth and power but within an ambience of legitimacy, expressed by the possession of higher culture.[199] Extending Leppert's argument, then, the depiction of these men with their families engaged in the elegant and rational pursuit of music suggested not only the harmony and order of British rule in India but its incapacity to provoke emotions other than those believed to be benign and socially virtuous.

But for men who nurtured the same ambitions, the situation was very different in New South Wales. They saw themselves as hampered at every turn, not only by the small group of 'Rum Corps' oligarchs who had appropriated to themselves so much wealth and *de facto* authority but by

---

[198] Ibid. 235–6.
[199] Richard Leppert, 'Music, Domestic Life and Cultural Chauvinism: Images of British Subjects at Home in India' in Richard Leppert and Susan McClary (eds.), *Music and Society, the Politics of Composition, Performance and Reception* (1987), 63–104; see also Leppert's 'Music, Representation, and Social Order in Early-Modern Europe', *Cultural Critique*, 12 (Spring 1989), 25–56.

government restriction represented in the person of the Governor of New South Wales, whether a Macquarie, a Darling, or a Bourke. In contrast to India, the British government in New South Wales fought for several generations to assert an inhibiting control over the activities of its private citizens: to curb in effect the natural move towards civic 'virtue' among them, which it accurately perceived as a political challenge—a liberalization which was a practical inconvenience, a luxury not consistent with the aims of a penal colony. It was a battle that it was inevitably to lose, but in the meantime a generation of thwarted Clives and Hastings sought to fashion whatever weapons they could against this most frustrating foe which refused to see them for what they perceived they really were—the heirs of British genius only awaiting the opportunity to impose the Enlightenment virtues of order, harmony, and social virtue upon a virgin continent. Music may have been for them, as Roger Covell has suggested, 'a precarious fiction of grace and ease and comfort', a charm against 'the night and the unknown', but this is to sentimentalize them as pathetic exiles—pitiable even. On the contrary, many were hard-headed, aggressive, and opportunistic folk in whose political armoury music was a temporary weapon—a symbol not of dominance achieved, as in India, but of dominance aspired to.[200]

The theatre had been a victory, the Wallace–Deane concerts an unexpected windfall, but, above all, the 'Oratorio' or 'Festival' to be held in September 1836 in the still incompleted St Mary's cathedral, like the portraits of the nabobs, was to be invested with its own particular discourse of legitimacy.

There was nothing new here. There were powerful models. The terms 'oratorio' and 'music festival' had, since 1784 in England, become almost synonymous with the name 'Handel' and, by extension, with 'King George' and the glorious constitution. It was the year of the election which toppled the disreputable Fox–North coalition. As William Weber has noted, the great Handel Festival marked what looked like the end of the old Whig hegemony and the beginning of a consensus between Whig and Tory (or, depending on your preference, between reform Whig and establishment Whig) led by the wonder-boy William Pitt the Younger. However, it was not so much a consensus that the Sydney 'uneasies' desired, as a routing of persisting Tory oligarchy in the colony: ironic in hindsight, since by the 1830s the political result celebrated in 1784 looked distinctly like the genesis of that very Tory oligarchy; ironic too

[200] Roger Covell, *Australia's Music: Themes of a New Society* (Melbourne, 1967), 11.

THE DANCING DOGS,

AS PERFORMED AT SADLER's WELLS, WITH UNIVERSAL APPLAUSE.

21. W. Dent's 1784 cartoon showing Fox, Burke, and Lord North as the Dancing Dogs. Ref. BM DG 6636.

since it was the Foxite Whigs (arguably the direct political ancestors of the Sydney 'uneasies') who were vociferous in their attack upon the 1784 festival as a symbol of corruption and the insidious power of the Court.[201] But in 1836 such resonances were obviously forgotten or banished—what was sought from the Sydney 'festival' was the sense of cultural authority that the Handelian ritual would bestow upon a political order clamouring to be born.

The Oratorio was indeed an ambitious project, involving almost the entire musical profession, the military bands, and many amateurs, all directed by Sydney's undisputed musical emperor, William Vincent Wallace. But, working behind the scenes, it was Cavendish, according to the *Australian* of 23 September, who had been its 'original promoter' (a phrase which suggests either that he maintained a leadership position within the Sydney musical profession or that such a position had been usurped by others).

Essentially the festival was to consist of large slabs of oratorio— Handel's *Messiah* and Haydn's *Creation* interspersed with other religious pieces. It was very much in the mould of the great Music Festival in Westminster Abbey of 1834, of which Susannah had been so scornful but of which she had nevertheless sent Cavendish the 'bills', along with the vocal score of the *Messiah*. It was an event which did not go unnoticed in Sydney, with the *Monitor* dedicating several columns to a London newspaper report which may very well have been supplied by Cavendish, via Susannah. On that occasion some 631 performers took part: 356 chorus voices, 233 instrumentalists, and 52 vocal soloists and organists, before a glittering audience which included Their Majesties.[202]

At that time the idea of imitating such an event would hardly have been thinkable, but with the arrival of the Deanes, the Wallaces, Mrs Chester, and Mrs Rust, and the public interest in music that they provoked, Cavendish may indeed have enjoyed the idea of emulating the great national event in New South Wales, if for no other reason than to answer Susannah's gibes about his chosen location.

But he did not just conjure up a 'festival' out of nothing. There had already been developing at St Mary's a solid core of musical experience.

---

[201] William Weber, 'The 1784 Handel Commemoration as Political Ritual', *Journal of British Studies*, xxviii (1, Jan. 1989), 43–69. The year 1784 was also when the Dancing Dogs first appeared at Sadler's Wells. Fig. 21 shows 'the dogs', Fox, Burke, and Lord North, dancing to the devil's fiddle.

[202] 'Royal Music Festival', *Mon.* 1 Nov. 1834, pp. 2–3.

As we have seen, Cavendish had already made use of quite a large corps of singers from St Mary's, where it is very possible he was choirmaster. St Mary's choral excellence was implied as early as 1835 when a correspondent in the *Australian* used it as part of an attack on the music of Anglican St James's just a hundred yards away in Macquarie Street.

Such dolorous sounds have the same effect on the mind and spirits as a wet blanket would on a half smouldering fire . . . I never hear a psalm in that church which does not produce in me dejection . . . The Roman Catholics, who wish to make religion attractive are well aware of the influence of vocal music and they follow in this respect the sweet psalmist of Israel.[203]

Cavendish's assistant in 1836 may have been the ex-jewel thief James Bushelle, a ticket-of-leave man, whose voice and physique were held to resemble those of Lablache and whose other accomplishments included fluency in French, German, and Italian.

In May of 1836, much to the chagrin of Dr Lang's *Colonist*, the 'heathen' *Australian* recommended 'lovers of sacred music' to attend divine service at St Mary's, for there Mrs Rust, Messrs Wallace, Deane, and Cavendish, Clarke and Bushelle, plus a 'phalanx' of till then unknown talent would be providing a rare treat. They performed, as it turned out, parts of Masses by Mazzinghi and Mozart with Cavendish presiding (this time) 'most scientifically' at the seraphine. The church was crowded and amongst the congregation—and this is probably what outraged Dr Lang—were a 'great number of Protestant ladies and gentlemen'.[204]

As in London, where, as we have already seen, the Catholic chapels of the various embassies, especially the Portuguese, where Vincent Novello presided, were besieged with music lovers of all denominations, so too in Sydney, religious antagonism, it seemed, could be waived in the pursuit of musical revelation. It was this circumstance which, if it did not inspire it, probably made the whole idea of a 'festival' at St Mary's feasible. Originally planned for 24 August, it took place on 21 September, and was by all accounts a resounding success. Although prices were high: 10s. 6d. or £1. 11s. 6d. for a family of four, nevertheless, nearly a thousand people crammed inside the church, 'principally of the middling classes, besides many Government officers and others of the first classes', with a thousand more outside in the moonlight.[205]

[203] *Aust.* 16 Oct. 1835.
[204] *Aust.* 7 June 1836.   [205] *SH* 26 Sept. 1836.

Proceedings began at 7.30 with a voluntary on the seraphine (presumably performed by Cavendish), and the Hallelujah chorus, it was reckoned, could be heard a mile away. The *Monitor* admitted that it had not thought the musical talent of the colony would be adequate to the occasion, but had been agreeably proved wrong. 'We expected nothing so good in New South Wales', it crowed.[206] The 'star' had unanimously been declared to be Mrs Rust, whose notes, the *Australian* felt, sounded 'like liquid drops from a bending flower', which took the mind back 'to the days in which we were familiar with the sweet and silvery tones of Sontag'.[207] On a more mundane level it noted that Mr Cavendish's 'bass viol' (presumably cello or double-bass) was of 'infinite service'.[208] The ex-chorus-master of the Surrey Theatre evidently knew a thing or two about thumping out the rhythm, a function he obviously performed without squeamishness. The advertised programme was as follows.

PART ONE
Selections from Handel's Sacred Oratorio

The Messiah
___

Introductory Hymn
___

Overture
___

1. Comfort ye my people   Mrs Rust
2. He shall feed his flock   An Amateur

Pastoral Symphony

3. Where is this stupendous stranger   Mrs Chester
4. He was despised   An Amateur
5. I know my Redeemer liveth   Miss Wallace
6. Holy Holy Lord   Mrs Rust
___

SECOND PART
Selections from Haydn's Grand Oratorio

THE CREATION
___

---

[206] *Mon.* 24 Sept. 1836.
[207] *Aust.* 23 Sept. 1836.   [208] Ibid.

Ave Verum—Solo & Quartet
Mrs Rust & Amateurs
OVERTURE

1. In the beginning (Recit.)
   No Vanish (Air)   An Amateur
2. Chorus, A new created World
3. And God said (Recit.)
   With Verdure clad (Air)   Mrs Chester
4. Of stars the fairest pledge of day   An Amateur
5. Sanctus—Trio   Mrs Rust & Amateurs
6. Graceful Consort   Mrs Chester & Amateur
7. Grand Double Chorus—The Praise of God—The Solos by Mrs Chester
   Single Tickets—10/6
   Family (4)—£1.11.6
   Single tickets to admit 2 children
   Books of words—1/-

Leader of the Band Mr Wallace—Principal 2nd violin Mr Deane
Assisted by the gentlemen of the Philharmonic Society.[209]

Apotheosis

But Cavendish evidently did not see himself merely as the provider of
cultural artefacts for self-seeking colonial parvenus. He was himself
anxious to join them; if not in any desire for ultimate political control,
then in the desire for financial independence. Perhaps Susannah's parting
shot, that without hope of such independence his journey would be
'rash', still rang in his ears. After the Festival at St Mary's in 1836, his
name almost fades from the musical annals of Sydney. This could suggest
several things: that he was not on good terms with the rest of the
profession; that he preferred to remain in the background, managing
musical events rather than performing in them; that he was engaged in
less publicized activities, at St Mary's perhaps; or that he was distracted
from music by other occupations. Certainly if he had decided to
'disappear' in regard to Susannah, it would have been risky to allow his
name to appear in newspapers which she may have been able to gain
access to, but this did not impede him in 1838 when he was advertising

---

[209] *Mon.* 17 Sept. 1836; the programme published in the *Monitor*, 29 Sept. 1836, has
some variations. The 'Hallelujah Chorus' followed Item 6 of Part I. From *The Australian*,
23 Sept. 1836, it is evident that the 'Ave Verum' of Part II was by Mazzinghi. Other works
included the overture to *Joseph* by Méhul, and to *Zaira* by Winter.

the sale of his 'magnificent' Tomkinson pianofortes.[210] He had by then obviously decided to channel at least some of his energies into the mainstream of colonial economic life.

The 1830s were, on the whole, boom years. Whaling and wool were the chief sources of wealth, the latter being a somewhat easier proposition than the former for the dilettante investor. But although speculation in wool eventually did attract him, even as early as 1835 there is some indication that Cavendish may have had some interest in whaling. He had friendly links with Captain Richard Hayward of the whaling ship *Louisa*, who had written to him from Cloudy Bay in June 1835 of some of his logistical problems. Captain Hayward may also have entertained hopes regarding Mary, to whom he addressed his regards in capitals, and regretted that he had been unable to procure for her any tortoiseshell or other 'curiosities'.[211]

By 1838, Cavendish's dancing academy was flourishing, with accounts with some of the most prestigious schools in the colony. By January 1839 the Revd Robert Forrest had run up a bill of £114. 12s. 0d. for dancing lessons at his King's School in Parramatta. In Parramatta he also had 22 students at James Bradley's Parramatta Academy. And at Dr Lang's Australian College in Sydney he had 7 pupils owing altogether £57. 18s. 6d., including the sons of Major-General Stewart and Lieutenant Thompson. Mrs Barton of an establishment in O'Connell Street also had several of his pupils, as did Mrs Bell's in Castlereagh Street, from whose account it would appear that he charged £1. 11s. 6d. a quarter for one hour and £2. 2s. 0d. for two. Other accounts, for Mr Demetz (£58. 6s. 0d.) and Mrs Davies (£30. 2s. 9d.), also suggest school commitments. Indeed, there were, among his debtors in 1839, 'a great number of Seminaries'.[212]

His success in the lucrative education market must have been the envy of his competitors and may perhaps be explained—although this is mere conjecture—by the good graces of no less a personage than William Grant Broughton, head of the Anglican Church in Australia, who had been appointed Archdeacon of New South Wales in 1829 through the patronage of the Duke of Wellington. One of Broughton's prime functions was to supervise colonial education on Anglican lines, and one of his earliest achievements had been the establishment of the King's

---

[210] *Aust.* 6 Oct. 1838, p. 3.
[211] Hayward–WJC, 14 June 1835.
[212] SCNSW/PD 968/1, correspondence generated by Curator of Intestate Estates on behalf of Cavendish's estate.

School in Parramatta, which quickly became, largely through the efforts of the Revd Robert Forrest, the most successful and prestigious school in the colony. It survives today, arguably as the Eton of the private school system in Australia. Broughton, roughly Cavendish's age (he was born in 1788), was the son of Grant Broughton and Phoebe Ann, née Rumball, of Barnet—almost certainly related to the Rumballs of St Albans whose family roots were in Barnet. Much to Susannah's chagrin, Cavendish had certainly maintained links with Horner Rumball after his exit from London and may have procured from him a letter of introduction to Broughton in Sydney. True, Horner could as easily have damaged his chances as promoted them, but perhaps he was a truer friend than Susannah had ever been prepared to acknowledge.[213]

In June 1838, however, Cavendish was negotiating, through J. T. Wilson, with the wine merchants and ship and insurance brokers, Messrs Buckle, Bagster & Buckle in London, for a dancing master to be sent out to manage the academy, and to provide such a person with the means to do so, 'to the extent of £250'.[214] This was presumably in anticipation of a new commercial undertaking—the setting up of a haberdashery business with Edward Webb. The partnership was formed in August 1838, with Cavendish the owner of the real property of the firm.[215] It lasted only a few months, a disagreement between the partners apparently proving irreconcilable and landing the unfortunate Webb in prison for debt over an outstanding account for business advertisements of £10. 15s.[216] It was still trading as Webb & Co., Cecil House, throughout October, as a 'Cheap Linen Drapery & Silk mercery Establishment',[217] but after some legal wrangling, on 27 November, a notice appeared in the *Australian* stating that, owing to a 'misunderstanding' between the partners, the firm was suspended, and that Edward Webb was not authorized 'to make any purchases or contract debts on account of said Firm'. A receiver was appointed.

At this time Cavendish was rather heavily in debt. In May he had signed an IOU to J. & G. Simmons for £146. 2s. 0d., probably for the purchase of sheep up in Patrick's Plains (near Singleton).[218] He owed

---

[213] For the Broughton/Rumball connection see S. M. Johnstone, *The History of the King's School Parramatta* (Sydney, 1932), 13, also the entry for Broughton in *ADB*.

[214] SCNSW/PD 968/1, J. T. Wilson to Buckle, Bagster & Buckle, 26 Mar. 1839.

[215] Ibid., Eastman to Manning [n.d.]; ibid., Manning to Eastman, 10 Jan. 1840.

[216] Ibid., Eastman to Manning [n.d.].

[217] *Aust.* 2 Oct. 1838, p. 1 and subsequently.

[218] SCNSW/PD 968/1, IOU to I. & G. Simmons, signed WJC, 10 May 1838. Isaac Simmons & Co. is mentioned in other documents in connection with the auction of sheep.

P. P. Willis Sandemann for five pianos, none of which he had evidently sold. They had cost him about £60 each, and, even though they had been returned, Willis Sandemann & Co. were still claiming £215 interest and £9. 14s. 0d. for fees to the Chamber of Law Proceedings.[219] In November he signed an IOU to J. T. Wilson for £224. 15s. 0d., agreeing to pay within three months, and another IOU to Alexander Busby for £243, signed in May, also became due then.[220] He had probably taken over Cecil House sometime after April 1838, on an annual lease of at least £44. 10s. 5d., and set up house above the shop to be.[221]

The nature of the Cecil House ménage seems on the face of it to have been quite comfortable. It boasted several servants, two horses and an English gig, canaries in arch cages, parrots in round ones, wine from Tenerife, and a full complement of household goods, from barrels of lemon syrup and cases of spices to a cribbage board, lustres, bidet, telescope, and a portrait of Cavendish (probably the miniature that was later sold for 19s.)—all the accoutrements of an established middle-class household, even down to the monkey dog (stuffed?) in a case, displayed probably in what was the parlour-cum-dining room along with the portrait, a timepiece in a glass case, and a miscellany of chimney ornaments above a fireplace graced with a brass fender.[222]

This must have been a rather spacious room, as it held, apart from nine cane-bottomed chairs, one sofa, one sideboard, two tables, one large writing-desk, and one smaller one. The household occupied seven other rooms as well, on two floors: four bedrooms, a store-room, a kitchen/ stable (probably in an outhouse), and what was perhaps a room dedicated to professional purposes, since it contained, among other things, 13 chairs, 4 forms, 8 lamps (1 swinging and 7 wall), one violin and one guitar. This was presumably the 'dancing academy'. It may also

---

[219] SCNSW/PD 968/1, Willis Sandemann & Co. Account [n.d.].

[220] Ibid. IOU to J. T. Wilson, signed WJC, 8 Nov. 1838.

[221] Ibid. S. N. Bryant & Co. affidavit in part claiming rent to 6 Mar. [?1839]. This might suggest that he moved in in Mar. 1838, but a Mrs Nash (either a friend or a client) wrote to Mary on 16 Apr. 1838 from Parramatta, addressing the letter to the Corner of Phillip and King Street which is rather further east than three doors from George Street. Prior to that, in June 1835, according to the letter from Captain Hayward of 14 June 1835, they had been living in Pitt Street.

[222] Ibid. Mostly from a room-by-room inventory of Cecil House taken sometime after 26 Jan. 1839. The canary and parrot cages are from an affidavit from Frederick Irwin, Wiremaker of George Street, and the servants from various items *re* payment of salaries; and the Inquest Report, *Aust.* 29 Jan. 1839, p. 2g; the wine is from Bryant & Co.'s affidavit already cited.

have been where Mary conducted her teaching activities—perhaps singing. Oddly enough there appears to have been no piano in this room or, for that matter, in the house.

Sleeping arrangements seem, ostensibly, to have been separate. Cavendish's room was presumably the one that contained such manly objects as shaving razors and straps and the gun-case and cover. This room also contained (among other things) 4 boxes of fiddle and piano strings, a quantity of books and music, a small box containing writing-paper, 2 slates and pencils, 1 small parcel of wire, a bottle of castor-oil, a spyglass, a map of New South Wales, and a mouth-organ. But most of his clothing—apart from a few 'old' items and those which were specifically functional, like his shooting-jacket, a Mackintosh cape, and his patent leather dancing-pumps—was found, when inventories of the property were taken in 1839, in what was clearly Mary's room.[223]

The major inventory of Cecil House fills eight large double-columned sheets and, notwithstanding some odd omissions like table cutlery, testifies to a domestic environment of some order and stability. A store-room and kitchen stocked with sets of crockery and glassware suggest also a modest level of entertaining. And one other important conclusion may be drawn from this source. Mary was no captive recluse. Two-and-a-half pages of the inventory deal with her room and reveal that she was very much an entrenched and even perhaps an indulged domestic partner. She possessed a wardrobe of some 26 dresses of either silk, muslin, cotton, poplin, or 'merino', at least half-a-dozen capes or tippets, shawls, veils, aprons, 7 bonnet caps and 3 bonnets in boxes, 14 pairs of shoes and boots, 12 boxes of perfumery, 1 riding habit, 3 pairs of white stays, 1 stomacher, 1 plume of feathers, 1 pair of long white kid gloves, petticoats, shifts, night-caps, silk stockings, etc. The only mention of jewellery, though, is a box found in what seems to have been the stable, which contained, apart from 3 wedding rings, 1 gold watch, 2 pairs of earrings and sundry bracelets, brooches and beads. Very possibly jewellery as well as other items may not have survived long enough to make it on to the inventory.

Behind this façade of comfort and respectability, we are not in a position to know what tensions existed—whether they were content

---

[223] Ibid. Two room-by-room inventories were taken, the less detailed one perhaps by J. T. Wilson. Both substantiate each other while offering slightly different perspectives. WJC's clothing in 'Mary's' room: half a dozen shirt collars, 5 pairs of white trousers, 8 white shirts, 9 collar cravats, 10 pairs of white socks, 1 pair of worsted socks, 3 pairs of cotton socks, 5 pairs of white drawers.

with each other or with their environment—whether they saw themselves as 'at home' in Sydney as the inventories might suggest.

We do know, however, that a Mrs Elizabeth Jones, having been deserted by her husband, William Mulford Jones, came to live with them (probably in 1838) and stayed for seven months. Whether this was just another manifestation of Cavendish's old vice, what Susannah always called his 'incontinence', or whether he was acting as a genuine Good Samaritan in the case, or, for that matter, whether he was simply interested in the £300 she had become possessed of, is a matter of pure surmise. Mrs Jones herself referred to Cavendish as her 'only friend' in her time of distress. Eventually, perhaps as a result of domestic pressure, Cavendish settled her in a store at Patrick's Plains (presumably at Singleton on the Hunter River) and undertook to supply her with goods.[224]

He had other interests in Patrick's Plains as well. Singleton was the service town for up-country sheep-grazing interests. In late 1838 Cavendish set out with a guide, Edward Saffery, on a gruelling 300-mile return trip from Singleton to Liverpool Plains, a sheep-grazing area about 150 miles north-west of Sydney.[225] This eight-week trek was presumably in connection with the flock of 500 sheep he had on two-third shares with Benjamin Singleton of Patrick's Plains. Singleton (after whom perhaps the town has been named) had been granted 1,280 acres in 1829.[226] It would seem that Cavendish too now hankered after the squatter's life. But time was running out.

In Sydney, musical life continued. On 2 October 1837 it had suffered the death of Barnet Levey, an event greeted, as we have already seen, with less than universal expressions of regret. Most, however, were generous enough to admit that, although his theatre was not everything that could be desired, and although Levey, as a personality, was not ideally suited to

---

[224] SCNSW/PD 968/1, Elizabeth Jones to Manning, 27 Nov. 1839.

[225] Ibid. Account tendered to the Court from Edward C. Saffery, for 'accompanying Mr Cavendish from Singleton to Liverpool Plains for the purposes of piloting him and returning a distance of upwards of 300 miles . . . £4. 0. 0', dated Nov. 1838. The bill also charged for '8 weeks salary at 30/- per week superintending taking sheep from Casillis to Liverpool Plains'. I am assuming he did both these things simultaneously.

[226] Ibid. W. Gilchrist Whicker to Manning [n.d.] refers to Cavendish having 500 sheep on thirds; Account of Sale of Sheep auctioned by J. T. Wilson, dated 4 Apr. 1839, mentions their being on thirds with Mr Singleton; letter, Singleton to Manning, 28 May 1839, mentioning the sale of his share of the wool; Singleton's grant, PP, New South Wales 1831–41, *New South Wales and Van Diemen's Land . . . A Return of the Alienation of Crown Lands during the last Ten Years . . .*, 4.

run such a theatre, without him there would have been no theatre at all.[227]

Levey, as a Jew and brother of an emancipist, had suffered more than his share of official obstruction in the days of Darling, who had once referred to him as a 'bankrupt' and 'person of the lowest class'.[228] He had, however, almost from the very start, at least from the time of those 1826 series of concerts in the Freemason's Tavern, been an integral part of Sydney's musical life. His comic songs and mimicry were vastly popular among Sydney audiences right up to the time of his death. They were probably closer to the traditions of the popular East End twopenny concerts (well known for their Jewish performers)[229] than to those of the 'classical' London concerts of the West End which Wallace and Deane emulated; but this, one suspects, would have endeared him to his working-class audiences as well as to those of the aspiring middle class who were honest enough to admit it. But there was as yet no public voice for the working classes in Sydney, and Levey's passing, at the youthful age of 39, elicited at best only a qualified appreciation from some sections of the existing Press.[230] Perhaps the most affectionate notice came from the *Sydney Times* ('If poor old Barney had his faults . . .'), which reported with real pleasure that the Governor (Bourke), although unable to attend the benefit concert on the 19th because of the news of the death of William IV, had sent a present of £10 to Mrs Levey.[231]

In spite of the introduction of gas lighting in 1837, the theatre had had a particularly bad year, provoking criticism from all quarters of the press for poor standards and sloppy management. How genuine the criticisms were, or how far they were influenced by comparisons with the new and more polite concert venues, is hard to tell. There is no absolute evidence that the upper classes deserted the theatre for the concert—indeed it was suggested that this had already happened anyway—and of course the

[227] *Mon.* 2 Oct. 1837. Written just before Levey's death, but published just after, the article 'Royal Australian Exchange . . .' (*Aust.* 3 Oct. 1839) includes the comment: 'Mr Levey, although he has proved utterly inefficient to manage a theatrical company, or to superintend theatrical affairs, has a just claim to our respect, for the zeal and perseverance which enabled him to surmount so many obstacles, and afford us an opportunity of enjoying in his "Theatre Royal" the pleasure imparted by the *Acted Drama*.' A footnote mentions that 'Since the above was in type, Poor Levy [*sic*] is no more'; 'Obituary', *ST* 21 Oct. 1837.

[228] Historical Records of Australia, Series 1, Governor's dispatches to and from England, vol. xiii, Jan. 1827–Feb. 1828. Reference from Mitchell Library Card Catalogue (Names), which specifically references this comment.

[229] Mayhew, *London Labour and the London Poor*, ii. 132.

[230] See above, n. 223; the *Aust.*, 27 Oct. 1837, did take the *Gazette* to task for printing the offensive letter of William Kerr's mentioned previously.

[231] 'Obituary', *ST* 21 Oct. 1837.

286 The Speculative Voyager, 1831–1839

relative infrequency of concerts (about six or seven in 1837) should not seriously have threatened the theatrical monopoly, yet there was quite possibly a lowering of morale in the theatre due to the development of this higher strand of entertainment. And lurking in the background was the knowledge that Joseph Wyatt's theatre in Pitt Street, to be named the Royal Victoria after the new queen, was in the process of construction.

In late May 1837, John Deane and his two sons, presumably Edward and John, had been appointed to the theatre orchestra,[232] and Wallace himself often performed there in the intervals. But if musically things had improved at the theatre, it was not enough to deflect the increasingly aggressive expressions of dissatisfaction which did not end with Levey's death.

The *Gazette* had never been friendly to the theatre—had always taken what may be termed the politically 'Merino' or religiously 'wowserish' line, in its eagerness to condemn it as a threat to order and morality. So that when the theatre presented a loyal Address of thanks to Governor Bourke upon his departure from New South Wales at the end of 1837, its outrage was quite predictable. 'Of what possible value for instance, in the eyes of the poorest inhabitant of Britain, can a certificate of character be, of a description such as that furnished to Sir Richard Bourke by the graceless 'unwashed' rabble who had the impudence to designate themselves his friends.'[233] Less predictable was the response of the *Herald*, which, in spite of its opposition to much of Bourke's administration, it said, declared the address 'an insult'.[234]

Yet it is very unlikely that without the theatre Sydney could have supported as many musicians as it did—not even the *crème de la crème* of the Sydney concerts, the Wallaces and the Deanes, all of whom eventually turned to the theatre for their bread and butter.

Both Wallace and Deane had set up teaching establishments in 1836, with Wallace aiming strictly for the top end of the market, claiming the patronage of the governor and Mrs E. Deas Thomson and asking £6. 8s. 0d. a quarter for Class 1 students, £4. 10s. 0d. for Class 2 students, and £3. 3s. 0d. for beginners. His 'Academy' was advertised for 'Young Ladies'. For individual lessons for gentlemen he charged 7s. 6d. for the pianoforte, and for the violin 10s. 6d. Examinations were to be held every four months, to which parents were invited.[235] Deane, with his 'Music Saloon', was more modest, charging only £2. 12s. 6d. a

---

[232] *SH* 15 June 1837, p. 2.   [233] Irvin, *Theatre Comes to Australia*, 224.
[234] Ibid.   [235] *Aust.* 1 Apr. 1836, p. 1.

quarter, or 5s. for individual lessons at the student's house. He also offered to give quarterly lectures on the theory and practice of music, to which he invited both pupils and their parents, and to provide careful and correct pianoforte tuning at 'the shortest notice'.[236]

Both also made the most of the talents of their relatives: Deane of his daughter Rosalie, and Wallace of his wife, sister, and brother, who all taught as well. But how successful were they? Did the Sydney gentry flock to have their sons and daughters given expert musical tuition according to the latest methods of Logier and Hertz, on pianoforte, violin, cello, guitar, flute, or in singing and the theory of music?

The fact that Deane took on the direction of the theatre orchestra in 1837 suggests that they did not. It was hardly the most gratifying or prestigious of tasks at that time. Not only would he have been limited by the standard of playing of individual members and subjected to public criticism for collective shortcomings, he would have had to contend with the peccadilloes of the 'stars'—like Miss Lazar, the dancer, for example. She, it was claimed, had danced before the King, and her father, who happened to be the theatre manager, thought fit on one occasion to halt her performance because he considered that the orchestra under Mr Deane was failing to do his daughter justice—not, apparently, having been made familiar with certain steps. Deane seems to have been a rather placid character, merely retiring 'bewildered' to the green room and later returning to complete the rest of the evening's performance, 'with commendable good humour',[237] but such occurrences can hardly have been very enhancing professionally.

In 1837, in October, Wallace also opened, or at least advertised his 'Australian Music Repository', through which he guaranteed to supply the colonists, both in Sydney and in the interior, with the best of everything musical. He assured residents that his invitation for them to inspect his 'really splendid assortment' of newly arrived pianofortes, selected for him with great care by Henry Herz, and each personally inspected by himself, was motivated only by 'a desire to promote the culture and advancement of a science, in which, from its having been the exclusive pursuit of his whole life, and being now adopted by him as a profession, he cannot but be supposed to feel a deep and intense interest'.[238]

Deane also seems to have engaged in music selling, but not on the same altruistic level as Wallace. At the end of the long list of musical

[236] *Aust.* 3 May 1836.   [237] *ST* 27 May 1837.
[238] *Aust.* 27 Oct. 1837, p. 3.

items Deane claimed that Cavendish owed him for in January 1839, mostly sheet music and strings, he was not too proud to add the three dozen duck eggs he had supplied at 3*s.* a dozen.[239]

By 1837, the boom in the economy was faltering. Over-production and speculation in England had produced an economic crisis, aggravated by the raising of tariffs in the USA in response to its own recession. Hard times were on their way. But in Australia there was as yet little appreciation of the true state of things. Squatting interests were still demanding the retention of transportation, in the face of urban middle-class objection, and threatening to import labour from India or China to maintain flocks for which there was soon to be a greatly reduced market. Music, which, except in the theatre, was still effectively little more than a service industry to middle-class political and social pretensions, was bound to be hit hard by the changes which were soon to occur in the colonial economy.

The first overt sign of this was in the response to the second Sydney music festival of 31 January 1838 (postponed from the 26th), celebrating the 50th anniversary of the foundation of the Colony, when the *Monitor* noted that, 'Owing to the badness of the times', it had not been so numerously attended as the previous one, and that the numbers deficient 'included many principal families'.[240] According to the *Herald*'s report, only 500 attended.[241] It had again been held at the still uncompleted St Mary's and was dominated again by Wallace, both as conductor and violinist. His sister Eliza also featured prominently, as did the 'amateur' bass and 'choral master' of St Mary's, James Bushelle, whose performance of Mozart's 'O Jesu potentissime' earned spectacular praise. His 'delicious duet' with the 19-year-old Eliza Wallace was declared a '*beau idéal* of perfection—the voices blended in a manner that ought to be held up as a model to all those who cultivate the vocal art in this Country'.[242] The subsequent blending of these two in matrimony in April 1839, however, was to be considered less than an ideal model, not only because of Bushelle's convict status but also, possibly, his reputation for atheism. Bushelle, transported in 1828 at the age of 22, had been treated severely by the administration because of his adherence to 'French' principles (i.e. the philosophy of Voltaire), his ticket of leave to Sydney having been cancelled and renewed only in December 1839 at the request of the Revd

---

[239] SCNSW/PD 968/1, Account submitted to the Court from John P. Deane [n.d.].
[240] *Mon.* 5 Feb. 1838.   [241] *SH* 5 Feb. 1838.
[242] *Aust.* 6 Feb. 1838, p. 2.

Dr Polding (later Catholic Archbishop of Sydney) in order that he could be 'assistant choir master' of St Mary's. Polding, it would seem, was less easily scandalized than the new Governor, Gipps, in matters of religion; or, as Dr Lang might have argued, he valued his choir's musical training more highly than he did the security of their immortal souls. Bushelle was not given a conditional pardon till 1 February 1841, two years and six months before his death, while on a concert tour with his wife in Tasmania, on 28 July 1843.[243]

Cavendish, who may still officially have been the choirmaster at St Mary's, did take his part in this festival, suggesting, even if he was not choirmaster, an ongoing commitment to musicmaking at St Mary's, which was still by far the most musically active of the Sydney churches, with no sign at all of the later puritanism which would outlaw such quasi-secular works as *The Messiah* and the unashamedly virtuosic masses of Mozart and Haydn. The Revd Dr John Polding and his friend and Vicar-General-to-be, Dr Henry Gregory, both English Benedictines of patrician caste, and by no means unhappy in Sydney establishment circles,[244] probably encouraged this musical pre-eminence as much for the social kudos as for any purely pastoral reasons, which may account for the hostile rejection by St James's of the request to lend the assistance of their 'choral band' to this 1838 music festival[245]—a lack of co-operation indicative of the continuing religious antagonisms still very much part of Sydney social life.

Cavendish's connection with the St Mary's musical establishment was unlikely to have returned him serious remuneration, if any, but may have satisfied whatever still remained of the musician in him—perhaps his

---

[243] Typescript résumé of information from the Dixon Library, fiche 669, 749 A. 1217, Reel 1050, 1052, 1053. It would seem from the official records of the granting of tickets of leave for particular locations within New South Wales that there was a discrepancy between these records and other recorded information, viz., newspaper reportage of Bushelle's presence in Sydney in 1836 when he was meant to have been in Port Macquarie and the renewal of his ticket of leave for Sydney issued 10 Dec. 1839 (until then he was meant to have returned to Port Macquarie some 200 miles away) when he is recorded as having married Eliza Wallace on 30 Apr. 1839 in Sydney.

Roger Therry in his 1863 *Reminiscences* remarks, 'Bushell had a voice almost equal to Lablache, to whom in size and person he bore a strong resemblance. He was principal singer for many years at our theatres and concerts in Sydney. There, he made a respectable connexion by marriage.' He ended his biography of 'Bushell, the Knave of Diamonds' (pp. 113–14) with the insoucient inaccuracy which was his wont. Bushelle had lived, he believed, 'a reputable life' and had died a few years ago—'few', in Therry's argot, apparently meaning about twenty—'in easy circumstances' at the age of 37.

[244] See Mary Shanahan, *Out of Time Out of Place. Henry Gregory and the Benedictine Order in Colonial Australia* (1970), 35–8, for Gregory's social background.

[245] *Aust.* 2 Feb. 1838, p. 2.

continuing interest in the organ. Perhaps, being a gregarious individual, he also enjoyed the rather mixed society. The ex-jewel thief, linguist, and moral philospher, James Bushelle, was probably excellent company. So, perhaps, was Eliza Wallace.

Whether or not he was actively involved this time in the organization of the event is not known. But, reading between the lines, it seems to have been a lack-lustre affair, insufficiently advertised and under-capitalized. The *Monitor* remarked that such events would only 'pay' by attracting a larger audience and that they would 'not answer their end, unless there be a sufficient and effective *outlay*, or investment of *capital*'.[246]

Less than a fortnight later, Wallace suddenly departed for Valparaiso, leaving debts, it was claimed by the ever-vigilant *Gazette*, of some £2,000,[247] a fact which has never been conclusively proved or disproved. He had actually announced his departure a year previous to this in order, he said, to take up the position as leader of the orchestra at Covent Garden,[248] but must have changed his plans. Wallace was throughout his life almost more famous for his eccentric ways and laconic story-telling than for his not inconsiderable musical achievements[249]—so that his sudden departure, when it eventually came, may have been more quixotic than criminal. It would have been even more surprising, though, had the hard-nosed *Gazette*, used to the more normal reasons for such departures, actually put a kinder interpretation upon it. But whatever the real truth, it would seem that Wallace had had quite enough of Sydney, and, we must assume, of his wife too, whom he left behind with the rest of his family.

The Wallaces, however, continued to dominate the musical scene, especially Eliza, who featured prominently in all the concerts that year and gave her own for the first time on 17 October 1838, in the saloon of the Royal Hotel, to be greeted with rapturous praise. Assisted by the Deanes, and, among others, by the 'amateur' bass singer, it was a programme of some calibre, consisting almost entirely of vocal music by Rossini, Mozart, and Madame Malibran, and hardly an English song or

---

[246] *Mon.* 5 Feb. 1838.
[247] *SG* 14 Feb. 1838.   [248] *Mon.* 1 Feb. 1837.
[249] See Hector Berlioz, the last evening in his *Soirées de l'orchestre* (Paris, 1852); English edn., *Evenings in the Orchestra* (1929), 356–65, in which Berlioz recounts one of Wallace's extraordinary tales of his adventures and amours in the South Seas. Berlioz believed it was true only because he thought 'the fellow [i.e. Wallace] too indolent to lie'. See also Willert Beale, *The Light of Other Days. Seen through the Wrong End of an Opera Glass* (new edn., 1890), 122–3; Arthur Pougin, *William Vincent Wallace. Étude biographique* (1866); William Spark, *Musical Memoirs* (new edn., 1909), 144–7.

an Irish air to be heard. Cavendish was unmentioned. By this time he was busy with other things—his dancing academy, his partnership difficulties with Edward Webb, his sheep speculations, his growing debt, and, probably, Mrs Jones.

Neither does he appear to have been involved with the new Royal Victoria Theatre, which, four days after the closing of the old Theatre Royal, had opened on 26 March 1838, with *Othello* and *The Middy Ashore*. The musical director was John Gibbs.[250] Deane, however, probably replaced Gibbs, for when *Der Freischutz* was given in September (hailed by the *Monitor*, in spite of its being German, as 'the first real opera' in Sydney), he was very much in charge. The *Herald* expressed itself most impressed with the performance and admired the manner with which Deane led the orchestra 'through the intricate mazes of some of the most extraordinary music ever composed'.[251]

By this stage, the orchestra contained not only Deane and his three (perhaps even four) sons, but Mr Peck from Hobart, whose talents were declared almost equal to Wallace's,[252] and the flautist Stephen Wellington Wallace. Indeed, with times becoming tougher economically, the theatre had probably become the mainstay of them all. Cavendish's cello or double-bass would doubtless have been a useful enough adjunct to the orchestra at any time, either instrument presumably being relatively rare, and there is no absolute evidence that he did not play in the Royal Victoria Theatre, but it seems unlikely, given the range of his other activities and perhaps the likelihood of reduced status within the orchestra itself. For Cavendish such a role may have seemed far too like the old days of drudgery in the London theatres. He had come, after all, a long way since then.

As we already know, Cavendish was trekking through the bush with his sheep in late 1838, leaving his friend J. T. Wilson back in Sydney to superintend his business affairs, including the sale of the effects of Webb & Co. on 5 December. He did not take his passage by boat back to Sydney from the Hunter, and Mrs Jones, till 11 January, the charge of £6. 2s. 6d. for the passage being paid by order through J. T. Wilson, whose company ran the Hunter River steamer.[253] Thus it was Mary and not Cavendish who attended Dr Bland on 31 December, a consultation

---

[250] *Aust.* 27 Mar. 1838, p. 3.
[251] *SH* 19 Sept. 1838. [252] *Aust.* 18 May 1838.
[253] SCNSW/PD 968/1, Account from J. T. Wilson to the Court, dated Feb. 1839, itemizing goods etc. The Hunter passage is dated 11 Jan.

for which he charged a guinea.[254] On 8 January, Cavendish's IOU to Wilson expired but was not redeemed by him. Back in Sydney, on 14 January 1839 he requested J. T. Wilson to pay Willis Sandemann & Co. £161. 4s. 8d. on his behalf, adding yet another debt to his growing tally. Yet it would seem that, in spite of bank balances amounting to hardly more than £50, his economic ambitions were undiminished.

On Saturday, 26 January, the annual Regatta Day celebrating the foundation of the Colony, he set out with a party of five, plus two boatmen, in one of J. T. Wilson's boats to look at land at Middle Harbour. The party consisted of himself, Mary (by now presumably recovered from what had ailed her three weeks earlier), Duvachelle the French teacher, James Lennon (or Leonard), an accountant friend of Cavendish's, and a servant, Anderson. They had set out from a Sydney wharf at about 10 a.m. Off Bradley's Head, while putting about, a sudden gust of wind capsized the boat, plunging all its occupants into the water.

Farther out in the Harbour a boat race was taking place as part of the Anniversary Regatta. Participants did not notice the difficulties of the boat off Bradley's Head. The party's two boatmen had struck out for the shore, probably less than fifty yards away. Lennon, who with Duvachelle and Anderson had gained the keel, left it to assist Mary. But she panicked and, grasping him, would, he later claimed, have pulled him under. So he retreated back to the safety of the boat.

Cavendish, who was supposedly a good swimmer, then went to her and tried to calm her. He was overheard to encourage her with the words, 'Never mind, dear Mary, I have got hold of you'. But her head was already submerged and, unable to support himself and apparently unwilling to relinquish Mary, he too sank. Their bodies were later recovered floating in Chouder Bay and brought in to Cox's Wharf.

There were public recriminations about whether or not the racing fleet should have been able to assist, or whether, had medical aid been available sooner, the pair might have been saved, but in the event the coroner brought down a verdict of accidental death,[255] and on Monday, 28 January 1839, at 4 o'clock, William Joseph Cavendish and his sister Mary were buried. The funeral, costing £83. 19s. 0d., was organized by

[254] SCNSW/PD 968/1, Account from William Bland submitted to the Court, 'for Medical Attendance . . . £1.1.0', 31 Dec. 1838.

[255] All of the foregoing account of the accident is from the 'Coroner's Inquest', *Aust.* 29 Jan. 1839, p. 2g; Cox's Wharf comes from SCNSW/PD 968/1, the Edward Hunt funeral bill, which charged £6. 0s. 0d. for removing the bodies from Cox's Wharf.

22. Bradley's Head (with navigation mast) juts out from the right (north side) almost into the centre of the picture. Almost a hundred years later, a small boat passes near the spot. Oil painting by John D. Moore. 1936.

J. T. Wilson, with some splendour. The two hearses and one mourning coach were drawn by four horses each and were attended by four grooms, four mutes, two coach pages, and eight underbearers. Inside their hearses the bodies, wearing their superfine burial dresses and caps and resting on pillows, lay within black-draped coffins (alone worth £20), finished with gilt mounting-plates and inscriptions.[256]

As Cavendish's friend, doubtless Wilson believed such a funeral to be appropriate and as he, Cavendish, would have wished. Generous,

[256] SCNSW/PD 968/1, Hunt funeral bill.

considering the sums Cavendish owed him and the fact that at least £83. 10s. 0d. of the estate would now go to Edward Hunt the undertaker rather than to himself. The *Australian* only commented:

the bodies of the deceased were followed by a numerous train of friends to whom they were endeared by their friendly and correct demeanor. The musical profession has lost a friend and a warm supporter in Mr Cavendish, who has always been foremost [to] render his services *gratuitously* to the advance and encouragement of the science. In private life he was greatly esteemed.[257]

It thus contradicts Therry's claim that, with the exception of the mutes and other hirelings, 'not a single person followed them to the grave'.[258] Therry the Gothic moralist had obviously triumphed over Therry the objective observer.

The truth of what actually happened off Bradley's Head, now the comfortably familiar site of Sydney's Taronga Park Zoo, ten minutes by ferry from Circular Quay and almost in the shadow of the great coat-hanger bridge, will now never be known. Olive-green with trees still, wreathed at its tip in shallow ridges of pale yellow sandstone, it appears an innocent peninsula, and the waters off it, calm and green, an unlikely location for tragedy, let alone murder. Yet, without indulging in macabre speculation simply for the sake of it, there seems cause to question the verdict of the inquest, a verdict which might have been very different had Cavendish survived.

It was odd that it was only after Lennon had retreated to the keel that Cavendish, known to be a good swimmer, made his own attempt to 'save' Mary. It was even stranger that the two watermen, presumably expert sailors and paid employees of Wilson, should have so peremptorily left the scene of the accident and do not appear to have been called as witnesses at the inquest. Were they 'protected', having been paid perhaps to engineer the capsize, with the most likely victim being the female passenger? She was presumably weaker, had perhaps recently been ill, and was in any case encumbered with the voluminous skirts of the current fashion. Was there a conspiracy between Cavendish and Wilson to rid Cavendish of his 'sister' which went badly wrong, with Cavendish either relenting at the last moment, or Mary, in a flash of awareness, or simply in blind panic, dragging him down with her?

From what is known of Wilson's character and career, a discreet

[257] 'Coroner's Inquest', *Aust.* 29 Jan. 1839.
[258] Therry, *Reminiscences*, 116.

murder of this kind was probably not beyond his imaginative scope. His ruthlessly unscrupulous treatment of women was notorious. Later, the captain of his escape ship the *Nereus* was reported to have 'committed suicide' over Wilson's seduction of his wife. So did this portly con-man act the demon and tempt Cavendish into murder—for love perhaps of Elizabeth Jones, left languishing in exile at Patrick's Plains, or of some other woman completely unknown to us—and thus lead him to his own death? Or had Cavendish no need of an evil genius? And as he struggled for his last breath in the waters of one of the safest harbours in the world, did Susannah's invocation of 16 November 1830 flash before his mind with the power of a remembered curse? 'Should the blackened cloud and foaming wave arrest the mariner's progress,' she had said, 'your thoughts will be wildly employ'd—on absent objects.' There was no blackened cloud or foaming wave, and the mariner was only ten minutes from home, but such facts were immaterial. The storm of Susannah's imagination was in all probability raging in his heart.

The sensation created by the sudden deaths of two well-known, if not entirely prominent, persons in a small community was to be expected. Indeed it was not to be forgotten for many years. In 1846, Francis Low included the event in his *Chronology of Momentous Events in Australian History*.[259] But, apart from the flurry of dozens of affidavits presented to John Edye Manning, shipping magnate and Registrar of the Supreme Court handling the estate, from persons all swearing that Cavendish owed them money, and the sometimes undignified squeals of protest from some of Cavendish's own debtors when applied to by the Supreme Court, the Cavendishes' exit, unlike that of J. T. Wilson later on in October, caused little real impact on the life of Sydney. James Lennon, accountant and friend, was paid £20 for putting Cavendish's accounts in order. Captain Hayward, of the greetings in capitals to Mary from Cloudy Bay, claimed from the estate £25. 2s. 0d., which seems to have been allowed. Not so Deane's claim of £24. 11s. 8d., nor many more claims besides, which the court apparently, in its wisdom, declined to consider of sufficient substance or merit, causing no doubt some frustration and anger.[260] But many more were luckier and were eventually paid 15 shillings in the pound; although this must have been partly the result

[259] George Mackeness (ed.), *A Chronology of Momentous Events in Australian History 1788–1846*, in two parts: Part I (1788–1828) by Robert Howe, Part II (1829–1846) by Francis Low (Sydney, 1952).
[260] SCNSW/PD 968/1, Claims and Affidavits.

of Wilson's claim of £655. 7s. 6d. presumably having been cancelled in the wake of his defection. If so, it probably gave Manning, as commissioner, some little satisfaction, since he had found Wilson difficult to handle and had had to officially reprimand him (albeit with kid gloves on) in a letter of 25 February, for distributing, among himself and two other persons, the funds of the 5 December sale without consulting him, thus effectively pre-empting the court and depriving other creditors of their rightful share.

The court was quickly informed by Mr S. C. Walton, a gentleman from Mount St Thomas, Woollongong, of Cavendish's real identity and of facts concerning him that he believed were not generally known. It was from this letter that Therry had probably gleaned much of what he knew about 'Devenish':

> In the year 1826, owing to some causes (family disagreements I believe) he quitted London Suddenly & secretly—it was his wish to have it believed that he had drowned in the Thames, his hat was picked up in the river & it is possible that his wife & children are under the impression that he has long since been no more—these facts were ascertained by my late father Captain Walton, late of the 39th Regiment, while residing at St Servan in France, who found it necessary to make some enquiries respecting him and elected the foregoing . . .[261]

But no effort seems to have been made to contact any of his family. The court was also aware of the fact that 'Mary Cavendish' was not who she pretended. In the letter to J. T. Wilson of 25 February, Manning had referred to her as 'the female who passed as his sister but is supposed to be his wife'.[262] But no action seems to have been taken to establish her identity.

Except, perhaps, for Elizabeth Jones, who not only lost her 'only friend' but the unrecorded £100 which she claimed she had only days earlier given him to buy goods for her in Sydney, J. T. Wilson, and perhaps Captain Hayward, existing documents point directly to no other individuals who might have had cause to mourn or regret the Cavendishes' loss. But records, no matter how profuse or detailed, cannot ever fully reveal or explain human existence either collectively or

---

[261] SCNSW/PD 968/1, S. C. Walton to Manning, 30 Jan. 1839; his father must have been Captain Robert Walton of the 39th Regiment, on half-pay from Mar. 1816 to July 1819 when he became paymaster to the 9th Regiment. He presumably retired to St Servan after 6 July 1826 when he was replaced in this position by Lieutenant Robert Uniake. The *Army List* though does not record this event till 1834. Might this have been Susannah's despicable 'Captain O.'?

[262] Ibid., Manning to Wilson, 25 Feb. 1839.

individually. In Cavendish's case they have only drawn the faintest outline. We do not know what person or persons unknown to history may have followed the funeral procession on its short journey from Christchurch St Lawrence to the Sydney Burial Ground, later perhaps to return to weep a tear—or mutter an insult—over the twin graves, around which one William Cowell had, for £7, by April 1839, built a painted palisade.[263]

[263] Ibid., Account from William Cowell, 20 Apr. 1839. 'For building a palacade fence round the graves of the late Mr & Miss Cavendish in the Sydney Burriel Ground, encluding painting and all materials.'

7

Epilogue, 1839–1888

THE Castells, although not professionally significant, belonged to the same secular musical tradition that had produced some of the most important musical dynasties of eighteenth- and early nineteenth-century England: families like the Wesleys, the Linleys, the Ashleys, the Weichsels, the Moris, the Lavenus, which from generation to generation passed on the 'trade' in what was in many respects a closed shop. Without a strong guild to protect their 'monopoly' as other trades had protected theirs, professional musicians created an informal one through family and professional networks which served fairly successfully to keep out interlopers. True, there were loopholes. The cathedral system often chose its choristers from outside the traditional musical family (although as often as not it seems to have selected from within it). Simple doggedness was another way of entering the profession. Thomas Arne, defying his upholsterer father, managed to get Michael Festing to teach him music. And of course anyone could, without professional training or legal barrier, set themselves up as a 'professor' of music. But on the whole, being born into a family of musicians had been the surest way to enter the profession.

For this reason it is often postulated that musical genius is inherited—that it is in some way carried in the genes. Francis Galton's *Hereditary Genius* (1869) argued just such a case on behalf of social Darwinism, an argument which is still being regurgitated as a justification for competitive élitism.[1] But the argument is a fragile one, seriously flawed, if by no other evidence than by the disappearance of these professional families, and in England by the virtual disappearance—for well over one hundred years, in a period of unprecedented national power and affluence—of original musical genius altogether.

Certainly the existence of these families provided a ready conduit for exceptional ability, should it, by whatever process, happen to emerge. But, even while some physiological and even temperamental qualities

[1] See, for example, David Stove, 'The Diabolical Place. A Secret of the Enlightenment', *Encounter* (May 1990), 9–15.

conducive to music may be inherited (indeed it could be argued that all human beings are born with incipient musical capacities), there was no guarantee that a Purcell, Mozart, or a Bach would have expressed his superior intellectual capacities in music had he not been nurtured in a musical family. Bach, for one, certainly did toy with other options. Likewise, there was no guarantee that a family tradition in music, no matter how long, would necessarily produce what we like to call 'genius'. Over many generations of the musical Bach family, for example, until the emergence of Johann Sebastian, no particularly exceptional individual is discernible. Yet the greatest chance for musical 'genius' to emerge and blossom in the eighteenth and early nineteenth centuries obviously lay in the existence of as many such families as possible; and, in England, the bustle of late eighteenth-century musical activity probably masked a serious decline in their numbers—although there is no hard data available to prove this.

What we do see, though, by 1820, is the English profession in a state of crisis: ideologically empty, creatively barren, and inundated from below and from above by casually trained hopefuls on the one hand and by highly qualified Continental musicians on the other. In the grip of such forces, traditional musical families of competent professional musicians like the Castells found themselves squeezed virtually out of existence. Yet being human beings, even when faced with economic and cultural irrelevance, they could hardly cease from being who they were— could hardly put aside background, training, culture, and personality to cope single-mindedly with the new realities. William Joseph Castell's personal weaknesses were obvious, but to expect him to have behaved differently because the world had changed would be to expect economic statisticians to have altered human nature—in effect, to have turned an improvident optimist like Castell into a cautious mechanist like Sir George Smart. Sir George read the signs of the times rather like he read his scores, quite literally but without imagination. He survived, Castell did not; although we might well argue (albeit to little point) which of them was potentially in possession of the greater 'genius'.

But the family failure did not end with Castell's drowning in Sydney Harbour.

We left Susannah in London in May 1835 having just quitted 19 Stangate Street for her new address not far away in Mount Gardens, just south of Westminster Bridge Road, quite near the Marsh Gate. She had indicated that it would probably only be a temporary measure, but the

1841 Census shows that she was still there six years later. They were all still there, except Susan. All five, headed by the 45-year-old Augustine, were designated as 'Teachers of Music'.[2] Susan may simply have been absent on the night of the census, she may have married, been employed somewhere else, or she may have died. In 1834 Susannah had informed Castell that both girls were in delicate health and had been suffering for nine months with whooping-cough[3]—a debilitating affliction which may have created dangerous vulnerabilities.

Later on in the same year, 1841, on 1 September, Augustine Humble died of a heart condition.[4] Susannah wrote to the Royal Society of Musicians on 2 October announcing with painful regret the death of her dear and lamented son, and begging leave, on account of his having died without leaving sufficient funds to defray his funeral expenses, to request the 'usual allowance granted upon those occasions'. His illness, she went on, had been attended with increased expenditure and an inability to fulfil his professional engagements for some time previous to his death. All resources had thus, she declared, been destroyed.[5] William was now head of the house and, we assume, chief breadwinner for the diminished family, perhaps consisting only now of himself, his mother, Alfred, and Emily.

But the family may not long have stayed together after Augustine's death. For, at some time between then and 1849, Susannah and Emily moved to an altogether new location in University Street, off Tottenham Court Road in the Parish of St Pancras. It is possible that, with Augustine's death financial pressures had made it necessary for the two women to take more modest accommodation while the two males found themselves cheap bachelors' digs.[6]

On 28 May 1849, at 5 University Street, Emily died of erysipelas. A month later, on 28 June, the 75-year-old Susannah also died—of erysipelas, sometimes called St Anthony's fire, a febrile disease accompanied by localized deep red coloration of the skin. Neither William nor Alfred seem to have been present at either of the deaths.[7] Somehow Emily had managed to accumulate a nest-egg of £200 which went, after

[2] PRO. HO. 107, Great Britain. Census of Great Britain for 1841. Population Returns.
[3] SEC–WJC, 9 Oct. 1834, p. 3.
[4] GRO, Deaths.
[5] RSM, MS Members' Files [Humble].
[6] I am assuming that William and Alfred did not move to University Street with Susannah and Emily because neither are mentioned on their death certificates as either being present or as informants. This may be an incorrect assumption.
[7] GRO, Deaths.

23. William J. [Jones]
Castell, photograph by
W. & D. Downey, *c.* 1850. From
the collection of photographs. Royal
Society of Musicians of Great Britain.

administration (there being no will), to Susannah. Upon Susannah's death it was granted to William.[8] It was her only legacy.

On 25 May 1850, William married the widow Emma Giles, née Clarkson, the daughter of a brass-founder. His brother Alfred witnessed the event in the parish church of St Martin-in-the-Fields.[9] William's subsequent career was unspectacular but apparently successful enough. In 1851 we find him 're-appointed' with the Philharmonic Society.[10] And the Royal Society of Musicians preserves a photograph of him, indicating that he may have been deemed more than merely respectable. Possibly a wedding portrait of 1850, it shows a thin puckish face in early middle age framed by a crop of sleekly bouffant dark hair and mutton-chop whiskers. Around his protuberant, yet hooded, eyes, there seems to linger

---

[8] PRO, PROB.6 225/304. [9] GRO, Marriages.
[10] BL, Loan 48 6/3, MS records of the Philharmonic Society. I am grateful to Professor Cyril Ehrlich for alerting me to this reference.

the vestiges of an embarrassed smirk. He is not wholly at ease. There is a slightly cruel set to his mouth, probably, to give him the benefit of the doubt, the result of ill-fitting dentures—although his lips are firmly closed. A nice poise is established in the way his head relates to his shoulders—by way of a neck of elegant length, exaggerated rather by the huge knotted and bejewelled cravat worn above a richly patterned vest and sharply tailored coat. A lump the size of a small egg, just off centre at the top front of his forehead, is obviously a cyst which the photographer, had he been a portrait painter, might have discreetly removed.

Almost thirty-eight years after his marriage, on 20 March 1888, William, apparently by then a widower, died at the age of 75 at his home, Alton Villa, No. 9, St Petersburgh Place, Bayswater. He left his entire fortune of £9,013. 16s. 5d. to his daughter Emma Le Conte Castell, wife of Frederick Baumgart Nicholson Castell.[11] A civil and electrical engineer originally from Liverpool, his son-in-law had changed his name in 1886 to that of his wife, evidently to please the old man in a gesture, along with the 'Le Conte' addition, suggesting a dynastic pride which was ironic in its ultimate futility.[12]

Emma had also been a musician, and a member of the Royal Society of Musicians until her resignation, within a year of her father's death, in January 1889.[13] She had not, however, been an only child. She had had at least one older brother, Pietro Le Conte Castell, who had once had a song called 'The Moth' published by C. Jeffreys.[14] But he had died of tuberculosis in 1885 at the age of 29, leaving an estate of £12.[15]

Of Alfred, beyond the fact that he was a witness to his brother's marriage in 1850, nothing is known. As far as it is possible to tell, then, by the end of the nineteenth century no Castells were engaged in the musical profession, ending a tradition that went back at least to the trumpeter William Jones and the middle of the eighteenth century.

William and Susannah Castell were, in their own way, small tragic figures. Belonging to the pivotal generation which came to maturity in an age of unprecedented social and economic upheaval, they perhaps reflect a wider tragedy as well. The uprooting of Castell, and his seemingly pointless wanderings around the world with his double-bass and/or cello

[11] GRO, Deaths; PPR. Index vol. 1888/316.
[12] Name change, *The Times*, 22 Mar. 1886, p. 1b.
[13] RSM, *List of Members*, 34.
[14] BL. H.1778f.48, Pietro Castell, 'The Moth', words by A. S. Wilks. London [n.d.] .
[15] GRO, Deaths; PPR. Index vol. 1885.

and his 'sister', might be seen as a kind of parable of the uprooting and dispersal of much else in English cultural life at the time. Likewise the embitterment of Susannah, as her belief in true love is superseded by her belief in respectability as the guiding moral principle of her life, might be seen as a parable of the more general transformation of spiritual faith in the age of machines, into political and social dogma.

Such an interpretation is certainly open to debate. Arguably, industrialism opened up as many avenues of creativity and fulfilment as it closed—made possible new lives and new faiths. But even if this is true, wholly or partially, there was still a price to be paid. Even if we could juggle data into approximate masses of negatives and positives and come up with a neat zero, there would remain the reality of those who were the winners and those who were the losers, and for the losers the statistical 'zero' would represent a rather sardonic joke made at their expense.

Castell's contributions in all the spheres in which he operated were, as far as can be determined, unproductive of any coherent result. His musical career was never able to satisfy what were perhaps unrealistic material ambitions. His private life was shrouded in error and ambiguity, with his chances of lasting economic and/or personal satisfaction marred again and again by poor judgement and, if we are to believe Susannah, by an inability to come to terms with the true nature of the human heart, especially his own. Indeed, in spite of his undoubted style, energy, and daring even, he does not seem to have had the positive resources of character which we expect from proverbially heroic failures. But this should not make him unworthy of our attention. Nor should his undoubted uniqueness rob him of his potential representativeness of those found in the negative column of our data sheet.

Susannah, in spite of her great disappointment in the eventual outcome of their relationship, sustained (perhaps as justification of her own initial judgement) her belief in his intrinsic worth. For her, it was the wicked world that had corrupted his fundamental innocence. Perhaps it was true; and, quite apart from this personal relationship, it is conceivable that, confused by the great economic and cultural flux of his age, he had lost an important sense of social and psychological equilibrium.

It might also be seen as significant that he should, after all his wanderings, have come to the very place that was founded to rid England of those other waste products of its new philistine culture, the conveniently labelled 'criminal classes'. And significant too that it was out of that unlikely environment that he should have made his last attempt to wrest success, by exploitation rather than art.

But for all the fundamental hopelessness of his quest, he at least enjoyed the final boon of a sudden and, on the face of it (if we exclude macabre speculation), almost heroic death—a fate to be denied to Susannah. Susannah's fate was to witness the deaths of two—possibly three—of her children, without having enjoyed their fulfilment, and to die old and, the odds are, embittered and alone. Music had betrayed everything she had hoped for: justice, security, and the respect of society. She may not have consciously hoped for meaning as well—but in the end that too was probably denied her.

With the exception of William, none of that family of six may be said to have survived through music into the relative cultural certainties of mid-Victorian affluence and respectability; and there is a real possibility that he may have done so through a fortuitous marriage rather than through music alone. Augustine never married. Neither did Emily. Susan had probably died before 1841, and Alfred fades into obscurity after 1850. If he did survive, then it was almost certainly not as a successful musician. Susannah herself may never have known of Castell's own ultimate fate, nor did she live to see their son William's modest victory.

Although it is not very safe to generalize from the experiences of one family of obscure English musicians, it is nevertheless of some value to note that these experiences do not conflict with the findings of Deborah Rohr's or Cyril Ehrlich's studies of the profession and that they reinforce the view that English musicians up to at least 1850 had failed as a group to integrate themselves into the evolving economic and social framework of middle-class professionalism. And it is also possible to see in Castell's own career and those of his sons' some of the forces at work which were hampering musicians' creative as well as their economic progress: the decline of the Church as patron and giver of intellectual and social status; the failure of the theatre to provide a socially acceptable alternative; a continued absence of a viable educational structure; continued dependence upon declining private patronage; aristocratic indifference; Evangelical neo-Puritanism and continuing low intellectual and social status; over-supply, foreign competition, and the fragility of the entrepreneurial climate. Of course, these forces hampered individuals unequally according to circumstance and ability, and it is possible that had they been totally absent the Castell family might still have failed. On the evidence, however, their failure does seem to be linked with these larger social and economic factors.

Castell himself, though, was ultimately removed from the English environment, and the question might be raised whether, if he had not died when and how he did, he would finally have met with success in Australia. As a performing musician, or even as a teacher of music, the answer is almost certainly no. Without a large and reliable middle class and in the absence, in spite of the efforts of some, of an Australian 'aristocracy', professional musicians had no natural support other than the commercial theatre. Of the Churches only the Catholic Church maintained a strong musical element. But while it may have offered stimulus and an occasional opportunity for display, it is very unlikely that it offered remunerative posts of any economic significance.

As we have seen, many prominent Sydney musicians, including Castell, attempted to engage in retail trading in musical instruments and printed music, but the market was small and the capital required led to the kind of extortion seemingly engaged in by middlemen like Willis Sandemann, who charged Castell interest on the value of unsold pianos almost to the value of the goods themselves.[16] And finally we see Castell, in spite of his successful dancing academy, attempting to move into haberdashery with Webb & Co. and into speculation in sheep. The first effort failed and in the latter he was also likely to have failed—for two reasons. The first was his personal and financial association with J. T. Wilson, whose collapse later on in 1839 would almost certainly have brought Castell down too. The second was the serious economic slump that was just around the corner in the early 1840s.

Nor did the land itself, or the indigenous culture of its Aboriginal people, offer to European settlers like Castell any sense of a possible alternative to the unfettered opportunism that fed unashamedly upon those materialist tenets of industrial civilization which they had brought with them. Guilt for the 'inevitable' fate of the Aborigines, and indeed for the blood and misery of the convict system itself, was subsumed into the rush to be rich. It was a rush that, far from wishing to avoid or stem, Castell was only too eager to join.

As we saw, music in the 1830s became briefly a yardstick by which some of the already successful wished to measure their perceived superiority over their natural foes, the oligarchy of the puritanical philistines. But this was more a posture than a founding principle of art, and barely saw out the decade. It can hardly be said that this group actually invested

---

[16] SCNSW/PD 968/1, Willis Sandemann Account. The value of the 5 pianos was £269. 17s. 0d. The interest on the overdue bill was claimed at £215. 3s. 0d.

in music, even while they were prepared to use it to support their claims to social legitimacy.

Of course it is possible that Castell might have weathered the economic storms of the forties and battled his way into some kind of economic equilibrium by the 1850s when the gold rushes changed the entire perspective, but as a musician it is unlikely that he would have achieved in Australia any more significant or lasting success than other Sydney musicians did.

Eliza Wallace, after the premature death of James Bushelle, went to London in the early 1840s and enjoyed moderate success, returning to Australia only in the mid 1860s with her son, also James Bushelle, an amateur singer. The Deanes, it is true, plodded on into the next two decades—father and sons and Rosalie—to become the founding dynasty of European music in Australia, although by the end of the century the family were known in legal rather than musical circles. They were joined in the forties by Isaac Nathan, Frank and John Howson, and the Marsh brothers and in the fifties by Sarah Flower, Catherine Hayes, Nicholas Bochsa, Anna Bishop, Louis Lavenu, and other wandering European musicians catering to a gradually expanding middle-class market. But of those who stayed, like the Deanes, Nathan, Sarah Flower, the Howson and Marsh brothers the going was very tough indeed, the outcome disappointing, and for some, ultimately even tragic.[17] Castell's possible place among them, supposing that he had continued in the profession, may have been assured enough, but almost certainly no more successful.

If colonial societies were able to forge new social, economic, and political relationships which could be classified as 'progressive', in cultural terms what was more evident here was a stubborn insistence upon preserving from the 'mother' culture attitudes towards music which were intrinsically narrow and limiting. But in any case, as we know, a short sharp southerly squall on Australia Day in January 1839 abruptly curtailed at least one English musician's contribution to colonial culture.

[17] I base this assessment upon preliminary research into this later period, research which is as yet not consolidated.

APPENDIX
'Devenish—His Strange Career'

(Extract from: Roger Therry, *Reminiscences of Thirty Years Residence in New South Wales and Victoria*, 2nd edn. (London, 1863), pp. 114–16, interspersed with a few additions and corrections.)

To these sketches of the career of convicted persons [including James Bushelle, the 'Knave of Diamonds'] the successful imposture of an unconvicted person may be not inappropriately added in conclusion.

It has been said, with more smartness than truth in the expression, that the Colony of New South Wales consisted of 'persons who had been transported, and those who deserved to be so.' That there were some unconvicted persons who might deservedly have shared the fate of transportation, and who made New South Wales an asylum of refuge, may, however, be truly alleged. The case of Devenish (not the real name, but representing a real personage) furnished a curious instance of successful imposture. Devenish was not a convict, yet his career was a strange, mysterious, and guilty one.

This man's story is gleaned partly from personal knowledge of the man, and partly from papers and letters that after his death fell into the hands of the Curator of Intestate Estates in Sydney. Devenish had been the leader of the orchestra at one of the theatres at the Surrey side of London. He was an accomplished musician and an excellent dancing-master. Finding his affairs embarrassed, he resolved to fly the country, leaving his wife and four children to provide for themselves as best they might. The following ingenious plan was adopted to avoid inquiry about himself after his exit from England. Having taken his passage in a *chasse-marée* that was to sail from Gravesend for St. Malo on Sunday morning, he appeared in his usual place at the orchestra on the previous Saturday, and was seen there so late as ten at night. On that evening he wore a new hat, inside which his name and address were written in very legible letters. On his way home, Devenish had to pass over Waterloo Bridge. In passing over it, he threw his hat over the parapet of the bridge, in order that it might be supposed he had thrown himself over along with it. The stratagem succeeded. The hat was picked up next morning close to the bridge; the owner was nowhere to be found, the river ineffectually searched, and the supposition prevailed that he was drowned. After remaining some time at St. Malo [actually St Servan], where he supported himself by the exercise of his talents, he deemed the place too close to the shores of England, and betook himself to the Isle of France. He might have remained there prosperous and undetected for many years, for he was an adept as a teacher of music and dancing; but he eloped—whether at St. Malo or St. Louis it does not appear from the papers—with the wife of a Captain C——, of the French navy. With her he arrived in Sydney in 1832 [actually 1833], and passed her off as his sister. For several years he had excellent business as a teacher of dancing and music, realizing an average income of from 600*l*. to 800*l*. a year.

It is customary to hold a regatta in Sydney Harbour on the 26th of January, the anniversary of the foundation of the Colony, and on that particular day in 1842 [actually 1839] Devenish had hired a boat for the amusement of himself and his *soi-disant* sister. As the evening advanced [it was morning], when they were a mile distant from the land [it would be difficult to be a mile from land in any part of Sydney Harbour, and certainly not off Bradley's Head], a sudden gale arose and upset the boat. The case was one in which the only hope of safety lay in swimming. The boatmen escaped by doing so, and Devenish might have also saved his life, for he was an expert swimmer, but he would not leave his female companion to perish. He was seen from the shore to bear her up bravely for nearly half a mile. [Complete invention.] At length they sank together and were drowned. The bodies were next day found. [They were picked up the same day.]

A few days afterwards I happened to pass by the Sydney cemetery as their funeral approached. With the exception of the mutes and other hirelings in attendance, not a single person followed them to the grave. [The only possible excuse for Therry's inaccuracy on this point might be that in 1842 there was another drowning in Sydney Harbour on Regatta Day and Therry may have confused it with the deaths of the Cavendishes three years previously.] That Devenish behaved well and nobly in risking his own life to save that of his companion must be admitted, but genuine pity should be reserved for the wife whom he had cruelly deserted, and whose letters indicated that she knew of his whereabouts, and the mode of life he was leading, and the deep distress she and her children suffered from his desertion. She was aware it would be unavailing to follow him from England, and from some passages in these letters, it was plain he had told her so.

BIBLIOGRAPHY

MANUSCRIPT SOURCES

(Correspondence, official documents, unpublished memorabilia, maps)

Ayrton, William. Papers. British Library.

Beard Collection. Theatrical memorabilia—Theatre Museum, Covent Garden, London.

Cavendish, William Joseph. Papers. Supreme Court of New South Wales, Probate Division, Sydney.

Christchurch St Lawrence, Sydney. Records of burials.

Colonial Office, Correspondence, Mauritius. Public Record Office, London.

Company of Musicians, Apprentice Books, 2 vols., Corporation of London, Guildhall Library.

—— List of Freemen, 1743–1831, Corporation of London, Guildhall Library.

—— The Court of Assistants Minute Book, 1772–1839. 4 vols., Corporation of London, Guildhall Library.

Godman, T., and Rumball, J. H. MS Map of St Peter's Parish, St Albans, 1826. Hertfordshire Record Office.

—— Book of Reference to the map of St Albans, HRO.

Hunt, Vere. MS 'Vere Hunt's Account with John Booker', 28 Aug. 1790–22 June 1791. Typescript of relevant parts supplied by Mid-West Archives, Limerick, Ireland.

Lawrence, W. J. MS 22 Volumes of Miscellaneous Papers concerning the History of the Theatre in Ireland, comp. by W. J. Lawrence. Irish National Library.

Philharmonic Society [London]. MS Account Book, 1813–1866, British Library.

Royal Society of Musicians [London]. MS Members' Files.

—— MS Admission Book.

—— MS Minutes of the Governors' Meetings.

[Sadler's Wells Theatre]. Collections relating to Sadler's Wells, the Percival Collection. British Library.

—— Collection of Newspaper Cuttings &c. British Library.

—— Playbills in the Guildhall Library Collection.

St Catherine Cree Church, Leadenhall Street [London]. Parish Records. Churchwarden's Accounts. Guildhall Library.

—— Vestry Minutes. Guildhall Library.

St Mary's Church, Lambeth [London]. MS Churchwarden's Accounts, 1802–1820. Lambeth Archives Department, Minet Library, Brixton.

St Mary's Church, Lambeth [London]. MS Poor's Rate Books 1809–1820. Lambeth Archives Department, Minet Library, Brixton.

—— MS Register of Persons summoned for arrears of Poor Rate . . . May 1824– May 1831. Greater London Record Office.

St Peter's Church, St Albans [Hertfordshire]. MS Church Rates, 1804–1810. Hertfordshire Record Office.

—— Churchwarden's Accounts, 1787–1825. Hertfordshire Record Office.

St Stephen Walbrook [London]. Vestry Minutes, 1775–1843. Guildhall Library.

Theatre Royal, Covent Garden. MS Memorandum of Agreements between the Proprietors of the Theatre Royal, Covent Garden and various Musicians, Sept. 1818–Sept. 1820. British Library.

War Office. Muster Roll, 87th Prince of Wales (Irish) Regiment, 25 June–24 Dec. 1794 [and subsequent musters]. Public Record Office, London.

—— Monthly Return, 1 Jan. 1832. 87th Royal Irish Fusiliers. Public Record Office, London.

NEWSPAPERS AND JOURNALS

Australian [Sydney]
Annual Register [London]
Blackwood's Magazine [Edinburgh]
Canon [Sydney]
Le Cernéen [Port Louis]
Currency Lad [Sydney]
Ennis Chronicle
European Magazine [London]
Faulkner's Dublin Journal
Finn's Leinster Journal [Kilkenny]
Freeman's Journal [Dublin]
Gazetteer and New Daily Advertiser [London]
Gentleman's Magazine [London]
Harmonicon [London]
Hibernian Chronicle [Cork]
Hibernian Chronicle [Dublin]
Intelligencer [London]
London Magazine
Monitor [Sydney]
Monthly Mirror [London]
New South Wales Magazine [Sydney]
The Orchestra [London]
The Public Advertiser [London]
Quarterly Musical Magazine and Review [London]
Spectator [London]

Sydney Gazette
Sydney Times
The Times [London]
Walker's Hibernian Magazine [Dublin]
Wexford Herald

OTHER PRINTED SOURCES

(Books, journal articles, theses, etc.)

Allen, Thomas. *The History and Antiquities of the Parish of Lambeth and the Archiepiscopal Palace in the County of Surrey* (London, 1826).

Allen, Warren Dwight. *Philosophies of Music History. A Study of General Histories of Music 1600–1960* (rev. edn., New York, 1962).

An Answer to the Memoirs of Mrs Billington with the Life and Adventures of Richard Daly Esq. and an Account of the Present State of the Irish Theatre . . . (London, 1792).

Atlas, Allan W. *Music in the Classic Period. Essays in Honour of Barry S. Brook* (New York, 1985).

[Austen, Jane]. *Jane Austen's Letters to her Sister Cassandra and Others*, ed. by R. W. Chapman (2nd edn., London, 1952).

Australian Dictionary of Biography (Melbourne, 1966–   ).

Bacon, Richard Mackenzie. *Elements of Vocal Science, being a Philosophical Enquiry into some of the Principles of Singing* (London, [1824]) [being reprints of several of his essays originally published in *QMMR* under various pseudonyms].

Baker, H. B. *History of the London Stage* (London, 1904).

Barnwell, P. J., and Toussaint, A. *A Short History of Mauritius* (London, 1949).

Barrington, Jonah. *Personal Sketches of His Own Times* (2 vols., London, 1827).

Beale, Willert. *The Light of Other Days, Seen through the Wrong End of an Opera Glass* (London, 1890).

Beckett, J. C. *The Anglo-Irish Tradition* (London, 1976; Belfast, 1983).

Beedell, A. V. 'William Joseph Castell, o. k. a. Cavendish (1789–1839), Musician. His Origins, Life and Career in Ireland, England, France, Mauritius and Australia'. Hons. MA thesis (2 vols., Univ. of New South Wales, Sydney, 1990).

Berlioz, Hector. *Evenings in the Orchestra*, trans. by Charles E. Roche with an introd. by Ernest Newman (New York, 1929).

—— *Memoirs of Hector Berlioz from 1803 to 1865*, ed. by Ernest Newman (New York, 1835).

Bernard, John. *Retrospections of the Stage by the late John Bernard, Manager of the American Theatres, and formerly Secretary to the Beef-Steak Club* (2 vols., London, 1830).

Bewick, Thomas. *A Memoir of Thomas Bewick, written by Himself*, ed. by Ian Bain (Oxford, 1979).

Biographia Dramatica; or a Companion to the Playhouse (3 vols., London, 1812).

A *Biographical Dictionary of Actors, Actresses, Musicians, Dancers, Managers and other Stage Personnel in London 1660–1800*, comp. by Philip H. Highfill and others. (Carbondale, Ill., 1973–).

Biographical Dictionary of the Living Authors of Great Britain and Ireland . . . (London, 1816).

Blom, Eric. *Music in England* (London, 1947).

Boaden, James. *The Life of Mrs Jordan . . .* (2 vols., London, 1801).

—— *Memoirs of the Life of John Philip Kemble . . .* (2 vols., London, 1825).

Boylan, Henry. *A Dictionary of Irish Biography* (Dublin, 1978).

Bradshaw, T. *Views in the Mauritius, or Isle of France drawn from Nature . . . with a Memoir of the Island, and a Description of each View* (London, 1832).

Brayley, Edward Westlake. *Historical and Descriptive Account of the Theatres of London . . .* (London, 1826).

Brown, James D., and Stratton, Stephen S. *British Musical Biography. A Dictionary of Musical Artists, Authors and Composers born in Britain and its Colonies* (Birmingham, 1897).

Brown, John. *A Dissertation on the Rise, Union, and Power, the Progressions, Separations and Corruptions of Poetry and Music . . .* (London, 1763).

Browne, Alice. *The Eighteenth Century Feminist Mind* (Brighton, 1987).

Burgh, A. *Anecdotes of Music, Historical and Biographical in a Series of Letters from a Gentleman to his Daughter* (3 vols., London, 1814).

Burney, Charles. *A General History of Music from the Earliest Ages to the Present Period* (4 vols., London, 1789).

Campbell, R. *The London Tradesman* (London, 1747; facsimile edn., London, 1967).

[Campbell, Thomas]. *A Philosophical Survey of the South of Ireland in a Series of Letters to John Wilkinson* (London, 1777).

Candid Remarks upon the Stage-bill, Now Depending (Dublin, 1785).

Clark, G. M. H. *A History of Australia. II: New South Wales and Van Diemen's Land, 1822–1838* (Melbourne, 1968).

—— *A History of Australia. III: The Beginning of an Australian Civilization, 1824–1851* (Melbourne, 1973).

Clark, William Smith. *The Irish Stage in the Country Towns 1720–1800* (Oxford, 1965).

Covell, Roger. *Australia's Music. Themes of a New Society* (Melbourne, 1967).

Cox, H. Bertrum, and Cox, C. L. E. *Leaves from the Journal of Sir George Smart* (London, 1907).

Cox, John Edmund. *Musical Recollections of the last Half Century* (2 vols., London, 1872).

Creevey, Thomas. *Papers*, selected and ed. by John Gore (this edn. Harmondsworth, Middx., 1985).

Crewdson, H. A. F. *The Worshipfull Company of Musicians* (London, 1956).

Davey, Henry. *History of English Music* (London, [1921]).

Dawe, Donovan. *Organists of the City of London 1666–1850. A Record of One Thousand Organists with an annotated Index* ([Padstow, Cornwall], 1983).

Decastro, J. *The Memoirs of J. Decastro, Comedian . . .* ed. by R. Humphreys (London, 1824).

Defoe, Daniel. *Augusta Triumphans* (London, 1728).

Dibdin, Charles. *Professional and Literary Memoirs of Charles Dibdin the Younger: Dramatist and Upwards of Thirty Years Manager of Minor Theatres*, ed. by George Speaight (London, 1956).

[Doane, J]. *A Musical Directory for the Year 1794 . . . containing Names and Addresses of the Composers & Professors of Music, with a Number of Amateurs, Vocal and Instrumental* (London, [1794], xerox copy in Guildhall Library).

Dodd, George. *Days at the Factories. The Manufacturing Industry of Great Britain Described* (London, 1843).

Doran, John. *'Their Majesties' Servants'. Annals of the English Stage from Thomas Betterton to Edmund Kean*, 3 vols., ed. by R. W. Lowe (London, 1888).

Doyle, Francis Hastings. *Reminiscences and Opinions of Sir Francis Hastings Doyle 1813–1885* (London, 1886).

Drummond, Pippa. 'The Royal Society of Musicians in the Eighteenth Century', *Music & Letters*, lix (1978), printed in RSM, *List of Members* (London, 1985), 191–215.

Dunlop, O. Jocelyn, and R. D. Denman. *English Apprenticeships and Child Labour* (London, 1912).

Ehrlich, Cyril. *The Music Profession in Britain since the Eighteenth Century. A Social History* (Oxford, 1985).

Elkin, Robert. *The Old Concert Rooms of London* (London, 1955).

—— *Royal Philharmonic. The Annals of the Royal Philharmonic Society* (London, [n.d.]).

Emsley, Clive. *British Society and the French Wars, 1793–1815* (London, 1979).

Engel, Carl. *Musical Myths and Facts* (2 vols., London, 1876).

Fiske, Roger. *English Theatre Music in the Eighteenth Century* (London, 1973).

Fitzpatrick, William John. *A Note to the Cornwallis Papers Embracing with other Revelations, a Narrative of the extraordinary Career of Francis Higgins, who received the Government Reward for the Betrayal of Lord Edward Fitzgerald* (Dublin, 1859).

Flood, William H. Grattan. *A History of Irish Music* (Dublin, 1905).

Foss, Michael. *The Age of Patronage. The Arts in Society 1660–1750* (London, 1971).

Foster, Myles Birket. *History of the Philharmonic Society of London, 1813–1912* (London, 1912).

Frost, Thomas. *The Old Showmen and the Old London Fairs* (London, 1874).

Gardiner, William. *Music and Friends, or Pleasant Recollections of a Dilettante* (3 vols., London, 1838).

George, M. Dorothy. *London Life in the Eighteenth Century* (this edn. Harmondsworth, Middx., 1966).

Gilbert, J. T. *History of the City of Dublin* (3 vols., Dublin, 1861).

Gilliland, Thomas. *The Dramatic Mirror* (2 vols., London, 1808).

Goodwin, Crauford D. W. *The Image of Australia. British Perception of the Australian Economy from the Eighteenth to the Twentieth Century* (Durham, NC, 1974).

Grove's Dictionary of Music and Musicians (5th edn., London, 1954).

Hackett, Maria. *A Brief Account of the Cathedral and Collegiate Schools; with an Abstract of their Statutes and Endowments. Respectfully addressed to the Dignitaries of the Established Church* (London, 1827).

—— *Correspondence and Evidences respecting the Ancient Collegiate School attached to St Paul's Cathedral* ([London], 1832).

Hall, James. 'History of Music in Australia 1788–1843', *Canon* (in a series between Jan. 1951 and June 1952).

Hare, Arnold. *The Georgian Theatre in Wessex* (London, 1958).

Harvey, A. D. *Britain in the Early Nineteenth Century* (London, 1978).

Hawkins, John. *A General History of Music* (London, 1776; this edn. 2 vols., New York, 1963).

Hitchcock, Robert. *A Historical View of the Irish Stage from the Earliest Period down to the Close of the Season 1788* (2 vols., Dublin, 1788–94).

Hobsbawm, E. J., and Rudé, George. *Captain Swing* (London, 1969).

Hogan, Ita Margaret. *Anglo-Irish Music 1780–1830* (Cork, 1960).

Hogarth, George. *Memoirs of the Musical Drama* (2 vols., new edn. London, [1851]).

Hogwood, Christopher, and Luckett, Richard (eds.). *Music in Eighteenth-Century England: Essays in Memory of Charles Cudworth* (New York, 1983).

Holbrook, Ann. *The Dramatist; or Memoirs of the Stage, with the Life of the Authoress* (Birmingham, 1809).

Hone, William. *The Everyday Book and Table Book or Everlasting Calendar of Popular Amusements, Sports, Pastimes, Ceremonies, Manners, Customs and Events . . .* (London, 1831).

Horwood's Plan of London, Westminster, Southwark & Parts adjoining, 1792–1799 (facsimile edn., London, 1966).

—— Also the 1819 edition held by GLRO, Dept. Maps and Prints.

Howell, Brenda M. 'Mauritius, 1832–1849: A Study of a Sugar Colony', Ph.D thesis (London, 1950).

Howitt, William. *The Rural Life of England* (3rd edn., London, 1844; facsimile edn., 1971).

Hughes, Robert. *The Fatal Shore. A History of the Transportation of Convicts to Australia 1787–1868* (London, 1987).

Hullah, John. *Music in the Parish Church. A Lecture delivered at Newcastle-on-Tyne, November 27th, 1855* (London, 1956).

Hume, Robert. *The London Theatre World 1660–1800* (Carbondale, Ill., 1980).

Humphries, Charles, and Smith, William C. *Music Publishing in the British Isles from the Beginning until the Middle of the Nineteenth Century. A Dictionary of Engravers, Printers, Publishers and Music Sellers* ... (2nd edn., London, 1970).

Irvin, Eric. *Theatre Comes to Australia* (St Lucia, Queensland, 1971).

Kassler, Jamie Croy. *The Science of Music in Britain, 1714–1830. A Catalogue of Writing, Lectures and Inventions* (2 vols., New York, 1979).

Kelly, Michael. *Reminiscences*, ed. with an introd. by Roger Fiske (London, 1975).

Lang, Paul. *Music in Western Civilization* (London, 1942).

Later English Broadside Ballads, ed. by John Holloway and Joan Black, vol. 2 (London, 1979).

Lecky, William. *History of Ireland in the Eighteenth Century* (4 vols., new edn., London, 1892).

Le Huray, Peter. *Music and the Reformation in England 1549–1660* (London, 1967).

Leppert, Richard. 'Music, Domestic Life and Cultural Chauvinism: Images of British Subjects at Home in India', in Richard Leppert and Susan McClary (eds.), *Music and Society, the Politics of Composition, Performance and Reception* (Cambridge, 1987), 63–104.

—— 'Music Teachers of Upper-Class Amateur Musicians in Eighteenth-Century England', in Allan W. Atlas (ed.), *Music in the Classic Period* (New York, 1985).

Lewes, Charles Lee. *Memoirs* (4 vols., London, 1805).

Lippman, Edward A. *Musical Aesthetics: A Historical Reader* (2 vols., New York, 1986)

Locke, John. *Some Thoughts concerning Education*, introd. by Revd R. H. Quick (2nd edn., London, 1884).

The London Stage 1660–1800. A Calendar of Plays, Entertainments & Afterpieces together with casts, box-receipts and contemporary comment ... (Carbondale, Ill., 1958).

Lucas, F. L. *The Search for Good Sense. Four Eighteenth-Century Characters. Johnson, Chesterfield, Boswell, Goldsmith* (London, 1958).

Lynch, James J. *Box, Pit and Gallery. Stage and Society in Johnson's London* (Berkeley, Calif., 1953).

McConville, Michael. *Ascendancy to Oblivion. The Story of the Anglo-Irish* (London, 1986).

Mackerness, E. D. *Social History of English Music* (London, 1964).

Mackerras, Catherine. *The Hebrew Melodist. A Life of Isaac Nathan* (Sydney, 1963).

McVeigh, Simon. Calendar of London Concerts 1750–1800, [computer data base] Goldsmith's College, University of London.

—— 'Felice Giardini: A Violinist in late Eighteenth-Century London', *Music & Letters*, lxiv (1983), 162–72.

Malcolmson, Robert W. *Popular Recreations in English Society 1700–1850* (Cambridge, 1973).

Marshall, Dorothy. *Industrial England 1776–1851* (2nd edn., London, 1982).

Maturin, Charles. *Women; or Pour et Contre* (3 vols., Edinburgh, 1818).

Maxwell, Constantia. *Dublin under the Georges 1714–1830* (rev. edn., London, 1956).

Mayhew, Henry. *London Labour and the London Poor . . .* (3 vols., London, 1851).

Mellers, Wilfred. *Harmonious Meeting. A Study of the Relationship between English Music, Poetry and Theatre, c.1600–1900* (London, 1965).

—— *Music and Society. England and the European Tradition* (London, 1946).

Memorial presented by the Inhabitants of Mauritius, in support of their Petition to His Majesty, setting forth the Sufferings they have endured, the Dangers they are exposed to, and the Rights to which they lay claim: and containing a brief Narrative of the Events which have taken place in the Colony during the Months of June and July, 1832 (London, 1833).

Milligan, Thomas B. *The Concerto and London's Musical Culture in the late Eighteenth Century* (Epping, Essex, 1983).

Moody, T. W., and Vaughan, W. E. (eds.). *A New History of Ireland. IV: Eighteenth-Century Ireland 1691–1800* (Oxford, 1986).

Morgan, Lady. See Owenson, Sydney.

Mundy, Godfrey Charles. *Our Antipodes: Or Residence and Rambles in the Australian Colonies. With a Glimpse of the Gold Fields* (3 vols., 2nd rev. edn., London, 1852).

Musical Travels through England by Joel Collier, Organist (London, 1774).

Nadel, George. *Australia's Colonial Culture. Ideas, Men and Institutions in Mid-Nineteenth Century Australia* (Melbourne, 1957).

Nagler, A. M. *A Sourcebook in Theatrical History* (2nd edn., New York, 1959).

Nathan, Isaac. *An Essay on the History and Theory of Music, and on the Qualities, Capabilities and Management of the Human Voice* (London, 1823).

Neale, R. S. *Class and Ideology in the Nineteenth Century* (London, 1972).

Nettel, Reginald. *Music in the Five Towns 1840–1914. A Study of the Social Influences of Music in an Industrial District* (London, 1944).

—— *The Orchestra in England. A Social History* (London, 1946).

The New Grove Dictionary of Music and Musicians (6th edn., London, 1980).

Nicoll, Allardyce. *A History of Late Eighteenth Century Drama, 1750–1800* (Cambridge, 1927).

O'Connell, Maurice R. *Irish Politics and Social Conflict in the Age of the American Revolution* (Philadelphia, 1965).

O'Keefe, John. *Recollections of the Life of John O'Keefe written by himself* (2 vols., London, 1826).

Orchard, W. Arundel. *Music in Australia. More than 150 Years of Development* (Melbourne, 1952).

Owenson, Sydney [later Lady Morgan]. *Lady Morgan's Memoirs: Autobiography, Diaries and Correspondence* (2 vols., London, 1862).

[Oxberry, William]. *Oxberry's Dramatic Biography and Histrionic Anecdote* (7 vols., London, 1825–6).

Park, Roy (ed.). *Lamb as Critic* (London, 1980).

Parke, William Thomas. *Musical Memoirs; Comprising an Account of the General State of Music in England from the first Commemoration of Handel in 1784 to the year 1830* . . . (2 vols., London, 1830).

Perkin, Harold. *The Origins of Modern English Society 1780–1880* (this edn. London, 1985).

Phillips, Henry. *Musical and Personal Recollections during Half a Century* (2 vols., London, 1864).

Pigot & Co. *London & Provincial Directory for 1826–27.*

—— *National London & Provincial Directory for 1832–3–4.*

Planché, James Robinson. *Recollections and Reflections, a Professional Autobiography* (this edn. New York, 1978).

Portal, William. *Abraham Portal, born 1726, died 1809, and his descendants* (Winchester, 1925).

Portnoy, Julius. *The Philosopher and Music. A Historical Outline* (New York, 1954).

Potter, John. *Observations on the Present State of Music and Musicians* (London, 1762).

Pougin, Arthur. *William Vincent Wallace. Étude biographique* . . . (Paris, 1866).

Pring, Joseph. *Papers, Documents, Law Proceedings &c &c, respecting the Maintenance of the Choir of the Cathedral Church of Bangor, as provided by an Act of Parliament passed in the Reign of King James II A.D. 1683, collected and arranged by Joseph Pring, Mus.Doc.Oxon. endowed Organist of Bangor Cathedral* (Bangor, 1819).

Rainbow, Bernarr. *The Land without Music. Musical Education in England 1800–1860 and its Continental Antecedents* (London, 1967).

Raynor, Henry. *Music in England* (London, 1980).

—— *A Social History of Music from the Middle Ages to Beethoven* (London, 1972).

Reynolds, Frederick. *The Life and Times of Frederick Reynolds written by himself* (2 vols., London, 1826).

[Ridgway, James]. *Memoirs of Mrs Billington, from her Birth, containing a Variety of Matter, ludicrous, theatrical and —— with Copies of several Letters now in the possession of the Publisher, written by Mrs Billington to her Mother, the late Mrs Weichsel* (London, 1792).

Ritchie, John. *Punishment and Profit. The Report of the Commissioner John Bigge on the Colonies of New South Wales and Van Diemen's Land, 1822–1823. Their Origin, Nature and Significance* (Melbourne, 1970).

Riviere, Lindsay. *Historical Dictionary of Mauritius* (Metuchen, NJ, 1982) (African Historical Dictionaries, No. 34).

Robinson, Portia. *The Hatch and Brood of Time. A Study of the First Generation of Native-Born Australians 1788–1828*, vol. i (Melbourne, 1985).

Roe, M. *A History of the Theatre Royal, Hobart from 1834* (Hobart, [n.d.]).

Rohr, Deborah Adams. 'A Profession of Artisans: The Careers and Social Status of British Musicians 1750–1850', Ph.D thesis (Pennsylvania, 1983).

Rosenthal, Harold. *Two Centuries of Opera at Covent Garden* (London, 1958).

Royal Society of Musicians of Great Britain. *List of Members, 1738–1984* (London, 1985).

Rudé, George. *Hanoverian London, 1714–1808* (London, 1971).

Sadie, Stanley. 'Concert Life in Eighteenth Century England', *Proceedings of the Royal Musical Association*, lxxxv (1958–9), 17–30.

Scholes, Percy A. *Music and Puritanism, with an Appendix on Dancing and Puritanism* [Lausanne, 1934].

—— *The Puritans and Music in England and New England. A Contribution to the Cultural History of Two Nations* (London, 1934).

Shanahan, Mary. *Out of Time Out of Place. Henry Gregory and the Benedictine Order in Colonial Australia* (Canberra, 1970).

Shaw, A. G. L. *Heroes and Villains in History. Governors Darling and Bourke in New South Wales* (Sydney, 1966).

Smart, William. *Economic Annals of the Nineteenth Century, 1821–1830* (London, 1917).

Smith, William Charles. *The Italian Opera and Contemporary Ballet in London 1789–1820—a Record of Performances and Players* (London, 1955).

Snell, K. D. M. *Annals of the Labouring Poor* (London, 1985).

Southey, Robert. *Letters from England*, ed. by Jack Simmons (Gloucester, 1984).

Spark, William. *Musical Memoirs* (London, 1909).

Spencer, Francis. *Portals. The Church, the State and the People leading to 250 years of Paper-Making* (Oxford, 1962).

Stanhope, Philip D., 4th Earl of Chesterfield. *The Letters of the Earl of Chesterfield to his Son*, ed. by Charles Strachey (2 vols., London, 1901).

Stockwell, La Tourette. *Dublin Theatres and Theatre Customs (1637–1820)* (Kingsport, Tenn., 1938).

Strutt, Vide. *The Sports and Pastimes of the People of England from the Earliest Period . . .*, ed. by J. Charles Cox (London, 1801).

Survey of London. xxiii. South Bank & Vauxhall. The Parish of St Mary, Lambeth, Part I (London, 1951).

—— *xxxiii. The Parish of St Anne Soho* (London, 1966).

Temperley, Nicholas. *Jonathan Gray and Church Music in York 1770–1840* (York, 1977) (Borthwick Papers, No. 51).

— (ed.) *Music in Britain. The Romantic Age 1800–1914* (London, 1981).

Therry, Roger. *Reminiscences of Thirty Years Residence in New South Wales and Victoria* (2nd edn., London, 1863).

Thespian Dictionary or Dramatic Biography of the Present Age (2nd edn., London, 1805).

Thompson, E. P. *The Making of the English Working Class* (this edn. Harmondsworth, Middx., 1980).

Thomson, H. Byerley. *The Choice of a Profession. A Concise Account and Comparative Review of the English Professions* (London, 1857).

Thorne, R. *Theatre Buildings in Australia to 1905. From the Time of the First Settlement to the Arrival of Cinema* (2 vols., Sydney, 1971).

Tristan, Flora (pseud.). *London Journal. A Survey of London Life in the 1830s* (London, 1980).

Troubridge, St Vincent. *The Benefit System in British Theatre* (London, 1967).

Tuveson, Ernest Lee. *The Imagination as a Means of Grace. Locke and the Aesthetics of Romanticism* (Berkeley, Calif., 1960).

Walford, Edward. *Old and New London. A Narrative of its History, its People, and its Places . . .* (6 vols., London, [n.d.]).

Walker, Ernest. *History of Music in England* (3rd rev. edn. [n.p.], 1952).

Walsh, T. J. *Opera in Dublin 1705–1797* (Dublin, 1973).

War Office. *A List of the Officers of the Army and Marines with an Index . . . and a List of the Officers . . . on half-pay* [*Army List*] [London].

Weber in London 1826. Selections from Weber's Letters to his Wife and from the Writings of his Contemporaries in London in 1826 . . . (London, 1976).

Weber, Max. *The Protestant Ethic and the Spirit of Capitalism* (London, 1930).

Weber, William. *Music and the Middle Class. The Social Structure of Concert Life in London, Paris and Vienna* (London, 1975).

— 'The 1784 Handel Commemoration as Political Ritual', *Journal of British Studies*, xxviii (1, Jan. 1989), 43–69.

Wesley, Samuel. *A Few Words on Cathedral Music and the Musical System of the Church, with a Plan of Reform* (London, 1849).

White, Eric Walter. *A Register of First Performances of English Operas and Semi-Operas from the 16th Century to 1980* (London, 1983).

Wilkinson, Robert. *Londina Illustrata* (London, 1819).

Willey, Basil. *The Eighteenth Century Background. Studies in the Idea of Nature in the Thought of the Period* (this edn. London, 1986).

Williams, Anthony (pseud. Pasquin). *The Children of Thespis. A Poem* (London, 1792).

Winstanley, Eliza. *Shifting Scenes in Theatrical Life* [a novel] (London, [1859]).

Woodfill, Walter L. *Musicians in English Society from Elizabeth to Charles I* (Princeton, NJ, 1953).

Woodward, Llewellyn. *The Age of Reform, 1815–1870* (2nd edn., Oxford, 1962).

Worgan, Thomas. *The Musical Reformer* (London, 1829).

Wroth, Warwick. *The London Pleasure Gardens of the Eighteenth Century* (London, 1896).

Wyndham, Henry Saxe. *The Annals of Covent Garden Theatre from 1732 to 1897* (2 vols., London, 1906).

Young, Arthur. *Tour of Ireland* (*1776–1779*), ed. by A. W. Hutton (2 vols., London, 1892).

Young, G. M. *Portrait of an Age. Victorian England* (London, 1977).

Young, Percy M. *The Concert Tradition from the Middle Ages to the Twentieth Century* (London, 1965).

Zeldin, Theodore. *France 1848–1945. Ambition and Love* (Oxford, 1979).

INDEX